Play and Educational
Theory and Practice

Recent Titles in
Play & Culture Studies
Stuart Reifel and Jaipaul L. Roopnarine, Series Editors

Volume 1: Diversions and Divergences in Fields of Play
Margaret Carlisle Duncan, Garry Chick, and Alan Aycock, editors

Volume 2: Play Contexts Revisited
Stuart Reifel, editor

Volume 3: Theory in Context and Out
Stuart Reifel, editor

Volume 4: Conceptual, Social–Cognitive, and Contextual Issues in the Fields of Play
Jaipaul L. Roopnarine, editor

Play and Educational Theory and Practice

Edited by Donald E. Lytle

PLAY & CULTURE STUDIES, Volume 5
Jaipaul L. Roopnarine, *Series Editor*

Westport, Connecticut
London

Library of Congress Cataloging-in-Publication Data

Play and educational theory and practice / edited by Donald E. Lytle.
    p. cm.—(Play & culture studies, ISSN 1096–8911 ; v.5)
    Includes bibliographical references and indexes.
    ISBN 1–56750–684–4 (alk. paper)
    1. Play. 2. Early childhood education. I. Lytle, Don, 1944– II. Series.
  LB1137.P5555 2003
  155.4'18—dc21   2002028309

British Library Cataloguing in Publication Data is available.

Library of Congress Catalog Card Number: 2002028309
ISBN: 1–56750–684–4
ISSN: 1096–8911

First published in 2003

Praeger Publishers, 88 Post Road West, Westport, CT 06881
An imprint of Greenwood Publishing Group, Inc.
www.praeger.com

Printed in the United States of America

The paper used in this book complies with the
Permanent Paper Standard issued by the National
Information Standards Organization (Z39.48–1984).

10 9 8 7 6 5 4 3

To my mentors in play and perspective taking: Brian Sutton-Smith,
Ann Marie Guilmette, Rebecca Lytle, and Utahna and Gene Lytle;
and to my children, Michelle, Amy, Kelsey, and Sean,
who also taught me about the importance of life.

Contents

Series Editor's Note

In staying close to the overall multidisciplinary focus of the Association for the Study of Play (TASP), Volume 5 of Play & Culture Studies reflects a broad range of theoretical and applied papers on play. Specifically, the first two sections of the volume provide further challenges to commonly held beliefs about play research and theory. The preeminent scholar in the field of play and folklore, Brian Sutton-Smith, proffers a new conceptual framework on the role of emotions in understanding the adaptive value of play, while our European colleagues in the fields of education and psychology shed further light on the applied value of central tenets espoused in the popular theoretical frameworks of Vygotsky and Piaget. The other segments of the volume are equally as impressive, focusing on the role of play in early learning and educational planning. Here, emphasis is on core areas of play: pretend play and metacommunication, play and creativity, humor and play, school recess time and children's activities, and rural children's play.

This volume, however, achieves much more than providing sagacious discussions of theory and the applied value of play. It also attempts to demonstrate advances in the ongoing dialogues that are occurring in the area of play research and their applied implications for human development and education on the global stage. Increasingly, researchers in North America are pursuing joint investigations with their colleagues and graduate students from other parts of the world in order to shore up our existing knowledge base about play in diverse cultures. This is not to detract from the hard work of previous editors of this series and those of the Anthropological Association for the Study of Play who have done a wonderful job of bringing play in diverse cultural settings to the forefront of our thinking. My point is that this volume builds on previous efforts in this domain by including a section on the play of Asian children. I see this volume as a prelude to future discussions on how extant play theories and research can be strengthened with new data from diverse ethnic and cultural groups around the world. Dr. Donald Lytle should be highly commended for his work on this volume.

Jaipaul L. Roopnarine, Series Editor
Syracuse University

Introduction

When Brian Sutton-Smith, Garry Chick, and other TASP professionals con-ceived of a play theory journal, which eventually evolved into Play & Culture Studies, they wanted contributions to be focused on play research. That was easily understood, but given the myriad playful possibilities and constructions in the world and related investigations, it made the practical and organizational task for editors difficult. The strong tradition of scholarly play research estab-lished in the first four volumes of Play & Culture Studies continues with this issue's 17 peer-reviewed chapters. The range of playful repertoires and scholarly investigation involves theoretical, quasi-experimental, and data-based research. A general theme emerges from the chapters herein, as most of the topics coalesce around the dynamic play of the young human and how that relates to children's learning and early educational practices, theories, and models. Most chapters reflect and respond to the growing and important international interest in early childhood education, with special attention to discussion and critique of the developmental and educational theories of Lev Semenovich Vygotsky.

Presented in Part I are theoretical and conceptual creations, the important play contributions of sociologist Georg Simmel and how college students' assump-tions about children's play don't always hold up. In the first chapter, the world's most prolific play and folklore scholar, Brian Sutton-Smith, continues his the-oretical work/play from the past two issues of Play & Culture Studies. He has refined his groundbreaking theory of play's function as an intricate mammalian evolutionary interplay of primitive, old brain emotions and secondary, neocortex emotions. Tom Henricks (Chapter 2), a consistent contributor to Play & Culture Studies, demonstrates that Georg Simmel is a most profound sociologist relative to commentaries on play and human association. Dana Gross first presented her applied work on introducing college students to children's play behaviors in an introductory psychology class at a TASP meeting in Baltimore. Patrick Biesty ends the first section with the question, "Where is play?" and by the time this book ends, play has traveled around the world from American universities to Spain to Jean Piaget's Western Europe and Lev Vygotsky's Soviet Russia to Norway, Australia, Taiwan, and Korea. Enjoy the trip, for play, learning, and teaching are all grand and important adventures.

In Part II the first predominant theme of Vygotskian theories and applications is presented. Beverley Lambert and Margaret Clyde, with the permission of their publisher, Social Science Press (Katoomba, New South Wales), consented to the solicited use of Chapters 2–5 of their book, *Rethinking Early Childhood Theory and Practice* (2000). Rosario Ortega of Spain writes of "Play, Activity, and Thought: Reflections on Piaget's and Vygotsky's Theories" in Chapter 6 and Kara Gregory, An Sook Kim, and Alice Whiren show how adults can effectively and systematically guide children through verbal scaffolding processes in block constructions (Chapter 7).

Part III presents research of children's creative and cognitive playfulness. R. Keith Sawyer (Chapter 8) further refines his extensive work on pretend play discourse. Janet Sawyers and Nathalie Carrick (Chapter 9) discuss the "Symbolic Play through the Eyes and Words of Children," and Betty Beach (Chapter 10) takes advantage of her rural roots and current research interests to discuss "Rural Children's Play in the Natural Environment."

Part IV includes chapters on humor in the classroom, recess, and preschool practices. Phil Fitzsimmons and Barbra McKenzie introduce a most playful Australian secondary school educator (Chapter 11), and Grace Masselos shows how humor through play can be applied to early childhood education (Chapter 12). Recess in an American charter middle school is the focus of Olga Jarrett and Michelle Duckett-Hedgebeth's study in Chapter 13. Jeanette Rhedding-Jones in Chapter 14 draws on her educational experiences in Australia and explores dichotomous constructions focusing on preschool day-care centers and schools in Norway. This leads into Part V, investigating children and educational practices in Taiwan and Korea. Li-Chun "Sandy" Chang and Stuart Reifel, a past editor of *Play & Culture Studies*, present "Play, Racial Attitudes, and Self-Concept in Taiwan" in Chapter 15. Pei-Yu Chang's "Contextual Understanding of Children's Play in Taiwanese Kindergartens" (Chapter 16) and Seunghwa Jwa and Joe L. Frost's "Contextual Differences in Korean Mother–Child Interactions: A Study of Scaffolding Behaviors" (Chapter 17) revisit Vygotskyian theory in the last chapters of the book.

ACKNOWLEDGMENTS

An annual, peer-reviewed book cannot be realized without the altruistic and professional work of the reviewers. On behalf of the Association for the Study of Play I wish to thank most sincerely the 44 individuals who conscientiously provided excellent, objective, and helpful feedback on the many articles submitted for Volume 5 of Play & Culture Studies: Doris Bergen, Patrick Biesty, John Bock, Rosemary Bolig, Craig Buschner, Garry Chick, Jim Christie, Don Chu, Rhonda Clements, Sue Dockett, Claire Farrar, Mary Fryer, Dana Gross, Ann Marie Guilmette, Thomas Henricks, Robyn Holmes, Olga Jarrett, James Johnson, Marge Kaiser, Nechie King, David Lancy, John Loy, Grace Masselos, Felicia McMahon, Jay Mechling, Alice Meckley, Bernard Mergen, Brooks Moore, David Myers, Don Nilsen, Stephanie Owens, Tony Pellegrini, Stuart Reifel, Elizabeth Renfro, Mary Ruth Reynolds, Mary Rivkin, Cosby Steele Rogers, Jaipaul Roopnarine, Kathleen Roskos, Walt Schafer, Dorothy Sluss, Phillips Stevens, Brian Sutton-Smith, and Synthia Sydnor.

Donald E. Lytle

Part I

Play Theory and Research

Chapter 1

Play as a Parody of Emotional Vulnerability

Brian Sutton-Smith

INTRODUCTION

The trouble with the Association for the Study of Play (TASP) membership is its diversity (Loy, 1982). It's hard to believe at first that everyone can be talking about play with equal validity. A useful defense is to retire into one's own discipline and ignore all of the others. But if one stays with TASP for the 25 years that some of us have, that becomes unseemly. TASP is an interdisciplinary society, and typically all the various works are of scholarly merit. One way out, therefore, is to mimic the society itself and become an interdisciplinary scholar. My book, *The Ambiguity of Play* (Sutton-Smith, 1997), was my effort of that kind. It tried to reduce all these diversities of play theorizing to seven intellectual and ideological rhetorics. Unfortunately, whatever its merits may be, it still does not tell us what play actually is, in, say, one sentence or two. In fact, at the end and following Stephen Jay Gould's view (1996) that variability is the key to evolution, it began to seem probable that perhaps play is basically just another kind of evolutionary variability. Which means that the more extensive that play is, the more it improves the natural and cultural selection possibilities of the players. If so, then in these terms play might be summarized most simply as adaptive variability (Sutton-Smith, 1975, 2001a, 2001b).

THE SEARCH FOR A DEFINITION OF PLAY

Unfortunately, the definition of play, as only a random source of possible alternatives, seems insufficient. It seems not responsive to the feeling that, in an evolutionary sense, something else related to "survival" is missing. This chapter is an investigation of the hypothesis that one of the functions of play has been to mask the very centrality of emotions upon which it depends. The contention here is that play is most fundamentally about a hidden emotional dialectic of stress versus non-stress (Sutton-Smith, 1978, 2002). The search that led to this conclusion proceeded as follows. It began with a reading of the Bekoff and Byers book entitled *Animal Play* (1998) and in particular with Gordon Burghardt's article in that book on the evolutionary origins of play. Of particular interest was his reference to the famous post-dinosaur era, 65 million years ago, when mammals appeared, with larger brains, with parental care, with a more differentiated emotional life, and remarkably, with the presence of the novel behavioral forms called play. All of a sudden it appeared that perhaps the emergence of play at the same time as the emergence of the new emotional systems might not have been accidental. Perhaps the inevitable conflicts between the older reflexive systems for emotional survival (by anger, fear, shock, etc.) versus the newer systems for cognitive emotional survival (by embarrassment, shame and guilt, etc.) could be the incentive for the genetic invention and selection of a method for mediating that conflict. Perhaps play could be such a mediator of emotions.

The rest of this chapter is about the attempts to make some sense out of that original intuition that play functions as this kind of emotional mediational phenomenon. The first supportive breakthrough came from the work of Antonio Damasio's 1994 book entitled *Decartes' Error*, in which he shows that Descartes' thinking as in *cognito ergo sum* (I think therefore I am) is not alone the basis of consciousness. Indeed, from his point of view *sentio ergo sum* (I feel therefore I am) might be more in order—that is, if one is to thus sum up the human condition in one simple statement. In his work Damasio distinguishes between two types of emotion, which he calls the primary and the secondary.

Table 1.1 indicates some of the distinctions that have been applied to these two groups of different emotions. There is some evidence (Ledoux, 1996) that the primary emotions have neural circuitry that can be instigated through the amygdala without the intervention of the cortex. That is, a perception of, say, danger can lead to immediate performances (flight, etc.) without any conscious cortical interventions. But it is also clear that the same emotions can occur also with prefrontal cortical mediation, as, for example, when people feel angry about the politicians of the other party and consider what they might like to do to the political party that they abhor; that is, all emotions have both involuntary and voluntary aspects, but the primary group has more of the first, and the secondary group has more of the second. Not all researchers are sympathetic to this notion of fairly discrete and fixed lifelong emotions. Some feel that cognitions govern the initiation of emotional states; others feel that cognition governs their transformations over the life span (Mascolo & Griffin, 1998). What is more probable is that the primaries all emerge in infancy more or less reflexively and then become transformed with social and cognitive experience. Nevertheless, whatever the criticisms of the simplicity of these names for emotions, the six primary

Table 1.1
A Duality of the Emotions

Primary Emotions	Secondary Emotions
Involuntary	Voluntary
Anger	Embarrassment
Fear	Pride
Shock	Empathy
Disgust	Shame
Sadness	Guilt
Joy	Envy

Interpretations	
Reptile emotions	Mammal emotions (Burghardt)
Universal emotions	Cultural emotions (Ekman)
Reflexive emotions	Reflective emotions (Mascolo & Griffin)
Survival emotions (Darwin)	Familial emotions (Freud)
Amygdala dominant	Neocortex dominant (Damasio)
First year of life	Second year onward (Lewis)
Negative emotion	Positive emotions (Fredrickson)
Hijacking	Intelligent (Goleman)

ones that are there in the first year of life do seem to look as if they are special to very appropriate kinds of play.

Table 1.2 sets forth these six emotions and the forms of play to which they seem as if they might be most appropriate. Obviously, the complexity of emotions and the complexity of play make this a fairly simplistic set of connections. Nevertheless, the similarities seem to be such as to justify further examination. It was interesting to note how children's folkloric material, much neglected in modern child development studies of play, could be so correlated. The material is taken from the classics of British and American children's folklore by such authors as Iona and Peter Opie (1959), Simon Bronner (1988), and Brian Sutton-Smith, Jay Mechling, Tom Johnson, and Faye McMahon (1999).

Obviously, there is a considerable simplification in supposing that each of these multiple forms of play is sustained by the single emotion appropriate to its category. There has to be much more to the story, and there is. Although single affect names are given to each category, the reality is probably more like a neural factor analysis with six names indicating the dominant factor terms. As an example consider the affective colligations to be found in the original work of Darwin (1965/1872) and more recently in the families of emotions described

Table 1.2
Six Primary Emotions and Six Play Types

Anger (attack, compete)
contests including the 129 world championships (from Gustines & Bierman, 2001): such as arm wrestling, bathtub racing, baton twirling, billiards, bobsledding, bocce ball, cat shows, checkers, cliff diving, elephant polo, Frisbee, horseshoe pitching, luge, marbles, orienteering, Scrabble, tug-of-war, trampoline, Wiffleball, and yo-yo.
    Children: insults, gangs, jeers, torments, mean play, spoilsports, cheats, bullies, school rivalries, anti-teacher jokes, riddles, wit, pranks, duels, taunts, and teases.

Fear
gambling, games of chance, deep play, X games, Halloween, ghosts, spooky movies, telling fortunes, horror stories, roller coasters, ghoulism, legends.

Shock
surprises, tricks, explorations, levitations, puns, parodies, skits, hazings, repartee, guile, phone calls, shockers, April fool, crooked answers, booby traps, window tapping, magic.

Disgust
obscenities, graffiti, urine and excrement play, panty raids, food fights, camp songs, fartlore, kissing, spitting jokes, hymns and carols, greedy guts, fatties, skinnies, redheads, funny faces, fools, dunces, crybabies, gross jokes, scatology.

Loneliness
initiations, argots, forts, rituals, school lore, nicknames, secret languages, love tokens, friends, festivals, parades, soft toys, parties, birthdays, the New Games movement.

Ego–Joy
central person games and performances, flow, zones, peak experiences, Mother May I, statues, beauty contests, infinite play, self-actualization, aesthetic and religious play.

---

by Goleman (1995). One has to suppose that each of these six major categories is contributed to by the variance of each of many subordinate terms. One theorizes, for example, that in the anger/play contest category, major emotions may well be such as animosity, exasperation, and annoyance, with the other more extreme alternatives, such as fury and hostility, being less acceptable, although they sometimes occur, as is well known. One supposes that what is being discussed here are basically six kinds of neural somatic clusters (Damasio, 1994), in which what we call a complex of emotions is embedded. It should be noted that the four primary emotions of anger, fear, shock, and disgust have more obvious play liaisons than the final two, sadness and happiness. These later two, which can be appropriate to the outcome in any and all forms of play, are somewhat less obvious in their ordinary play connections. Our own folk analysis of child play suggests that the major play-driven emotion for sadness is loneliness, and the major emotion for happiness is egocentricity, both deriving from the social and maturational level in early children's play relationships (Sutton-Smith et al., 1999).

While very few affect theorists frame play as an emotional dialectic (see Allen Schore, 1994, for notable exceptions) many, nevertheless, wittingly or otherwise, constitute play as a dialectical relationship between performance elements (in particular, Bateson, 1972). Usually the contrast is between some performance normality (learning, cognition, etc.) and some form of performance transgression (incongruity or irreality, etc.). It is important to realize, however, that this is a performance antithesis that can be conceived as controlled and motivated by the secondary and voluntary emotions. No one seems to have pegged the ancient and reflexive or involuntary emotions as themselves providing the underlying metaphor for the first side of these ludic antitheses or seen the voluntary emotions as providing the contrary side. In addition, people typically, in modern thought, tend to separate emotions from real performances, but modern research suggests, on the contrary, that there are many occasions in which they form a liaison for survival purposes. The extensive affect-related research of the past 20 years suggests, indeed, that the two, emotion and performance, are typically wedded together in human motivation. Authority for this statement is to be found in the formulations of Damasio (1994, 1999), Ledoux (1996), and Edelman (1992). In particular, Damasio (1994) argues that the major function of the emotions is to act as a biological control system that itself elicits strategies for survival. Humans are born with the primary reflexive strategies associated with anger, fear, shock, disgust, sadness, and happiness, all of which are present in the first year of life and the first two of which, anger and fear, are often summarized behaviorally as the reflexive fight and flight strategies. Damasio argues that the conceptual activity of the frontal cortex always works in combination with the affective activity within the limbic regions of the brain, particularly the amygdala. Persons accidentally injured so that the amygdala is extirpated can think and act like others but have no feeling that anything that they do has any validity. They are, in a sense, autistic. They can point to their parents as looking like the parents whom they knew but will declare that those persons are not really their parents but are only pretending to be such. These views make it most probable that particular emotions often are linked to the play performances that represent them in some practical sense as proposed here in the emotion–play relationships of Table 1.2. It might further be supposed that the persistence of many of these play forms throughout human history, particularly the contests and festivals, are driven by these underlying biological emotions. That is, when we find ourselves enjoyably involved in these pleasures of performance and feeling, we are, as it were, still celebrating a system of affect regulations that has been with hominids for millions of years.

Having made possible the view that the emotions are central to play and that the specific emotions are generally connected to the motivation of specific kinds of play performances, it now has to be understood just how the primary emotions come to be expressed, or at least represented, in play. In this respect Fein and Kinney suggest that pretense involves the expression of emotionally consequential issues *without* a direct experiencing of emotion. "Play will not occur if there is any doubt about the derivative non real status of the expressed affect or about its acceptability in a given situation" (1994, p. 199).

The crux of the play problem then rests in trying to comprehend how play can involve the expression of emotionally consequential feelings without the direct experiencing of these emotions. This might be called the actors' dilemma.

The extensive work over the years of William Corsaro (1985) is most relevant in showing just how difficult it is for preschool children to form play groups together and how quickly they fall apart. In a book entitled *Friendship and Peer Culture in the Early Years* (1985) he shows that the children have trouble with the actors' dilemma, which is how to pretend what one is feeling without actually feeling it. The younger they are, the more they want to introduce their own real Freudian or other feelings. But all that does is to frighten off other children. They all have to arrive at a consensus of pretense with which to hold themselves together, and they usually achieve this by exaggerated meta-representations of what they want to indirectly express. There is evidence that they get together more easily if they are indeed metarepresenting similar original emotions (Howes, Unger, & Matheson, 1992). All of this, incidentally, makes clearer that this chapter is discussing Darwin's collectively represented emotions. This is not about the idiosyncratic emotional worlds with which play therapists have to deal.

Table 1.3 begins with a list of cultural rhetorics or contexts for the emotions to be dealt with. These are not quite the same as those presented in *The Ambiguity of Play* (Sutton-Smith, 1997). Progress has been conflated with initiations in general, including the more extreme forms of hazing and the milder curriculum forms of play. Frivolity and the imagination have been incorporated into iconoclasm. In a general sense columns A and B are about the realities of culture and emotions, and C, D, and E are about pretense, that is, about the actors' dilemma of converting these realities of A and B into the metarepresentations that follow.

Column A, named culture, is a statement about the cultural value context within which these emotions find their traditional place. These are like metaphoric ghosts that dominate our public ideas on leisure. They make us think that we "know" what we are talking about when we discuss sports or chess or mountain climbing or gambling or teasing or jokes or the Mardi Gras or being in the zone. Their emotional connotations are made most obvious when crowds of spectators or audiences gather together and reveal their feelings en masse during the performances.

Column B gives some of the reasons that these six emotions underlie the cultural rhetorics. This column names the six classic emotions presented here and serves as a reminder that these are ancient survival emotions and as such are a guarantee at least of an engagement and at best of wild excitement to those who participate.

Table 1.3
The Dialectics of Playful Emotions

THESES		ANTITHESES		SYNTHESES	
A	B	C	D	E	F
Culture	**Emotion**	**Play**	**Metarepresentation**	**Mastery**	**Parody**
Hegemony Power	Anger	Contest	Attack	Strategies	Invulnerability
Fatalism	Fear	Deep play	Risk	Courage	Invulnerability
Initiation	Shock	Hazing	Playfulness	Resilience	Invulnerability
Iconoclasm	Disgust	Gross play	Comedy	Imagination	Invulnerability
Identity	Loneliness	Festival	Inebriation	Sociability	Invulnerability
Self-esteem	Egomania	Display	Flow	Charisma	Invulnerability
CONTENTS					
Traditions	Survival	Frames	Play ethic	Antitheses	Unpredictable
Culture	Excitements	Rules	Playfulness		Incongruous
Spectators	Disruptions	Referees	Spontaneity		Celebrations
	Seepages	Hierarchy	Exuberance		
	Vulnerability				
	Tyson effect				

This belief that they underlie the play-forms rests in their:

- centrality to the six rhetorics and the strength of feeling that most players have in favor of their own ludic expression of these rhetorics. It is emphasized that each of these emotions is a kind of vulnerability the implicit meaning of which all the players share;

- manifestation in fights, riots, hooliganism, and cheating when there's a breakdown in or about the playing that leads to a regression into these direct original emotions;

- occurrence when a player flares up with anger or reacts with real shock or disgust. These momentary "seepages" during the course of the play might be taken as a validation of the view that hidden within the games, these emotions are nevertheless the motivating presence. Although the point being made is about the six collective emotions being dealt with, Freud makes a similar point in dealing with the individualistic emotional manifestations, which were his concern. Thus, he says that "the unwelcome phenomena . . . is pushed away from consciousness (repressed, etc.) but is nevertheless not robbed of all capacity to express itself" (1938, p. 178);

- antithetical position to the specific emotions found in Column E. These are performance masteries, which by implication indicate the continuing presence of the classic six emotions against which they are reacting; and

- Tyson effect, wherein persons maladjusted in these emotions are drawn to their playful representations and often cause their disruption. This happens one time in four, says Pellegrini (1995), when boys play-fight on the playground.

ANTITHESES

But what is more important is that Column C and Column D begin the process of secondary emotional mediation. Thus, the basic forms of emotion are meta-represented in a series of play-forms. These play-forms (C) and meta-representations (D) are not direct representations of the emotions. They are often much curtailed or incongruous, variations on direct expression of the emotions.

Thus, in the first group of contest plays, motivated by anger in this theory, there are various, often aggressive expressions of highly structured and yet limited kinds of attack. In risk plays, motivated by fear, the range is from provocations to highly controlled flight or withdrawal. In hazing and teasing plays, motivated by shock, there are countering expressions of the ultimate playfulness and ridiculousness of these initiatory ventures. In gross form plays, motivated by disgust, the world is allowed to be an upside-down comedy. In festivals, motivated by loneliness, there are typically social excesses such as exuberant and inebriant impulses. In self-displays, motivated by narcissism, there can be a search for more controlled cynosures and charismatic display experiences.

To this point secondary emotional controls over the original emotions show in these forms of play:

1. the character and incongruity of the many metarepresentations of the original emotions; but in addition,

2. all forms of play are also run with routines, rules, hierarchies, and mini-legal systems (Ariel, 2002), and where appropriate, by coaches, teachers, supervisors, and referees; and

3. all play (as in Column D) is governed strongly or weakly by a play ethic. This is perhaps best understood through the research on "playfulness," which shows that there are always some children who are especially capable in this way and whose characteristics generally control what happens in play. These are persons who, in childhood at least, are more spontaneous, more exuberant, more optimistic, and more empathic. These are a few of the traits that have appeared in considerable research on this subject (Barnett, 1998; Fein & Kinney, 1994; Singer, 1999).

Column E cites the controlling antithetical masteries of the successful players within each play-form. Most remarkably, the players in each kind of play-form triumph by *doing the opposite* of what the basic emotions might suggest. Thus, the players *control* anger through their deployment of tactics or strategies instead of giving way to it. Or they show *courage* in play instead of being fearful. Or they show *resilience* to shock. Or they use the freedom of fantasy to ingest any disgusting iconoclasm. Or they overcome sadness by *bonding*. Finally, they convert egoistic manias into concrete kinds of cynosures or charismatic *status*.

These masteries within play, which were acknowledged by the famous psychoanalytic play theorist Erik Erikson (1950), are, however, not just the slim kind of reality in play that he suggested. His view may have had considerable relevance to the disturbed children whose play therapy he was attending but simply did not do justice to the endless hours of skill in performance alluded to by the mastery concepts of strategy, courage, resilience, imagination, bonding, and charismatic success. It is remembered that Goffman (1961) believed that in play it is as if the player is learning in a virtual way how to act in control when metaphorically under fire.

SYNTHESIS

In Column F the performances are in a way like a return to Columns A and B. The performances of the prior accounts (Columns C–E) now are revealed to have characteristics of the original reflexive emotions insofar as they are unpredictable and incongruous. What is imagined in all cases of play is that the subjects have overcome their basic vulnerabilities even if they do happen to lose the game. They have given it all that they have and in so doing have behaved with an openness and wildness (an unpredictability and incongruity) that are a performance parody of the original emotions that have initiated this whole mediating dialectical performance. If the point is not clear, then the wildness of their celebrations may indeed make it so.

CONCLUSIONS

Play as Emotional Dialectics

Implicit throughout this chapter is the struggle represented between the spirit of the six emotions and the wide range of voluntary controls to which they are subjected. If there is any single message here, it seems to be that the six emotions can indeed be expressed as long as they are substantially controlled in all of the ways that are listed and discussed. Each game and play-form combines a dialectic of expression and control such as anger-strategy, fear-courage, shock-resilience, disgust-imagination, loneliness-bonding, and mania-charisma. In all of this, play is itself an amazing exultation of the notion that the involuntary emotions can indeed be allowed their expression if spirited within these playful terms. Play is here a dialectic of the older and newer forms of emotional survival. The involuntary and the reflexive, versus the voluntary and the reflective, are combined in a most motivating and yet survival-connected form of excitement. Play appears to be a message that this is a civilized as well as an "earthy" way of arranging the relationship of these conflicting emotions that are at the bottom of mammalian evolutionary history. For example, there would appear to be a relationship between human contests and animal play-fighting, between risk taking and animal locomotor activity, and between animal object play and disgust as well as several of the other human categories (Power, 2000). On the other hand, the present emphasis on play-forms as mediators between emotions gives some justification even to those scholarly greats the historian Johan Huizinga (1955/1938) and the sociologist Norbert Elias (Elias & Dunning, 1986), both of whom have associated play with cultural progress in one way or another.

Play Simply Defined as Parody

Obviously, the players, although they are only pretending that nothing really matters in one sense, are, in another sense, extremely and seriously excited about the validity of their own performances within the play paradigm of contests, fantasy, and so forth. Their mastery opposes the very classic emotions and yet in a sense both expresses as well as inverts them. Play in the performance sense makes fun of these six extreme emotions, and yet in the play paradigm sense it is also preoccupied with the game play-related implication of these six emotions as attacks and risks and so on. Further, the play performances are like the six emotions in being unpredictable. In addition, play actions, which are non-normative and done in pretense even, show some analogy with the incongruous and wild behavior of the six emotions in the primal state; despite all the direct ways in which play controls the six emotions through metarepresentations, rules, playful ethics, and antithetical performance masteries, the play performances also directly simulate the character of those ancient emotions in their own unpredictability and incongruities. On the one hand, then, the performance controls mask the primary emotions, and, on the other, they mimic the primary emotions. Furthermore and astonishingly, there are the even more unpredictable celebrations, which often occur during or at the end of group play. Whoever wins or whoever loses may behave with the extreme involuntary emotions of happiness or sadness, even destroying the playing field and the surrounding town, or more briefly, rolling about on the ground, leaping on others, or weeping with others, or more frequently, becoming engaged subsequently in inebriant celebrations. It is remarkable that, in a cultural event in which so much time has been spent in the measured control of these basic emotions, these ultimate celebratory outcomes can sometimes so completely defy that same control. What is at one moment heralded perhaps as a fascinating example of civilized "controls" is at the very next expressed as the very opposite. There is, indeed, an irony in hitching the concept of civilization to the ludic supposition that group play associations can take place without evolutionary stress. Perhaps this is why the earliest meanings of the word "fun" in the English language (*Oxford English Dictionary*, 1985) mean that to play is to make a fool of someone or something. It would seem that we are making a fool of ourselves every time we get too serious about either the animality or the civilized nature of play, and that is why it is so much paradoxical fun. Clearly, we have in play a more complex series of paradoxes than Bateson (1972) noted in his essay on play as a paradox of reality versus irreality. In the present case we have the paradox that in order to both express and contain the involuntary emotions, play presents itself as like these emotions in its own inversions, incongruity, unpredictability, and celebrations. The cure for the conflict between primary and secondary emotional control systems in this play phenomenon is the creation of a simulative involuntary behavioral system, which in concert with the players' ethic of playfulness might be called a "behavioral" parody of the players' emotionality or vulnerabilities. Following Hutcheon's (1985) *Theory of Parody*, perhaps play can be defined as behavioral parody of emotional vulnerability because it both mimics and inverts the primary emotions ironically. It makes fun of it all. At the very least this provides the kind of summary definition that was sought at the beginning of this search for the meaning of play. At least it also focuses on what seems to be the key in all playing, which is to make fun of the emotional vulnerabilities of anger, fear, shock, disgust, loneliness, and narcissism.

In sum, it might be speculated that a reason that these dialectical emotional bases of play have never been dealt with seriously is that play itself is a protection against such recognition. The emotional vulnerabilities, which are the essence of play, are masked from the players by the rules, the play ethic, and their own inversive masteries. Thus, play is meant not only to represent these vulnerabilities but also to bring protection against them by masking their relevance.

ADAPTABILITY THEORY

What follows is a discussion of the relevance of the foregoing emotional dialectical view of play as to the usual questions about adaptation. The procedure here is to follow Burghardt's (2001) division between primary processes, which set the context for the emergence and survival of play, and the secondary processes, which refer to play behaviors and their usefulness for adaptive purposes. To this is added a tertiary process to discuss play's claims to functional autonomy.

Primary Processes

Let's begin with John Allman's 1999 account of the evolution of the brain, which suggests the priorities that were necessary in the survival of the earliest mammals as infants. Any list of the requirements for these early playing infants would have to cover their needs for homeostatic bodily heat, parental protection, and brain stimulation as well as social stimulation by the extended social groups to which they belong. While there are various explanations of the way that play can serve the infants' needs for additional stimulation, what is to be given particular attention here, in the light of the above descriptions of the place of emotions in play, is the primary process of protecting the infant from its emotional survival vulnerabilities. Thus, what strikes some scholars most about evolution, for example, is that survival in the face of predation is the central primary kind of vulnerability at all levels of creature complexity (Ehrenreich, 1997; Wrangham & Peterson, 1996). Presumably, anxiety over anger, fear, and shock could be primarily geared to this kind of vulnerability. By contrast, disgust, loneliness, and egoism seem more geared to anxieties induced by the immediate family and social contexts. Nevertheless, all of these anxieties might have generated duplicate play genes that parallel these conditions but with the kind of included safeguards and mutations that have been discussed earlier. As Allman (1999) puts it, "the duplicated gene escapes the pressures of natural selection operating on the original gene and thereby can accumulate mutations that enable the new gene to perform previously non existent functions while the old gene continues to perform its original and presumably vital role" (pp. 49–50).

Secondary Processes

Secondary processes are the typical growth correlates of various forms of play, from social to cognitive, with which modern play investigators are familiar. In the present context, the key adaptive argument might be that play is biologically an instrument of emotional regulation because it is an experience of the voluntarily controlled emotionality managing the involuntarily uncontrolled emotionality, even though the total events are as much a parody of such control as they are a representation of it. Still, acquiring mastery in such controls might subsequently make a contribution to human adaptation. It might be supposed that individuals who play more will be more capable of controlling their emotional lives in terms of their capacities for performance strategy, courage, resilience, imagination, sociability, or charisma. There is some empirical support for this occurrence in the finding that parents who play with their children have children who are more successful in playing with their peers as well as having a deeper understanding of the nature of different emotions (Carson, Burks, & Parke, 1993). But perhaps the largest support for seeing play as the present dialectic of emotional regulation is found in the neurobiology of emotional development as presented by Allan Schore in his book *Affect Regulation and the Origin of the Self* (1994). Briefly, he argues that emotional health and emotional development of a child and parent require the parent's dealing with both emotions that are distressful and those that are a relief (what we might term here primary and secondary emotions). But what is essential, he says, is that this "dialectic"(his term) of distress and relief should be injected in a positive manner into the mother–infant relationship. What is remarkable here is that his account of good parenting is parallel to the account of play as presented in this chapter. The good parent–infant relationship and the good game both involve a dialectical engagement of contrary emotions within a positive framework. This might imply that good parenting is the key to the generation or selection of this play duplicate gene, the position taken by the greatest of all animal play theorists, Fagen (1995).

Tertiary Processes

This concept applies to play when it is said to be intrinsically motivated. In the present context it implies that the primary and secondary emotional mediation that occurs in play and that began perhaps some 65 million years ago now runs mainly under its own steam with little need for any particular consequences other than those mediated within the play frame. The consequences within the play frame are the amelioration of those key primary emotional vulnerabilities forever connected with evolutionary survival throughout history in either the biological or cultural senses. More specifically, play as a parodic event with inversion and irony offers amusement as well as excitement and thus constitutes an alternative form of reality (Goodman, 1992). That this alternative form is one of adaptive virtuality means that playing the game is as good as, or better than, living realistically. It means that in the play the inanities, the chaos, or the mortality of everyday life can be transcended at least temporarily and can thus be adaptive by making the rest of life worth living, even though it often doesn't merit that assistance. This is perhaps echoed in Bakhtin's (1984) study of the inebriant, gluttonous, obscene, and disgusting festivals of medieval Rabelaisian peasants when he suggests that the festivals lifted them out of their ordinarily miserable and depressive lives into a brief time of greater non-vulnerable liveliness. It made their ordinary life temporarily worth living when indeed it was generally not worth living at all—thus the glory of play as a parody of emotional vulnerability.

REFERENCES

Allman, J. M. (1999). *Evolving brains.* New York: Scientific American Library; dist. by W. H. Freeman.

Ariel, S. (2002). *Children's imaginative play.* Westport, CT: Greenwood Press.

Bakhtin, M. M. (1984). *Rabelais and his world.* Bloomington: Indiana University Press.

Barnett, L. A. (1998). The adaptive powers of being playful. In M. C. Duncan, G. Chick, & A. Aycock (Eds.), *Play and Culture Studies, 1* (pp. 97–119). Greenwich, CT: Ablex.

Bateson, G. (1972). *Steps to an ecology of mind.* New York: Ballantine.

Bekoff, M., & Byers, J. A. (Eds.). (1998). *Animal play: Evolutionary, comparative and ecological perspectives.* New York: Cambridge University Press.

Bronner, S. (1988). *American children's folklore.* Litttle Rock, AR: August House.

Burghardt, G. M. (1998). The evolutionary origins of play revisited: Lesson from turtles. In M. Bekoff & J. A. Byers (Eds.), *Animal play: Evolutionary, comparative and ecological perspectives* (pp. 1–26). New York: Cambridge University Press.

Burghardt, G. M (2001). Attributes and neural substrates. In E. Bass (Ed.), *Handbook of behavioral neural biology* (vol. 13, pp. 327–366). New York: Plenum Press.

Carson, J., Burks, V., & Parke, R. D. (1993). Parent–child physical play determinants and consequences. In K. MacDonald (Ed.), *Parent–child play, descriptions and implications* (pp. 197–220). Albany, NY: SUNY Press.

Corsaro, W. (1985). *Friendship and peer culture in the early years.* Norwood, NJ: Ablex.

Damasio, A. R. (1994). *Descartes' error: Emotion, reason and the human brain.* New York: Putnam.

Damasio, A. R. (1999). *The feeling of what happens.* New York: Harcourt.

Darwin, C. (1965/1872). *The expression of the emotions in man and animals.* Chicago: University of Chicago Press.

Edelman, G. M. (1992). *Bright air, brilliant fire.* New York: Basic Books.

Ehrenreich, B. (1997). *Blood rites.* NewYork: Holt.

Ekman, P. (1992). Are there basic emotions? *Psychological Review, 99*(3), 550–553.

Elias, N., & Dunning, E. (1986). *Quest for excitement: Sport and leisure in the civilizing process.* Oxford: Blackwell.

Erikson, E. (1950). *Childhood and society.* New York: Norton.

Fagen, R. (1995). Animal play, games and angels: Biology and brain. In A. D. Pellegrini (Ed.), *The future of play theory* (pp. 23–44). Albany, NY: SUNY Press.

Fein, G. F., & Kinney, P. (1994). He's a nice alligator: Observations on the affective organization of pretense. In A. Slade & D. Wolf (Eds.), *Children at play: Clinical and developmental studies of play* (pp. 188–205). New York: Oxford University Press.

Frederickson, B. L. (1998). What good are positive emotions? *Review of General Psychology, 2*(3), 300–319.

Freud, S. (1938). *The basic writings of Sigmund Freud.* NewYork: Modern Library.

Goffman, E. (1961). *Encounters.* Indianapolis: Bobbs-Merrill.

Goleman, D. (1995). *Emotional intelligence.* New York: Bantam Books.

Goodman, F. D. (1992). *Ecstasy, ritual and alternate reality.* Bloomington: Indiana University Press.

Gould, S. J. (1996). *Full house.* New York: Harmony Books.

Gustines, E. A., & Bierman, F. (2001). A year of champions. *New York Times,* December 30, S5–S8.

Howes, C., Unger, O., & Matheson, C. C. (1992). *The collaborative construction of pretend.* Albany, NY: SUNY Press.

Huizinga, J. (1955/1938). *Homo ludens: A study of the play element in culture.* Boston: Beacon Press.

Hutcheon, N. L. (1985). *A theory of parody.* New York: Methuen.

Ledoux, J. (1996). *The emotional brain.* New York: Simon & Schuster.

Lewis, M. (2000). Self-conscious emotions: Embarrassment, pride, shame and guilt and the emergence of human emotions. In M. Lewis & J. M. Haviland-Jones (Eds.), *Handbook of emotions* (pp. 265–280). New York: Guilford Press.

Loy, J. W. (Ed.). (1982). Preface. In *The paradoxes of play.* West Point, NY: Leisure Press.

Mascolo, M. F., & Griffin, S. (1998). *What develops in emotional development.* New York: Plenum Press.

Opie, I., & Opie, P. (1959). *The lore and language of schoolchildren.* Oxford: Clarendon Press.

Oxford English Dictionary. (1985). 24th printing. Oxford: Oxford University Press.

Pellegrini, A. D. (1995). *School recess and playground behavior.* Albany, NY: SUNY Press.

Power, T. G. (2000). *Play and exploration in children and animals.* Mahwah, NJ: Erlbaum.

Schore, A. N. (1994). *Affect regulation and the origin of the self.* Hillsdale, NJ: Erlbaum.

Singer, D. G. (1999). Imagination, play and television. In J. A. Singer & P. Salovey (Eds.), *At play in the fields of consciousness* (pp. 302–326). Mahwah, NJ: Erlbaum.

Sutton-Smith, B. (1975). Play as adaptive potentiation. *Sportswissenschaft 5,* 103–118.

Sutton-Smith, B. (1978). *The dialectics of play.* Schorndorf, Germany: Hoffman.

Sutton-Smith, B. (1997). *The ambiguity of play.* Cambridge, MA: Harvard University Press.

Sutton-Smith, B. (2001a). Reframing the variability of players and play. In S. Reifel (Ed.), *Play and culture studies* (vol. 3, pp. 27–50). Westport, CT: Ablex.

Sutton-Smith, B. (2001b). Emotional breaches in play and narrative. In A. Goncu & E. L. Klein (Eds.), *Children in play, story and school* (pp. 161–176). New York: Guilford Press.

Sutton-Smith, B. (2002). Recapitulation redressed. In J. L. Roopnarine (Ed.), *Play and culture studies* (vol. 4, pp. 3–21). Westport, CT: Ablex.

Sutton-Smith, B., Mechling, J., Johnson, T. W., & McMahon, F. F. (Eds.). (1999). *Children's folklore.* Logan: Utah State University Press.

Wrangham, R., & Peterson, D. (1996). *Demonic males.* Boston: Houghton Mifflin.

Chapter 2

Simmel: On Sociability as the Play-Form of Human Association

Thomas S. Henricks

If a modern sociologist were asked which founder of that discipline offered the most profound commentaries on the subject of play, the answer would come quickly enough: Georg Simmel. Especially in his 1910 essay on sociability, the "play-form" of human association (Simmel, 1950, pp. 40–57), Simmel offered a dazzling array of insights about the nature of play and the roles of those who would be players. These observations are included in the major English-language anthologies of Simmel's work (see, e.g., Simmel, 1950, 1971) and are studied by sociology graduate students as part of their formal training in theory and culture studies. With the recent "renaissance" in Simmel studies, including attempts to link his thought to post-modernist approaches (see Pescolido & Rubin, 2000; Weinstein & Weinstein, 1993), the impact of Simmel on the social sciences seems destined to increase markedly.

For such reasons, it is odd that the field of play studies has paid so little attention to Simmel's work. His thoughts are not examined in the major compendia of play theory (see, e.g., Ellis, 1973; Spariosu, 1989; Sutton-Smith, 1997) nor do they figure prominently in contemporary research. Some of this neglect may be due to the fact that Simmel's work is stylistically difficult and quite fragmentary in its treatment of subject matter (see Axelrod, 1979, pp. 36–40). A more likely cause is the fact that modern play studies is dominated by scholars from psychology, anthropology, education, and animal studies rather than sociology. In that setting, contemporary studies of play have focused especially on the activities of children and animals, subjects that Simmel largely ignored. However, dismissing Simmel on these grounds is hardly justifiable. Sociology was only one of the intellectual commitments of a man who was equally a student of philosophy, psychology, and aesthetics (see Wolff, 1950, p. xix). Indeed, Simmel turned from sociology during the last 10 years of his career to address more directly what Frisby (1984, p. 32) calls "the philosophy of culture." In this broader sense, then, Simmel's observations are pertinent to all manner of questions regarding the possibilities for human creativity and self-determination in the modern age.

In this chapter, I elevate Simmel's standing in the contemporary field of play studies. To accomplish this task, it is necessary to explain who Simmel was in the context of his life and times, to describe his major contributions to the study of play, and to indicate how his ideas might be extended for future work in this field.

SIMMEL'S LIFE AND SOCIOLOGICAL CONTRIBUTIONS

Simmel's biographers (see, e.g., Coser, 1977, p. 194; Frisby, 1984, p. 21) are fond of noting that he was born in Berlin in 1858 at the corner of Friedrichstrasse and Leipzigerstrasse, a great intersection resembling at some point Times Square in New York. In this light, Simmel is pictured as the consummate urban intellectual at a time when Berlin itself was changing from a city to a metropolis. In 1840, Berlin had 400,000 people; 60 years later, it had 4 million (Coser, 1977, p. 203). As a stylish commentator on intellectual affairs who lived nearly his entire life within the city, Simmel was a significant contributor to Berlin's emerging cosmopolitanism and cultural spirit. Indeed, when Simmel left the city to take a university position in Strasbourg in 1914, newspaper editorials screamed, "Berlin without Simmel: Unthinkable!" Unthinkable perhaps for Simmel as well—as social isolation and declining health precipitated his death 4 years later.

During his 60 years, Simmel was a prolific speaker and writer who produced 25 books and more than 300 articles and reviews (Frisby, 1984, p. 22). Most of these writings comment in some fashion on the development of modern culture and, more specifically, on the character of urban life. For example, his most famous book—on the "philosophy of money"—is not a treatise on economics but rather an analysis of how social relationships have been altered by this impersonal medium of exchange (Simmel, 1990). Similarly, his classic essay (Simmel, 1950, pp. 409–424) on the "metropolis and mental life" is essentially a discussion of social relations and personal experience under the terms of city life.

Simmel's preoccupation with the city and modern culture shaped his more strictly sociological writings as well. Much like a great city, society is portrayed as a complex web of interactions sustained by the interests and objectives of millions of people. While individuals themselves provide the energy and inspiration for all that happens, their activities are channeled (and constrained) by increasingly objectified and abstract forms. As conditioned by these cultural and social forms, human intercommunication is seen as a network of busy intersections, with all kinds of people coming together, forming groups, acting out their perceived responsibilities to one another, and then modifying or dissolving these connections. Simmel's sociology is thus a sociology of process or encounter. People compete, compromise, and cooperate in ever-changing ways; no moment is like another (see Simmel, 1955).

Furthermore, there is always a creative tension or "distance" between individuals and their involvements (see Levine, 1971, pp. xxxiv–xxxv). We are always "partly within and partly without" our public lives; some elements of ourselves are brought forward, and others are withheld. Much like the urban revelers whom he studied, people in Simmel's world wear a variety of social masks. This distinctive viewpoint has become familiar to modern readers through the writings of Erving Goffman (e.g., 1969; see also Manning, 1992, p. 19), one of Simmel's academic descendants. However, it should also be apparent how a sociology that focuses on social life as personal encounter; on the mergers of competition and cooperation in social exchange; and on the possibilities for individual resistance, creativity, and disguise in the social world is connected intimately with the concerns of contemporary play studies.

Two examples that illustrate Simmel's thinking well are his treatments of the "stranger" as a distinctive role (1971, pp. 143–149) and sheer number of people as a determinant of group relations (1950, pp. 105–169). In each case, his argument is that certain "forms" channel interaction and experience in distinctive ways, even though the subject matter or "contents" of those interactions may vary widely. His essay on the stranger focuses not on the traveler who simply passes through but rather on those who come and stay within the group. Examples of this are foreign visitors and merchants, minorities like European Jews, and even professional observers like sociologists. The existence (and semi-acceptance) of such outsiders in the group is important because that status creates a set of new possibilities for group relationships. For example, strangers commonly possess a relative objectivity of judgment about group matters and provide new ideas leading to social creativity. For such reasons, they are often recipients of personal disclosure or confession from others. Because strangers are less firmly established in the group, they may actually experience more social mobility—or at least more access to wider social circles—than more permanent members. In general, then, strangers participate in a range of relationships that are somewhat cooler and less personal than those enjoyed by full-fledged members. To use Simmel's phrase (1971, p. 148), they are both "near and far at the same time."

In a similar way, the sheer number of persons determines group possibility. In Simmel's discussion of the "dyad" and "triad," he explains how adding a third person creates a much fuller sense that the group is an entity in itself. Indeed, the group can now survive the loss of a member. Furthermore, relations themselves become somewhat more specialized and impersonal. In addition to changing the level of responsibility for each person, the three-person group features new clusters of roles like "spectators" or "isolates" and permits the formation of two-person alliances ("coalitions"). This growth in artificiality, formality, and even individuality accelerates as additional members are added (see Simmel, 1971, pp. 251–293).

Despite Simmel's prolific speeches and writing—and the celebrity that attended these—his scholarly career generally is acknowledged to be incomplete or even a failure. This may seem an odd judgment about a man who was the center of his own literary circle in Berlin and who taught famous students like Karl Mannheim, Georg Lukacs, and Ernst Bloch. Furthermore, Simmel was a popular teacher whose lectures drew hundreds of students. Still, his reputation as an academic outsider or "stranger" persists. Despite the support of Max Weber, his work was not well regarded by many of the leading figures of the German academic establishment. In consequence, he remained a *privatdozent* (i.e., one who depends for his living on student fees) for almost his entire career.

There are reasons behind this official disapproval (see Coser, 1977; Frisby, 1984). Simmel was Jewish in an academic world dominated by Christians. He was too popular with students. He was as interested in the popular press and lecture circuit as he was in more sober academic forums. Indeed, he seemed to reject the norms of contemporary German social science, which emphasized patient, exacting studies of narrow topics. Furthermore, he tended not to use footnotes in his writing or otherwise signify the importance of others, and he was a bit of a showman in both his personal style and manner of public discourse. For such reasons, Simmel was dismissed by one contemporary critic as having invented a "sociology for the literary salon" (Frisby, 1984, p. 35).

Perhaps it is more accurate to say that Simmel was something of an academic "player." A servant only of his inclinations, he flitted about a vast field of topics—mealtimes, Rodin's sculpture, fashion, secrecy and secret societies, coquetry, adventure, the gift, faithfulness, and so on. Everything was touched in a distinctive way that emphasized the interplay of sociocultural form and individual appetite. He was the great proponent of the essay and the public lecture. Every topic he held at arm's length in a way that signified both curiosity and dispassion. Indeed, it was said of his lecture style that he could hold up the most ordinary subject and make it seem like a diamond, by turning it so the audience could see and appreciate each facet (see Wolff, 1950, p. xvii). He did this without apparent structure or notes; indeed, he seemed to be making it up as he went along. For such reasons, Frisby (1981, pp. 68–101) has described Simmel as a "flaneur," a stroller of boulevards who partakes of the sights of a city and considers them at his ease. Much like a restaurant critic analyzing a meal, Simmel savored the pleasures of the modern world. However, he was always at the edge of that world; he was never taken in.

Simmel's status in the modern sociological community owes much to the early sociologists at the University of Chicago who, upon the establishment of that department in 1892, disseminated his thought (see Levine, 1971). Indeed, the *American Journal of Sociology*, published by that university, included nine of his essays in its first few years. The interest of the Chicago sociologists in the city as a living, breathing environment owes heavily to Simmel, as do later emphases on symbolic interactionism and exchange theory, both central theories in the field. In the largest sense, Simmel's interests in roles as units of analysis, in the interplay between "forms" and "contents" at different levels of social reality, in the objectification of cultural and social form, in the importance of conflict to social order, and in the characteristic tension between people and their environments continue to influence the field.

SOCIABILITY: THE PLAY-FORM OF HUMAN ASSOCIATION

As noted above, Simmel himself was something of a player. For him, the act of theorizing and analyzing—of manipulating his subject matter—was more important than the finished product. Indeed, the subject hardly mattered. Fundamentally, Simmel's essays and lectures were aesthetic as well as intellectual experiences, attempts to display tensions and discover harmonies. Not surprisingly, many of his writings focused on famous artists and musicians, on the character of their work and the experience that this work generates in the public mind. To this degree, Simmel was himself the artist, ever contemplating the human experiences of formfulness and disarray.

For such reasons, Simmel was most curious about a class of social occasions where participants gather for purposes of companionship and public festivity. These occasions—and the social structure that they assume—he termed "sociability" (see Simmel, 1950, pp. 40–57). Sociability was of paramount importance to Simmel just because these events are separated—or, at least in their official rationales, are separated—from customary concerns and entanglements. In sociability, people are not to focus on such "contents" as making money, producing products, or training others; instead, they are to commit themselves solely to the experience of association. In that light, sociability distills or makes abstract the elements of social life. Social engagement itself becomes the focus of interaction; what is normally "form" becomes "content" (1950, pp. 40–41). Participants feel the ebb and flow of conversation, the rise and fall in status, the formation and dissolution of groupings in ways that are otherwise less apparent.

To this degree, sociability serves as a kind of training ground in social awareness. People test their social skills, see what reactions they can provoke from others, and conspire in public creation. Simmel felt that people are drawn to such activity fundamentally because they enjoy it. He even imputed a "sociability drive"—somewhat like Schiller's "play drive"—which "extracts the pure process of sociation as a cherished value" (1950, p. 45).

Furthermore, there is a general form for sociability that transcends its individual expressions. Although Simmel himself was especially interested in the occasions of his own milieu—the dinner party, the masquerade, the intellectual bantering of the salon and so on—his judgments are applicable to a great range of other events as well. Thus, block parties, baby showers, bachelor parties, wedding festivities, charity benefits, fraternity bashes, proms and their after-hours derivatives, family reunions, church suppers, and so on all are united by broader themes and structures. Significantly, this form (with all its attendant conventions) becomes objectified in public culture. In sociability, people do not invent their relationships but rather play at or within this distinctive form. Indeed, how well people play the form becomes the focus of collective pleasure and the measure of personal success.

What are the distinctive characteristics of this form of relationship? Simmel identifies some of the general traits of sociability as follows:

1. Sociability is both connected to "real life" and disconnected from it. For the most part, ordinary social life is ruled by past and future. Some of what we do is marked by a respect for historical events and circumstances. People commonly protect established identities, acknowledge the past efforts of friends and family, and employ the creeds of church and state. To that extent, human relationships are carried forward by the inertia of previous patterns and commitments. However, social life is equally a readying for the future, an attempt to replace disability and disadvantage with other states of affairs. Put differently, everyday life is complicated and persistent. Commitments endure; damage lingers. In Simmel's own terms (1950, p. 48), "modern life is overburdened with objective contents and exigencies."

By contrast, sociability is intentionally cut off from external consequence. The silly costumes, lively music, and effusive manners of the festive occasion signify a break from the customary sobriety of everyday life. However, this separation allows the themes of public life to be brought back in a lighter, more harmless way. Sociability is like art, then, to the degree that it abstracts cultural issues and re-presents them for social estimation (1950, p. 43). However, in a manner different from art, sociability routinely makes a parody of profound matters or even excludes issues so serious as to darken the mood of the participants.

2. Sociability features a certain de-personalization of participants. While many believe that people are perhaps most fully themselves when they are at play (see, e.g., Huizinga, 1950; Rahner, 1972), Simmel argues that the opposite is true. To participate in public festivity is to play a distinctive role. Among the elements of that role is the expectation that one will not press overly personal matters into the conversation. To do otherwise is to be out of control or, worse, a "bore." Certainly, individual concerns and experiences animate the interaction, but these are to be treated in a light, even self-mocking fashion. This satiric quality becomes more important as the size of the conversational circle expands.

In this regard, Simmel identifies what he (1950, p. 47) calls "upper and lower sociability thresholds." These are passed, in the first instance, when the individual interacts "from motives of objective content and purpose" and, in the second, "when entirely personal and subjective aspects make themselves felt." These boundaries are exhibited by the telling of jokes and stories at parties. Although these latter activities are, in Simmel's view (p. 53), a "testimonial of intellectual poverty," they are nevertheless valuable as a "means for the liveliness, harmony, and common consciousness of the party." Furthermore, they reveal a movement away from individual intimacy. To Simmel, then, the most successful jokes and stories are those featuring persons or events outside the group itself. Then all listeners can participate with equal pleasure in the banter or admire the artifice of the storyteller.

In an interesting twist, Simmel explains that the relative impersonality of sociability permits a certain freedom. His example (1950, p. 46) is the revealing clothing sometimes worn by women at fancy-dress parties. In a smaller, more serious gathering, a dress with a plunging neckline would be inappropriate. In sociability, such attire is acceptable just because it isn't to be taken seriously. Rather, it is part of a broader masquerade, a stylized contribution to an atmosphere of gaiety and allure. In that sense, the wearer aspires to be provocative only in a general, public way, not to provoke earnest reactions from her viewers.

3. *Sociability depends on cooperation and tact.* Although sociability often showcases lighthearted rivalry and debate, the overall theme is good fellowship. People must know when to stop pressing a point and how to take a joke. The successful party creates and then sustains a bubble of affability. To do this is a collective project requiring considerable social skill by all members. Chief among these abilities is "tact," the ability to help others avoid embarrassment or other serious losses of status (Simmel, 1950, p. 45). The tactful person knows how to ignore rude remarks or behaviors or, more impressively, how to redefine them so that they seem less rude or harmful. In that light, the gifted host or hostess can bring the right people together, kindle their enthusiasm for conversation, and then separate them when that fire has died or burned in dangerous directions. Ideally, all this is done without the participants' knowledge of the manipulation.

4. *Sociability is promoted by social equality.* Max Weber (1958, p. 187) once explained that German bosses had difficulty socializing with their workers because they could never forget (or choose to forget) their superior status. For his part, Simmel emphasizes how such forgetting stands at the heart of sociability. As he (1950, p. 49) explains:

If sociation itself is interaction, its purest and most stylized expression occurs among equals—as symmetry and balance are the most plausible forms of artistic stylization. Inasmuch as it is abstracted from sociation through art or play, sociability thus calls for the purest, most transparent, and most casually appealing kind of interaction, *that among equals.*

However, he is also clear that all this is only a pretense of equality, a "game in which one 'does as if' all were equal, and at the same time, as if one honored each of them in particular" (1950, p. 49). Put differently, sociability depends on the consent of all participants; that is, a kind of informal democracy prevails. At a party, groups form and re-form in very fluid ways. People are not held in place but move about the room as interest dictates. A successful conversation, then, must somehow speak to all its members. As noted previously, bigger groups exhibit conversations that are more superficial and lighthearted; exercises in cleverness and showing off prevail. Nevertheless, these too must respect—or lose—their audience.

For such reasons, Simmel terms sociability an "ideal sociological world in which the pleasure of the individual is closely tied with the pleasure of others" (1950, p. 48). His phrasing the issue in this way is clearly indebted to Kant, who sought a universal ethical scheme that could reconcile individual self-expression and collective well-being. For Simmel, however, this is not an ethical matter but rather one dictated by the "intrinsic principle of the social form itself" (1950, p. 48).

Simmel's famous example of such mutual participation is the coquette (1950, pp. 50–51). As he emphasizes, coquetry is the "play-form" of eroticism. The coquette seems to intimate interest in the male, yet her commitment is always ambiguous. She simulates the gestures of affection but stops short of anything that would signify serious intent. Thus, her admirer is kept suspended between "yes" and "no." However, Simmel emphasizes that the admirer must also play the game. He knows that she is only half-serious and that he must respond in kind. That is, his protestations of love are equally ambiguous. What one finds, then, is a beautiful game of quasi intent, a luxuriating in the "forms" of sexual attraction without their usual consequences.

APPRAISING SIMMEL: PITFALLS AND POSSIBILITIES

Even great thinkers are easy to criticize, especially from a distance of nearly 100 years. Writers are almost always creatures of their times, either trotting out fashionable ideas or railing against them. As noted above, Simmel lived for the lectern, salon, and coffeehouse, places where he could feel his own powers and be appreciated for them. Like other successful types of people then, he perhaps overestimates the voluntarism, even democracy of his chosen settings. As an idealized form, sociability may well develop as a cooperative venture; by contrast, its reality commonly features the very manipulations and malignancies so common to other moments of life. Put differently, parties are also adventures in clique formation, gossip, and sexual predation. People talk about others across the room or when they leave the circle. Indeed, rudeness or social snubbing at parties may be more hurtful just because these events focus on social acceptance and identity so clearly.

Furthermore, Simmel does not choose to analyze the various social consequences or functions of such gatherings. Certainly, sociable events are promoted as times of gentle festivity, when an ethic of polite manners and easy conversation prevails. All this notwithstanding, anyone hosting a party knows that other matters are afoot. Hosts plan their guest lists with an eye to status or social respectability issues. To ensure appropriate attendance, they strategize about the best dates and advertise a list of pleasures. They encourage people to linger so that the affair will be deemed retrospectively a success. Furthermore, invitations themselves may be repayments of personal debts (especially, previous invitations) or attempts to cultivate social contacts. The guests who come are equally cognizant of the range of personal, professional, and even romantic opportunities. In other words, Simmel's (1950, p. 47) imputation of a "sociability drive" as the principal motivation for attendance at such affairs seems in retrospect like a quaint oversimplification.

It is also noteworthy that Simmel doesn't distinguish the implications of specific roles in sociability. Mingle as we will, there are variations in responsibility. The host is a quite specialized and central role, as is the guest of honor (should one exist). Likewise, close friends of the host are expected to come early, stay late, and otherwise help to make the affair a success. Those who have been explicitly invited should be distinguished from the people whom they choose to accompany them. Finally, there may be Simmel's famous "strangers" in the midst, those semi-exotics whom we mine for insight and experience. In other words, sociable gatherings might be better described as concentric circles of commitment that place some roles near the center and others at the margins.

It is easy enough to continue with the criticisms. For example, Simmel's essay doesn't adequately address cross-cultural or historic variation in sociability. To be sure, he does include a brief set of "historical illustrations" (1950, pp. 54–55) explaining how chivalric and aristocratic forms of courtesy in Europe became disconnected from their practical, military origins. In another passage (p. 48) he acknowledges that the social occasions of earlier times tended to be more ceremonial and less personal. Nevertheless, the thrust of his essay suggests that his own Northern European, professional-class occasions are an adequate basis for generalization. As modern social scientists have explained (see, e.g., Handelman, 1990), the character and composition of festive events are one of those things that vary by society and by such matters as age, class, and gender. That is, people tend to have different patterns of inclusion and exclusion, mix their personal and occupational commitments differently, connect these matters quite variably to spiritual concerns, employ different conceptions of time and timeliness, and so on. People everywhere may aspire to be sociable, but they realize these intentions in somewhat different ways.

Furthermore, although Simmel's broader work has been an inspiration to those later sociologists who have focused on social life as process or encounter, his work on sociability doesn't really consider these issues. That is, there is no description here of how social gatherings begin, proceed, and end. Instead, sociability is seen as a rather static form, like the rules for a game of cards. In Simmel's world, people sit at the "tables" of public festivity; they play with what skill and spirit they can muster; they avoid the bad manners that would prevent their being invited back. At the conclusion, they say good-bye to their host and leave. Again, as any partygoer knows, real events feature a continual tension between staying and leaving, connecting with others and finding oneself isolated, feeling overstimulated or bored. As Simmel (1955) himself explained in other writings, social life is a complex web of interactions. Partygoers make their way through these as they do on city streets.

If Simmel's argument seems flawed in these ways, why should he now be praised? As I (2001) have tried to argue in the somewhat similar case of Huizinga, great thinkers are to be esteemed more for the directions that they give us than for the answers that they provide. Through their eyes, we are able to see landscapes formerly hidden from view. Moreover, their writings commonly intimate more than they say plainly. Indeed, as the postmodernists would have it, their texts say much more than the authors themselves comprehend.

In my own view, then, Simmel's thought remains quite pertinent to contemporary play studies. Some of these contributions are described below:

1. *Simmel's emphasis on the formfulness of play is a useful complement to psychological perspectives.* Not surprisingly, psychological approaches tend to emphasize what players themselves bring to public events. Personal interests, creativity, and spirit are all elements of what Lieberman (1977) has termed "playfulness." In relatively inventive ways, players manipulate the conditions of their existence. They laugh and tease and make spectacles of themselves. In a way that no one disputes, people themselves are the life of the party.

Somewhat differently, Simmel envisions sociability as a sociocultural form that channels human communication in restricted ways. Partygoers themselves are clear about the range of expectations that they will encounter. Such issues as dress, mood, times to arrive and leave, conversational topics, polite ways to engage and disengage others, and so on are matters to be addressed. To that degree, sociability is a language that shapes both public conversation and private consciousness.

In Simmel's view, then, public creativity (including the pursuit of pleasure) is bounded. At sociable gatherings, an appropriate set of cultural themes is brought forward for public estimation. These issues are treated in circumscribed ways. To say this is not to negate the private, creative aspects described above but to emphasize the frameworks that facilitate social discourse. Indeed, as Simmel stresses, these frameworks may become the very focus of the interaction; form becomes content. For such reasons, Simmel's insights are a useful correction, particularly in Western societies that celebrate individual impulse and freedom of expression. Play emerges as a sociological as well as psychological adventure.

2. *His exploration of the tension between psychological and social order is interesting and productive.* Simmel's greatness lies in his ability not merely to recognize the twin themes described above but to reconcile them. With that in mind, sociability is not merely formfulness but rather the encounter with form. All of social life features the meeting of personal appetite and public expectation; however, at sociable occasions, these elements frequently collide. Parties stand far away from more serious events like funerals or investitures of public office. The former are noisy and disruptive. People play at rebellion.

In a sense, then, every partygoer is an amateur sociologist. As Simmel himself did with his lecture topics, revelers hold the manners and mores of their societies at arm's length. For public amusement, they turn and twist and tease these themes. Jokes and stories prevail.

As others (see, e.g., Schilling, 1965) have explained, comedy differentiates itself from tragedy by its celebration of individual resistance and relative impartiality of vision. In contrast to the tragic perspective, comic actors do not consider themselves as trapped by circumstance. Instead they oppose and puncture inevitability. By that collective process, social manners and mores are found to be something of an artifice—and an incongruous one at that. By revealing that the emperor is, in fact, naked, people claim some control over their lives. This sense of "distance" or tension between people and sociocultural form is a profound theme in all of Simmel's work.

As in other play settings, then, sociability provides people with opportunities to assess their world. From the safety of their festive identities, individuals mock their world and themselves (as participants in that world) at the same time.

3. *His emphasis on the relative impersonality of play counters traditional views.* As argued above, most writers on play have extolled the relative freedom of personal expression that is found in such settings. By contrast, the circumstances of routine adult existence are seen commonly as a rat race or maze generating anxiety and unhappiness. To the rescue comes play. Stated more strongly, play allows people to be "themselves" in ways that are otherwise forbidden.

While Simmel acknowledges the relative freedom that is gained by fencing the playground away from external schemes and obligations, he does not believe that people are more fully themselves in play. Sociability, in his mind, is a distinctive type of occasion that demands a certain kind of role-performance. One of the critical elements of that role is that people must not insert their own personal concerns too deeply into the event. Individuals restrain their expressive impulses or, rather, let these come out in narrowly defined ways.

To that degree, sociability depersonalizes people. As in a masquerade, people appear as stylized representations of themselves. Just as sporting activities encourage an aggressive, energetic version of the person or business ventures a shrewder, more manipulative side, so sociability cultivates a jaunty, clever, outgoing persona. Participants are merely actors in an improvisational theater of public festivity.

4. *His interest in mutuality/cooperation counters current emphases on the competitive, assertive aspects of play.* In relatively individualistic societies like the United States, much attention has been given to the personal experiences associated with play and to the view of play as a confrontation between people and their environments (see Csikszentmihalyi, 1975; Pellegrini, 1995). In that sense, adults are depicted playing ball games, gambling, climbing mountains, playing chess and computer games, and so on. In play, people test the limits of their world and discover their own powers in the process.

Although Simmel recognizes the above themes, his work is interesting because of its emphasis on the cooperative aspects of play. Sociability is a public creation. Together, people work their way through sets of socially appropriate issues by using a framework of established behavioral expectations. To this extent, he emphasizes what I have elsewhere (1999) termed "descending meaning," that is, the conformitive or accommodative response of humans to the conditions of their lives. Accepting these constraints as a voluntary social act—engaging in what Turner (1969) calls "communitas"—is a foundation of mutual self-recognition and a source of considerable joy.

Again, Simmel's significance to modern play studies lies in his ability to reconcile the conforming, yielding project of people (i.e., "communitas") with the more manipulative, assertive project (i.e., "play"). In sociability, people accept formfulness and yet trifle with it at the same time. Moreover, they do this as a more or less voluntary act; reality is less a burden to be endured than a construct that one arranges and manipulates. That precarious balance between yielding to expectation and skillfully deflating it is the tension that sustains the festive occasion.

REFERENCES

Axelrod, C. (1979). *Studies in intellectual breakthrough: Freud, Simmel, Buber.* Amherst: University of Massachusetts Press.
Coser, L. (1977). *Masters of sociological thought.* New York: Harcourt Brace Jovanovich.
Csikszentmihalyi, M. (1975). *Beyond boredom and anxiety.* San Francisco: Jossey-Bass.
Ellis, M. (1973). *Why people play.* Englewood Cliffs, NJ: Prentice-Hall.
Frisby, D. (1981). *Sociological impressionism: A reassessment of Georg Simmel's social theory.* London: Heinemann.
Frisby, D. (1984). *Georg Simmel.* London: Tavistock.
Goffman, E. (1969). *Strategic interaction.* Philadelphia: University of Pennsylvania Press.
Handelman, D. (1990). *Models and mirrors: Toward an anthropology of public events.* New York: Cambridge University Press.
Henricks, T. (1999). Play as ascending meaning: Implications of a general model of play. *Play and Culture Studies, 2,* 257–278.
Henricks, T. (2001). Huizinga's contribution to play studies: A reappraisal." In J. L. Roopnarine (Ed.), *Play and culture studies* (Vol. 4, pp. 23–52). Westport, CT: Ablex.
Huizinga, J. (1950). *Homo ludens: A study of the play element in culture.* Boston: Beacon Press.
Levine, D. (1971). Introduction. In G. Simmel, *On individuality and social forms* (pp. ix–lxv). D. Levine, Ed. Chicago: University of Chicago Press.
Lieberman, J. (1977). *Playfulness: Its relation to imagination and creativity.* New York: Academic Press.
Manning, P. (1992). *Erving Goffman and modern sociology.* Stanford, CA: Stanford University Press.

Pellegrini, A. (Ed.). (1995). *The future of play theory: A multidisciplinary inquiry into the contributions of Brian Sutton-Smith*. Albany, NY: SUNY.

Pescolido, B., & Rubin, B. (2000). The web of group affiliations revisited: Social life, postmodernism, and sociology. *American Sociological Review, 65*(1), 52–76.

Rahner, H. (1972). *Man at play*. New York: Herder and Herder.

Schilling, B. (1965). *The comic spirit*. Detroit: Wayne State University Press.

Simmel, G. (1950). *The sociology of Georg Simmel*. K. Wolff, Trans. and Ed. New York: Free Press.

Simmel, G. (1955). *Conflict and the web of group affiliations*. K. Wolff & R. Bendix, Trans. New York: Free Press.

Simmel, G. (1971). *On individuality and social forms*. D. Levine, Ed. Chicago: University of Chicago Press.

Simmel, G. (1990). *The philosophy of money*. London: Routledge.

Spariosu, M. (1989). *Dionysus reborn: Play and the aesthetic dimension in modern philosophical and scientific discourse*. Ithaca, NY: Cornell Unveristy Press.

Sutton-Smith, B. (1997). *The ambiguity of play*. Cambridge, MA: Harvard University Press.

Turner, V. (1969). *The ritual process: Structure and anti-structure*. Chicago: Aldine.

Weber, M. (1958). *From Max Weber: Essays in sociology*. H. H. Gerth and C. Wright Mills, Trans. & Eds. New York: Oxford University Press.

Weinstein, D., & Weinstein, M. (1993). *Postmodern(ized) Simmel*. London: Routledge.

Wolff, K. (1950). Introduction. In G. Simmel, *The sociology of Georg Simmel* (pp. xvii–lxiv). K. Wolff, Trans. & Ed. New York: Free Press.

Chapter 3

An Introduction to Research in Psychology: Learning to Observe Children at Play

Dana L. Gross

Students often make definitive decisions about whether to continue studying science in their introductory-level classes (Rigden & Tobias, 1991; Tobias, 1990; Wineke & Certain, 1991). In these classes, students are introduced to the scientific method and learn to frame particular questions, to conduct an investigation, to analyze results, and to interpret their findings. They experience the excitement of discovery and the thrill of sharing ideas and findings within a community. When this happens, students are eager to continue their study of science.

Unfortunately, many introductory science courses do not accomplish this. Instead, students complain about large class sizes, impersonal lectures, machine-graded exams, little sense of community among students, and almost no collaborative learning (Rigden & Tobias, 1991). Often when there are laboratory requirements accompanying first courses in science, students are taught to conduct experiments as if they were following recipes from a cookbook, rather than encountering science as a way of knowing.

In the 1995–1996 academic year, the Psychology Department at St. Olaf College piloted an introductory course with the goal of designing an integrated laboratory program that would provide opportunities for beginning students to translate the curiosity that psychology arouses into testable hypotheses and researchable questions and to design experiments as well as collect and analyze data. The resulting course, which was developed further with support from the National Science Foundation, augments the regular three hours per week of lecture and discussion with 10 weeks of three-hour laboratory sessions and a field research project about children's play—the Play Project. The Psychology

Department at St. Olaf is part of the division of natural sciences and mathematics, and the introductory laboratory course in psychology fulfills one of two
general education curriculum requirements. Students bring many expectations to
the course, but the last thing that they expect is to study play for natural science
credit.

The Play Project uses children's play to tie together three of the laboratory
sessions in the course—a Play Lab, an Information Literacy Lab, and a Statistics
Lab—and is the focus of a poster symposium at the end of the semester. The
components of the Play Project are illustrated in Figure 3.1. Whereas the other
self-contained, three-hour labs in the course introduce students to topics such as
psychophysiology, sensation and perception, neuroanatomy, and schedules of
behavior reinforcement, the Play Project lasts all semester and takes students
out of the classroom to observe gender or age differences in children's play. In
the Play Project, students work in teams of three, using naturalistic observational
techniques. Because this project is conducted over the course of the semester,
it helps students appreciate a more "natural" time course for empirical research
(i.e., most scientific inquiry cannot be initiated and concluded within a span of
three hours!).

Figure 3.1
The Components of the Play Project

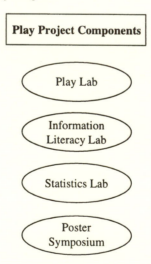

THE PLAY LAB

The Play Lab begins with an overview of research designs, research settings,
and data collection techniques. Students identify the Play Project as a correla-
tional field study using naturalistic observation. They discuss the concepts of
"state" and "event" and then watch a videotape segment showing animals and

humans exhibiting states (e.g., goats eating, fish swimming, a baby sleeping) and events (e.g., a whale slapping its fin, a dolphin jumping out of the water, goats butting heads). The discussion that follows asks students to report the kinds of states and events that they saw and to speculate about the reasons that researchers distinguish between states and events.

Students are introduced to ethological methods for studying behavior in natural settings by watching a videotape segment of snow monkeys interacting at the Minnesota Zoo. The first time that students watch this segment, they write a narrative account, recording as much as they can about the setting, participants, and behaviors observed. Before watching this segment, students read a brief description about the snow monkeys and the Minnesota Zoo. The concept of observer bias is highlighted during this portion of the lab because, unbeknownst to the students, two different versions of the description are distributed. Half of the students read the following "neutral" description:

The animals shown in the videotape are snow monkeys at the Minnesota Zoo. The Minnesota Zoo is located in Apple Valley, Minnesota. Snow monkeys are social animals who live in colonies in the wild. The exhibit at the zoo contains a large climbing structure, a grassy area, and a small pond. In addition to snow monkeys, zoo visitors can see another group of primates—gibbons—in a rainforest exhibit. The zoo also has a children's petting zoo, featuring goats, ducks, and a donkey, and a new aquatic exhibition is called Discovery Bay. A monorail train offers a bird's-eye view of the zoo grounds. The zoo is open year-round and maintains groomed cross-country ski trails in the winter.

The other half of the students read a different description, which tends to produce a bias for aggressive behavior:

The animals shown in the videotape are snow monkeys at the Minnesota Zoo. Snow monkeys are social animals who live in colonies in the wild. The exhibit at the zoo contains a large climbing structure, a grassy area, and a small pond. The climbing structure provides the monkeys with a "stage" upon which dominance hierarchies can be established, challenged, and defended. The monkeys chase each other on the grassy area around the pond. They frequently continue their aggressive displays in the water. Zoo-keepers are experimenting with changes in the exhibit in an effort to decrease the snow monkeys' behavior.

Students discuss the advantages and limitations of using narrative accounts, with most students reporting that the narrative approach was frustrating and difficult to use because so much behavior was going on in the segment. They discover that not everyone chose to focus on the same monkeys or the same behaviors. Although they recognize the narrative account as a rich source of information, perhaps useful at an early stage in research, they do not see it as a particularly scientific approach.

Building on the critique of the narrative approach, in the next portion of the Play Lab, students choose just a few behaviors from their narrative accounts and learn about event sampling. The behaviors that each student chooses are listed on the board for the entire class to see, divided according to the version of the snow monkey information that the student read. Students soon notice that one group seems to have more "aggressive" behaviors recorded in their narrative accounts; at this point in the lab, the class is debriefed about the different versions of the information sheet that were distributed, and the issue of observer bias is discussed.

The necessity of a good operational definition in observational research is reinforced when students choose one of the behaviors that they noted in their narrative accounts and develop an operational definition for it. As a team of three, they select one team member's target behavior and, as the videotape segment is viewed once more, use the operational definition to record all instances of that behavior. The notion of inter-observer reliability is introduced and discussed when each team of three calculates the inter-observer agreement within its group.

The remainder of the Play Lab focuses on the topic of play and the development of a specific research question for each research team. Each lab during the semester has an assigned reading, which is discussed during lab. The reading for the Play Lab is a popular press article from *U.S. News & World Report* called "The Case for Frivolity: Play Isn't Just Fun. Young Animals Can't Do without It" (Brownlee, 1997). The article explains that play is a legitimate area of empirical study and scientific inquiry and presents the idea that play, which may appear to have no purpose, serves important functions for humans and other animals. The article also introduces the ideas that play is generally studied through observation, and observation may be more difficult than one might assume (e.g., researchers are just beginning to decode the signals that animals use to communicate to one another that aggressive-looking behavior is not actually intended to cause harm). Consistent with the objectives of the Play Lab, the article also explains that systematic observational techniques are just as useful for studying play in humans as they are for studying play in nonhuman animals. These techniques are sometimes supported with instrumentation (e.g., videocameras), but they are also used with only the "naked eye," as in the Play Lab.

The lab manual for the Play Lab also provides students with an overview of children's play, based on a number of key sources (e.g., Bretherton, 1984; Flavell, Miller, & Miller, 1993; Rubin, Fein, & Vandenberg, 1983; Sawyer, 1996; Sutton-Smith, 1998). Two major questions guide the discussion of play during the Play Lab:

1. Why do children play? In what ways might children's play contribute to their development? Putting this another way, what might happen—in both the short- and long-term—to a child who never played?

2. Research suggests that all immature mammals, as well as birds and even reptiles, engage in play. How is children's play behavior different from the play behavior exhibited by animals? How are children's play and animals' play similar?

Figure 3.2
Pre-Observation Worksheet to Obtain Approval to Carry Out Their Study

Pre-Observation Worksheet
for the Study of Children's Play

By completing this worksheet and receiving approval from your instructor or preceptor before you begin collecting data in the field, your group will ensure that:

- the research method you use is naturalistic observation
- your study compares two groups
- your results will be able to be compared with the results of classmates' studies

Location/setting for observations

_____

_____

_____

Behavior to be observed

_____

_____

_____

Operational definition for the behavior (attach separate sheet if necessary)

_____

_____

_____

Grouping variable: _____ Age   OR   _____ Gender (Check one)

Hypothesis/Research Questions about Play (attach separate sheet if necessary)

_____

_____

_____

Following this discussion, students watch three video clips of children at play: a 3-year-old boy playing on his own at home; two 4-year-old girls playing in a day-care setting; and two sisters, aged 2 and 5 years, and their father playing at home. After watching these very different examples of children's play, in each setting students brainstorm about possible behaviors that they might observe and research questions they might explore.

The last part of the Play Lab consists of brainstorming in research teams about a specific study of children's play. Students complete a Pre-Observation Worksheet (see Figure 3.2) that they must submit in order to obtain approval to carry out their study. Upon receiving approval, they are given blank data sheets and a "letter of introduction" (shown in Figure 3.3) that they can share with anyone who has questions about their observations. While research teams frequently gather their data nearby in preschools and on playgrounds in North-

Figure 3.3
"Letter of Introduction" to Share with Anyone Who Has Questions about Students' Observations

To Whom It May Concern:

The following student, _____ is a student at St. Olaf College. As part of research associated with their course in Psychology,[1] the student and their research team members have the assignment to learn more about child behavior, specifically patterns of play.

Their research plan has been reviewed.

They are conducting what is called an "observational" study, in which they are to observe children in various settings. They are first to ask the permission of any adults who have responsibility for the children they hope to observe before proceeding with any observation.

In some cases the children may be playing in a public area, and there may not be any specific person in charge, or specific person supervising the children. In such a case, and in the event that someone inquires what they are doing, the students have been instructed to show this letter of introduction.

We respectfully request your cooperation in assisting these students in their observational study in any way you are able.

If anyone has further questions about the purposes of this study, or questions or concerns about the manner in which the students are carrying out their observation, they are invited to call the St. Olaf College Department of Psychology, at 507-646-3142, and ask to speak with any of the faculty involved in teaching this course.

Thank you.

Jim Dickson, Ph.D., Dana Gross, Ph.D., Bonnie Sherman, Ph.D., Howard Thorsheim, Ph.D.
Faculty in the Department of Psychology

[1]Principles of Psychology: Experimental Foundations.

field, many students choose to observe children playing at the Children's Museum or the Science Museum in St. Paul, at the Minnesota Zoo, or at Camp Snoopy and Lego Land at the Mall of America.

The requirements for the Play Project are that it must be an observational study, employing event sampling and comparing either gender differences or age differences in the target play behavior. Research teams are advised to seek out children between the ages of 2 and 10 years and to avoid studying children who are engaged in formal games with rules. Apart from these stipulations, students are free to choose any dependent measure of play that they wish. As a result, the final set of posters presented at the Poster Symposium is always a diverse collection. Topics that have been studied in the past include initiation of play episodes, bossiness, sharing, laughter, verbal behavior, imitation, creativity, aggression, and choice of same- versus opposite-gender toys.

THE INFORMATION LITERACY LAB

During the Information Literacy Lab, students learn to locate, retrieve, and evaluate library resources, using the play topic that they have chosen for the Play Project. They also develop and refine their hypothesis in light of their literature review. Discovering connections between their interests and the work of other researchers reinforces the feeling that students are joining a community of scientists.

The assigned reading for the Information Literacy Lab is an article about social pretend play in Korean- and Anglo-American preschoolers (Farver & Shin, 1997). This article was selected because it provides an example of a study examining children's play activities in free play and quasi-experimental conditions and comparing two groups of children. It reviews the research literature on social pretend play and cross-cultural studies of play. There is a summary of some of the factors that previous studies have shown to influence children's verbal and nonverbal play behavior and play talk, examples of children's pretend play discourse, and operational definitions of five levels of play behavior. The procedure that the researchers used to observe play is clearly described, as is the method for establishing inter-observer reliability. Taken together, these features reinforce a number of concepts introduced in the Play Lab. They also make the Farver and Shin article a valuable resource for each research team's Play Project.

THE STATISTICS LAB

Students bring their Play Project data to the Statistics Lab, during which they learn about descriptive statistics. They examine patterns and relationships in their data, examine and compare distributions for the two groups that they observed (either younger vs. older children or boys vs. girls), and plot their findings graphically. In addition, by "playing" with their data set on the computer, for example, by increasing the number of data points, increasing the range of scores, or adding a small number of very extreme scores, students learn how sample size, variability, and outliers can affect patterns and distributions of data. They use the descriptive analyses of their real data set to generate information that is reported on their final Play Project poster: the arithmetic mean, standard deviation, and range of the data, as well as two graphic descriptions (a bar chart and one other graph of their choice).

The assigned reading for the Statistics Lab is a chapter from Paulos' (1990) book *Innumeracy: Mathematical Illiteracy and Its Consequences*. This chapter examines many aspects of popular culture, from stock scams and newspaper psychics to diet and medical claims, to demonstrate the popular misconceptions resulting from the inability to deal with large numbers, probability, and ratios. During the discussion of this chapter, students often express surprise that they enjoyed reading and talking about statistics. The lab manual for the Statistics Lab begins with two quotes that also generate surprisingly animated discussion: "There are three kinds of lies: lies, damned lies, and statistics" (Disraeli); "Statistical thinking will one day be as necessary for efficient citizenship as the ability to read and write" (H. G. Wells).

THE POSTER SYMPOSIUM

At the conclusion of the Play Project, students gather together to present their projects. As they answer questions from their classmates and the faculty, and as they engage in discussion with the other research teams about their projects, they are truly members of a collaborative learning community. They express pride and relief about having completed the project, and many are overtly enthusiastic about doing additional empirical research in future psychology courses. At the same time, they are quick to admit that the project was more difficult and demanding than they had thought it would be; observing behavior systematically and objectively turns out to be quite different from simply "watching kids play."

REFERENCES

Bretherton, I. (Ed.). (1984). *Symbolic play: The development of social understanding.* Orlando, FL: Academic Press.

Brownlee, S. (1997). The case for frivolity: Play isn't just fun. Young animals can't do without it. *U.S. News & World Report, 122*(4), February 3, 45–49.

Farver, J.A.M., & Shin, Y. L. (1997). Social pretend play in Korean- and Anglo-American preschoolers. *Child Development, 68*, 544–556.

Flavell, J. H., Miller, P. H., & Miller, S. A. (1993). *Cognitive development* (3rd ed.). Englewood Cliffs, NJ: Prentice-Hall.

Paulos, J. A. (1990). Pseudoscience. In *Innumeracy: Mathematical illiteracy and its consequences* (pp. 49–71). New York: Vintage.

Rigden, J. S., & Tobias, S. (1991). Tune in, turn off, drop out: Why so many college students abandon science after the introductory courses. *The Sciences*, January/February, pp. 16–20.

Rubin, K., Fein, G. G., & Vandenberg, B. (1983). Play. In P. H. Mussen (Ed.), *Handbook of child psychology: Vol. 4, Socialization, personality, and social development* (4th ed., pp. 693–774). New York: John Wiley.

Sawyer, R. K. (1996). *Pretend play as improvisation: Conversation in the preschool classroom.* Hillsdale, NJ: Erlbaum.

Sutton-Smith, B. (1998). *The ambiguity of play.* Cambridge, MA: Harvard University Press.

Tobias, S. (1990). *They're not dumb. They're different: Stalking the second tier.* Tucson, AZ: Research Corporation.

Wineke, W. R., & Certain, P. (1991). The freshman year in science and engineering: Old problems, new perspectives for research universities. *Journal of College Science Teaching, 20,* 277–287.

Chapter 4

Where Is Play?

Patrick Biesty

Like master chefs not quite satisfied with the formulation of a basic cooking sauce, play researchers are continuously refining the definition of play, trying to get it just right. The attempt to define play in this chapter pays homage to those many efforts, especially recent ones (Henricks, 1999; Sutton-Smith, 1999). Nevertheless, this "chef" emphasizes the most basic ingredients and the taste of their combination to the player. The approach is experiential and argues that the individual experience of play is a socially constructed event, the expression of a social nature.

The difficulty of defining play was pointed out by Huizinga (1938/1955) who, rather than defining it, described six of play's salient characteristics. He noted that play is a free activity standing consciously outside "ordinary" life, not serious but intensely absorbing, connected to no material gain, bounded by rules, and tending toward social affiliations. Play is also characterized more generally as fun activity that has meaning while serving no end outside itself. The implication is that because play is fun, there is no more essentiality to it than the fun that it engenders. But play and fun are not the same (Biesty, 1986). Whereas fun may be an end in itself, play, it is argued, has ends. The most elemental end is the harmonious proximal forms created by "taking the role of the other." Mead's (1934) phrase "taking the role of the other" is expanded in this chapter to mean the broad selection of actions where the player acts as the challenging form or force of the situation.

Huizinga's lack of a definition for play raises several questions that this chapter attempts to answer. Foremost among these questions is the inherent solipsistic dilemma: if play is an end in itself, how is it related to the cultural forms?

Rather than follow Huizinga and characterize play as an irreducible motivation, I argue that play arises from a somatic and social construction, harmonizing two fundamental motivations, growth and belonging. The solipsistic issue of self-reference disappears when, by taking in the "other," the actor unifies the basic motivations and articulates them in somatic and social shapes and eventually into the cultural forms. Play is not so much an end in itself as it is an end of itself, an end that is an evolving form of its author(s).

In bypassing a definition of play, Huizinga's work raises other questions. How does play relate to the creation and elaboration of the cultural forms? How does play differ from and synchronize with socially destructive actions and repressive cultural forms? How does play relate to the occasional rapt attention and outright fun of work? How does non-play fun sometimes share all the characteristics of play? This chapter proffers a definition of play that suggests partial answers to these questions and distinguishes play from other fun activities.

The relevance and importance of a definition are demonstrated by contrasting play with one of many recent acts of "fun" violence:

60 Minutes: Women Tell Police of Assaults in Park: One woman, a newlywed French tourist, had two gold chains snatched from her neck as chanting men removed her skirt. Three others, teenagers from London, were surrounded by the group of men, who sprayed them with water, tore at their clothing and sexually assaulted them. (Chivers & Flynn, 2000)

These events followed a festive Puerto Rican Day parade along Central Park in New York.

The sexual assaulters might have called upon Huizinga's characteristics of play to "spin" a defense, the way a vindictive child explains, "I was only playing." In fact, the assaulters' behavior could be understood as arising from that "irreducible motivation to play," although the resulting behavior was not play. Among themselves, the assaulters' actions have all the characteristics of play. They were free, outside "ordinary" life, not serious, intensely absorbing, having no material gain (the robbery seems isolated and incidental), bounded by rules, and leading to group bonding with fellow thugs. The thugs might point to similar crowd behavior at "raves," at "mosh" dance pits, and at Mardi Gras in New Orleans and Rio, which share similar definitions of men and women and festive fun. At Mardi Gras women celebrants voluntarily participate in an adult show-and-tell. Women bare their breasts and bottoms, while being groped by crowds of men. The goal is a collection of beaded necklaces. The women with the most necklaces gain some distinction. From a theoretical perspective, the voluntary participation of one woman in the Central Park grope would muddy the social reality of that event between rowdy play and sexual abuse. The essayist Anna Quindlan (2000) echoed this sentiment when she wrote, commenting on the attack in Central Park,

The difference between the woman in a wet-T-shirt contest and the woman with the wet T-shirt being ripped from her body as she pleads for mercy, for respect, for humanity, can be contained in a single word. That word is consent. (p. 68)

Many activities, like this assault, are constructed to satisfy the growth and belonging motivations. But only play maintains the motivations in a harmonious tension consistent with the gravity of the situation. Eroticism, desire, offer and refusal form the gravity that challenged the revelers at the parade. Thus, a definition that articulates that balance helps clarify the differences between play and related "fun" activities.

As this chapter is mainly an argument in support of the definition, a brief outline of the major references serves as a guide to the steps in that argument. The starting point is Huizinga's claim that play is an end in itself. A counter-hypothesis is offered, that play is both the harmonizing of two core motivations identified by developmental psychologists (Hermans, 1989) and the resulting actions, to the extent that the resulting actions keep the motivations in harmonious tension. The first element, the protomorphic synthesis, accords with Plato's nostrum that play is what makes the animal leap. A phenomenological argument is used to analyze a fictive scenario of a playful leap. That leap is accomplished by taking the role/attitude of the other (Keleman, 1985; Mead, 1934). This cognitive and affective action creates an internal proximal world, similar in character to the zone of proximal development (Vygotsky, 1978). Play acts radiate from these precedent actions. The sequence is *ready*, that is, synthesized; *set* by attenuating action and fantasizing (Sarbin & Coe, 1972); and *go*, that is, play, work, have fun. Although play appears to be for itself, it is intrinsically a creation of a protomorphic self by taking the role of another and acting "as if" one were the other while still being oneself. The proximal world provides at least two enlarged meanings outside play, an identity as a player (group member) and second, the potentiated realization (growth) of new skills and adaptations (Henricks, 1999; Sutton-Smith, 1999).

LOCATING PLAY

The example of violent fun at the Puerto Rican Day parade suggests that play can be defined by, and in contrast to, the contexts that frame actions and the boundaries that players create, respect, extend, and cross. To understand the sources of a definition of play, let us look at the following fictional sequence and ask, Where is play?

As I walk down a path, I imagine actions involving the puddles left from the recent rain: avoid them by walking round, kick the water to make them splash, run around and skirt the edges, jump in and splash, leap over, hopscotch around. I fantasize the puddles as a challenge. Then I leap over the smaller ones and then the widest of the lot, hopscotching around the scattered puddles that physically frame the play, and, continuing with a bounce to my step, I wend my way to an academic meeting. Ugh!

What makes this animal leap the puddles? Is it fantasy? Or is the fantasy itself called out by some other cause? Plato said that play makes the animal leap. Following this insight, I could conclude that neither the fantasy nor the leap is play but rather that play is the movement that calls out fantasy and initiates the leap. However, without the leap, there is no play. The urge to leap is insufficient. In forming itself as the leap, the animal propagates an alternative self within the frames of gravity, time, puddled terrain, and the social definitions that constrain it and then playfully leaps. This chapter offers a definition of play as a sequence of three socially constructed actions that proceed by taking in and acting as the challenging other. The three constructions are synthesizing two sometimes conflicting motivations, generating proximal forms that dramatize possibilities and alternatives, and initiating actions that display the new form.

In its leap, the animal constructs actions that embody the synthesized motivations. The bodily leap coordinates the challenging pull from gravity and the subjective escape from that pull, by an embrace that embodies the contending forces. The leap is a willful expression of the body being in and out of earth's gravitational force, as well as the social actor moving toward the social goal, the meeting. The physical leap keeps me in the social world of my schedule while I embrace and am embraced by the physical environment. By leaping, I am subjectively free from physical and social gravity yet objectively an illustration of those gravities. The leap is also continuous, moving from the somatic actions (ready) that bring forth a fantasy (set), to the initial leap (go) and subsequent hops, skips, and jumps.

In the purely platonic sense, play is neither the fantasy nor the leap. Play is a form of the self, or, perhaps in keeping with the Greek attitude, play is Eupheme, the nurse of the muses who inspire fantasies and actions that we label play and play-inspired forms. I would rather label each part of the sequence as play, because that is how we conceive it in everyday life. Play is a continuity of somatic actions that, by embracing the gravities of a situation, constructs and apprehends an extraordinary self in the sequences of those frames and carries into action physical and social movements that emanate from it: the sequence of play in the above example is the protomorphic synthesis, the fantasy and the hops, skips, and leaps.

As noted above, the term "gravity" is being used both as denotation and as connotation to stand for the physical, social, and psychological challenges that confront the player. Gravity challenges and is played with. Like Shakespeare's stages of man, sequential but overlapping forms challenge the player. Among the more notable are physical gravity, solidity of objects, time, space, language, social roles, social rules, sexuality, social organizations, structures, knowledge, power.

As the construction of a synthesis is not routinely apprehended nor easily objectivated by the leaper or by an observer, it has become practical to conceive of play as the ensuing sequences of fantasy and/or action. This practicality should not dissuade us from examining the synthesizing process through reasoned examination, *verstehen*, and apperceiving its form in process. The sequence of protomorphic synthesis, fantasy and leap provide a paradigm for marking other play-forms. Reasoned examination of observed play, theoretical inquiries, and the examination of empirical studies show that the originating essence of play is a protomorphic synthesis. The practice of *verstehen* yields a similar conclusion. Examine, for example, the synthesis of motivations in one's own actions when playing with young children. This examination reveals an attempt to foster growth and a sense of belonging between child and self. Because propriocepting the play synthesis is a complex process of gauging the nerves, muscles, organs, senses, and skeleton, it is an acquired skill. A useful guide to self-apperception is provided by Keleman (1985). The process is based on "observing" the formative movement emerge and contract, usually accompanied by a meditative alert and assertive breathing.

PLAY AS FORMATIVE PROCESS

A review of the literature points to four salient features that help explain human behavior. Two of the characteristics, growth and belonging, I borrow from developmental studies and call motivations because they underlie and move the human out into the environment. The other two, pleasure and pain, I borrow from behavioral studies and refer to as motivators, because they guide, inhibit, and/or reinforce the initiated action.

Hypothetically, human behavior can be reduced to two motivations, self-enhancement (growth) and attachment to others (belonging) (Giles, 1957; Hermans, 1989). These two motivations form actions that carry out the core function of the organism: "to define, locate, demarcate the world from a consistent perspective, by organizing, integrating and representing experience from that vantage point" (Brownell & Kopp, 1991, p. 299). The ordinary life of the person is thus delimited by enactments of these two motivations within physical and social environments. Within this world of action conflicts exist. First, the two basic motivations are often in tension and conflict, pulling away from or opposing each other within the organism and within social worlds. As a simple example, take the toddler who wishes to climb to dangerous heights and is punished by the parent by, among other things, a withdrawal of approval; or, conversely, consider a child who is afraid to challenge the environment because the parent keeps the child under a blanket of protective "love." Second, the physical and social environment is a multiplicity of challenges, conflicts, insults, and inhibitions that, sui generis, frustrate the motivations. The child or adult finds the world, at one and the same time, both challenging and alienating. I designate these environments as the gravities that the actor takes in and within which he or she enacts its growing and belonging.

The social and physical environments guide these movements by means of myriad rewards and punishments. Thus, the motivators are often defined as the seeking of pleasure and the avoidance of pain. Although conditioned responses can explain a great deal of behavior, humans often discount these motivators because of commitments to the loyalties and competencies that they have grown into and achieved through commitment. Thus, the adult risks pain to give birth and then to maintain and protect the life of offspring.

Children and adults suffer great travail to protect projects that they have built as expressions of their being. As important as the motivators are, they are secondary to the two prime motivations. While the ordinary life of the person is the process of externalizing and elaborating these contending motivations around the pilot posts of pleasure and pain, play is temporary and idealized, that is, a protomorphic synthesis of those motivations. Play forms from the person's ongoing internal (somatic and fantasy) organization and external (physical and symbolic) activity, in pursuit of its consistent orientation or attitude. The play synthesis is a proximal reality, a proximal orienting attitude, graced with the six characteristics of play. The play attitude, therefore, creates and presents a potential form for orientation in the real world. In contrast to Vygotsky's moral imperative that, "the only 'good learning' is that which is in advance of development" (Vygotsky, 1978, p. 89), I would contend that the relation of play's proximal realm to development is indeterminate.

The motivation to grow includes physiological abilities (balance, locomotion, strength, grace), psychological skills (self-conception, reality testing, managing emotions), social skills (cooperation, competition, conflict, group formation, symbol production and sharing). The motivation to grow places the person in the world. In contrast, the motivation to belong makes of the physical, the psychological, the social, and the cultural a world of inclusion and exclusion. The person tries to be the world within which it is growing. Play is an attitude that puts one harmoniously both in and of the world.

Play is action that integrates the two primal motivations into an attitudinal unity of being in and of the world. The model for this unity is the fetus in the womb, growing and belonging. In its earliest life, Freudians tell us, the infant acts as if she or he is still attached to the mother's body. This unacknowledged "as if" consciousness of the infant is later replicated by taking the role of the other, that is, acting as if one were the other in order to harmonize the motivations. Like the infant, the player is mostly unaware that he or she is both self and other.

The motivation to grow and the motivation to belong are the yin and yang of play. We experience our own play, and we see the play of others in the creation, maintenance, and repetition of those essential movements. As these actions take place within specific somatic, physical, and sociocultural worlds that variably support and inhibit action, play is as variable as the gravity of its surrounding frames. Play is thus defined as self-formative actions in which all players willfully embrace challenging gravities to articulate proximal worlds that reflect the harmony of the growth and belonging motivations.

Each element of this definition bears some elaboration. *Formative action* is the protomorphic synthesis of the contending motivations, the creation of a somatic, cognitive, and affective organization that is a distinct experience of being something other, a being distinct from each motivation and distinct from the conflict between them. *Willful embrace* means that the synthesis is accomplished by the acquiescence of each motivation to the other in the subjective act of mutual "role taking." The acquiescence is accomplished by whatever somatic actions achieve the mutual embrace. Acting "as if" one were the other establishes an unquestioned belonging with the challenging other. Thus, the action is "out of the ordinary" because the boundary that each motivation gives to the other dissolves, and the player is conscious of one harmonized action. The mutual acquiescence is perhaps best defined as a kind of adaptive instantiation that progresses in a ready-set-go pattern or the pressure and release of a coiled spring or the contraction and expansion of an accordion. In the leap, I get *ready* by submitting to, becoming the gravity controlling my balance. My *set* position adapts to the gravity as a dynamic but constrained spring. In the *go* stage my muscles add a buoyant release and boost to gravity's push. The *gravity of its frames* refers to whatever self, somatic, physical, social, psychological, cognitive, or other obstacles stand in the way of a synthesis of the motivations. In solitary play one takes on the gravity of an alternative aspect of self. Gravity is here used in both its indicated and figurative meanings and is somewhat similar to Sutton-Smith's (1978) concepts of ludic and adaptive dialectics. Of play he writes, "It mirrors, mocks and diminishes the greatest concerns of existence for life and success, but it also relieves the boredom of our everyday succession of habitual events" (Sutton-Smith, 1999, p. 245).

The concept of adaptive instantiation is a generalization and extension of Mead's (1934) concept of taking the role and attitude of the other. In his discussions of the development of the self, Mead postulated the mostly cognitive process of taking the role/attitude of the other as the means that the child uses to organize and grow a self. When the child plays at a role, for example, "mommy," it does not imitate but rather takes in the mother and adapts its specific mother's role and attitude to its own form. In playing "mommy," the child is not its mother but could not be itself without "mommy." Sarbin and Coe (1972) label this action hypothetical instantiation, emphasizing the "as if" experience of the child as its mother, adding an experiential—that is, somatic and affective—dimension to Mead's concept.

At the game stage the player takes in the roles and attitudes of both teammates and opponents in order to play his or her role in the game. To bat well, one must take in the opposing pitcher, and the good pitcher takes in the batter. To Mead, one cannot play a role without taking in the other. But players do more than take the role of the other cognitively. Players adaptively instantiate the other in themselves, being somatically pitcher and batter in the instant and in the subsequent fantasy and action arising from a protomorphic synthesis of self and other. Those moments are the experiential play of the game.

The essence of play is the synthesizing of the growth and belonging motivations by means of adaptive instantiation, which is somatic, cognitive, and affective. Play incorporates the other to power the leap. In the leap, the other is gravity taken as a somatic force. In more complex play, skilled physical, cognitive, and affective elements are engaged as well. In each instance the player adapts and makes the other a somatic as well as cognitive and affective substance of being. The instantiation is hypothetical because it is not real outside of play. The instantiation is adaptive since it provides a proximal alternative behavior for the self.

Consequently, the solipsistic nature of play is an illusion. Play exists in relation to the ordinary activities that surround it and from which play absorbs its content and creates its meaning. In the example of the leap, play has a meaning different from that of an ordinary walk around the puddles. The leap means I am in and of the gravity of earth. In addition to the membership and skill attainment, play has a further meaning, the experience of being different from the ordinary. The player can be "extraordinary" by repeating the play or by realizing some altered self in the real world.

Play also has other meanings in the functions that derive from it. We owe the idea that play is the formative kernel of culture to Huizinga. Humans create not just games and amusements from play but religious rituals, the law, philosophy, art, poetry, and civilization itself. Other writers, notably, Mead and Piaget, coming from a psychological or sociological perspective, have argued the formative role of play in individual development. The purported importance of play to so many aspects of human life belies the contention that play is an end in itself, unless we understand that the end is a formation of something more than itself. Play is a formative process, which, by creating and apprehending something more than itself, promotes cultural and self-development.

THE 10 OR MORE CHARACTERISTICS OF PLAY

I suggest that the end of play is the creation and apprehension of an extraordinary self that is formed in play and fades when not in play. That chimeric self has the characteristics that Huizinga noted: free, extra-ordinary, not serious, utterly absorbing, bounded, and affiliating. However, by looking at play as a constructed protomorphic synthesis, rather than solely as activity, four additional characteristics suggest themselves. Play is cognitively dissonant, zero-gravitational, egalitarian, and essential. As there may be other characteristics to add to the six offered by Huizinga, I call these the 10 or more characteristics of play.

Play Is Cognitively and Affectively Dissonant

Absorbing social reality and denying it simultaneously, play is cognitively and affectively dissonant. Although this characteristic is related to fantasy creation, it should not be confused with its product. Play is a reality in which the external social world is made permeable so that the player moves in and out of it at will. The reality of a challenging gravity is absorbed to become part of the player, while simultaneously remaining an external constraint. Gravity exists in the person weighed down by its force. Gravity includes the leaper and treats him or her as an object. To say that the experience of weightlessness in the leap is a fantasy is to miss the essence of play. The player is both weightless and weighted down by gravity. Play is always two contradicting concepts and feelings at one time, the tension of which provides a frisson to the event. Cognitive and affective dissonances are referred to as paradoxes (Bateson, 1972; Loy, 1982), but I am here speaking of experience from the point of view of the players, not an objective evaluation of them.

Play Is a Zero-Gravity Form

By this I mean that the player's embrace defies, neutralizes, and joins with the gravity or challenge of his or her situation. Although the leap is totally bounded by the gravity of the earth, the leap is experienced as gravity neutralized and defied. Gravity, as an external force, is embraced as part of the leaper. Zero gravity is not the absence of gravity nor the experience of a liminal state. It is the equalization within gravity by a counterforce suited to it. This is true of any challenging form or force, whether that gravity is social control, social definition, or pressing external or internal need. Consider the gravity of making an error in a baseball game. It can ruin one's sense of play and, conversely, if learned from, make the next play possible. Thus, play seems to body its boundaries, push the envelope, and dance with deviance. Defiance of gravity requires the exercise of power and is the fun of play, deriving an exultation of glee from the active novelty of sudden weightlessness within gravity.

Play Is Egalitarian

Play's zero gravity points to its egalitarianism. The internal motivations that organize play are not normally balanced. In the leap, the force of gravity dominates the leaper by any calculable measure. However, the player constructs a qualitative experience of equal power in defiance of gravity, through the leap. By measurement the two forces, the power of leaper and the power of gravity, are unequal, but in the leap the force of gravity is made equal to the force of the leap. A similar experience exists between two contending players. For example, two arm wrestlers struggle to pin each other. In the contest one wins, and one loses. This agon is about inequality. The agon is play, however, in the moments of power equality in the match. Without those moments, however fleeting, there is no play, merely a zero-sum game of strength. In addition and possibly due to the experiential equality, play tends to be socially egalitarian.

Although issues of sex, race, nationality, and other group affiliations are often brought to bear on players, an egalitarian spirit tends to emerge.

Each Player Is Essential to the Play

Because play requires at least momentary egalitarianism, it reveals another characteristic, the essentiality of the players. Play gives to those who play a sense of being essential to action. Without each particular player, play could not exist. The leaper needs to leap to be essential to the world of puddles, and puddles are not playful challenges without the leaper. The arm wrestler needs an opponent to play. I play; therefore, I am essential in the action, and the opponent is also essential. Thus, the player is essential to gravity because the player leaps. If players cannot grant the essentiality of the other, they cannot play, although they can have a lot of fun. Play varies according to the ability of players to give and get a sense of essentiality. If a player is snubbed or spurned by the other players, play seeps out of the interaction unless it is reconstituted, excluding the other. The newly organized game as, say, serious play for serious players, might still sour the play.

DISCUSSION

The meaning of play is examined from two directions, one in relation to the environment and the other in relation to experience. Henricks (1999) argues that, like work, play is always an ascending meaning, which is an imposition of the ego's formulated patterns on the self and the environment. Thus, festivals, parades, proms, pageants, and fairs are not play, because they result in conforming—that is descending—meanings. In contrast, if play is an adaptive instantiation, as argued here, ascending meanings relate to the growth motivation and descending meanings relate to the belonging motivation. Play's meaning can vary between poles of uniqueness and conformity, creativity and recreation.

The second area of meaning derives from the experience of harmonized motivations, evoking a proximal zone redolent of that harmony. Such a zone is meaningful experientially outside the normal space/time mentality. It is meaningful because it points to the potentiality of idealized relationships between self, other, and environment. Thus, play is repeated for this meaningful experience.

Play's relationship to development seems best understood in terms of Vygotsky's (1978) concept of a zone of proximal development. Vygotsky observed that children learn skills and capacities in the learning environment, usually a socially interactive arena, but often find difficulty performing the tasks in isolation. The students know how to do the task but cannot demonstrate that learning on their own. They are in a zone of proximal development, in which learning has taken place but has not been transformed into a blend of ascending development. It appears that taking the role of the other is more difficult when the other is absent.

Something akin to this occurs in play. The play synthesis locates the players in a zone of harmonized motivations, which may not develop into anything further than the play itself. The play, for example, leaping, becomes more refined, complex, and/or challenging but still remains play. The play competence, however, may provide the player with skills for some real-life situations when leaping is required. To use a Sutton-Smith example, the baseball or cricket players become the most facile grenade throwers. It is also necessary to consider whether the experience of play and the creation of proximal worlds might retard development. The proximal zones of harmony are, for some, more appealing venues than the real world of conflict and struggle. Certainly, we have all heard warnings against living in fantasy or complaints about men lost in an adolescent fascination with sports.

As previously noted, the relation of play to self-development has long been studied, yet it is not seen as the central impulse moving people between stages, except in childhood. The definition offered here might prove useful in examining the content and transitional steps between stages of adult development postulated by different theorists. For example, controlling for cultural and structural factors, what types of erotic play, coquetry, sexual practice, and "courtship" develop and/or inhibit responsible adult sexuality?

Huizinga's focus was on the role of play in the development of cultural forms, religious rituals, the law, philosophy, art, poetry, and others. However, his approach was linguistic and comparative, seeing the six characteristics reflected in these cultural expressions. It is, therefore, fruitful to analyze the development and organization of cultural expressions as harmonized gravities. For example, do religions proffer elaborate proximal harmonies of death and immortality? Does the law proffer some proximal harmony of justice and injustice? Finally, if play is the way that humans form possibilities of themselves from the gravities of their environment, does play ever become the realization of self in ordinary life?

CONCLUSIONS

In this attempt to define play on the shoulders of others, some disagreements have been voiced. Play is not an end in itself. Play is not an essential motivation. Some biases might have also crept in. Play is not the end of life or the good life. However, play is fun, wonderful, and ephemeral. It is constructed in the actions of players and is easily disassembled by exceeding any 1 of the boundaries of its 10 or more characteristics. What constitutes boundary crossing is also variable, as pushing a boundary may itself be a way of grappling with the gravity of life. For example, insulting and debasing other players may be a test of inclusion rather than an actual dismissal, and handling those insults may, in fact, be a way to grow into membership as well as a means of gaining social interaction skills.

So it is with role playing in games. An intriguing hypothesis is to consider games and other play-forms as gravities that threaten to take play away or that give practice in the construction of broader frames for play in more alienating environments. Consider how in a game of baseball, for example, freedom to enter or leave is restricted; repeated play becomes ordinary and predictable; whether it is seriously absorbing depends upon the score and the competition; the rules can become restrictive and oppressive; social affiliation can become debased by cliques and jealousies; the frisson provided by dissonance can go flat through boredom and predictability; the gravity of the game, winning, can overwhelm play; egalitarianism can give way to adverse and disheartening ranking of players and teams; and it is easy to consider some players essential and others, the benchwarmers, superfluous. Leaping in this environment is a challenge to the self and a harbinger of living in the world.

Games condition players for the hard world where syntheses of the basic motivations are hard to find or construct or where ludic opportunities exist within cultural forms crafted in earlier times or in new formulations by disparate, non-membership groups. The value of the definition is that play is constructed from gravity and is not a given in any situation. Only after wrestling with a challenge, as with the gravities of a slow baseball game, does one achieve play. Thus, after a hard day's struggle at work, grappling with a meaningful issue, one might look back and realize, That was play, because by taking on the challenges of the day, a protomorphic synthesis of growth and belonging was constructed. Work begs the question, What other role is taken for work to be experienced as play? Some possibilities are the Puritan God's grace or the worker's own ego ideal. Perhaps work is experienced as play when it is not so much a labor of love, which implies duty, but work done by a loved and loving laborer.

Work is not play because it is done out of necessity or to attain an extrinsic goal, but this attitude might be one shared by a child chasing a ball, an activity that others call playing. Both are play only when the protomorphic synthesis is achieved. Work, after all, is more noble than play. It keeps us fed and safe from the cold and contributes to the accomplishments of humankind, and work in its broadest meaning is capable of a true synthesis of our motivations, in friendships, in a family, and in the diverse cultural realms mentioned by Huizinga.

Where is play? It is in the actions of the games of life and in embracing any and all the gravities that surround it. The ability to embrace these gravities derives from experience and the role modeling of coaches and other players who display how to achieve a leap under challenging circumstances. In this way games create a learning ground for the conflicts and challenges of life. Zones of proximal harmony are created to counterbalance the gravities of the game so that baseball is played, and work is a pleasure.

REFERENCES

Bateson, G. (1972). *A theory of play and fantasy.* In G. Bateson, *Steps to an ecology of mind* (pp. 177–193). New York: Ballantine Books.

Biesty, P. (1986). If it's fun, is it play? A median analysis. In S. Reifel (Ed.), *Cultural dimensions of play, games and sport* (pp. 61–72). Champaign: Human Kinetics.

Brownell, C. A., & Kopp, C. B. (1991). Common threads, diverse solutions: Concluding commentary. *Developmental Review, 11*(3), 288–303.

Chivers, C. J., & Flynn, K. (2000). 35 scary minutes: Women tell police of assault in park. *New York Times,* June 13, 1.

Giles, H. H. (1957). *Education and human motivation.* New York: Philosophical Library.

Henricks, T. S. (1999). Play as ascending meaning: Implications of a general model of play. In S. Reifel (Ed.), *Play and culture studies* (vol. 2, pp. 257–277). Stamford, CT: Ablex.

Hermans, H.J.M. (1989). The meaning of life as an organized process. *Psychotherapy, 26*(1), 11–22.

Huizinga, J. (1938/1955). *Homo ludens: A study of the play element in culture.* Boston: Beacon Press.

Keleman, S. (1985). *Emotional anatomy. The structure of experience.* Berkeley, CA: Center Press.

Loy, J. (Ed.). (1982). *The paradoxes of play.* West Point, NY: Leisure Press.

Mead, G. H. (1934). *Mind, self and society.* Chicago: University of Chicago Press.

Quindlan, A. (2000). Sexual assault, film at eleven. *Newsweek,* July 3, 68.

Sarbin, T., & Coe, W. C. (1972). *Hypnosis. A socialpsychological analysis of influence communication.* New York: Holt, Rinehart, & Winston.

Sutton-Smith, B. (1978). The dialectics of play. In E. Landry & W. Oban (Eds.), *Physical activity and human well being* (vol. 2, pp. 759–770). Miami: Symposia Specialists.

Sutton-Smith, B. (1999). Evolving a consilience of play definitions: Playfully. In S. Reifel (Ed.), *Play and culture studies* (vol. 2, pp. 239–256). Stamford, CT: Ablex.

Vygotsky, L. S. (1978). *Mind in society. The development of higher psychological processes.* Cambridge, MA: Harvard University Press.

Part II

Vygotskian Theory and Scaffolding

Chapter 5

Putting Vygotsky to the Test

E. Beverley Lambert and Margaret Clyde

PART I. VYGOTSKY: THE PERSON, PLACE, AND TIME

In recent times, writers and researchers in the early childhood field have moved strongly toward the work of Lev Vygotsky as a theoretical basis for educational debate. This shift has signified a search for more contextualized approaches that provide better acknowledgment of the influence that sociocultural contexts can have on learning and development.

Frequently, the metaphors used to illustrate contextual approaches in the literature are weaving, a rope, webbing, networks, or other branching structures such as nodes or modules. The integrated nature of these images makes it easier to understand the emphasis of this developmental perspective, namely, that growth and progress should be seen *in terms of* the contexts in which they occur such as gender, culture, individual differences, family experiences, and so on. Contextualists would argue that previously we tended to consider the child *and* the environmental influences or contexts that affected development or the child *alongside* these contexts, but rarely the child *in terms of them* (Cole, 1992).

Consequently, over time this may have contributed to a view of development as being separate from the contexts that actually shape it and, therefore, must be a part of it. Contextualized approaches, nevertheless, are easily identified in early childhood practice, as evidenced by the expertise of caregivers and teachers at making learning tasks more meaningful for young learners by carefully matching them to children's prior learning experiences, interests, and ability levels. In themselves, contextualized views of development are not a new idea in the field of early childhood education.

In this chapter, however, we begin the argument that the Vygotskian phase in early childhood education may not have been a step forward and may in fact have occurred to the detriment of furthering contemporary theoretical debate. Many contemporary theoretical perspectives provide far better contextualized accounts of learning and development than Vygotsky's. Some of these, following a Vygotskian tradition, are framed within social constructivist views such as Rogoff's guided participation/apprenticeship perspective (Rogoff, 1990), but many are not.

Social constructivist perspectives argue that knowledge is initially found not within the individual but within our social and cultural surrounds. As a result of our interactions with others in this social context, knowledge then becomes internalized on an individual basis. While current social constructivist perspectives are relevant to early education, we argue strongly that Vygotsky's work has only limited value. Ironically, it seems that the desire to embrace Vygotsky as a great contextualist has occurred as a result of taking his writing out of context and sometimes even embellishing it with our own contemporary understandings and professional leanings.

As this chapter is about program planning, we concentrate only on that work of Vygotsky's that relates to the learning process and education. Vygotsky believed that the higher cognitive processes, which developed during the school years, occurred best in mediated interactions with a teacher. That is, new knowledge was presented more meaningfully via the teacher, who provided a helpful, connecting link between the child and the content. As a result of these mediated interactions, the social knowledge of one's culture became transformed or internalized into personal or individual knowledge. As the learner's knowledge became more complex due to this collaboration with a more knowing other, it moved from an actual level to reach a potential level. This process occurred in what Vygotsky called the zone of proximal development (ZPD). One of the significant features of his ideas about education is that it was a mediated process. According to him, the most important tool required for the mediation process to be successful was language.

Our Concerns about "Vygotsky's Theory"

We suggest that there is no such thing as a Vygotskian theory of learning because Vygotsky's writings about education simply do not constitute a theory according to scientific definitions of psychological theory (Miller, 1989; Murray, 1991). Vygotsky wrote on diverse facets of learning and education, but due to the unfortunate fact of his premature death, he was never able to develop his ideas to any great depth of detailed analysis. Hence, we believe it is more fitting to describe his works as theoretical perspectives, rather than as a theory or model.

Vygotsky is currently embraced by many in the early childhood field as a theorist who uniquely acknowledged the influence of social and cultural contexts on children's learning. Certainly, it cannot be denied that at the period in which he was writing (1920–1930 in the USSR) this was so, and at that time it was indeed a unique focus. However, we feel concerned that such a willingness to accept Vygotsky's work today may, in fact, result from misknowledge about it and reliance upon thirdhand and even further removed sources of information. This latter problem is, of course, compounded by the fact that we all have to rely upon English translations (secondary sources) of Vygotsky's writing. Nevertheless, it is still possible to gain a more detailed picture of the man and his work from selective and careful reading of reputable secondary sources, rather than accounts that are further removed. We were fortunate enough to find an academic translator who assisted us in clarifying the meanings of Vygotsky's most commonly used terms and who possessed Vygotsky's works in Russian, some of which have still not been published in English.[1]

Overall, our criticisms stem from a concern that Vygotsky, whom we praise as a great "contextualist," has, ironically, been studied *out of context*. Popkewitz (1998), using the example of Vygotsky and Dewey, argues strongly against the folly of merely inserting historical theories into contemporary pedagogical debate, due to the fact that the place of the individual in society today can never be the same as when historical theories originated from different social contexts. That is, he questions their relevance. If this is so, then we must ask ourselves, What *was* the cultural context within which Vygotsky was living and working? It is both necessary and appropriate to pause now and consider this question before we look at the criticisms noted above in more detail. There are three major influences to be considered:

- the influence of "defectology," Vygotsky's focus on special needs children
- the pattern of Vygotsky's professional development and thinking
- the USSR and historical materialism; the influence of USSR politics and ideology on Vygotsky's thinking

Vygotsky in Context: The Influence of "Defectology"

Much of Vygotsky's work on learning and development was focused on children with intellectual disabilities. When we consider this, it becomes easier to see that his notion of the ZPD was quite a structured, rigid, and controlled one, more typical of interventionist approaches; we argue this in depth, shortly. Gindis (1995) cites the work of Luria, one of Vygotsky's students, and other authors as evidence

that Vygotsky's involvement in defectological practice [a Russian term] aroused his interest in the profession and science of psychology. Defectology was the main empirical domain from which Vygotsky obtained data to support his theoretical concepts. . . . He founded a laboratory that later was upgraded to the Research Institute of Defectology, which exists (under a different name) today. It was the place where Vygotsky's ideas and his disciples literally survived Stalin's purges of the late 1930's.... Many of Vygotsky's major theoretical concepts were formulated and developed within the defectological theoretical framework and terminology ... as a part of the general cultural historical theory. (Gindis, 1995, pp. 77–78)

Luria himself states, "Between 1925 and 1934 Vygotsky gathered around him a large group of young scientists working in the areas of psychology, defectology and mental abnormality" (Luria, "Biographical note on L. S. Vygotsky," in Cole, John-Steiner, Scribner, & Souberman, 1978, p. 15).

Gindis goes on to describe Vygotsky's concept of the ZPD with its actual and potential levels of understanding as having developed from his work on compensatory education for special needs children. Certainly, Penuel and Wertsch also note that the ZPD is an important mechanism in the understanding of individual intellectual development and that "it has been a particularly useful tool in designing effective instructional intervention" (Penuel & Wertsch, 1995, p. 86). Wertsch (1985, p. 67) states more specifically that Vygotsky "introduced the notion of the ZPD in an effort to deal with two practical problems in educational psychology: the assessment of children's intellectual abilities and the evaluation of instructional practices." It was felt that for "mentally defective" children, the ZPD with its acknowledgment of potential levels of ability would enable a better prediction of a child's future growth or learning.

This is rarely, if ever, acknowledged by current early childhood writers who embrace Vygotsky. However, it is important to know about, because when the ZPD is interpreted in terms of this "defectology" background, it can be seen as a mechanical, rigid, didactic mode of operation, more aligned to remedial interventionist practices than those of active learning or learning-as-discovery.

On this point, it needs to be noted that there appears to have been a change in the way that the ZPD has been described in different editions of Vygotsky's work. Glick (in Rieber, 1997, pp. x–xi) notes that the 1962 edition of *Thought and Language* interprets the ZPD as a diagnostic concept whose usefulness lay in relation to developmental/remedial assessment. That is, it was given a very specific role and did not feature as a major component of Vygotsky's work. However, in the 1978 edition of Vygotsky's *Mind in Society*, the ZPD is represented quite differently. It had become a topic in its own right, more like the global, educational process that people describe it as today. Glick argues that this changed perception of the ZPD may well have occurred in response to a perceived need to provide a counterpoint to Piagetian theory, which was a dominant developmental focus during that decade. Nonetheless, this raises an important implication, not so much for the ethics of translation, but more for the ethics of how authors choose to "fit" Vygotsky's concepts into modern educational theories. Rieber and Carton (1987, p. v) argue that authors should not use translations of Vygotsky's work as "an occasion for subtle revisions which would make the texts seem even more consonant than they are with one or other current beliefs or scientific trends."

The ZPD can be illustrated as a rigid, didactic mode of interaction. This is evident in the examples that Vygotsky himself described from his work with children. In one study when he was using the ZPD strategy with second and fourth grade children—which, in the USSR school system at that time, related to 9- and 11-year-olds, respectively—who were not special needs children, it was found that when problem solving, they were able to correctly apply scientific concepts more than spontaneous concepts. (Vygotsky defined scientific concepts as the abstract, systematic nature of scientific knowledge that resulted from formal schooling, that is, from seven years onward. Spontaneous concepts were the concepts that occurred in very young children as a result of daily living and playing, which were, so he argued, crude, basic, and of lesser importance [Vygotsky, 1986]).

Vygotsky concluded that his subjects' preference for using scientific concepts was a result of lessons that were mediated by the teacher within the children's ZPD. He defined the teacher's role as *"always beginning with a verbal definition/s of the concept/s"* and that a teacher, when *"working with the pupil, explains, informs, inquires, corrects, and forces the child himself to explain"* (Vygotsky, cited in Rieber & Carton, 1987, p. 214; emphasis added). To illustrate this point, Vygotsky gave the example of a second grade child who, when the ZPD process was being evaluated, was given an unfinished sentence about social science. The child was able to successfully complete the sentence by adding "because" in the correct place, thus saying that "planned economy is possible in the USSR because there is no private property—all land, factories, and plants belong to the workers and peasants" (Vygotsky, cited in Rieber & Carton, 1987, p. 215). According to Vygotsky, the ability of the child to make this statement was due only to the teacher's interactions with him within the ZPD. "The child's concept had been formed in the process of instruction, in collaboration with an adult" (Vygotsky, 1986, p. 191).

The more we looked into the ZPD and came across examples such as this one, however, the more certain we became that the premises about learning upon which it is based (cited in the italicized quote above), are the very opposite of those upheld by the early childhood field. What they represent instead is a very mechanical view of learning-by-training or, in Vygotsky's own words, instruction. Such principles are, in fact, directly related to the behaviorist-influenced expository mode of teaching, about which one can read in any educational psychology textbook. They are also related to the reciprocal teaching model developed by Palinczar and Brown (1984), which retains behaviorist influences and was designed for remedial literacy teaching.

Such structured, rigid methods based upon an assumption that the teacher and curriculum control the learner are not, however, normally those chosen for use in contemporary early childhood programs. Instead, these endorse a view that there is a need to respect and foster individual abilities and approaches to learning and that the rights of the child-as-learner to question and experiment with ideas are highly valued. While there may well be times when a structured approach is an appropriate strategy, such as when a child wants to develop a specific skill like skipping or when one is working with special needs children, this kind of approach is not expected to dominate the teacher–child interactions that occur in early childhood centers. We feel, therefore, that Vygotsky's ZPD presents a restricted view of learning processes and reduces the learner's role to one of passivity and dependence upon the adult.

Consequently, it is indeed disappointing to read comments like the following one: "Vygotsky's basic premise is that the development of higher mental functions only takes place through social interaction (when the child engages in dialogue with others)" (Pacini, 1998, p. 34). The author then continued upon the assumption that this premise of Vygotsky's referred to the usual play interactions that today commonly occur between children and between children and staff in early childhood centers. However, our close reading of primary translations of Vygotsky's work lead us to conclude that (free) social interaction, play, and (open) dialogue as implied in Pacini's quote, were not a part of Vygotsky's notion of the zone of proximal development. The ZPD was not a democratic construct, and we continue to discuss this in more detail shortly when we consider some key issues in depth.

Vygotsky in Context: The Pattern of Vygotsky's Professional Development

The reason that the ZPD appears as a limited construct continues to become more evident when we consider Vygotsky's work in terms of the background of his professional development. Minick (1987) traced the development of Vygotsky's theoretical work and describes it as falling into three different spheres or shifts. First was Vygotsky's use of psychology to focus on the importance of psychological tools such as language to mediate or make sense of experience. Vygotsky's work here was of a behaviorist nature—a key focus in psychology at this time—incorporating stimulus–response interpretations of behavior. This first phase commenced in 1924, when Vygotsky was 28 years of age. Following that phase he shifted toward a focus on the psychological systems that underlie the relationships between various mental functions, the obvious one for Vygotsky being between thought and speech. From this point on, his psychological vision began to broaden. This second phase evolved out of the first and finished in 1930, when Vygotsky was about 34 years old.

However, of greatest interest is the fact that, according to Minick (1987), it was only in the last two years of his life, from 1933 to 1934, that Vygotsky turned to psychological explanations of the social contexts of thought and action. During this time he focused on the individual psychological processes of interaction, and it is only from this brief period of two years that his ideas about the ZPD were developed. This, we strongly argue, is probably why the ZPD is, in fact, an undeveloped and incomplete notion and should be known as such. Figure 5.1 shows the professional timeline of Vygotsky.

Figure 5.1
Vygotsky's Professional Timeline

1925–1930	1930 on	1933–1934
Key developmental assumptions: the response unit is the basis of learning and behavior in people and animals.	**Key developmental assumptions:** a focus on relationships of mental functions (e.g., memory and speech).	**Key developmental assumptions:** view of stimulus-growth as social systems of interaction that affect individuals.

Source: Lambert & Clyde (2000). Reproduced with permission.

Vygotsky in Context: The USSR and Historical Materialism

Vygotsky's work on the ZPD was based upon an understanding of the learning process as something that remained strongly in the control of the teacher and the curriculum and occurred within school settings. It was, we argue, a process of mechanized instruction, and certainly Vygotsky himself used the word "instruction" in his writing to describe it. Progress in the ZPD occurred as the learner progressed to more advanced levels of thinking, that is, from an actual to a potential level of understanding. This, according to Vygotsky, occurred as a result of the teacher's instruction.

When placed against the political background of communist ideology in the 1920s and 1930s in the USSR, Vygotsky's interpretation of the ZPD can be more easily understood and respected, as it was indeed a product of its time. It was developed in a period when education, particularly scientific education, was prioritized by the government and also when knowledge and education were held and manipulated by favored experts and delivered to what were considered to be novices. Here one can see a parallel with Vygotsky's notion of the ZPD, which, we have previously argued, was a controlling structure where knowledge was delivered in a one-way process from a learned other (teacher) to a learner. If so, then it must be recognized that Vygotsky's notion of the ZPD was philosophically opposed to the bases of learning currently endorsed by the early childhood field.

During Vygotsky's lifetime the Soviet leadership controlled scientific and educational thinking in the USSR. Such knowledge was valued probably above all else and was seen to be a critical pathway to future development for the new communist state. In line with the new communal society and the desire to reject the capitalist approaches in bourgeois countries where it was felt that the emphasis was incorrectly placed upon the individual, Vygotsky's work supported the communist idea of social influences taking precedence. Consequently, Vygotsky's work was oriented toward developing a theory that would support the furthering of scientific thought within an ideological framework of Marxist dialectical materialism. Wertsch (1985) describes Vygotsky as a Marxist psychologist and states that from 1922 onward (the last 12 years of Vygotsky's life) "people such as Vygotsky and his followers devoted every hour of their lives to making certain that the new socialist state, the first grand experiment based on Marxist–Leninist principles, would succeed" (1985, p. 10). (Considering his commitment to this cause, it is indeed tragic that during Stalin's era after Vygotsky's death, all his works were banned for 20 years, because two aspects of it offended the dictator. His comments on the use of standardized psychometric approaches and some aspects of his work on linguistic development simply did not agree with Stalin's view.)

The fact that Vygotsky's work emanated from a Marxist theoretical framework, specifically, historical materialism, has previously been well noted in the literature (Cole & Scribner, 1978; John-Steiner & Souberman, 1978; Saxe, 1981). Cole and Scribner (1978) clearly illustrate the influence of Engel's arguments, as well as Marx's, regarding the significance of human labor and the use and development of tools, which, in turn, facilitate further development and societal change. They claim that Vygotsky extended Engel's concept of tools-as-mediators to include cultural sign systems or language. Wertsch (1985) strongly agrees. Certainly, language-as-mediator was an important element of the ZPD and a key contributor to the raising of the learner's ability from actual to potential levels of understanding. Consistent with Marx and Engel's ideology was the belief implicit in Vygotsky's writing that people using tools can effect change. Hence, Vygotsky's interpretation of the development of higher psychological processes "reveals the close relationship between their fundamentally mediated nature and the dialectical, materialist conception of historical change" (Cole & Scribner, 1978, p. 8).

It seems odd that the early childhood field, in a push to find theoretical bases that acknowledge cultural and societal influences upon development, has embraced an old, incomplete 1930s work. Vygotsky is frequently quoted throughout some of the field's literature when, instead, we should be expecting to read about those who have scientifically examined his theoretical premises and developed newer and more culturally relevant insights. This does not refer only to Bruner's work either; there are now other theorists whose work we introduce throughout this chapter. We must be prepared to recognize that Vygotsky's work was developed during and for the political period of first-phase communism in the USSR. It was based upon a zealous, ideological adaptation of Marx and Engel's historical materialism to a new communist educational curriculum intended for the masses. In practice, this process of learning became an abstract, formalized, and controlled method of inquiry, separated from the material that it was investigating, rather than a way of openly posing problems and seeking alternative options and presenting possibilities (Gamble, 1981).

To assist in the process of rethinking early childhood theory, it is useful to ponder the following questions:

- Is it reasonable to assume that continuity exists between the educational ideas of the 1920s and 1930s and those of the twenty-first century? Have thinking and technologies not evolved during that time span?

- Current beliefs about "the child as learner" are based upon certain assumptions about the rights of the individual in our society. Is it reasonable to assume that these views today in Western culture are the same as those held in 1920s–1930s USSR—the new communist state?

- Is it reasonable to assume that the unique culture and history of the USSR in 1920–1930 are consistent with those of modern, Western democracies and that therefore we can merely transplant philosophies from the former to the latter?

Summary So Far

We have begun the pathway to rethinking early childhood theory and practice by putting Vygotsky to rest amid the cultural and political contexts from which he came. Readers may not have expected discussion about the USSR in the 1920s and 1930s. However, it is nonetheless of paramount importance to consider, due to the fact that it is not legitimate to merely transplant Vygotskian perspectives into current early childhood debates about the processes of teaching and learning. Nor is it legitimate to use Vygotskian premises as a guide to educational practice with very young children.

PART II. VYGOTSKY'S WORK: EARLY CHILDHOOD, PLAY, AND THINKING IN PRESCHOOLERS

What are the stumbling blocks that Vygotsky's work poses for early childhood education? It is important to take time now to consider these in detail. Let us review each of the following dilemmas issue by issue.

Issue 1: Children under 7 Years Were Not the Key Focus of Vygotsky's Work

Exactly what did Vygotsky believe with regard to early childhood development and education? We should expect to find many meaningful links between the two because we read so much about Vygotsky in Australian and international early childhood literature. However, we have found it disappointing that, overall, Vygotsky did not think that the early childhood period was a very important one, nor did he pay it much attention in his work.

The school years as a whole are the optimal period for instruction in operations that require awareness and deliberate control; instruction in these operations maximally furthers the development of the higher psychological functions while they are maturing.

This applies also to the development of the scientific concepts to which school instruction introduces the child. (Vygotsky, 1986, p. 190)

It is critical for us to remember that, in the Soviet Republic at the time during which Vygotsky was writing, school education did not commence until 7 years of age (Vaisey, 1967). The thinking of school-aged children, that is, children from 7 years onward, was of far greater importance to Vygotsky in his work on learning than the early childhood period from 0 to 7 or 8 years. The majority of Vygotsky's work focused on children over 7 years of age. Vygotsky likened the thinking capacities of younger children merely to an ability to remember things. "Our analyses suggest that thinking in the very young child is in many respects determined by his memory and is certainly not the same thing as the thinking of the more mature child" (Vygotsky, cited in Cole et al., 1978, p. 45). The work that Vygotsky undertook with younger children occurred (1) in relation to language development, but this was merely a precursor to his main theoretical focus on the relationship between language and thought in school-aged children, and (2) as a paper of approximately 8,500 words on the role of play in development (Vygotsky, 1933, in Bruner, Jolly, & Sylva, 1985).

Issue 2: Vygotsky Did Not Develop a Theory of Play

We feel that it is necessary to look into Vygotsky's work on play because sometimes he is described as a play theorist, yet his understanding of play is, we feel, both theoretically limited and inconsistent. In view of the significance of play today in early childhood programs, as well as its relationship to learning and the curriculum, we need to take a more analytical look at Vygotsky's comments. As mentioned previously, his work on play consisted of only one 8,500-word paper (Vygotsky, 1933). The complete and unabridged version of "Play and Its Role in the Mental Development of the Child" can be found in Bruner et al. (1985), and we feel this is the best source. In other papers, such as "Prehistory of the Development of Written Language" (in Rieber, 1997), he sometimes made brief comments about play, but these were not the main focus of his discussion. The 1978 *L. S. Vygotsky: Mind in Society* publication, edited by Cole, et al., also contains a chapter on Vygotsky's work on play. However, it presents only selections of his work and does so in a style of English that is quite different from the complete paper found in Bruner et al. Hence the Cole et al. version appears to be one that is somewhat "watered down."

Vygotsky claimed that play was not intrinsically valuable to the child as a source of pleasure and self-satisfaction. "To define play as an activity that gives pleasure is inaccurate for two reasons" (Vygotsky, 1978, p. 92). First, he claimed, other activities can provide greater pleasure, such as a baby's sucking a pacifier, and second, Vygotsky believed that the games that schoolchildren play can provide pleasure only if the child finds the result interesting, such as when one wins at rule games. Many of his comments on play seem to refer more to rule games of children over 7 years. This raises the question of how play was perceived in Russia during the 1930s. (The translator's note in the Bruner et al. book indicates that play and games with rules or organized games were given a similar meaning.) It seems that Vygotsky did not consider the exploratory play of younger children to actually *be* play in the same way that we consider it so today. We should not be too critical of this because we suspect it may well be due to three reasons:

1. *Theoretical reasons*. Vygotsky did not consider the thinking that resulted from play in early childhood (which he labeled spontaneous concepts) important. He considered it to be the lowest kind of thinking and the least important to the process of learning. Spontaneous concepts were, according to Vygotsky, merely used in the absence of a better organized system of instruction that began once children reached school (Vygotsky, 1986). We return to look more closely at this when issue 3 is discussed.

2. *Cultural differences*. Only in more recent times and in some cultures more than others is the play of very young children recognized as an important contributor to development. It seems unlikely that this would have been so in the Soviet Republic during the 1930s, when Vygotsky was formulating his ideas.

3. *Historical reasons*. Play is a complex phenomenon to research, and modern research methods are far more sophisticated and better suited to the task.

What's Wrong with Vygotsky's Views about Play?

The premises that Vygotsky held about the play of young children, which we feel are not supported by current research about play in the early years, are:

(a) Play merely provided an arena for children's needs to become more mature. It was not seen by Vygotsky to be a developmental area in its own right. Play "seems to be invented at the point when the child begins to experience unrealisable tendencies" (Vygotsky, 1978, p. 93), and it is simply "a stage between the purely situational constraints of early childhood, and adult thought which can be totally free of situations" (1978, p. 98). In other words, when the desire for something occurs along with the typical need of the younger child for immediate fulfillment, the child "enters an imaginary illusory world in which the unrealisable desires can be realised, and this world is what we call play" (Vygotsky, 1978, p. 93).

Vygotsky attempted to describe this change from low levels of immaturity where one's needs are immediate, to higher levels of maturity where one can wait, accept compromise, or obtain one's own goals, as the boundaries of the ZPD, but his argument remains vague and lacks detail. In the same way he also described play as leading development. Early childhood personnel today would certainly agree with this statement. However, in true contradictory style, Vygotsky made this statement against a background of emphasizing that the role of play was predominantly imitative. Imitative functions alone, however, cannot lead development.

Consequently, Vygotsky seemed to view pre-rule play as being of a transitory nature, geared toward providing a form of comfort to children who, due to maturational immaturity, were rendered dependent and powerless. Such a view of play is not consistent, however, with his statement that play leads development, which, conversely, implies that play has an extremely important, and long-lasting role. Vygotsky never resolved this odd contradiction. Which of his confusing statements are readers to believe? Although we cannot deny the cathartic value of play, we reject Vygotsky's assumption that this is the only or predominant value that play offers to the development of young children. This is because current literature in the field abounds with research examples of the diversity of ways in which play contributes to all areas of development and learning.

(b) Play was not seen to have an important role in cognition. Vygotsky did recognize that play was symbolic, but he seems to have had an idiosyncratic interpretation of what "symbolic" meant. He did not consider the play of pre-schoolers to be symbolic because the meaning of objects dominates the young child's knowledge of those objects; that is, he or she cannot divorce the object from its meaning. That is why, according to Vygotsky, young children need a "pivot" such as when they use a stick to be a horse. Vygotsky claimed that the young child, however, will not want to use other, far removed objects such as a match for a horse. "For a child it cannot be a horse: one must use a stick; therefore this is play, and not symbolism" (Vygotsky, 1933, in Bruner et al. 1985, p. 547).

In Vygotsky's view, play became internalized as a result of formal schooling and then changed into formalized symbolic knowledge. "Play is converted to internal processes at school age, going over to internal speech, logical memory, and abstract thought" (Vygotsky, 1933, in Bruner et al., 1985, p. 548). In his writing on the prehistory of written language (Cole et al., 1978), Vygotsky defined symbolism as speech through gesture. This is unlike present-day interpretations that emphasize the significance of symbolic thought in terms of cognition as well as language and also regard it as a critical element in representational/abstract thinking across various art forms and curriculum areas. We do acknowledge that Vygotsky's unusual use of the word "symbolic" may well have been a familiar one in Russian psychological theories at the time when he was writing about play. If so, then it is a culturally bound concept and should be recognized as such. Nevertheless, we cannot ignore the difficulties that this poses for present-day attempts to interpret Vygotsky's writing.

Another example of this difficulty is when Vygotsky does agree at one point that the play of younger children could be symbolic. By "symbolic" he, in fact, meant imaginary—"the imaginary situation." On this he commented, "Finally, last and most important. Study has shown that the creation of an imaginary situation in the true sense of the word does not yet exist in early childhood" (Vygotsky, in Rieber, 1998, p. 267). In his paper on early childhood development, Vygotsky stated, "Studies show that play in the figurative sense, with imaginary situations, appears in a rudimentary form only toward the end of early childhood" (Vygotsky, in Rieber, 1998, p. 267). Yet he rejected symbolism in any other play-form, for example, its different modes of representation in art (which is fascinating considering that his early work was in this area [Vygotsky, 1971]), movement, or music. However, when writing about the prehistory of written language (Cole et al., 1978), Vygotsky did acknowledge that some symbolic development occurs in play and drawing. The only other kind of symbolism that he mentioned was the abstract symbolism of mathematics, which, Vygotsky felt, had nothing to do with the play of 0–7-year-olds.

We object even to his comments on imaginary play. He was generally unclear, and, in relation to the play of younger children, he interpreted imaginary play as being symbolic but then gave a very limiting definition of imaginary play as consisting entirely of imitative play. Imitative play, he claimed, consisted of rules—sociocultural rules, such as those that we see in home play. Vygotsky argued that the social conventions underlying children's imitative play (e.g., parents cook meals for their children) were observed and imitated and then became the "rules" that guided play.

We do not agree that the symbolic development that occurs in imaginary play should be defined in such a narrow way, because it ignores the child's now known ability to explore with and invent symbols. We are not prepared to accept such a narrow version of symbolism either, because this ignores the now known importance of symbolic and representational development as a true and independent part of cognition, in domains other than language. We know, for instance, that the development of symbolic thought has implications for cognition in the creative arts, math, and science.

Even more confusing than this is that later on Vygotsky again made a statement about the progressive changes in play but gave little specific developmental information. Instead, he described global changing patterns from (1) the imaginary situation, which he always claimed merely imitated real life, to (2) a greater realization of the purpose of play, such as wanting to win a game, to (3) the final stage of rule play. He argued that the play of preschoolers, which, he had stated earlier, began with the imaginary situation, was, in fact, hardly imaginary at all because it merely imitated real-life rules. "Play is more nearly recollection than imagination—that is, it is more memory in action than a novel imaginary situation" (Vygotsky, cited in Bruner et al., 1985, p. 552). Contradictory and inconsistent statements such as these are only one reason that this paper cannot be accepted as a theory of play.

(c) Little or no importance is attributed to the play of children under 3 years old, as Vygotsky did not consider that children of this age could play imaginatively. "Play in an imaginary situation is essentially impossible for a child under three" (Vygotsky, 1978, p. 96). Vygotsky felt that such young children were bound too much by concrete situational constraints; that is, they were too young, and their thinking was not advanced enough. Today we can confidently reject these assumptions, as many theorists (e.g., Bruner et al. [1985]; McLune [1986], not to mention research studies that can regularly be found in reputable journals such as *Child Development*) for the last 25 years, have scientifically documented the symbolic development that occurs through imaginative play during the first 3 years of life and have clearly identified how this contributes to cognitive advancement.

Vygotsky's view of the child at 3 years of age was a negative one. This may have been due to the paucity of research in the area at the time when he was writing. Nonetheless, he saw the developmental phase of the 3-year-old as a crisis period and described it as consisting of seven "experiences of the crisis" or the "first zone of symptoms" (Rieber, 1998, pp. 283–286). They are described as follows:

• Negativism

• Stubbornness

• Obstinacy

• Willfulness

• Protest/rebellion

• Devaluation of things dear (e.g., calling mother a fool)

• Despotism manifested as either egocentricity (in only children) or jealousy (in children with siblings)

Vygotsky believed that these problems emanated from the necessary restructuring of social relationships that occurred as the child matured. He claimed that this age of crisis was a result of child raising in bourgeois countries where there was always a focus on individualism. However, he did not offer any alternative developmental viewpoints or debate.

It may well be that Vygotsky's paper on "the crisis at 3" was little more than a political statement. Notwithstanding this, his extremely negative developmental profile could be described only as antithetical to the more informed psychological viewpoints of today. These note the developmental status of the 3-year-old in terms of important growth achievements, paying due respect to the ways in which egocentricity, as well as immature cognitive ability, can exercise natural constraints upon the 3-year-old's ability to deal with frustration.

Schwitzgebel (1999), for instance, claims that the third year of life needs to be understood as a phase of transition to a higher level and that this shift should be seen as a gradual rather than sudden one. He describes this view of development as gradualism and argues that the traditional view of the 3-year-old as either having or not having certain skills or abilities is an unfair one.

Major cognitive developments are unlikely to happen instantaneously. Consequently, children must frequently pass through periods of being 'in between' genuine understanding and failure to understand. The current literatures on false belief understanding and object permanence largely fail to recognise the importance of such in between states of understanding (Schwitzgebel, 1999, p. 283).

This viewpoint is supported by other theorists who also describe a general shift to higher cognitive levels by the fourth year (*Human Development*: special issue, 1992). Thus, today, preference leans strongly toward a credit (can do) perspective of the 3-year-olds' abilities and developmental progress, rather than a debit (cannot do) perspective.

Issue 3: Children's Thinking, 0–7 Years, Was Not Considered by Vygotsky to Be Significant

Two important notions in Vygotsky's understanding of thinking were the roles played by scientific and spontaneous concepts. Scientific concepts, according to Vygotsky, developed as a result of formal schooling and were of far greater significance than the spontaneous (unschooled) concepts, which developed in 0–7-year-olds as a result of their play. Although Vygotsky did briefly acknowledge the value of play to development, it was primarily to explore the relationship between language and representational thought. This had significance for his work with older schoolchildren where language was shown to be an important tool (mediator) in learning, when used by teachers to further schoolbased learning or scientific concepts.

Vygotsky argued that scientific concepts constitute the higher mental processes and that they developed as functions of mediated activity in schools.

The school years as a whole are the optimal period for instructions in operations that require awareness and deliberate control, instruction in these operations maximally furthers the development of the higher psychological functions while they are maturing. This applies to the development of the scientific concepts to which school instruction introduces the child. (Vygotsky, 1986, p. 190)

On the other hand, spontaneous concepts, which result from the spontaneous, concrete play experiences that children have, were considered by Vygotsky to be unsystematic, unconscious, empirical, and, for these reasons, less important (Karpov & Bransford, 1995). Vygotsky generally referred to spontaneous concepts as the lower function of the mind and simply did not consider them to be significant (Gindis, 1995). Although he did acknowledge that spontaneous concepts provided a necessary element for the development of scientific concepts, Vygotsky still did not consider that the former could play a direct part in the development of correct conceptual knowledge.

Vygotsky believed that the development of scientific concepts occurred ahead of spontaneous concepts and cited evidence from his work with second and fourth grade children (9- and 11-year-olds) to illustrate this. In fact, he claimed that the two kinds of concepts developed from different directions. In his own terms, they have "adversative relationships" (Vygotsky, 1986, p. 191). By this he meant that they started at opposite poles and, with time, slowly moved closer together. The development of the child's spontaneous concepts occurred at a low level and advanced upward over time, while the development of scientific concepts commenced at a higher level and moved down toward the child's spontaneous understandings. In the ZPD, they met, as intellectual development became more advanced.

At this point we came face-to-face with another of Vygotsky's contradictory and vague statements. Vygotsky himself stated that the two processes of scientific and spontaneous concepts were related, that "they are parts of a single process" (Vygotsky, 1962, p. 85) (presumably of concept formation). But he then proceeded to go to great length to discuss them as absolute dichotomies. If he believed that they were, in fact, parts of a single process, then surely he would have had to take the play and everyday life experiences of younger children far more seriously (in a theoretical sense) than he did. It seems that on this point, as with others discussed in this chapter, Vygotsky makes a statement that, from our perspective, is philosophically sound and of theoretical interest but then explores the notion in ways that are contradictory and inconsistent.

Reflections So Far

The first three issues make difficult reading for those who embrace Vygotskian perspectives. It is hard to believe that Vygotsky's focus was not primarily on early childhood when we consider that his work has been endorsed by many early childhood authors, and, in particular, that Vygotsky largely devalued the developmental significance of the 3-year-old phase.

It is unpleasant also to be told that Vygotsky's writing on children's play was both inconsistent and lacking in theoretical rigor. Why has it been endorsed elsewhere as a suitable theory of play? It seems likely that in an attempt to develop a broad acceptance of Vygotsky's work in the early childhood field, as much of his work as possible was quickly pulled in under the early childhood umbrella, including one of our favorite topics, play. It is therefore regrettable that such a rush toward supposedly new ideas did not include pausing and attempting to read more primary translations or some in-depth questioning of Vygotsky's developmental assumptions.

In any journey that involves rethinking concepts that are already popular and accepted, there will be moments of discomfort and disjointedness. We have already traversed this uncomfortable path in the writing of this book over the past four years. But fortunately, the path is also stimulating and challenging, and even if you are now feeling a little disgruntled, we hope that this feeling of discomfort also means that you are nevertheless curious and ready to accept the challenge that comes with thinking these issues through further.

Issue 4: Scaffolding versus the Zone of Proximal Development (ZPD)

Issue 4 presents some of the most challenging rethinking of Vygotsky's theory. One may well find a need to return to the issues about to be discussed here

(Issues 4 and 5) over time. We have returned to them many times as part of our own process of rethinking early childhood theory and practice.

The concept of scaffolding is not Vygotsky's. Vygotsky identified the notion of the zone of proximal development (ZPD), the processes of which he never clearly defined but the function of which has been taken by contemporary writers and others to be very similar to that of scaffolding. It is not uncommon for some to use the terms interchangeably or to suggest that the process that Vygotsky described could today be called scaffolding (examples: Gonzalez-Mena & Widmeyer-Eyer, 1997, pp. 20, 146; Low Deiner, 1997, p. 176). However, we strongly argue that to do so exemplifies ignorance not only about Vygotsky's work and the cultural context in which it is embedded but about contemporary theories of cognition as well.

The term "scaffolding" was possibly first used by Wood, Bruner, and Ross to describe tutors' interactions with preschoolers when assisting them to solve a block reconstruction problem (Wood et al., 1976). Bruner also used it when investigating the ways in which very young children negotiate meaning in their early attempts to use language with adults (Bruner, 1978). The scaffolding metaphor was used to describe a new notion called *contingent instruction*. This referred to a process of helpful, structured interaction between an adult and a child to help the child achieve a specific goal. The amount and type of help provided were contingent upon the child's need of assistance. "This scaffolding consists essentially of the adult 'controlling' those elements of the task that are initially beyond the learner's capacity, thus permitting him to concentrate upon and complete only those elements that are within his range of competence" (Wood et al., p. 90).

It is important at this point to pause and examine what these authors meant by scaffolding, because the process that they identified is not necessarily the same as current writers would have us believe. Contemporary interpretations of scaffolding usually include descriptions of helping a child to focus on significant elements of a task, breaking a task into subsequences if necessary, or finding other ways of subtly supporting the learner to meaningfully complete the structure or task and subtly phasing out assistance as the child's competence increased. Many early childhood accounts of the process tend to imply that this process can be as free as one would wish, to the point that any kind of sensitized interactions between adult and child might be considered as examples of scaffolding. However, this is not what Wood et al., (1976) meant by scaffolding. They defined the key characteristics of scaffolding specifically as:

- recruitment (engaging the child's interest and adherence to the requirements of the task)
- reduction of degrees of freedom (simplification/reduction of task elements so the learner can recognize whether or not he or she achieves a "fit" with task requirements. That is, the tutor "fills in the rest and lets the learner perfect the component sub-routines that he can manage" (p. 98).

- direction maintenance (maintaining the child's interest if the child stopped the activity or got into difficulty)
- marking critical features (highlighting relevant features of a learner's response so that he or she can identify an incorrect response)
- demonstration (modeling or demonstrating solutions to the task so the child can imitate them)

We urge readers to think seriously about the above characteristics of the tutor. Are they really commensurate with the philosophy of "the learner as explorer" or the child as an independent learner and thinker, which early childhood programs have historically embraced? We suggest that the above teaching behaviors represent a structured, teacher-dominated approach that is indeed a perfect example of how a tutor works when manipulating a learner toward a predetermined answer, but early childhood professionals are not tutors. This original notion of scaffolding operates on a premise that there is only one correct answer or way to do something and that achieving that answer is of greater importance than the process of learning involved. This notion is framed within the methodology used in the study, where learners were not allowed to explore alternative pathways. In their reconstruction of a block model, the subjects who were 3, 4, and 5 years old had to make a correct reconstruction, according to a model.

It is also important to note that Wood et al. were not pursuing their study from within a Vygotskian framework. Yet many authors assume that they did. However, we repeat part of the quote presented earlier from their research: "This scaffolding consists essentially of the adult 'controlling' those elements of the task that are initially beyond the learner's capacity, *thus permitting him to concentrate upon and complete only those elements that are within his range of competence*" (Wood et al., 1976, p. 90; emphasis added). That is, it is our argument that the original notion of contingent instruction was not about shifting the child to a potential level of development, as exists with regard to the ZPD. Instead, it appears to be more about consolidating current levels of expertise and gaining a basic level of mastery. Yet discussion about scaffolding and the ZPD in contemporary early childhood literature frequently ties the two together when describing how to raise the child's level of understanding from an actual (lower) level to a potential (higher) one, whereas the role of the tutor as Wood et al. described it was to let the learner focus only upon those elements of the problem that related to his or her current level of ability. Thus, this original study, which defined the scaffolding process, did not define scaffolding as being a process of cognitive transition from an actual to a potential level of ability, within a Vygotskian framework.

A second point to note with regard to the Wood et al. study concerns contemporary interpretations of scaffolding where the gradual, sensitive withdrawal of the adult's scaffolding occurs, to enable learners to take more control over their learning as their knowledge increases. This understanding of scaffolding is commonly attributed to the work of Wood et al., but in their original work on scaffolding as previously discussed here, this is not a key issue and is not articulated as such. They refer to the transition that occurs in babies' verbal exchanges with their mothers, whereby the babies began to initiate more verbal exchange episodes, but that is not the same thing. The mother's tutoring role was noted as "a stabilising scaffold during the two phases of label learning we have been exploring, a stabilising scaffold with respect to which the child can vary his responses as his mastery permits" (1978, p. 75). But this is defined in terms of continued, albeit qualitatively different, exchanges with the tutor, rather than as a change toward self scaffolding (Bickhard, 1992) or self-learning, where the tutor can eventually withdraw. The notion of withdrawn support and eventual self-scaffolding is a contemporary one; it is not Vygotsky's, nor are we fully convinced that it belongs to Wood et al. Yet frequently, Bruner and Vygotsky are the only two names mentioned in much of the early childhood literature on this subject.

Clearly, the original notion of contingent instruction can be seen to be a limited one. It also has some qualitative differences from modern usage of the term "scaffolding." These differences should be acknowledged because they are not compatible with early childhood premises about the child, who, as an active learner should question, create, and independently explore new pathways of knowledge. This is not to reject the notion that adults' meaningful interactions with children can further their learning. However, one can reject the assumption that such didactic, adult-dominated interactions as described by Vygotsky and even those used in the Wood et al. study should typify or dominate our teaching interactions with very young children—more so when it is known that there are different modes of interaction that adults can offer, depending on the needs of younger learners.

Table 5.1 compares the two constructs of scaffolding and the ZPD in terms of the processes that have been identified by their authors. Do these teaching styles truly fit those needed for very young children who learn as creative, questioning explorers?

The ZPD

Vygotsky never clearly defined the ZPD or its boundaries, much less the process of internalization by which the social knowledge supplied by the teacher became transformed to conceptual knowledge within the individual learner. His examples of how it worked always showed knowledge and learning to be strongly in the control of the teacher and the school curriculum and the learner to be somewhat disempowered. Wood et al.'s notion of scaffolding is also, we suggest, a restrictive one.

Vygotsky's ZPD referred to a zone of responses between adult and child needed for the child to progress from an actual to a potential level of ability. Actual level meant the child's ability to problem-solve unaided, and potential level meant the improved ability of a child to problem-solve under the guidance of a teacher or in collaboration with a more capable peer. The potential level

Table 5.1
Two Constructs of Scaffolding and ZPD by Vygotsky and Wood et al.

Vygotsky's ZPD (1930s)	Wood et al.'s (1976) idea of contingent instruction, for which they used the metaphor "scaffolding"
Children learn through talking with a teacher who:	Children learn through interacting with an adult who:
• verbally defines the concept	• recruits (engages) their interest and adherence to the task requirement.
• explains the concept	
• informs the student	• reduces degrees of freedom so the learner can fit into the task
• inquires (or questions) the student	
• corrects the student	• conducts direction maintenance (keeps the child on task)
• forces the child to explain the concept	• marks critical features (so the child can identify incorrect responses)
	• demonstrates (models solutions so the child can imitate them)

was an ideal level of understanding that could be reached if conditions were optimal. The parameters of both these levels, however, were not investigated in depth or defined clearly by Vygotsky.

Interestingly, there is a degree of conjecture and dissension among current theorists about what the ZPD means. Kozulin (1990) argues that Western theorists have greatly misinterpreted what Vygotsky meant by it. Vygotsky, so Kozulin claims, intended the ZPD to explain the interaction that occurred between spontaneous and scientific concepts when they actually meet. Others, he argues, have mistakenly spread the ZPD as a catchword, to refer to a somewhat more subjective transformational experience involving dialogue between learner and teacher. O'Conner nicely demystifies the ZPD by simply stating that as Vygotsky used it, the construct "seems to invite multiple interpretations" (O'Conner, 1998, p. 40).

Wertsch (1985, p. 72) flatly states that the ZPD "is wanting in several respects," and to illustrate this he lists three key criticisms of Vygotsky's claim that instruction precedes development.

1. He criticizes Vygotsky for not making clear exactly what he meant by "development," claiming that this void detracts from any likely strength that the ZPD has as a construct. Wertsch feels that Vygotsky's idea of development probably referred to "learning as instruction" (1985, p. 73) or, what resulted from the teacher–child interaction. If so, this is quite an idiosyncratic interpretation, and Wertsch, we feel, has rightly criticized Vygotsky for not making this aspect of the ZPD clear.

2. The ZPD all but ignores the processes of development in children below 7 years of age. We agree with this point also and feel that Vygotsky's brief attempt to include it in his writing on children's play (Bruner et al., 1985) was both cursory and superficial.

3. The content of the instruction process is never "natural" but is contrived knowledge. This occurred because in the USSR in the 1930s, knowledge in schools resulted from the political preselection of curricula and was presented as traditional academic areas called "formal disciplines."

We support Wertsch's concerns and argue that for these reasons it is not acceptable to meaninglessly transplant Vygotsky's notion of the ZPD into contemporary early childhood educational practice! It simply does not fit.

Renshaw (1988) notes that a contemporary understanding of the ZPD should include acknowledgment of the rights of both partners to contest knowledge. He argues that Rogoff and Wertsch's attempts to reconstruct the ZPD as a negotiated process have failed because their apprenticeship interpretation, which was intended to endow the learner with a more interactive role, did not achieve that "this reassertion of the contribution of the learner remains benign in tone" (1988, p. 87). That is, the role of an apprentice has to be, by a process of logic, one where the learner adopts a passive, receptive mode and merely receives knowledge passed on by the expert. In practice that knowledge is usually modeled by the expert and imitated by the apprentice. According to Renshaw, if this is so, and there is no possibility of knowledge being actively contested and consequently changed, then logically the ZPD cannot exist in learning situations like this because potential levels of knowledge will probably not be tapped.

In Defense of Vygotsky

In criticizing Vygotsky for the gaps that exist in his work, we are sensitive to the fact that his untimely death would have prevented him from exploring many of his theoretical arguments further than he did in his introductory writings on these new topics. We are a good deal more critical of the attachment by early childhood educators to a half-finished theory in which the developmental needs of children 0–7 years were considered to be somewhat peripheral and that never really acknowledged the importance of learning as a result of everyday life, or spontaneous play experiences. These very things, which Vygotsky chose not to recognize, are strongly endorsed as a basis for early childhood programs.

What, then, we ask ourselves, could possibly be the reasons for this strong affinity between the early childhood field and Vygotsky's work? Vygotskian premises have been developed further by contemporary theorists who have contributed to what is now an enormous amount of literature on contextual psychology and social constructivist approaches. Shortly, we look at some of these theories in greater detail. But meanwhile we must ask ourselves: Why have these more current, scientifically based, theoretical contributions been largely ignored by the early childhood field? Why do we still sometimes read about Vygotskian scaffolding, even though no such thing exists? The 1960s and 1970s idea of contingent instruction was originally described as scaffolding purely in order to provide a metaphorical description. Nonetheless, it has been developed further in more recent times, and these contemporary perspectives, we argue, are more relevant to the field of early childhood education generally and the planning and monitoring of programs specifically.

Current Theoretical Debate about Scaffolding

Brown et al. (1983) argued, for instance, that during the process of scaffolding an ultimate aim should be for the child to provide his or her own scaffolding. Similarly, Meadows stated that scaffolding should enable the child to move from "other regulation to self-regulation" (Meadows, 1993, p. 248). In fact, Meadows implied there might be a kind of developmental sequence involved, whereby scaffolding is just one area of cognitive processing on a general continuum, and that it might be more appropriate in the early stages of knowledge acquisition.

It might possibly be the case for example that an early history of good scaffolding so to speak, "sets up" learners to become their own scaffolders so that they can both take their own rote learning and mechanical information processing "beyond the information given" and act in a Piagetian mode as never-ceasing equilibrators, continuously seeking a deeper and broader and more flexible understanding of their own worlds. (Meadows, 1993, p. 251)

Asmitia and Perlmutter (1989) agree with this statement and suggest that scaffolding approaches may be useful only in the acquisition of the early stages of a concept and that later, independent learning may be more beneficial in fostering conceptual advancement.

Bickhard (1992) also articulates a theory not of scaffolding but of self-scaffolding in which conceptual advancement occurs as progress is made from stable points of knowledge onward to other stable points of knowledge. He suggests a model describing the functional nature of scaffolding, from which self-scaffolding develops. As this occurs, developing conceptual networks can progress in different directions and can shrink, stretch, and grow in varying ways at varying times. This description is consistent with multidimensional definitions of cognition that describe intellectual processes as complex and multi-layered. It is also commensurate with studies in neuropsychology that describe "the mind as consisting of many parallel, simultaneous processes" (Nuthall, 1996, p. 41).

Bickhard (1992) acknowledges that it seems illogical to suggest that people can provide scaffolding for themselves—that is, new knowledge—when they do not have that knowledge. However, he argues that one does not have to already know what is needed to be known in order for the conceptual scaffolding to then be constructed. Instead, nearby points of conceptual stability can be bracketed or traversed like intuitive jumps of understanding, to enable progress onto a further point of thinking. This is possible, he argues, when learning is truly interactive and sensitive to context because such open approaches to learning better support underlying multidimensional, conceptual networks, as well as their continuing construction. Thus, contextualism is well and truly contained in Bickhard's theory. Bickhard's argument regarding intuitive leaps has parallels with those of other researchers who discuss developmental progress in terms of discontinuity and continuity, where in times of discontinuity, before progressing to higher levels of operating, children intuitively and inconsistently use aspects of slightly higher-level thinking (Biddell & Fischer, 1993; Doise & Mugny, 1984; Fischer & Silvern, 1985; Hort, 1982; Snyder & Feldman, 1984; Sternberg & Okagati, 1989).

Does "Instruction" Precede Development, as Vygotsky Claimed?

Initially we thought that Bickhard's work on self-scaffolding was also consistent with Vygotsky's claim that learning can precede development. In thinking this, we assumed that "learning" here referred to the stimulation of new learning. Translated into early childhood terms, this could mean many things, including setting up attractive and challenging play environments, encouraging social play interactions among peers, and so on. All these things do play a role in preceding or stimulating development and are dear to the heart of any early childhood professional. But then, in looking more closely at the translated works of Vygotsky using Hanfman and Vakar's 1962 abridged translation of *Thought and Language*, we found the actual words that Vygotsky used were that "*instruction* precedes development" (Vygotsky, 1962, p. 101). Wertsch (1985, p. 71) also quotes Vygotsky's comment from a 1934 paper that "instruction is good only when it precedes development." Minick's translation of Rieber and Carton's 1987 first volume of Vygotsky's papers contains the complete (unabridged) writings of Vygotsky on spontaneous and scientific concepts. In this chapter, Vygotsky discusses at length the issue of instruction and development, always using the word "instruction."

But what did "instruction" mean to Vygotsky? He used the word to refer to instruction in the formal disciplines as manifested in traditional school subjects, which, as we have previously discussed, referred to quite a rigid mode of teacher–pupil interaction. (The teacher must verbally define the concept, then explain, inform, inquire, correct the student, and make the student explain.) In "Notes to the English Edition," Rieber and Carton (1987, p. 388) examine the issue of the use of the word "instruction." Minick, the translator, strongly disputes translation of the Russian *obuchenie* as anything other than "instruction" and concludes that "we use the term 'instruction' here, because like the term obuchenie, it implies an intentional transmission of knowledge while the term 'learning' does not seem to." We sought independent advice from a translator who possessed Vygotsky's works in Russian. She strongly agreed with Minick's interpretation.[2] English-dictionary definitions of "instruction" also define it as a form of education resulting from given instructions, directions, or demands. This is a far cry from early childhood interpretations of Vygotsky that claim that learning in the Vygotskian sense means active, socially interactive, exploratory experiences, not unlike the kind of approach traditionally endorsed in early childhood centers.

Salomon and Perkins (1998) take this tendency of others to redefine these basic terms a step further:

Loosely speaking, socially mediated individual learning might be considered the same as instruction, and the point no more than that instruction inevitably involves a certain amount of social mediation. But far more is at stake than this. Instruction, in its proto-typical forms (involving lecturing or question-and-answer sessions), may be considered a special case—albeit not a very interesting one—of social learning. *However as a learning system, it often does not meet the critical conditions of learning very well.* And, when regular instruction is, in fact, effective, the processes involved may not be very socially mediated (as, for instance, when skilled students learn effectively from lectures because of their own auto-regulation skills, but rarely from each other). (p. 4; emphasis added)

In other words, instruction is wanting as a mode of learning, and consequently, learning often occurs in spite of "instruction," not because of it!

We are, therefore, naturally concerned when we read authors claiming that Vygotsky stated that *learning precedes development.* The general meaning of "learning" is, of course, quite acceptable in our professional language today because we share an understanding of its meaning in the twenty-first century. On the basis of that understanding, we might well agree with the view that learning does precede development. However, we cannot find evidence that Vygotsky once made this declaration. Vygotsky only ever used the word "instruction," which, as we have illustrated, had a totally different meaning 70 years ago in the USSR, which completely opposed the educational principles upon which early childhood education is based today. Consequently, it could well be claimed that those authors who use the statement in italics above commit the crime described by Rieber and Carton, whereby translations of Vygotsky's are used as "an occasion for subtle revisions which would make the texts seem even more consonant than they are with one or another current belief or scientific trend" (Rieber & Carton, 1987, p. v).

We, of course, reject Vygotsky's notion of instruction preceding development. In contrast to this, we prefer Bickhard's interpretation of cognitive advancement, which acknowledges that progress to higher levels of thinking can also occur for reasons that are intrinsic to the learner such as intuitive reasoning, conscious metacognitive reasoning (such as planfulness, persistence, being able to identify goals), motivation, and curiosity. Bruner (1978), among other theorists, has also argued that intuition plays an important role in cognitive advancement. We believe that learning can result from a combination of these intrinsic factors with environmental influences such as democratic approaches to learning that invite the learner's active participation and respect the learner's right to question established knowledge.

Attachment and Children's Dispositions Matter!

Bickhard's recognition of context can also be seen in his focus on the significance of emotional dimensions, in particular, attachment. He states that provided that children feel emotionally secure and comfortable with a caregiver, they can actively use that person as a resource, and so self-scaffolding begins. A practical example would be the toddler who actively explores the environment and learns from his or her own efforts, provided that he or she can return to a trusted adult as the need arises and provided that the adult offers genuine encouragement and further *self-challenge*. In agreement, Addison-Stone (1993) also argues that a missing link of Vygotsky's ZPD concerning the adult interaction needed to move the child from a lower to higher level is acknowledgment of the interpersonal relationship between the learner and teacher. In *Rethinking Early Childhood Theory and Practice* (2000) we extend these arguments further when we look specifically at program planning for 0–5s within a framework that recognizes the importance of attachment and the emotional relationship between the adult and child. Under "Reflection" we also acknowledge our notion of reciprocal scaffolding.

The issue of relationships is relevant to the educational aim of encouraging self-scaffolding and empowerment of the learner. According to Bickhard, provided that learners feel emotionally secure, and their use of the adult-as-resource is an active one, self-scaffolding can begin, and the learner is empowered. However, a focus on self-scaffolding need not mean that teachers become redundant or are no longer responsible for stimulating the learner to show initiative in learning; rather, once embarked along the road of motivated discovery, the learner is encouraged to take an increasingly active and autonomous role. The scaffolding provided by the teacher merely becomes more sensitized to the developing mastery of the learner.

In commenting on the relationship between the adult and learner, Wertsch and Rupert (1993) warn against the mediational influence of cultural tools such as language, curriculum, or scientific concepts, as espoused by Vygotsky. They claim that these ignore the influence of power and authority in the relationship between the novice and expert and the extent to which this may control or manipulate the kind of knowledge to be transmitted. Gee (1989, p. 20) stoutly declares that the language of discourse is "intimately related to the distribution of social power and hierarchical structure in society." But perhaps this element of language-as-power, which shapes the teacher–child relationship, is not in fact a shortcoming in Vygotsky's work as Addison-Stone (1993) thinks. If Vygotsky's ideas were a product of Soviet dialectical materialism, then the assumed power and authority of the teacher that were implicit in the teacher's language and that, in turn, illustrated Soviet control of education might well have been a conscious element of Vygotsky's methodology. If this is the case, it cannot be fairly criticized as a theoretical gap in his work when it is, instead, a cultural dimension. But if so, it merely provides another example of why Vygotsky's 1930s writing simply cannot be meaninglessly transplanted into our times, culture, or the current period of knowledge about psychological processes.

Bickhard, along with other current "contextual" cognitive psychologists, uses scaffolding to include situations where peers can be the "experienced other" (Bickhard, 1992; Rogoff, 1990). Vygotsky did not focus detailed attention on peer dyads (Tudge & Winterhoff, 1993). Bickhard also refines the notion of scaffolding to identify different types, such as *mutually scaffolded domains* that result from pretend play, rule games, and other peer relationships and hence serve to foster sound development in social areas. *Institutional scaffolding* is that provided by schools and other group experiences such as youth and sporting groups. There is also *environmental scaffolding*, which relates to broader environmental elements such as the type of educational equipment, quality of the learning environment, and general expectations about behavior. Bickhard maintains, however, that self-scaffolding "is among the most central of tasks the child must master" (Bickhard, 1992, p. 43).

It becomes easier to understand Bickhard's theory if we place it against the broader, contemporary theoretical framework of contextualized psychology, within which development and learning are seen to be multidirectional and to evolve with sociocultural influences. Developmental psychologists who adopt this more holistic perspective abound, and some of their work is known within the early childhood field (Cole, 1992; Demetriou, Effklides, & Platsidou, 1993; Moss, 1992; Pintrich, Marx, & Boyle, 1993; Reese, 1991; Rogoff, 1990; Rowe, 1998; Valsiner & Winegar, 1992; Winegar & Valsiner, 1992). We feel that these perspectives provide more meaningful theoretical accounts of development and learning than Vygotsky's 1930s works.

Naming "It"

The scaffolding process assumed by modern-day educators in their work with young children must be properly named. It is more than Bickhard's idea of mutual scaffolding that results from children's social play. Used in this sense, "mutual" refers to feelings or actions experienced by each partner, or *commonalities* felt by both in reference to each other. As children engage in home play, for instance, they experience common feelings, and upon the basis of that, their experience develops. But we do not feel that this paints the whole picture or a truly contemporary view of the learning process. Also involved are *differences*, contestation of ideas that alternatively push one's understanding to higher levels, and this is where true scaffolding occurs if it is to result in a furthering of learning. Mutual experiences or interactions tend not to make ground but to stay in one place where mutual responses repetitively occur from one person to the other. Mutual scaffolding is *repetitive scaffolding*, probably useful for consolidating skills, but that is all.

Consequently, the notion of mutual scaffolding does not acknowledge other legitimate dimensions of the learning experience that contribute to cognitive advancement. It does not, for instance, acknowledge environmental scaffolding such as suitable equipment and materials or the general ethos of social support in which these things operate. Most importantly for younger learners, it does not emphasize the importance of the emotional relationship with the adult, including trust, freedom to think, and support to move toward self-scaffolding approaches. All of these things are critical for younger learners.

Therefore, we argue that the notion of scaffolding relevant to the early childhood field is that of *reciprocal scaffolding*. "Reciprocal" comes from the Latin components—re (meaning back) and pro (meaning forward). In reciprocal interchanges, there is a greater emotional quality due to the process of giving and taking and to-ing and fro-ing that vigorously occurs. As such, a definition of reciprocal scaffolding would be: the situational scaffolding used to coconstruct higher levels of understanding or ability with a learner. An ultimate aim is movement toward degrees of self-scaffolding. Reciprocal scaffolding includes the attachment relationship between the child and adult (emotional supports), the physical environment (material supports), and the social ethos (social supports).

Reflection

Some readers may not be pleased to find that Wood et al.'s notion of scaffolding has been dealt such a hard blow. But on this point it must be noted that while we do reject the construct that they identified 20 years ago, we think the metaphor that they identified a useful one for early education and its premises about development, learning, and the rights of the child. The task, therefore, is to place scaffolding within a background of modern-day theoretical knowledge and *develop the construct accordingly, as we see fit.* This is opposed to passively accepting interpretations from within the discipline of psychology that may not be contextualized to the needs of younger children.

We feel, therefore, that the notion of *reciprocal scaffolding* is more respectful of the very young child's developing self-esteem, emotional need for closeness with others, and ability to initiate, not merely act as a passive receptor. It also provides the rationale for a program-planning framework to develop from *an ethos of attachment.*

The last three of the seven issues that we are addressing are now presented. These are important issues in that they do assist our ability to refocus upon contemporary studies in the area.

Issue 5: The Problem with Vygotsky's Actual and Potential Levels of Ability in the ZPD

Relevant to any discussion on Vygotsky's idea of internalization is his identification of the actual and potential levels of knowledge within the ZPD. This idea of real and possible levels of understanding is indeed a valuable notion, particularly to educators. It has been a valuable gift from Vygotsky, although he never clearly defined what these parameters were or emphasized their significance as probably being the most influential of cultural influences. This is frustrating because it is within his idea of actual and potential levels of knowing that "cultural contexts" are surely epitomized. Yet it is often Vygotsky's undeveloped notion of actual and potential levels that is quoted in early childhood literature, rather than more contemporary research in the area that has extended the Vygotskian concept considerably and made it relevant to contemporary social and cultural values.

Kagan (1970), for instance, in his work with infants discussed the idea of "optimal discrepancy" where social input can improve performance, but only within a particular range. Campione, Brown, Ferrara, and Bryant (1984) have analyzed the relationship between third and fifth graders' actual and potential levels of development and found that greater adult support resulted in higher levels of cognitive functioning. Kitchener and Fischer (1990) describe the gap between a child's functional level (which is equivalent to Vygotsky's actual level of ability) and optimal level (Vygotsky's potential level) as the "developmental range" and claim that environmental factors directly affect a child's ability to remain at a functional level or progress to an optimal level. In systematically investigating Vygotsky's actual and potential levels, Fischer, Pipp, and Bullock (1984) were able to define its parameters in relation to aspects of social development, as well as other elements of it. These authors and Fischer in a further study concluded that the developmental range increases with age until the late 20s (Kitchener & Fischer, 1990) and that it is found in children after 3 years where initially, according to the authors, it is very small or nonexistent (Lamborn & Fischer, 1988). This itself raises a critical question. If the distance between actual and potential levels is so small in preschoolers, yet we know that distance between these levels is a key constituent of the ZPD, how can Vygotsky's ZPD be relevant at all to such young learners? Vygotsky constructed the ZPD as an explanation of learning in Soviet schoolchildren, which meant, we must remember, children from 7 years of age onward. "In order to elaborate the dimensions of school learning, we will describe a new and exceptionally important concept without which the issue cannot be resolved: the ZPD" (Vygotsky, 1986, p. 985). It is hoped that future research efforts will investigate this question.

Coupled with this is the concern that Vygotsky's actual and potential levels assume a continual, progressive (i.e., upward), rate of development, yet we know that in reality, the developmental phase of early childhood is not smooth. It fluctuates, and regressions play nearly as important a part in progress as does progression itself.

Hoppe-Graff (1993), for instance, found that the typical (actual) and optimal (potential) levels of play development in toddlers were divergent by nature, rather than consistently progressive in a lockstep fashion. His study was a cross-cultural one and used German and Mexican subjects. Hoppe-Graff found that

more regressive patterns occurred in typical levels of ability and that development in the two levels did not correlate. Thus, he argued that optimal and typical
levels of ability in pretend play develop along different pathways. In free play,
for instance, he found that children do not always play at an optimal level.
Consequently, progress in typical-level ability did not necessarily mean similar
progress in optimal ability. "There was nearly the same chance of progress in
optimal level among children who made developmental progress in typical level,
as there was among children who remained at their initial typical level throughout the whole observation period or even regressed to a lower level" (Hoppe-
Graff, 1993, p. 68). This indicates that children may stay at a low level of
pretend play but at the same time gain more complex competencies. Consequently, the order of skill acquisition (in this case regarding pretend play) may
not be invariant for typical-level skills but multidirectional. In focusing on individual developmental patterns as opposed to sequential group patterns, Hoppe-
Graff found that for the majority of children there were much more variability
and fluctuation in developmental pathways at both optimal and typical levels.

Meadows queries the necessity of the ZPD in terms of raising children's
ability to potential levels in primary school settings. She claims that if schools
undertake so little of the Vygotskian approach (because of the demanding
teacher–child ratio of 1:1 and the need for an analytical knowledge of subskills
and how to foster each one and continue to do so over time), how is it that
schools are nonetheless relatively successful in educating children? Because, she
argues, there are other ways of learning, other kinds of constructivist approaches,
rote practices, information processing on an intra-individual level, use of demonstration strategies, and metacognitive strategies (Meadows, 1993). To this we
could add modern, social constructivist (scaffolding) approaches such as collaborative learning.

We must be prepared to move onward from the restrictive Vygotskian notion
of the ZPD and turn instead to current theories describing development and
learning as contextualized and multidimensional processes, while emphasizing
what Rogoff (1990) described as the learner's participation in a community of
practice. To this, however, we would add that the process should occur along
democratic lines where reciprocity and negotiation play an integral part. A learning process such as this is far more "contextualized" to life in the modern world.
For this reason we prefer contemporary ideas about scaffolding and the processes of internalization, including the sphere of peer collaborative learning—
hence, the more useful construct of *reciprocal scaffolding* introduced at the end
of Issue 5. We also subscribe to Fischer's idea of *developmental range*, where
a person's level of ability within different domains of knowledge is seen as a
zone or multistep region (Fischer & Silvern, 1985; Lamborn & Fischer, 1988)
rather than a single point or step on a unidirectional, developmental ladder.

Asmitia and Perlmutter (1989) provide yet another contemporary example of
how actual and potential levels of ability can be described in more scientific
and specific terms, yet we rarely see their work referred to in Australian early

childhood writing. They developed a model describing social influences on problem solving. It presents a sequential description of four levels of ability, acknowledging a continuum of subjects' behavior from solitary to social (when working with another) in preschool and school children. Their model acknowledges the influence of both Piaget and Vygotsky's work but, more importantly, moves beyond them. Of even greater interest is a second hypothetical model that they illustrate that demonstrates the difference between performance with and without social input. That is, they not only illustrate but define the levels of children's ZPD, or of the differences between actual and potential abilities. Their theoretical models also bear relevance to contemporary discrepancy theories of cognitive development. Similarly, Tharp and Gallimore (1998) describe a detailed, four-phase model of progress through the ZPD as the learner moves from socially scaffolded learning to self-scaffolded learning. Again, we repeat, provided one is prepared to move on from Vygotsky, contemporary works provide more answers and a far greater illumination of the variables involved in what has come to be called social constructivist perspectives of learning.

Issue 6: The Problem with Vygotsky's Notion of Internalization

Those who are unable to move onward from a Vygotskian/ZPD interpretation of learning are disadvantaged. This is because Vygotsky, possibly due to his untimely death, was never able to explore in depth the educational construct of internalization as it related to the transformation of social into personal knowledge. He did develop the idea of internalization a little more fully regarding the change of communicative language to inner speech and then to thought, but we wish to focus upon internalization as it relates more generally to the ZPD and school-based learning, as this aspect most commonly influences educational thought about curriculum and program planning today.

Vygotsky's ZPD and Bickhard's model of scaffolding differ markedly with regard to the process of internalization. Vygotsky claimed that knowledge is initially socially and culturally defined. It becomes internalized as individual knowledge as a result of interactions in the ZPD between a teacher and learner using the mediating tools of language. For Vygotsky, the idea of internalization applied only to the development of higher mental functions. Bickhard, on the other hand, openly rejects the relevance of Vygotsky's explanation of internalization on logical grounds—one cannot internalize a dimension that is already internal. His argument comes from the theoretical stance that if, during the process of interaction with a teacher, the learner does use intuitive reasoning, metacognition, or curiosity or self-selects from conceptual knowledge to construct newer understandings or even at times self-corrects what is known, then one is using motivational incentives that are indeed intrinsic to the learner.

Therefore, according to Bickhard, the meaning of internalization in a Vygotskian sense, namely, that knowledge moves from the outside to the inside, cannot be applied to current theories about scaffolding. Kitchener also questions Vygotsky's argument about

what is the underlying process of internalisation. . . ? Internalisation is, after all, something the individual does. It is, as Vygotsky (1978) puts it an internal *reconstruction* of
an external operation (p. 58). But if it is a construction on the part of the individual,
what are the mechanisms underlying this construction, and are these mechanisms individual (psychological) or social? How they could be social remains unclear. But if they
are individual and psychological, it would seem that at least some fundamental psychological processes are individualistic in nature. (Kitchener, 1996, p. 247)

Vygotsky (1978) himself admits that he had not supplied an adequate psychological account of the internalization process. He described how he believed
behavior changes because of it, such as when the very young child who asks
his mother for something, then when older, instead asks himself, Where is it?,
and when older again, finally thinks the question and does not need to ask it.
However, this is not tantamount to an explanation of the transformational processes involved.

Rogoff (1990), on the other hand, refuses to be ensnared by the logic of this
argument and instead almost digressively argues that if children are learning via
a social interaction, then the social is entwined with the personal or intrinsic
element anyway, "and there is no need for a separate process of internalisation"
(1990, pp. 194–195). That is, the solution in Rogoff's view is to build a different
understanding of internalization to fit in with Vygotsky's argument and reinterpret "social" and "personal/intrinsic" so that we can describe them as the same
thing. We do not consider this to be an appropriate response to the theoretical
debate.

Fortunately, the work of contemporary theorists has enabled greater analysis
of the process of internalization, and we now turn to these. Addison-Stone
(1993) suggests that the mediating process of scaffolding includes *prolepsis* or
an ability to presuppose some as yet unprovided information, and *transfer and
generalization* must also occur. These things should be contextualized or
matched within a meaningful context for the learner.

Addison-Stone (1993) supports Vygotsky's assumption of the importance of
language in this process, and, certainly, we cannot deny its influence in shared
learning between adults and children. Bickhard, however, while also acknowledging the importance of language, nevertheless argues that too narrow a dependence on language could be legitimately questioned, as the scaffolding
process involves more mediators than just language. It involves, for instance,
social, physical, and environmental factors such as those that he identified as
constituting different modes of scaffolding—the institutional, mutual, social, and
physical dimensions described previously. It could be argued that early childhood personnel who overemphasize scaffolding processes as linguistic processes

run the risk of denying learners the right to learn in other ways and, hence, of denying the diverse needs of learners.

Relevance of the "Ethos of Attachment"

Further details about the internalization process can be added from Bickhard's work concerning the relevance of *interpersonal factors* between the expert and child. We would argue that if the notion of scaffolding is going to be applied to early childhood learners, then it is imperative to include this dimension of affective development. Vygotsky did not do so, probably because it would not have been an approved element of Soviet educational ideology (yet another example of how Vygotsky's work simply doesn't fit into contemporary early childhood philosophy). Is the child attached to the expert, or does he or she feel comfortable and relaxed in his or her presence? Is the child a confident individual with high self-esteem and therefore is more likely to be motivated to respond to this learning challenge? Does the "expert" genuinely recognize the child's cognitive (or other developmental) starting point or merely assume so? Does the learning issue or problem in some way tap the child's interests or past experiences? If not, then is it appropriately related to the child's current knowledge so that meaningful links exist between the known and unknown? All of these questions point to the need for a sensitive, caring match between caregivers and children.

Consideration should also be given to the cognitive distance between the adult or peer expert and the novice learner, as this can impinge upon the process of internalization. Too much of a gap among peers, for instance, does not result in progress forward.

Such dimensions had not been considered in Vygotsky's work by the time of his death. This issue is not new to the area of cognitive research today, however. Being unable to undertake a historical review, we are able, nevertheless, to note that some of these studies, based on Piagetian theory (Doise & Mugny, 1984; Goncu & Rogoff, 1998), have helped illuminate details about the degree of difference that should exist between the conceptual levels of the expert and novice where peer/peer interaction problem-solving situations are used. Other studies, following a Vygotskian line (Tudge, 1992; Wertsch & Rupert, 1993), have identified elements that constitute the perceived authority of the expert in both adult–child and child–child interactions. This issue has also been looked at closely by researchers not operating from either a Piagetian or Vygotskian framework (Asmitia, 1988; Asmitia & Perlmutter, 1989; Phelps & Damon, 1989; Pintrich et al., 1993). Clearly, there are plenty of contemporary researchers currently taking this area of knowledge much further.

Issue 7: The Relevance of Metacognition Today

Contemporary interpretations of scaffolding as discussed earlier include recognition of the need to foster independent and responsible learning in children, particularly the ultimate ability to be able to "self-scaffold" when it is needed. For this to occur, adults should assist children to consciously use sound reasoning strategies such as thinking of similar examples or experiences, focus on part of the problem at a time, look for shortcuts or new connections between ideas, test out options, retain concentration and not get sidetracked, and, ultimately, self-scaffold and restructure elements of a task as needed. These kinds of skills typify metacognitive thinking or, as it is often described in the literature, "knowing how to know." Meadows (1993) defines metacognition as including skills like devising a good plan for attacking a problem, checking and retrialing, the ability to define a problem and identify goals, and so on. Having a metacognitive awareness is significant in any learning process whereby an ultimate goal is to empower the learner.

The application of metacognitive strategies by the learner was not an element of Vygotsky's writing. This is because of the historical limitations of Vygotsky's work (the fact that metacognitive theories have evolved over the last few decades) and the fact that such theoretical assumptions about the right of the learner to become independent and empowered would not have been compatible with the ideological framework of dialectical materialism within which Vygotsky worked. However, we feel that it is an essential element to be considered in relation to scaffolding today.

We found one description by Vygotsky of the ZPD interactions used by a teacher working with a child. In this description the ideal role for the teacher was to introduce and define the concept verbally (Vygotsky always insisted on this as a first step), then to work with the pupil, explain, supply information, question, correct, and make the pupil explain (Vygotsky, 1986, p. 191). It is our opinion that, seen in context, this process is a didactic, imitative, and structured approach in which the learner's role is reduced to one of passivity. As such, it describes a training model of learning that sits more comfortably within a behaviorist framework of learning rather than one that espouses creativity, diversity, and independent thinking within a framework of metacognitive reasoning.

This line of argument finds support in the work of others such as Rosenshine & Meister (1998), who argue that scaffolding works best when used to teach specific skills or to teach secondary students higher-level cognitive strategies in one-on-one tutorial situations. Similarly, Palinscar and Brown (1984) found scaffolding useful to teach remedial readers. The kinds of programs that these authors describe are more consistent with Vygotsky's descriptions, in which a high amount of structure, repetition, and teacher control were involved. Such methods, however, are not compatible with everyday early childhood practice.

It must be noted that whether or not metacognition occurs in preschool children is somewhat of a contentious issue in research literature (McLeod, 1997; Meadows, 1993). Sieglar (1998) argues that preschoolers are metacognitive, but on an implicit, not an explicit level. Studies that support the existence of metacognitive abilities in younger children specify that it tends to occur under certain conditions, such as (1) when adults actively help children to become aware of sound reasoning strategies on a conscious level, and (2) when children are actively encouraged to use those strategies, and (3) when teachers model good strategy usage in their everyday work with children (Cullen, 1992; Pressley & Levin, 1980; Schneider & Bjorklund, 1992; Slawinski & Best, 1995; Tishman, Perkins, & Jay, 1995). We are in agreement with the latter point of view. Our observations of 3–5-year-olds over many years tell us that they are more than capable of being metacognitive and tend to begin to do so more comfortably from about 4 years onward.

CONCLUSION: THEORETICAL FRAMEWORKS FOR MAKING SENSE OF CHILDREN'S LEARNING AND PLAY

Philosophically, we prefer the contemporary approaches of social constructivist perspectives, because they interpret children's learning and play as a creative, diverse process whereby the learner is empowered and where the outcomes of play can be many and varied depending upon the contexts in which they occur. For those early childhood educators who prefer a social constructivist approach and choose to follow a scaffolding philosophy, we advocate that the concept of *reciprocal scaffolding* is more suitable in terms of its recognition of current theoretical bases and its meaningfulness for younger learners.

However, we also prefer psychological constructivist perspectives, as our discussions about learning, which frequently refer to individual psychological processes and cognition, clearly demonstrate. Cobb and Bauersfeld (1995) describe this dual view that incorporates social constructivism and psychological constructivism as the emergent perspective. Apart from the work of those theorists mentioned in the preceding discussions, Prawat (1998) identifies symbolic interactionism, in which both social and psychological views are recognized. This is similar to Cobb and Bauersfeld's idea of the emergent perspective (for more detail see Cobb and Yackel, 1996). To this we could add the sociological ideas of Bronfenbrenner's ecological theory, and so one could go on. Regardless of whatever particular paradigm or philosophical base a person chooses, however, it must be noted that ecological validity in theory is well represented in contemporary, contextual psychosocial frameworks without having to cling to Vygotsky.

Current perspectives are more likely to describe processes whereby the adult's role is an active, participatory one from within which reciprocity, guidance, and a democratic interchange of ideas can occur. Viewed in this sense, play is seen as the primary vehicle through which learning occurs, whereas according to the Vygotskian view, it had no place in the learning process. The notion of play as learning was not a familiar one to Vygotsky. Whereas some do espouse that his ZPD was developed to foster active learning, Kozulin (1986, 1990) argues most critically and cogently that on this point Vygotsky has been greatly misinterpreted by current writers and that his contribution has indeed been overestimated. This issue has been addressed in detail in *Rethinking Early Childhood Theory and Practice* (Lambert & Clyde, 2000).

Developmental cognition has come a long way since theorists like Vygotsky and Piaget made their contributions. Their effect upon our knowledge of how children think has been of the greatest importance to our present-day understanding of this process. Their original work has been refined and extended by others in ways that they could never have done themselves. This is, of course, not something for which we can criticize them as, since their time, research methods have become markedly more sophisticated and consequently, our knowledge about cognition has expanded enormously. So also has our understanding about sociocultural influences upon development and learning. Rather, our concern lies with the fact that many early childhood researchers and writers, ironically, have *decontextualized* Vygotsky's work and in doing so have almost rendered it meaningless. It is not legitimate to accept Vygotsky's writing without seeing it within the shortcomings of dialectical materialism where knowledge was controlled by the state and where learners, according to the underlying political philosophy, were not to be encouraged as independent or creative learners or those whose individuality was recognized and respected.

Of course, we are not suggesting that Vygotsky's work be rejected on the grounds of political ideology. To do that would be yet another example of the control and manipulation of knowledge that we have just implied are unethical. But should we merely accept a work in its original skin (in this case a 1930s skin) without analyzing it and without thinking about how it does or does not relate to current theoretical contexts? Instead, we suggest that one should acknowledge Vygotsky's work for being a starting point from which our own thinking can progress futuristically and then, accordingly, take up the challenge of developing our own thinking in just that direction.

NOTES

This chapter (with minor revisions) originally appeared in E. B. Lambert & M. Clyde, *Rethinking early childhood theory and practice* (Katoomba, New South Wales: Social Science Press, 2000, chs. 2–5) and is reprinted here by kind permission of Social Science Press.

1. Our thanks go to Daniela Pacheva, currently of the University of British Columbia, Vancouver, Canada, and formerly from Sofia University, Bulgaria. Daniela holds Vygotsky's published works in their original language. She assisted us by providing a translation for *obuchenie* from this collection, including a 1934 article, "The Problem of Instruction and Cognitive Development at School Age," which, to the best of our knowledge, is not available in English. Her translation of the term *obuchenie* agrees with Minick's.

2. See note 1 above.

REFERENCES

Addison-Stone, C. (1993). What is missing in the metaphor of scaffolding? In E. Forman, N. Minick, & C. Stone (Eds.), *Contexts for learning: Sociocultural dynamics in children's development* (pp. 169–183). Oxford: Oxford University Press.

Asmitia, P. (1988). Peer interaction and problem solving: When are two heads better than one? *Child Development, 59,* 87–96.

Asmitia, P., & Perlmutter, M. (1989). Social influences on children's cognition: State of the art and future directions. In H. Reese (Ed.), *Advances in child development and behaviour* (vol. 22, pp. 89–144). San Diego: Academic Press.

Bickhard, M. (1992). Scaffolding and self-scaffolding: Central aspects of development. In L. Winegar & L. Valsiner (Eds.), *Children's development within social context: Volume 2. Research and methodology* (pp. 33–51). Hillsdale, NJ: Erlbaum.

Biddell, T., & Fischer, K. (1993). Beyond the stage debate: Action, structure and variability in Piagetian theory and research. In R. Sternberg & C. Berg (Eds.), *Intellectual development* (pp. 100–140). New York: Cambridge University Press.

Brown, A., Bransford, J., Ferrara, R., & Campoine, J. (1983). Learning, remembering and understanding. In J. Flavell & E. Markman (Eds.), *Handbook of child psychology: Volume 3. Cognitive development* (pp. 77–166). New York: Wiley.

Bruner, J. (1978). Learning how to do things with words. In J. Bruner & A. Garton (Eds.), *Human growth and development* (pp. 62–84). Oxford: Clarendon Press.

Bruner, J., Jolly, A., & Sylva, K. (1985). *Play—Its role in development and evolution.* Ringwood, Vic.: Penguin.

Campione, J., Brown, A., Ferrara, R., & Bryant, N. (1984). The zone of proximal development: Implications for individual differences and learning. In B. Rogoff & J. Wertsch (Eds.), *Children's learning in the zone of proximal development* (pp. 77–92). San Francisco: Jossey-Bass.

Cobb, P., & Bauersfeld, H. (1995). Introduction: The coordination of psychology and sociological perspectives in maths education. In P. Cobb & H. Bauersfeld (Eds.), *Emergence of mathematical meaning: Interaction in classroom cultures* (pp. 1–16). Hillsdale, NJ: Erlbaum.

Cobb, P., & Yackel, E. (1996). Constructivist, emergent and sociocultural perspectives in the context of developmental research. *Educational Psychologist, 31,* 175–190.

Cole, M. (1992). Context, modularity and the cultural constitution of development. In L. Winegar & L. Valsiner (Eds.), *Children's development within social context: Volume 2. Research and Methodology* (pp. 5–31). Hillsdale, NJ: Erlbaum.

Cole, M., John-Steiner, V., Scribner, S., & Souberman, E. (Eds.). (1978). *L. S. Vygotsky: Mind in society.* Cambridge, MA: Harvard University Press.

Cole, M., & Scribner, S. (1978). Introduction. In M. Cole, V. John-Steiner, S. Scribner, & E. Souberman (Eds.), *L. S. Vygotsky: Mind in society* (pp. 1–16). Cambridge, MA: Harvard University Press.

Cullen, J. (1992). Young children's learning strategies: Continuities and discontinuities. *International Journal of Early Childhood, 23,* 44–58.

Demetriou, A., Effklides, E., & Platsidou, M. (1993). The architecture and dynamics of the developing mind. *Monographs of Social Research in Child Development, 58,* 581–590.

Doise, W., & Mugny, G. (1984). *The social development of the intellect: Volume 10.* Oxford, U.K.: Pergamon Press.

Fischer, K., Pipp, S., & Bullock, D. (1984). Detecting developmental discontinuities: Methods and measurement. In R. Emde & R. Harmon (Eds.), *Continuities and discontinuities in development* (pp. 95–121). New York: Plenum.

Fischer, K., & Silvern, L. (1985). Stages and individual differences in cognitive development. *Annual Review of Psychology, 36,* 613–648.

Gamble, A. (1981). *An introduction to modern social and political thought*. Hampshire, U.K.: Macmillan.

Gee, J. (1989). What is literacy? *Journal of Education, 171*, 18–25.

Gindis, B. (1995). The sociocultural implications of disability: Vygotsky's paradigm for special education. *Educational Psychologist, 30*, 77–81.

Goncu, A., & Rogoff, B. (1998). *Nature of adult guidance as a moderator of social influence on children's learning*. Paper presented at the meeting of the Society for Research in Child Development, Baltimore.

Gonzalez-Mena, J. (1998). *Foundations: Early childhood education in a diverse society*. Mountain View, CA: Mayfield.

Gonzalez-Mena, J., & Widmeyer-Eyer, D. (1997). *Infants, toddlers, and caregivers* (4th ed.). Mountain View, CA: Mayfield.

Hoppe-Graff, S. (1993). Individual differences in the emergence of pretend play. In R. Case & W. Edelstein (Eds.), *The new structuralism in cognitive development* (pp. 57–70). New York: Karger.

Hort, L. (1982). *The concept of contradiction in the study of cognitive development*. Unpublished doctoral dissertation, Australian National University, Canberra.

John-Steiner, V., & Souberman, E. (1978). Afterword. In M. Cole, V. John-Steiner, & E. Souberman, *L. S. Vygotsky: Mind and society*. (pp. 121–133). Boston: Harvard University Press.

Kagan, J. (1970). The determinants of attention in the infant. *American Scientist, 58*, 298–306.

Karpov, V., & Bransford, J. (1995). L. S. Vygotsky and the decline of empirical and theoretical learning. *Educational Psychologist, 30*, 61–66.

Kitchener, R. (1996). The nature of the social for Piaget and Vygotsky. *Human Development, 39*, 243–249.

Kitchener, R., & Fischer, K. (1990). A skill approach to the development of reflective thinking. In D. Kuhn (Ed.), *Developmental perspectives on teaching and learning thinking skills* (pp. 48–62). Basel: Karger.

Kozulin, A. (1986). The concept of activity in Soviet psychology: Vygotsky, his disciples and critics. *American Psychologist, 41*, 264–274.

Kozulin, A. (1990). *Vygotsky's psychology: A biography of ideas*. Cambridge, MA: Harvard University Press.

Lambert, E. B., & Clyde, M. (2000). *Rethinking early childhood theory and practice*. Katoomba, NSW: Social Science Press.

Lamborn, S., & Fischer, K. (1988). Optimal and functional levels in cognitive development: The individual's developmental range. *Newsletter of the International Society for the Study of Behavioural Development, 2*, 1–4.

Low Deiner, P. (1997). *Infants and toddlers: Development and program planning*. Orlando, FL: Harcourt, Brace, & Co.

McLeod, L. (1997). Young children and metacognition: Do we know what they know they know? And if so what do we do about it? *Australian Journal of Early Childhood, 22*, 6–11.

McLune, L. (1986). Symbolic development in normal and atypical infants. In G. Fein & M. Rivkin (Eds.), *The young child at play: Reviews of research: Volume 4* (pp. 45–62). Washington, DC: National Association for the Education of Young Children.

Meadows, S. (1993). *The child as thinker*. New York: Routledge.

Miller, P. (1989). *Theories of developmental psychology* (2nd ed). New York: Freeman & Co.

Minick, N. (1987). The development of Vygotsky's thought: An introduction. In K. Rieber & S. Carton (Eds.), *The collected works of L. S. Vygotsky: Volume 1* (pp. 17–36). New York: Plenum Press.

Moss, E. (1992). The socio affective context in joint activity. In L. Winegar & L. Valsiner (Eds.), *Children's development within social context: Volume 2: Research and Methodology* (pp. 117–154). Hillsdale, NJ: Erlbaum.

Murray, F. (1991). Questions a satisfying developmental theory would answer: The scope of a complete explanation of developmental phenomena. In H. Reese (Ed.), *Advances in child development and behaviour* (vol. 23, pp. 39–48). Hillsdale, NJ: Erlbaum.

Nuthall, G. (1996). Commentary: Of language and learning and understanding the complexity of the classroom. *Educational Psychologist, 31*, 207–214.

O'Conner, M. (1998). Can we trace the "efficacy of social constructivism"? In D. Pearson & A. Iran-Nejad (Eds.), *Review of research in education* (vol. 23, pp. 25–72). Washington, DC: American Educational Research Association.

Pacini, V. (1998). Multiage grouping in a pluralistic society. *Interaction, 11*, 33–35.

Palinzcar, S., & Brown, A. (1984). Reciprocal teaching of comprehension-fostering and comprehension-monitoring activities. *Cognition and Instruction, 2*, 117–175.

Penuel, W., & Wertsch, J. (1995). Vygotsky and identity formation: A sociocultural approach. *Educational Psychologist, 30*, 83–92.

Phelps, D., & Damon, W. (1989). Problem solving with equals: Peer collaboration as a context for learning maths and science concepts. *Journal of Educational Psychology, 81*, 636–649.

Pintrich, P., Marx, R., & Boyle, R. (1993). Beyond cold conceptual change: Role of motivational beliefs and classroom contextual factors in the process of conceptual change. *Review of Educational Research, 63*, 167–199.

Popkewitz, T. (1998). Dewey, Vygotsky and the social administration of the individual: Constructivist pedagogy as systems of ideas in historical spaces. *American Educational Research Journal, 35*, 535–570.

Prawat, R. (1998). Current self-regulation views of learning and motivation viewed through a Deweyan lens: The problems with dualism. *American Educational Research Journal, 35*, 199–226.

Pressley, M., & Levin, J. (1980). Development of mental imagery retrieval. *Child Development, 61*, 973–982.

Reese, H. (Ed.). (1991). *Advances in child development and behavior.* Hillsdale, NJ: Erlbaum.

Renshaw, P. (1988). Sociocultural pedagogy for new times: Reframing key concepts. *Australian Educational Researcher, 25*, 83–100.

Rieber, R. (1987). *Collected works of L. S. Vygotsky: Volume 1—The problems of general psychology.* New York: Plenum Press.

Rieber, R. (1997). *Collected works of L. S. Vygotsky: Volume 4—History and development of higher mental functions.* New York: Plenum Press.

Rieber, R. (1998). *Collected works of L. S. Vygotsky: Volume 5—Child psychology.* New York: Plenum Press.

Rieber, R., & Carton, S. (Eds.). (1987). *Vygotsky, L. S. 1896–1934.* New York: Plenum Press.

Rogoff, B. (1990). *Apprenticeship in thinking: Cognitive development in social context.* New York: Oxford University Press.

Rosenshine, B., & Meister, C. (1998). The use of scaffolds for teaching higher-level cognitive strategies. In A. Woolfold (Ed.), *Readings in educational psychology* (pp. 137–145). Needham Heights, MA: Allyn and Bacon.

Rowe, H. (1989). Towards ecologically valid methods of intelligence assessment. In G. Davidson (Ed.), *Ethnicity and cognitive assessment; Australian perspectives* (pp. 27–36). Darwin, NT: Darwin Institute of Technology.

Salomon, G., & Perkins, D. (1998). Individual and social aspects of learning. In D. Pearson & A. Iran-Nejad (Eds.), *Review of research in education* (vol. 23, pp. 1–24). Washington, DC: American Educational Research Association.

Saxe, G. (1981). Body parts as numerals: A developmental analysis of numeration among the Oksapmin in New Guinea. *Child Development, 52,* 306–316.

Schneider, W., & Bjorkland, D. (1992). Expertise, aptitude and strategic remembering. *Child Development, 63,* 461–473.

Schwitzgebel, E. (1999). Gradual belief change in children. *Human Development, 42,* 283–296.

Sieglar, R. (1998). *Children's thinking* (3rd ed.). Upper Saddle River, NJ: Prentice-Hall.

Slawinski, J., & Best, D. (1995). *Effects of meta memory instruction on children's predictions of recall.* Paper presented at the meeting of the Society for Research in Child Development, Indianapolis.

Snyder, S., & Feldman, D. (1984). Phases of transition in cognitive development: Evidence from the domain of spatial representation. *Child Development, 55,* 981–989.

Sternberg, R., & Okagati, L. (1989). Continuity and discontinuity in intellectual development are not a matter of "either-or." *Human Development, 32,* 158–166.

Tharp, R., & Gallimore, R. (1998). A theory of teaching as assisted performance. In D. Faulkner, K. Littleton, & M. Woodhead (Eds.), *Learning relationships in the classroom* (pp. 93–110). London: Routledge/Open University.

Tishman, S., Perkins, D., & Jay, E. (Eds.). (1995). *The thinking classroom: Learning and teaching in a culture of thinking.* Needham Heights, MA: Allyn & Bacon.

Tudge, J. (1992). Processes and consequences of peer collaboration: A Vygotskian analysis. *Child Development, 63,* 1364–1379.

Tudge, J., & Winterhoff, P. (1993). Vygotsky, Piaget and Banduras: Perspectives on the relations between the social world and cognitive development. *Human Development, 36,* 61–81.

Vaisey, J. (1967). *Education in the modern world.* London, U.K.: Weidenfeld & Nicolson.

Valsiner, J., & Winegar, L. (1992). Introduction: A cultural historical context for social "context." In L. Winegar & J. Valsiner (Eds.), *Children's development within social context: Volume 1. Metatheory and theory* (pp. 1–18). Hillsdale, NJ: Erlbaum.

Vygotsky, L. (1933). Play and its role in the mental development of the child. In J. Bruner, A. Jolly, & K. Sylva (Eds.), *Play: Its role in development and evolution* (pp. 537–554). Ringwood, Vic.: Penguin.

Vygotsky, L. (1962). *Thought and language.* Cambridge, MA: Massachusetts Institute of Technology.

Vygotsky, L. (1971). *The psychology of art*. Cambridge, MA: Massachusetts Institute of Technology.

Vygotsky, L. (1978). *Mind in society: The development of higher psychological processes*. Cambridge, MA: Harvard University Press.

Vygotsky, L. (1986). *Thought and language*. Cambridge, MA: Massachusetts Institute of Technology.

Wertsch, J. (1985). *Vygotsky and the social formation of mind*. Cambridge, MA: Harvard University Press.

Wertsch, J., & Rupert, L. (1993). The authority of cultural tools in a sociocultural approach to mediated agency. *Cognition and Instruction, 11*, 227–239.

Winegar, L., & Valsiner, J. (Eds.). (1992). *Children's development within social context: Volume 1. Metatheory and theory*. Hillsdale, NJ: Erlbaum.

Wood, D., Bruner, J., & Ross, G. (1976). The role of tutoring in problem solving. *Journal of Child Psychology and Psychiatry, 17*, 89–100.

Chapter 6

Play, Activity, and Thought: Reflections on Piaget's and Vygotsky's Theories

Rosario Ortega

ACTIVITY AND THOUGHT IN CHILD'S PLAY: A HISTORICAL LOOK

Research on child's play and its role in human development is as old as psychology itself. Play, so different from and yet so similar to the rest of children's activities, has always aroused interest among scholars. From the naturalist studies of the eighteenth and nineteenth centuries by the empiricists, with their biographies of children and their meticulous observations of children's lives, to the experimental studies by the European and American child psychologists of the beginning of the twentieth century, to current studies, there has been a continual interest in explaining the psychodevelopmental nature of play and its role in learning. The first psychological theories, like those by Spencer (1855, 1861) and later by Groos (1901), Buhler (1930), and Buytendijk (1935), presented an integrated vision of child's play, relating it to the general immaturity of childhood. However, starting in the 1930s and clearly in the 1940s, psychology focused its general interpretation of development on specific developmental domains. Behaviorism denied psychological relevance to everything that was not measurable and modifiable through induced learning, and it was not very interested in a natural, spontaneous activity like play. Freud (1932) was interested in the subconscious world and argued that play was the language of the subconscious, a language that must be interpreted by means of mysterious codes not available to everyone. To some extent, because of psychoanalysis, play is seen as something dark and mysterious that has little to do with the evidence that this is a spontaneous, quite transparent phenomenon. Finally, in the 1930s the cognitive theories of child's play were developed.

The first theory to relate play to cognitive development was that of Piaget, who focuses his work on the components and functions of mental representation of knowledge. This was also the object of interest of the incipient but well-oriented psychology developing in Russia in the same period. However, the radicalization of political change in the Soviet Union and later World War II and the breaking off of relations between West and East in the dark Cold War period created two separate worlds of psychology on either side of the Iron Curtain.

I am interested in the degree to which the political and scientific history of the midcentury years in the two Europes affected the development of the basic theory regarding the role of activity, thought, and interpersonal relationships in child's play. I want to determine how the two European cultures focused their respective social models in constructing a theory of play. I believe that culture in general and its sociopolitical orientation in particular can affect the principles by which a theory is developed. As a result of the influence of sociopolitical concerns on science, I wonder to what degree the ideas that we have about play have been divided into two large groups: one extremely individualistic and the other extremely collectivist. A historical analysis shows that both visions, represented by their greatest exponents—Piaget and Vygotsky—began with similar principles in the first decades of the century but continued on divergent paths in the middle of the century.

I have thoroughly examined the theoretical principles on which both authors base their ideas about child's play and have reviewed the analytical assumptions of the processes that relate thought and activity; consciousness and praxis; symbol and action; reasons and realizations. As Sutton-Smith poetically stated (1980, 1985), "being" and the possibility of "not being" are essential ingredients in child's play.

In this chapter, I would like to resurrect an old theoretical problem as to the role of activity, thought, and social mediation in play processes in general and in those processes having to do with sociodramatic play in particular. I believe that this debate can be extended to other aspects of human development. Furthermore, it is an expression of the large gap that still exists in the realm of psychological science between the two great psychological traditions: the individualistic tradition of Western Europe and the collectivist tradition that was developed in Eastern Europe (Bronfenbrenner, 1970/1993). In recent years there has been an attempt to join the two so that the balance between the individual and the sociocultural returns to its optimal point (Bruner, 1997). It is a question of knowing which units of analysis should be used to study development and learning processes, one of which is undoubtedly child's play.

The Two Piagetian Theories of Child's Play

Piaget was a biologist and a rationalist who, in turn, became a great psychologist. Well trained as a naturalist and fascinated by the world of formal logic, he interpreted human development in adaptive and epistemological terms. The former referred to the human child adapting to the environment, and the latter to logical intelligence and scientific thought providing the best way for humans to adapt and the greatest and highest-quality transformation. His line of thought, keeping within functionalist and structuralist parameters, always moved from the natural to the rational; from the sensory-motor to the representational, from symbol to sign, from the concrete to the abstract, and from the simple to the complex. In this framework, his interpretation of child's play was used to develop a general theory of human development and adaptation. Piaget's treatment of the subject of child's play resulted from a need to explain other psychological processes and was never a priority in and of itself.

The first time that Piaget wrote about play (Piaget, 1932), he was trying to explain children's understanding of moral rules. The second time, he was trying to explain the movement from action to thought and the development of the first schemas of cognitive representation. Though, as a scientist, Piaget was not content with the status quo, he was a man of his times who took into account the intellectual context in which he presented his challenges. Both of these problems were relevant to Piaget's personal interests during different periods in his life. The first represents his interests in the 1930s, and the second is representative of his scientific interests in the 1940s and 1950s.

In the first analysis, Piaget was influenced by a general view maintained by the old Wundtian postulate (Wundt, 1887) that methodologically separated the superior psychological processes (reason, will, and morality) from the inferior ones (attention, perception, action). The superior processes should be studied in the context of the culture and history of the different societies, while the inferior processes should be studied using experimental methods. When Piaget carried out his second study about play, he was already the greatest scientific psychology representative in the Western world; he maintained a clearly individualistic perspective of development and was shaping a powerful theory about how the individual builds cognitive potential. For Piaget, this potential was self-generated based on powerful internal schemas inherent in the nature of intelligence and seemed to function autonomously with respect to the outside. At this point, Piaget had lost interest in culture and history as determining factors in cognitive change and had become interested in finding the keys to cognitive change in the individual.

The middle of the century is when, from my view, the two great models of psychological thought were really developed. The Western model was based on the value of individuals, their autonomy, and their personal initiative. These were values consistent with the effort to reconstruct a Europe physically destroyed by the war but morally affirmed by the victory over the irrationality of fascism. The Eastern model was strongly marked by emerging sociopolitical values, as seen further on. This period also marked the beginning of the lack of communication between the East and the West and the creation of the two European cultures: one open, free, and individualistic, based on the value of democracy and economic liberality, and the other closed to its own culture based on principles of state control, authoritarianism, and collectivism. In both the East and West, the splendid psychological ideas of the first decades of the century germinated, but they grew in opposite directions marked by their societies' cultures and values.

Play and Moral Thought in Piaget's First Theory of Play

In 1932, Piaget first took a good look at games in order to establish a theory about moral thought in children. Upon observing the interactions that boys and girls established while playing traditional games and studying how their rules evolved, he designed a theoretical model and criteria for moral development that is still generally considered valid. He was interested in the personal development of rules as a concept, and he understood that in that process there is clearly an ingredient of cultural transmission. The first rules are accepted automatically as an imposition of authority. Only later does the child discover his or her arbitrary and conventional components, and in the end the rules are incorporated into the adolescent mind as personal spheres of decision making related to principles of fairness and justice. In short, it was a study of sociomoral psychology that looked down neither on the analysis of thought content nor on the social structure of participation upon which knowledge is built.

In the analysis of cognitive representation that takes place during play, the first period of Piaget's intellectual and scientific activity is very interesting because his observations are carried out in natural situations with boys and girls playing traditional games that they organized and regulated within the group dynamics of friends and classmates. In the observation and analysis of spontaneous games, Piaget finds the negotiation of rules of adjustment among the personal initiatives, the cultural conventions, and the criteria of fairness and justice. It is a matter of personal adjustments within a framework of interpersonal relationships. *The Moral Judgment of the Child* (Piaget, 1932) is a monument to the social and moral logic found in spontaneous play from which judgment about what is right and wrong and about what we should do and not do grows and develops. Calling games "admirable social institutions," he writes that "if one wants to understand anything about morality in children he must understand how the rules of games work" (Piaget, 1932, p. 9).[1]

This model of analysis disappears in later works. Piaget stops giving importance to the specific content upon which mental representation is produced as well as the social situations that serve as the setting for the activity that is represented. He abandons the global and contextual analysis that includes social activity and psychological intentionality and concentrates on the logical balance between the represented elements. In 1932, Piaget is conscious of the need to analyze in detail the linguistic and cultural procedures that ritualize players' made-up game rules. None of these elements would be present in his theory in the 1950s.

In his second theory of child's play Piaget has relinquished all cultural and interpersonal principles as elements of analysis (Piaget, 1959). His only criteria are the cold structure of cognitive representation and the abstract elements of its operation. Piaget does not seem to observe in those games that represent actions, scenes, and events any normative element that affects the thought of the preschool child or the restructuring of his schemas in any relevant way. This does not mean that he does not value play activities in general or that he rejects their value as psychological processes but rather that, in his theoretical analysis, he strips linguistic symbols and symbols of play of all interpersonal, social, and cultural criteria that, ritualized by the combined action of playmates, aid in the development of knowledge. As he wrote in 1932,

Thus, in the same way as the so-called moral realities, the rules of the game of marbles are transmitted from generation to generation and are only maintained thanks to the respect that they inspire in individuals. The only difference is that in this case we are talking about relationships only among children. Little ones who are beginning to play are taught by adults, little by little, to respect the law and, moreover, they wholeheartedly tend towards this virtue, eminently characteristic of human dignity, which consists of correctly following the rules of the game. (Piaget, 1932, p. 10)

The abandonment of the sociocultural and interactive model, which he himself recognizes as very near to Durkheim's (1922) sociological orientation, made it more difficult, from my point of view, for Eastern and Western psychology to follow somewhat similar paths, not only in regard to play, although it is clearly true for play.

Thought and Action: The Cold Cognitive Theory of Child's Play

In 1959, when the complex book entitled *La Formation du Symbole Chez L'enfant* (Piaget, 1959) was published, Piaget used a method of analysis very different from his first sociocultural model, and he took as the main theme the operation of what he described as cognitive structures. He was interested in explanations based on the self-equilibrating of cognitive functions. He thus ignored the influence of the specific content of knowledge and interpersonal factors when one plays. He focuses his attention on the configuration of great thought structures, in which interpersonal context, experiences, and specific content with regard to games do not seem to have a relevant function. However, this is his most popular scientific work on play and the one that has become a paradigm. In this work, Piaget considers child's play, along with imitation and language, as one of the bases for children's ability to use symbols and as the real key to the child's entry into the world of thought.

The father of cognitive-developmental constructivism looked for and found the difference between serious intelligent activity and play in the nature of the transformation itself; that is, in the movement of action to mental representation as adaptive forms. Inevitably, Piaget constructed this theoretical building with the same material used to build his general theory: structure and function. In other words he used good form, which tends toward logic, and bad form, which tends toward subjectivism and play.

In this work, which is difficult to read despite the empirical examples that help the reader along, for Piaget, thought and play share the same psychogenetic origin—psychomotor action and its movement toward symbol. However, neither the structures nor the functions of the two activities progress in the same way. The simple sensory-motor schemas for play become lazy and irregular as a result of the false assimilations that the subject permits. In play, the subjects want to please themselves and are not at all strict regarding meaning; they do not express a need to adjust their interpretations of play to the external realities. Thus, although play and intelligent activity have their origin in the coordination of sensory-motor action, they are different both functionally and structurally. This differentiation leads games and the rest of our mental and practical cognitive activity down different paths, and this notion would force Piaget to offer a clearly imprecise view of play from the point of view of what is learned in play. Thus, Piaget, without intending to, placed play on a lower level than serious, intelligent behavior. In this way, games became activities for which little concentration is needed, activities that can be carried out in any fashion and whose final result is relatively unimportant because what is really important in play is having fun. Play becomes an intellectually unstimulating activity unrelated to what is important to the child as a curious discoverer of the world. A Piaget quotation is somewhat long but worth rereading:

The essential difference between the symbol of play and the representation adapted is, then, the following: in the intelligent act, assimilation and accommodation are always synchronized and in equlibrium with each other; on the other hand, with the symbol of play, the actual object is fitted in to a previous schema with no objective relationship to it and in order to evoke this prior schema and the missing objects that are being related, imitation intervenes as a "signifying" expression. In short, with the symbol of play, imitation is not related to the object present, but rather to the missing object that the person is trying to evoke, and, thus, imitative accommodation is still subordinate to assimilation. However, with deferred imitation, imitative accommodation is still an end in itself and is subordinate to reproductive assimilation. Finally, in the intelligent act, imitation is related to the object that the person is trying to assimilate and accommodation, even when it becomes representative imitation, is in equilibrium with assimilation. In conclusion, whether referring to intelligence or imitation and playful behavior, imitation prolongs accommodation, play prolongs assimilation and intelligence joins them all together, without interference, thus complicating this simple situation. (Piaget, 1959, p. 145)

Piaget based that differentiation on the irruption of emotion-based compensatory factors. However, the true function of these processes is never revealed.

He did not go into detail regarding compensation and affective equilibrium as a possible explanation. There is an untranslatable subjectivity in the symbolization process that comes from the signifier, that is, play itself, to which the memory of experiences and personal satisfaction is added. This seems to be the key to the objective differentiation that Piaget establishes between play and nonplay in relation to the type of thought produced or articulated.

Detrimental to the objective representation of reality, the emotional symbol seems to take on the function of play. This strange substitution remains unexplained by the epistemological elements that Piaget himself uses since neither subsequently nor in the rest of this work does Piaget take up the study of the emotional microprocesses to which the compensation of the ego, which he attributes to the imaginative assimilation of play, responds. The function that these emotional and affective processes have in activity or mental representation is not known, but they may act as a motivational basis both for serious activity and for play.

Vygotsky, on the other hand, does not do away with the emotional elements of play but places them at the very foundation of activity and sees them as the motivational force that roots games so deeply in desires and subjective intentions. This would explain the passion that children have for games and the joy that these activities bring to the subject's life.

It seems that Piaget, by separating assimilatory microprocesses into two types, serious and play, attributes a greater adaptive potential to the serious ones. There's an intellectually superfluous emotional connotation to play, and he diverts the discourse toward a cold cognitive model that leaves little room for playful motives and interests.

Another interpretive gap in Piaget's second theory of play is the ignorance of the role of *internal rules* in the representation of play. When he isolates two different types of mental representation—that of play (subjective, egocentric, and unrealistic) and that of serious representation (progressively objective, balanced, and realistic)—what happens in symbolic and sociodramatic play is emptied of its classifiable content. This, however, is a spontaneous type of activity that is always full of information about what the boy or girl thinks about the world, things, and others and about himself or herself, This can be seen very clearly in subsequent studies (see Bretherton, 1984, 1989; Fein, 1979, 1981, 1989; Griffin, 1984; Griffing, 1980; Nelson & Gruendel, 1979; Nelson & Seidman, 1984; Ortega, 1988, 1990, 1991a, 1992, among others). The rules that govern game action and those that direct conversation are extremely important. The rules of symbolic games serve an extraordinary role as auxiliary mechanisms for cognitive classification and for the mastery of the transformations of child knowledge schemas. The knowledge that preschoolers carry with them to play settings is full of conventions and rules linked to the development of daily social experience, but this type of knowledge is expressed in narrative and dramatic form (Bruner, 1984, 1990). However, Piaget did not value the conceptual importance of this type of knowledge as he focused on the study of logical thought.

However, Vygotsky did see the connection between the narrative rule and the logic of classifiable thought. This understanding led him to value games as spheres of knowledge linked not only to action but also to the complex thought that is generated by social interaction and whose specific content is very important because it refers to the interpersonal world in which the boy or girl moves.

In Piaget's works, play becomes a psychological process dependent upon the great cognitive-developmental structures (Ortega, 1991b). Piaget's research on children's games has not been unfruitful, although it has produced somewhat contradictory effects. The Western world has come to consider play as a cognitive process and an interesting and important activity for development, but it has lost the explanatory link between play and mental representation, which gives rise to the current theoretical debate. From a historical point of view, Piaget's studies from the 1940s and 1950s render the real content of experience as relatively unimportant and turn the human child into a being acting alone and guided by a strong impulse toward self-perfection inherent in the internal structures of intelligence.

It is known that children learn by playing, but little is known about the reasons. Games have become interesting exercises frequently programmed by adults to stimulate thought and cognitive conflict, but the cognitive and interpersonal conditions of knowledge construction are not certain (Smith, 1986). Games of action, games of symbol, and games of rules, which correspond to the three main cognitive stages, were the most cited by researchers until the 1990s (Takhvar & Smith, 1990). However, now the relationship between activity and thought and understanding the complex nature and meaning of spontaneous play has been greatly strengthened.

Play and Cultural Mediation: Vygotsky's Theory of Play

It is well known that Soviet authors did not always enjoy complete freedom of expression. After the first years of revolutionary euphoria and honest enthusiasm about the change taking place, there were years of ideological revisionism followed by Stalinist persecution. It is known that texts of the original authors may have been corrected or censored by state experts. So there is added challenge to a thorough examination of Vygotsky's hypotheses, not knowing what he thought and what was manipulated by the ideological censors. There is more than reasonable doubt that this happened (Kouzulin, 1990).

In opposition to the reductionist current that fueled the political revolution, Vygotsky wanted to define human thought mediated by social and historical phenomena as the greatest expression of culture. As discussed relative to Piaget, for Vygotsky, many of the basic concepts in regard to the role of thought, activity, and interpersonal relationships in human development are found in an analysis of play. Many keys to learning and human development are found when one attempts to understand the role of thought, rules, and emotion in play.

Vygotsky's first psychological studies were on method and they criticized post-Pavlovian behaviorist reductionism. These methodological writings were used to improve an understanding of the superior psychological processes by paying attention to microprocesses inherent in spontaneous or induced activity (Vygotsky, 1934).

Just like Piaget, Vygotsky, in his search for explanations, tried to articulate the rigors of empirical observation and the complexity of psychogenetic formulation. Both were extraordinarily rigorous in their approach, but their writings, which begin at the same point, diverge as they try to explain the psychological processes that they believe to be inherent in play. One must look for Vygotsky's ideas on the subject in the empirical studies of one of his most notable disciples, D. B. Elkonin, and one of his most thoughtful revisers, A. N. Leontiev. A careful reading of both of these men's texts reflects the brilliance of Vygotsky's ideas and, likewise, the degree to which many of them turned out to be unacceptable for an ideological system that made dialectical materialism not a method but an excuse for authoritarianism and the imposition of a single line of thought.

Although for Vygotsky, children's games are very important activities, especially for preschool children, it does not necessarily mean that they are collective processes. On the contrary, preschoolers' interpersonal relationships are what's important, not their psychological nature nor their function in development. Collectivization, or the sociocultural explanation for the psychological phenomenon, as a social and historical arena in which psychological events take place is the key. I closely examine the concepts of activity, rules, and thought mediated in play as proposed by Vygotsky and show how these concepts have been erroneously interpreted by subsequent Soviet authors and turned into basic assumptions for an ideological materialism applied to a form of psychology that turns out to be empty collectivism.

Play: An Important Activity Directed by Thought

Vygotsky did not personally carry out any studies regarding children's games. Consequently, his theories are seen in the advice that he gave to Elkonin and his corrections of Elkonin's work. Elkonin had thought of children's games as one of the most common and pleasurable activities of the preschool and school years. He studied the psychological and social relevance of these activities, applying the microgenetic method that Vygotsky had proposed. He analyzed the intermediary processes of complex activities internally, without separating these processes from the original sense of the games.

Elkonin (1980) likewise starts from a brilliant, exhaustive critique of the Piagetian theory of the relationship between thought and action and questions the nature of the mental representation that Piaget presents in relation to the action–thought binomial and the artificial division between play and non-play. He refutes the notion that the thought and language of preschoolers is egocentric and, following the line of thought set out by Vygotsky, carries out a careful analysis that completes and corrects that done by Piaget. Thus, he wrote,

Protagonized play, in general, is not an exercise. What is important, when representing the activity of chauffeur, salesperson, or doctor is not that the child acquires a habit. The sense of play is in the interpretation of the role. In activity, the desired result is the satisfaction of having fulfilled the function of the role taken on. (Elkonin, 1980, p. 225)

The importance of play is in the representative intent of the players as they attempt to imitate social occurrences or events. The problem with the action–thought link is in believing that action governs thought, which is not true in games. At the same time, the problem with the activity–culture binomial is in thinking that culture commands or governs activity or, in materialistic terms, in thinking that there is an inherent cultural element that imposes itself blindly on the free intentionality of the players. This is what Leontiev seems to propose when he tries to correct Vygotsky's original sociocultural ideas regarding the formation of human consciousness, to be discussed later.

For Elkonin, as for Vygotsky, there are two microprocesses in the relationship between activity and the mental representation of activity: the change of sense that objects and reality acquire through the expressed desire of the player (a change in the voluntary sense that the players create as they play) and the microprocess of the *objectification of one's own actions* in order to adapt them to those required by the "rules," the internal norms inherent to the plots that accompany the pretending implicit in all play. Both microprocesses seem more similar to Piaget's first theory of play than to his second.

For example, when a group of preschoolers plays "bus," representing the roles of bus driver, passengers, and conductor, what directs the activity that unfolds (action) is the sense that the players want to give to what they are going to do. Undoubtedly, cultural models shed light on that sense, but they do not determine it. Simulating a bus ride involves a great variety of actions, conversations, and behavioral norms that are the result of complex processes of negotiation among the players, not any sort of determinism inherent in the individual cognitive structures of a player or imposed by collective models of the adults being imitated. The margin of creative freedom is what makes play an environment for creating new knowledge. For Elkonin, the players reinterpret reality first in a personal way and then interpersonally. They attempt to adjust, insofar as possible, to sociocultural conventions, as long as this is appropriate to the "script" that they are following: "If the role interpreted by the child includes some sort of rule, action wants to attack it. The rule is fused together with the role and is not separated from it" (Elkonin, 1980, p. 238). Later he states,

Thus, play is presented as reality not only in regard to the change in attitude of the one who adopts the role, but also in regard to the relationship with the playmate from the point of view of the role represented by the playmate; not only as actions with objects consistent with the attributed meanings, but also in regard to the coordination of the perspectives regarding the meanings of these objects without directly manipulating them. This is a process of continual decentering. Play is presented as a cooperative activity among children. (Elkonin, 1980, p. 262)

Child's Play and the Problem of Consciousness in Vygotsky

The explanation of microprocesses for play leads Vygotsky to wonder about the general relationship between activity and thought: "Is play the preponderant or main type of activity? Might it not simply be a mirror of the processes that take place in other spheres?" Vygotsky answers his own questions: "The relationship of play to development is that of learning for development. Behind play are changes in needs and changes in consciousness of a more general nature. Play is a source of development and it creates areas of immediate development" (Vygotsky, 1933, in Elkonin, 1980, p. 269).

Later in the same text, he states,

In play, there is a new attitude between the word and action. Before, the word was inserted into the situation (indicative function) and the situation determined the actions through the word. Here the action comes from the meaning of the thing and not the thing itself (the vocative, attractive nature) for the meaning of the word. The word carries a bipolar indicator, becoming meaning in thought, as well as sense in the thing, the movement from the sense to the interior, to one's own processes and actions. (Vygotsky, 1933, p. 274)

It seems clear that Vygotsky is trying to define how the relationship among activity, consciousness, and cultural mediation should be understood and what the role of rules is in the whole affair. However, Lenotiev tries to "correct" the way that Vygotsky's ideas are understood, by directing them toward a supposed materialist model that would make consciousness depend on action and individual thought on the collectivist models. Leontiev states, "Faithful to his theoretical presuppositions, Vygotsky did not study psychic phenomena themselves but rather analyzed practical activity" (Leontiev, 1965, p. 429).

As González (1995) argues, what the Soviet school seems to be trying to do is show that the development of the subject is objective (from outside) by eliminating any Vygotskian reference to the subject and the subjective nature of consciousness. For Leontiev, the emphasis that Vygotsky had put on semiotic mediation processes was something transitory and contradictory that deserved to be refuted. He writes,

According to the ideas of L. S. Vygotsky, in the psychic processes of man we must distinguish between two levels: the first level is reason devoted to itself; the second is reason (the psychic process) armed with instruments and auxiliary means. And, in the same way, we must distinguish between two levels of practical activity, the first being the "simple hand /the bare hand," and the second, "the hand armed with tools and auxiliary instruments." . . . As the Marxist classics demonstrated, man's hand represents the organ and the product of work. . . . The terminology chosen by Vygotsky gave rise to confusion; the question arose, Are not all the psychic processes of modern man cultural? Such inconsistency in the ideas of Liev Semionovich provoked a justified criticism both during the psychologist's life and after his death. (Leontiev, 1965, p. 429)

In Leontiev's theory of play, spontaneous play is not a psychological process in which thought is restructured and new knowledge is produced but rather an access road for collectivity to reach individual thought; it is the acquisition of a mental model in the image of the collective adult model. It seems that Leontiev justifies his own thought by relating it to the symbolic and instrumental mediation proposed by Vygotsky as well as to the double process of the development of consciousness and the role of activity in that process. Although he admits that the expression "man's activity with the aid of objects" does not appear in Vygotsky's works, he considers that those were "his subjective projects." He states,

Naturally, it would seem that by placing the consciousness in the world of such pure cultural products as sign and meaning are, Vygotsky must have been renouncing the psychological program initially directed towards the study of practical labor activity with the aid of men's objects, a study on which all of Vygotsky's efforts were focused. Vygotsky's historical-cultural theory with his ideas on the mediated nature of psychic processes with the aid of psychological instruments (by analogy to the mediated form of man's practical activity) was the first formalization of that model. (Leontiev,1965, p. 449)

However, in games, what causes learning and development is the personal intention to attribute sense along with the consensus of the group in negotiating a new meaning, not any type of imposition of cultural elements, still less models of labor production. The game's protagonists choose topics, distribute their roles, and simulate their scenes and scripts in accordance with their own intentionalities and their own social processes; culture is a large backdrop for the stage, but it is not the stage; the stage is interpersonal and psychological in nature.

Vygotsky relates the subject of activity to that of consciousness, as two complementary processes (action and thought) that are joined together and have to be studied together. It is a unit that he calls duplicated experience; this duplicated experience (activity and consciousness) makes the psychological phenomenon tangible and should constitute the unit of analysis. But what is most important and what is secondary in this duplicity? The answer to this question leads directly to the main theme of Vygotskian psychology: the problem of consciousness.

Let us examine a long, complex quotation:

Play, as a type of activity and development of the superior psychological functions (and which is also sociogenesis) is a unit of opponents. The contradiction of play is the free, i.e. arbitrary, activity, all governed by impulse in such a way that it used to be considered an instinct; in other words, in an arbitrary, subconscious way, the interior in the exterior, that is, a contradiction of its psychological functions (elementary and direct). With its system and type of activity (free, arbitrary) the transition to interior speech and the superior psychological functions, the cause of development of these new school-age formations in play is resolved. (Vygotsky, 1933, in Elkonin, 1980, p. 274)

It seems clear that in the last years of his life, Vytotsky began to reconceive the role of instrumental and symbolic mediation of activity in the development of the superior psychological processes, perhaps with the intent to refute the ruling party interpretations of his work (Kouzulin, 1990). In this regard, everything seems to indicate that he considered games as the most important psychological process with which to initiate this refutation of the erroneous interpretations of his theory.

Games should be considered spontaneous activities in which the symbolic processes of mediation converge through concrete experiences with objects and with playmates and the negotiation of the sociocultural meanings that the contents of play represent. This mediation is carried out through discourse (conversation), which combines the individual sense that each player attributes to the processes of simulation and the meanings that the playmates share and that necessarily provide the cultural background for the situation; this does not require any sort of collectivization of individual thought, simply social consensus.

I do not know if this reflection sheds any light on the theoretical-historical problem that I proposed. But I would like to conclude with a subject that I think needs to be clarified not only through empirical research but also through conceptual formulation. The theoretical clarification of the cognitive, affective, and social nature of games used to favor the elaboration of educational proposals that began with spontaneous play activities and that became true environments of learning and development; this is possible only if there is a clear understanding of the relationship between the activity and the thought that is activated by the games.

If we rescued Piaget's old sociogenetic theory regarding the important role that the game rules have, and if we articulated it using Vygotsky's cognitive-cultural proposals, eliminating the strong individualistic slant of the Piagetian model and the collectivist bias that later authors gave to Vygotsky's work, the result would be a potentially very productive conceptual approach to the subject. This approach would attempt to articulate a theory that describes the psychological elements of play with a certain coherence in regard to the relationship that is established among them: thought as a governing element, intentionality and motives as a stimulating element, activity as continually putting into practice what is individually thought, and interaction and conversation as a real and symbolic context. Perhaps thus we would be able to make sense of many of the achievements of subsequent research as well as give more coherence to developmental theory and education.

SOCIODRAMATIC GAMES, ACTIVITY, AND THOUGHT

Games themselves are important for participants because they bring about idea exchange through actions. Playmates negotiate the sense that they give to their activity and their thought as they search for the cultural significance of what they are doing. Apart from adult interaction, the children imitate adult schemas. The contexts of relationships between playmates and their produced conversations aid interpersonal approval (ritualization of the rules) and cultural coherence to play, which turns it into a relevant activity, as both Vygotsky and Piaget, in his first theory, knew very well.

Moreover, the relevance of play has its roots in personal motives and desires, which stimulate these activities; as Vygotsky states, play is all about impulse and passion. Objects are relevant only as instruments for the development of action and conversation. The establishment of the real and symbolic stage for the game is adjusted both to the individual sense of what is being done and to the meaning of the content that is reproduced and that is shared by the playmates. Thus, the role of dialogue in play is fundamental.

In previous studies (Ortega, 1994; Ortega and Lozano, 1993), I have argued that sociodramatic play is a complex, spontaneous activity that becomes a setting for cognitive, social, affective, and moral development because individual knowledge is reproduced; meanings are negotiated until a network of shared knowledge is produced that contains the norms and conventions that are important to continue playing. A flexible system of roles and norms intrinsic to the script that is being played out and an intelligent guided conversation let the players know what is real and what is make-believe in a complex plot where knowledge and metaknowledge are articulated by means of a sophisticated system of direction from the script, which usually directs a child with the implicit consent of the rest of the players. Thus, the interpersonal experience of play enriches social relationships and begins integrating school-age children into them by teaching them to respect the rules so that the game does not break down.

Sociodramatic game activity is not an isolated action that can be analyzed independently from cultural referents. Actions must be adjusted to fit the context, while the game lasts. Interaction, taken both in its most basic framework (acting face-to-face with another person and respecting the other's performance) as well as in its broadest sense (acting together, with others), is a fundamental unit for the analysis of the cognitive representation that is produced in sociodramatic games.

The scripts have been defined by cognitive psychology as a schema that represents knowledge of the immediate context. Also included within the sociocultural framework are the characters, the roles, the sense of the situation, and its meaning and related goals.

The knowledge that is displayed in the sociodramatic game adapts well to the script as a model of shared cognitive representation. The conversation is a process of communication that allows the players to express and understand the individual mental representation (the personal script) and, at the same time, the interpersonal representation generated in the context (the generic script). If the cognitive and sociocultural hypotheses are true, the analysis of the conversation will lead us to discover the knowledge that is developed jointly (i.e., the construction of common schemas for shared activities).

In the conversation of play, if play is to continue, people must both understand and make themselves understood by their interlocutor in order to continually adjust their speech to that produced by their interlocutor. The conversation is key to understanding how the *personal schemas* are adjusted to those of the playmate and, thus, how *generic schemas* are constructed. This adjustment is necessarily the result of the search for minimal schemas that have the potential to be shared. To share a schema (a script in the case that we are looking at here), it is imperative to understand the meaning of most of what is said, to be in the same semantic context as the person who is speaking, to direct one's communicative intention toward common goals and to be able to see things from the other person's point of view (which assumes a psychological process of an affective and emotional nature implicitly in the attitude of play).

The goal of play is the most difficult component to isolate because there seem to actually be two goals: to represent a script (reach the end of the story presented) and to keep playing (keep any possible disagreements from disrupting the game). Form and content, in the case of representative play, are interactive and seem to implicitly and explicitly give way to negotiated partial goals.

Children between two and eight years of age frequently play these games in which several diverse psychological processes converge: motives, interests, emotions, affections, knowledge, and different types of communicative processes. The formats of sociodramatic play are excellent scenarios for learning and development. They are the best examples of what Vygotsky (1934) defined as a proximal developmental zone and the best examples of what Piaget understood as the ritualization of rules.

The great number of empirical studies about games over the last 40 years has failed in the absence of rigorous theoretical approaches; that is not to say that they have not been somewhat productive. But it would be more coherent to describe the achievements of empirical research based on theoretical formulations. In this sense, the development of a reasonably humanized version of the cognitive paradigm along with a version of the Vygotskian sociohistorical model, reasonably purged of its collectivist follies, would be a real triumph. This is what I think Jerome Bruner has tried to do throughout his career, especially in his later works (Bruner, 1997), by proposing a comprehensive stage in which the individual cognitive elements and the sociocultural foundations of psychology converge. This allows us to establish a sort of psychocultural paradigm from which the psychological proposals for education are derived. This, at least, is the path that I am following in my work (Ortega, 2000).

NOTE

1. All of the quotations in this chapter have been translated from Spanish editions of the various works. Additionally, the author wishes to sincerely thank Dr. Donald Lytle for all his help in translating this work.

REFERENCES

Bretherton, I. (1984). *Symbolic play: The development of social understanding*. New York: Academic Press.

Bretherton, I. (1989). Pretense: The form and function of make-believe play. *Developmental Review, 9*, 383–401.

Bronfenbrenner, U. (1970/1993). *Educación de los niños en dos culturas*. Madrid: Aprendizaje Visor.

Bruner, J. (1984). Juego, pensamiento y lenguaje. In Jerome Bruner, *Acción, Pensamiento y Lenguaje*. J. L. Linaza, Comp. Madrid: Alianza.

Bruner, J. (1986). *Actual minds, possible worlds*. Cambridge, MA: Harvard University Press.

Bruner, J. (1990/1991). *Acta od meaning*. Madrid: Alianza.

Bruner, J. (1997). *The culture of education*. Madrid: Aprendizaje Visor.

Buhler, C. (1930). Personality types based on experiments with children. Report of the Ninth International Congress of Psychology, New Haven, CT.

Buytendijk, F. J. (1935). *El juego y su significado*. Madrid: Revista de Occidente.

Durkheim, E. (1922/1973). *Education et sociologie*. Paris: PUF.

Elkonin, D. B. (1980). *Psicología del juego*. Madrid: Pablo del Rio.

Fein, G. G. (1979). Play and the acquisition of symbols. In L. Katz (Ed.), *Current topics in early childhood education* (pp. 96–110). Norwood, NJ: Ablex.

Fein, G. G. (1981). Pretend play: An integrative review. *Child Development, 52*, 1095–1118.

Fein, G. G. (1989). Mind, meaning and affect: Proposal for a theory of pretense. *Developmental Review, 9*, 345–363.

Freud, S. (1932/1972). Nuevas aportaciones al psicoanálisis. In *Obras completa* (pp. 3102–3205). Madrid: Biblioteca Nueva.

González Rey, F. (1995). *Comunicación Personalidad y Desarrollo*. La Habana, Cuba: Pueblo y Educación.

Griffin, H. (1984). The coordination of meaning in the creation of a shared make-belive reality. In I. Bretherton, *Symbolic Play* (pp. 82–103). Orlando, FL: Academic Press.

Griffing, P. (1980). The relationship between socioeconomic status and sociodramatic play among black kindergarten children. *Genetic Psychology Monographs, 101*, 3–34.

Groos, K. (1901/1976). *The play of man*. New York: Arno.

Kouzulin, A. (1990/1994). La psicologia de Vygotsky: Biografia de unas ideas. Madrid: Alianza Editorial.

Leontiev, A. N. (1965/1991). Introducción sobre la labor creadora de L. S. Vygotsky. In *L. S. Vygotsky. Obras Escogidas* (pp. 417–477). Madrid: Aprendizaje Visor.

Nelson, K. (1981). Social cognition in a script framework. In J. H. Flavell and L. Ross

(Eds.), *Social cognitive development: Frontiers and possible futures* (pp. 6–24). New York: Cambridge University Press.

Nelson, K., & Gruendel, J. (1979). At morning it's lunchtime: A scriptal view of children's dialogues. *Discourse Processes, 2*, 73–94.

Nelson, K., & Seidman, S. (1984). Playing with scripts. In I. Bretherton (Ed.), *Symbolic play* (pp. 45–72). Orlando, FL: Academic Press.

Ortega, R. (1988). El juego y la construcción social del conocimiento. [The game and the social construction of knowledge.] Unpublished doctoral disseration, Universidad de Sevilla.

Ortega, R. (1990). *Jugar y aprender*. Sevilla, España: Diada.

Ortega, R. (1991a). El juego sociodramático y el desarrollo de la comprensión y el aprendizaje social. *Infancia y Aprendizaje, 55*, 103–121.

Ortega, R. (1991b). Un marco conceptual para la interpretación del juego infantil. *Infancia y Aprendizaje, 55*, 87–103.

Ortega, R. (1992). *El juego infantil y la construcción social del conocimiento*. Sevilla, España: Alfar.

Ortega, R. (1994). El juego sociodramático como contexto para la comprensión sociall. In A. Alvarez and P. del Rio, *Explorations in sociocultural studies: Education as cultural construction* (pp. 79–86). Madrid: Fundación Infancia y Aprendizaje.

Ortega, R. (2000). Psicologia y educacion: La necesidad de un paradigma. Cultura y Educacion, *19*, 101–115.

Ortega, R., & Lozano, M. T. (1993). *Espacios de juego en la educación infantil*. Education Board, Junta de Andalucia [Andalusia Governing Body], Module 4 of the Curricular Material for Child Education.

Piaget, J. (1959/1961). *La formation du symbole chez l'enfant*. México: F.C.E.

Piaget, J. (1932/1971). *Le jugement moral chez l'enfant*. Barcelona, España: Fontanella.

Smith, P. K. (Ed.). (1986). *Children's play: Research development and practical application*. London: Gordon and Breach.

Spencer, H. (1855/1985). *Principios de Psicología*. Madrid: España Calpe.

Spencer, H. (1861/1985). *Educación*. Madrid: España Calpe.

Sutton-Smith, B. (1980). Children's play: Some sources of play theorizing. *New Directions for Child Development, 9*, 1–16.

Sutton-Smith, B. (1985). Play research: State of the art. In J. L. Frost & S. Sunderlin (Eds.), *When children play* (pp. 104–110). Wheaton, MD: Association for Childhood Education International.

Takhvar, M., & Smith, P. K. (1990). A review and critique of Smilanky's classification scheme and the "nested hierarchy" of play categories. *Journal of Research in Childhood Education 4*(2), 112–122.

Vygotsky, L. S. (1933). Fragment from notes for lectures on the psychology of preschool children. In D. B. Elkonin, *Psicología del juego* (pp. 269–282). Madrid: Pablo del Rio.

Vygotsky, L. S. (1934/1979). *El desarrollo de los procesos psicológicos superiores*. Barcelona, España: Crítica.

Wundt, W. (1887/1980). Psicología de los pueblos. Cited by A. Caparros in *Historia de la Psicología* (pp. 11–25). Barcelona, España: CEAC.

Chapter 7

The Effect of Verbal Scaffolding on the Complexity of Preschool Children's Block Constructions

Kara M. Gregory, An Sook Kim, and Alice Whiren

INTRODUCTION

Reports of play with blocks can be traced back to the fourth century B.C. (Gura, 1992). Today, most preschool and kindergarten classrooms have an area in the classroom that is designated for block play. Over the past 100 years or so, play with blocks has repeatedly been reported as an important medium to enhance the development of young children. Forman (1982b) makes a strong case for block play as a way to view children's representational thought in action. In addition, block play has been advocated as a way to enhance children's development of cognition (Cuffaro, 1995; Franklin, 1973), language (Donnelly, 1985; Isbell & Raines, 1991), and socialization (Meckley, 1994; Rogers, 1985). Some claims of the benefits that block play can provide for children are well documented, while others have been reported and accepted as "social wisdom." The area with the least amount of information, either research-based or otherwise, is on the methods that adults can utilize to support children's block play (Conrad, 1995). This is ironic given the current popularity in early childhood education of Vygotsky's theory, which calls for the active involvement of adults to support children's learning. Most practitioners set up a block corner in their classrooms, stepping in to assist only with conflict resolution or behavior issues. However, if the use of blocks in play does provide so many positive effects on children's development, is there a need for more active involvement on the adult's behalf to assist children?

Prior research suggests that merely including an adult in the block area increases the amount of time that children spend there (Halliday, McNaughton, &

Glynn, 1985). One would wonder if added time for children in the block corner reaps significant benefits or if more intervention is needed to derive the greatest results. Vygotsky's theory would advocate that adults take a more active role in the block corner. According to Vygotsky's theory of sociocultural learning, mental functions are first shared between others and then become part of the individual's thinking process. Higher mental functions are always first social, in the form of spoken language, before they become internalized thoughts (Berk & Winsler, 1995). In the social situation, an adult or "expert" other is the ideal partner. The challenge provided by the expert partner is the key to the child's internalization of the information and experiences (Stone, 1993). In reference to blocks, if children's representational thinking is displayed through their constructions, can the child's level of representational thought, as a higher mental function, be increased? Using Vygotsky's theory in practice, one highly effective method of presenting a challenge that is at a level just above a child's current ability in order to increase children's level of thinking is known as scaffolding (Wood, 1989; Wood, Bruner, & Ross, 1976).

The present study had three goals. The first was to investigate Vygotsky's theory in action in the area of block play, specifically, to determine the effect of adults' use of verbal scaffolding on the structural complexity of children's block constructions. The second goal was to establish a more comprehensive measure for the complexity of children's block structures. The third goal was to establish further support for the levels of complexity reported as stages, arches, and dimensionality. To establish the grounds for these goals, a brief look at the history of the measurement of block constructions is discussed below.

HISTORICAL OVERVIEW OF THE MEASUREMENT OF BLOCK CONSTRUCTIONS

Stage Complexity

In the 1900s, with the burgeoning use of blocks in preschool classrooms in the United States, a group of researchers attempted to document the common uses of blocks by children. The three main researchers, Hulson (1930), Johnson (1933), and Guanella (1934), shared some commonalities in their findings. Hulson (1930) proposed that children used blocks for four types of activities: knocking them down, carrying them, jumping from blocks, and dramatizing with them. Johnson's (1933) study seemed to elaborate on Hulson's types and reported seven stages:

1. Carrying blocks around;
2. Making rows or stacks;
3. Bridging: two blocks with a space between and a third on top;

4. Enclosures: blocks placed to enclose a space;

5. Decorative patterns with symmetry;

6. Naming of structures;

7. Reproducing or symbolizing what is familiar in what is built accompanied often by dramatic play.

Guanella's (1934) work was the most extensive of the three and continues to be cited by nearly every block researcher since its inception. Although based on only 12 children from upper-middle-class families, the stages that she identified have held true in subsequent studies. Guanella noted four stages of block building with unit blocks. Each stage consists of multiple categories. The first stage is the *preorganized* or non-structural stage. Second is the *linear* stage, which is piles and rows. Third, the *bidimensional* stage, includes solid areal forms (wall-like and floorlike arrangements), enclosed spaces, and arches. The fourth and final stage, the *tridimensional* stage, incorporates solid tridimensional structures and enclosed tridimensional structures. Guanella concluded that as children mature, their block constructions become more complex.

At about the same time, Bailey (1933) devised a scale, using blocks as the medium, to measure and evaluate the constructive and manipulative ability of children in preschool through kindergarten. The scale consists of 10 items for *plan and achievement of plan* and 10 items for *symmetry of design*. Pictures of actual block constructions were used to establish the scale.

Blocks as Evidence of Representational Thinking

In the late 1970s and the early 1980s, the next wave of interest in children's block play and its structural complexity began. The research emphasis was on the contribution of block play to cognition. According to Forman (1982b), one can see children's structures of thought by observing block play. While his work did not cite Guanella's, the stages that he described were very similar. His stages begin with infants. First, the child *grasps* the block with two hands. Next, the child *bangs the blocks together* at the midline. Later, the child *stacks* them (forming a vertical line). Still later they are in a *horizontal line touching* each other and finally in a *horizontal line with spaces* between.

Arch Complexity

Goodson observed children's mental representations for block models, developing a hierarchy of structures of arches in children's block building (1982). She proposed four levels of developmental progression in arch structure. (See Figure 7.2 for a description.) Goodson's research concluded that children in the higher levels of arch building also had better levels of planning and perception.

Dimensionality and Integration Complexities

Reifel and Greenfield (1982) concluded from their review of the literature and their own research that the hierarchical complexities of construction increase with age and suggest that cognitive structures also become more complex with age. In their study, they defined levels of integration in block building as well as levels of dimensionality. Comparing 4-year-olds to 7-year-olds, they found that the older children utilized greater levels of both integration and dimensionality. (See Figure 7.2 for a description of dimensionality levels.)

Spatial Complexity

Stiles-Davis (1988) is the most recent person to study spontaneous block play in relation to its developmental progression in spatial grouping. She used the previously discussed studies to devise a method of examining the complexity of block play based upon six measures: spatial products, spatial loci, directions, number of relations, types of relations, and processes. Her results are consistent with other research on the developmental progression of block structures; older children construct more spatially complex structures than do younger children.

Overall research findings thus far have supported a sequential developmental progression in various types of complexity of block structures, with predominantly more complexity the greater the age of the builder. Each of the studies looked at only one or two aspects of complexity at a time. Other than Guanella, these complexity components were each individually assessed. While useful, this provides only part of the picture of a child's ability. In the current study, complexity was considered with each of the following individual components: stage, arches, and dimensionality. A complexity composite component was then developed and utilized using all three aspects simultaneously.

Hypothesis of Current Study

In each of the prior studies, the child was working without adult assistance. Using Vygotsky's theory as a framework, it is hypothesized that adding an adult to the block area to actively use verbal scaffolding will positively impact the complexity of children's block structures.

According to Vygotsky's theory, it is possible for adults to work jointly with children on mental activities to support their movement from their present level of independent activity to their level of *potential* development through the process of verbal interaction (Vygotsky, 1962). The key is to work with children within their *zone of proximal development*, which is the area between where they are performing independently and where they work with assistance (Bodrova & Leong, 1998). To do this, the child's present level of development on the given task must be assessed. The adult or knowing other then actively works to assist the child in achieving the next level using some type of external mediator. This process is known as scaffolding. External mediators may take many forms. In this current study, the adult's use of language serves as the external mediator during the scaffolding process. While naturally occurring gestures, such as smiles when a child added a block to the construction, did happen, gestures were not the focus of this investigation. The verbal interaction that the adult structured in the situation with the intent of moving the child to higher levels of block complexity was the focus.

This study attempted to answer the main question, Does verbal scaffolding by adults while children are playing with blocks increase the complexity of their block structures in four areas: stage, arches, dimensionality, and composite complexity? In addition, the role that age plays in the varying complexities of structure was investigated. Gender was explored individually and as an interaction factor with scaffolding for each of the four areas.

METHOD

Sample

The research sample consisted of 85 preschool children from four classes in a University Laboratory Preschool in the midwest United States whose parents gave written permission for their participation in the study. No parents denied permission for any of the classes. Both the morning and afternoon sessions from two classrooms participated. The four classes serve families from ethnically and economically diverse backgrounds. Of the 85 children, a subsample of 50 (22 female and 28 male) between the ages of 38 and 71 months was used for analysis. The reduction was due to the necessity of including in the analysis sample only those children who participated in block play at least once during each time segment in the study (baseline, intervention, and follow-up). This subsample included 22 children in the control group and 28 children in the treatment group. As the children were assigned to the classes prior to the onset of the study, their classes were randomly designated as control or experimental groups.

Materials

Unit blocks were the only blocks available to the children during the course of the study. Each classroom had equivalent numbers of various types of unit blocks that are commonly found in early childhood classrooms. In addition, each block area had 10 vehicles, 10 animals, and 10 human figures available for the children from which to select during their time in the block area. Floor measurements were made of the block areas in both classrooms before the study began to ensure the availability of the same square footage for the block play. Two open shelves were provided in each classroom for the storage of blocks and accessories. The blocks were available for children's use during free play/ choice time, which spanned between 50 and 65 minutes daily.

Data Collection

Design

To control for the variable of time of day, the two classrooms, each with a morning and afternoon session, were randomly assigned control and experimental groups with each receiving the opposite treatment during the morning and afternoon sessions. One classroom functioned as the control group in the morning and the experimental group in the afternoon. The other classroom was the experimental group in the morning and the control group in the afternoon. Each session in each classroom had its own set of student teachers who were primarily responsible for interaction in the block play as well as overall classroom function. This greatly reduced the opportunity for contamination between the control and experimental groups in both classrooms. The control and experimental groups were observed before the intervention (baseline), during the intervention, and after the intervention (follow-up).

Intervention

The intervention was carried out four days a week, Monday through Thursday. Three of the classes did not attend on Fridays, and the fourth class did not open the block area on Fridays. The study occurred during the winter semester for a 10-week period (3 weeks of baseline, 3 weeks of intervention, 1 week off, and 3 weeks of follow-up).

In both the experimental and the control groups, an adult who was a student teacher majoring in child development was located in the block area, verbally interacting with the children. There were specific directions regarding the type of verbal interactions that the student teachers were expected to have with the children in their area, depending on their class' assignment of experimental or control. (See Figure 7.1 for specific details.) The adults for both the experimental and the control groups were each trained at the conclusion of the baseline and prior to the intervention. At this training, group-specific directions were explained and demonstrated when appropriate.

All student teachers in both the experimental and control groups were instructed during their training on the following common points:

• Always intervene for safety, rights of others, and property issues.
• Entice children to enter the block area by placing blocks on the floor.

Figure 7.1
Directions for Adult Interactions with Children in the Block Area

---

• Intervene for safety, rights of others, and property issues.

• When no children are in the block area, pull out blocks and place them on the floor to entice children into the block area, but DO NOT construct a structure.

• Talk with children, but DO NOT build with or assist with building blocks.

• Allow children to choose the blocks with which they will build.

• Stay in the block area at all times, unless an emergency occurs.

• Support children's play, DO NOT direct it.

• Use behavior reflections.

• Ask open-ended questions.

• Pose problems (e.g., What would happen if . . . , How could . . .).

• Make leading statements (e.g., Sometimes people use a block to join as structure . . .).

• Think of possibilities out loud (e.g., I wonder if . . .).

• Continually work to encourage children to build at the next level of complexity (keeping the three types of complexity from Figure 7.2 in mind). Evaluate where the child is and the next level to which to move him/her).

• Accept the child's choice in the matter. Your suggestion(s) may or may not be accepted. This is OK.

• Directions for both the control group adult interactions as well as the experimental group adult interactions.

• Directions for only the experimental group adult interactions.

• Refrain from building structures, demonstrating how to build, or taking over the child's play.

• Allow children to choose their own blocks.

All of the student teachers had been trained in their prior course work on using behavior reflections and asking open-ended questions and were strongly encouraged to do so when the children were in the block area.

The control group's adults were instructed that their goal for the next three weeks in the block area was to encourage and support block building. They were not trained in any of the complexities of block structures and reported at the end of the study no prior knowledge of these, nor were they trained in the process of verbal scaffolding. While all had heard of the term "scaffolding" during prior course work, none reported knowing how to accomplish this. In addition, as all were observed throughout the course of the study, none showed evidence of attempts at scaffolding.

The experimental group's adults were instructed that their goal was to increase the complexity of children's block play through verbal scaffolding. Training

Figure 7.2
Three Methods of Evaluating the Complexity of Block Structures

Stages Complexity*	
Tower	Blocks one on top of another in vertical fashion.
Row	Row of blocks, one next to the other.
Row-Tower	Combination of tower and row; also includes adding flooring and/or walls.
Enclosure	Blocks form an enclosure with "walls" on all sides.
Covered Enclosure	A "roof" is added to the enclosure.
Covered Enclosure with Tower	Tower is constructed on top of a covered enclosure.

*Adapted from Guanella (1933).

Arches Complexity**	
Arch—Level One	Two blocks parallel with third block on top of both.
Arch—Level Two	Two or more arches side by side or on top of each other or a tunnel.
Arch—Level Three	Three arches with at least one on top of the other.
Arch—Level Four	More than three arches on top of each other or in a variety of combinations.

**Adapted from Goodson (1982).

Dimensionality Complexity***	
Zero Dimension	Single block or scattered blocks forming single points.
One Dimension	At least two blocks forming one line.
Two Dimension	At least three blocks forming two lines or one plane.
Three Dimension	More than three blocks forming one line AND one plane.

***Source: Reifel & Greenfield, (1982).

began with teaching the adults to recognize the various levels of complexity of stages, arches, and dimensionality. They were given copies of Figure 7.2, which were then fastened to the back of their name tags for easy reference. The adult participants who would work with the experimental group practiced building each level in the three areas of complexity and recognizing various examples of these levels of complexity in block structures built by the researchers. The concept of verbal scaffolding was explained to them. They received a modified version of Figure 7.1, which gave them suggestions to assist in their verbal scaffolding. They viewed a role-play of one researcher's scaffolding another researcher while she built with blocks. They then watched a video of an adult's doing this with a child and finally practiced on each other.

The student teachers in both the control and experimental groups were monitored on a daily basis by the research team and their classroom head teachers to ensure that they were implementing their given intervention correctly. Immediate intervention by the research team members or classroom head teacher took place if something was occurring in the block area that was outside the intervention. Above all, the student teachers were strongly encouraged not to direct the children's play. All ideas had to come from the child's play frame. If the adult's verbal comments were ignored or rebuffed by the child, the adult was to accept this. If an adult was observed to be interfering or directing a child's play, she was immediately redirected by the research observers or head teacher. In addition, members of the research team were available to all student teachers in both the control and experimental groups to answer questions that arose throughout the entire study period.

During each of the three time segments (baseline, intervention, and follow-up), the children were strongly encouraged to go to the block area at least once during their free choice time and build. Individual structures were also encouraged. Group structures did occur but were coded only if it was blatantly clear what the continuous contribution of individual children was; it could be separated from the rest of the structure; and it could be coded according to the given complexity categories.

Measurement

The block areas in both classrooms were continuously observed by the research team and recorded by video for the entire duration of the study. Ten constructions from the videotapes were randomly selected and independently coded by members of the research team in each of the four areas: stage, arches, dimensionality, and overall complexity composite. These initial block construction ratings were compared. An interrater reliability of .95 was computed. The subsequent coding was identical to the initial coding and completed by the same members of the research team. Each child's most mature structure during every block play session was assessed using the three categories stage, arches, and dimensionality, using a scale of 1–4. If there was no observation of a particular component, it was left blank. (See Figure 7.2 for a complete description of each area and level.) In addition to these three categories, a fourth category, the block composite, was created. It was used to assess the overall complexity of the structure.

Stage

The measurement scale for stage was based primarily on a combination of Johnson's (1933), Guanella's (1934), and Forman's (1982b) stages of block construction. As each stage represented a higher level than the one before, the data were treated as parametric data. The stages received the following numerical ratings:

Tower	1
Row	2
Row-Tower	3
Enclosure	3
Covered Enclosure	4
Covered Enclosure with Tower	4

Arches

The arches scale was taken directly from Goodson's work (1982). See Figure 7.2.

Dimensionality

The dimensionality scale, also found in Figure 7.2, was taken directly from Reifel and Greenfield's (1982) description of dimensionality in block play. The numerical values are the dimension level plus one point due to the fact that a zero dimension does not mean lack of presence of dimension (e.g., zero dimension is a 1 on the scale). Again, the levels of dimensionality represent a true hierarchy, with each level more advanced than the previous one; therefore, the data were treated as interval data.

Composite

A composite score was created to look at the overall complexity of a given block structure. This appeared to be a logical combination as each of the three areas to be combined occurred simultaneously in the structure, not in a linear fashion. To create this composite, each of the three complexity areas of stages, arches, and dimensionality had to possess an equal number of stages, which they did. Each had four levels. In addition, the data had to be parametric. Given that the areas met these criteria for combination, the numerical values for stages, arches, and dimensionality from the most complex block structure of each observation period were averaged. The resulting number was the complexity composite structure score. If one of the areas was not able to be coded (such as the non-existence of an arch), that score was not included in the average.

RESULTS

An analysis of covariance (ANCOVA) was conducted on the dependent variables (stage, dimensionality, and complexity composite) using the Statistical Package for the Social Sciences (SPSS). The baseline measurements for each dependent variable were used as the covariates to control for the differences in the children's original block-building abilities. Table 7.1 depicts the description of the data for both groups. It includes the baseline and follow-up data on all component areas: stage, arches, dimensionality, and complexity composite. In

Table 7.1
Descriptive Data of Block Study

No Scaffolding	N	Mean	Standard Deviation
Control Male Age	11	57.9091	8.348
Stage Baseline	10	3.2	1.6193
Stage Follow-Up	11	3.0	1.4832
Arch Baseline	5	1.6	.5477
Arch Follow-Up	2	2.0	1.4142
Dimensionality Baseline	11	3.5455	.8202
Dimensionality Follow-Up	11	2.4545	.5222
Complexity Comp. Baseline	11	2.3	.4584
Complexity Comp. Follow-Up	11	1.9	.543

No Scaffolding	N	Mean	Standard Deviation
Control Female Age	12	59.3636	10.5667
Stage Baseline	12	2.9167	1.1645
Stage Follow-Up	10	2.7	1.4944
Arch Baseline	4	2.25	.9574
Arch Follow-Up	4	1.75	.9574
Dimensionality Baseline	12	3.5	.7977
Dimensionality Follow-Up	12	2.3333	.6513
Complexity Comp. Baseline	12	2.3681	.5897
Complexity Comp. Follow-Up	12	1.833	.6317

Scaffolding	N	Mean	Standard Deviation
Experimental Male Age	17	55.1176	5.3722
Stage Baseline	17	3.3529	1.147
Stage Follow-Up	13	3.5385	.9674
Arch Baseline	8	1.3750	.5175
Arch Follow-Up	9	1.7778	.9718
Dimensionality Baseline	17	3.2941	.7717
Dimensionality Follow-Up	17	3.5882	.7123
Complexity Comp. Baseline	17	2.1765	.4876
Complexity Comp. Follow-up	17	2.4902	.6193

Scaffolding	N	Mean	Standard Deviation
Experimental Female Age	11	58.0	3.8471
Stage Baseline	11	3.1818	.7508
Stage Follow-Up	10	3.2	.9189
Arch Baseline	4	1.75	.5000
Arch Follow-Up	6	1.1667	.4082
Dimensionality Baseline	11	3.5455	.6876
Dimensionality Follow-Up	11	3.1818	.7508
Complexity Comp. Baseline	11	2.5606	.5541
Complexity Comp. Follow-Up	11	2.0606	.3963

all of the analyses, there were no significant effects of practice, which was the number of times during the study that a child played with the blocks. Therefore, the practice factor was eliminated from the analyses. A significance level of $p < .05$ was set.

Table 7.2
Effects of Age on Stage Complexity

Source	Degrees of Freedom	F Ratio	Significance
Baseline Stage	1	.4000	.531
Age	1	5.6959	.023
Gender	1	2.093	.156
Scaffolding	1	2.279	.140
Gender&Scaffolding	1	.00440	.953

Notes: Adjusted R Squared = .092; Mean Square Error = 1.308; Alpha = .05.

Baseline Analyses

To obtain information regarding the children's prior block-building structural complexity and to assess comparability across groups, the control and treatment groups' scores for the baseline for all four components (stage, arches, dimensionality, and complexity composite) were examined using a T test. No significant differences were found between the groups on any component.

Stage Complexity Results

Age was a factor that predicted F (1, 37) = 5.659, p < .05 and was significant. See Table 7.2. Older children built more complex structures according to the stage complexity criteria. This finding is consistent with previous work.

The baseline for stage complexity F (1, 37) = .400, gender F (1, 37) = 2.093, and scaffolding F (1, 37) = 2.279 did not significantly influence the stage complexity, nor did the interaction of gender and scaffolding F (1, 37) = .004. Considering that the adjusted R squared is so low (.092), the combination of these variables does not account for much of the variance in the model as related to stage complexity. The hypothesis that verbal scaffolding would increase the stage complexity of children's block structures was not supported.

Arches Complexity Results

No statistical analyses were run on the complexity of arches due to the low number of children who built arches both at the baseline and at the follow-up time segments (n = 13).

Dimensionality Complexity Results

The ANCOVA for dimensionality revealed significant effects for scaffolding F (1, 44) = 30.455, p < .05 (Table 7.3). Age F (1, 44) = 1.131, baseline for dimensionality F (1, 44) = 2.748, gender F (1, 44) = 2.619 and the interaction between gender and scaffolding F (1, 44) = 1.267 were not significant. The

Table 7.3
Dimensionality Complexity

Source	Degrees of Freedom	F Ratio	Significance
Baseline			
Dimensionality	1	2.748	.104
Age	1	1.131	.293
Gender	1	2.619	.113
Scaffolding	1	30.455	.000
Gender & Scaffolding	1	1.267	.266

Notes: Adjusted R Squared = .427; Mean Square Error = .409; Alpha = .05.

Table 7.4
Complexity Composite

Source	Degrees of Freedom	F Ratio	Significance
Baseline Composite	1	3.161	.082
Age	1	.108	.744
Gender	1	4.165	.047
Scaffolding	1	4.788	.034
Gender & Scaffolding	1	2.053	.159

Notes: Adjusted R Squared = .183; Mean Square Error = .266; Alpha = .05.

Adjusted R squared = .427 indicated that these variables account for nearly 43% of the variance in this model of dimensionality complexity. The hypothesis that verbal scaffolding would increase the dimensionality complexity of children's block structures was supported.

Complexity Composite Results

The ANCOVA for the composite revealed a significant effect for gender $F (1, 44) = 4.165$, $p < .05$, and for scaffolding $F (1, 44) = 4.788$, $p < .05$ (Table 7.4). The baseline for composite $F (1, 44) = 3.161$ and the interaction between gender and scaffolding $F (1, 44) = 2.053$ were not significant. The Adjusted R squared (.183) indicated that the variables in this model, gender and scaffolding, accounted for nearly 18% of the variance in the complexity composite. The hypothesis that verbal scaffolding would increase the composite complexity of children's block structures was supported.

DISCUSSION

The first goal of this study was to investigate the effect of verbal scaffolding on the complexity of children's block structures in the areas of stage, arches, dimensionality, and complexity composite. For the overall complexity composite and for the dimensionality component, specific adult verbalization in the form of verbal scaffolding did positively impact the complexity of children's block structures. It did not impact the stage complexity when considered alone. Not enough data were present to infer its impact on arch complexity. Further research in this area is recommended.

The second goal of this study was to provide a more detailed description of the complexity of children's block structures than is currently used. First, the components of stages, arches, and dimensionality progressions supported by empirical research in prior studies were used to assess block structure complexity; then the three separate components were combined. This resulted in the creation of the complexity composite. Future research is warranted to further examine the ongoing feasibility of the complexity composite.

The third goal of the study was to gain further support for scales of block complexity discussed in previous research studies. Results of this study confirm findings of previous studies that there is a progression in stage complexity (Forman, 1982b; Guanella, 1934) and dimensional complexity (Reifel & Greenfield, 1982). There were not enough data to confirm or refute previous findings on the arches scale by Goodson (1982).

Guanella's (1934) and Forman's (1982b) findings that stage complexity of children's block play was primarily due to the age of the child did hold true in this study. Age was the significant factor in the children's stage complexity of block structures, with older children building more stage-complex structures. However, age was not a significant factor with the other components of structural complexity examined (dimensionality and overall complexity composite). This is contrary to Reifel and Greenfield's (1982) conclusion that maturation leads to more complex dimensionality in block structures.

Contrary to popular belief, gender did not play a role in the complexity of the children's block structures when the complexity components of stage and dimensionality were examined individually. However, when these components were combined into the complexity composite, gender did make a difference. Boys did build significantly more complex structures than girls did overall. Other studies have found that boys chose to play in the block area more often than girls (Beeson & Williams, 1979; Varma, 1980). This suggests a need for further research into whether more exposure is the advantage for boys or if other factors are at work.

This study provides support for Vygotsky's proposition that learning leads performance and perhaps may lead development (Berk & Winsler, 1995). When paired with a more knowing adult, children were able to use higher levels of complexity in their block structures overall (complexity composite) and in the area of dimensionality. During the intervention, the adults were able to successfully work with children in their zone of proximal development to consciously assist them to attain their potential level of development through the use of verbal scaffolding. This later became their new independent level, as evidenced in the follow-up data. There was no difference between the control groups and the experimental groups in the areas of complexity during the baseline data collection. Following the intervention, there was a significant difference in overall complexity and in dimensionality.

There are some areas to consider in this study. While the student teachers in both groups were observed during the baseline, intervention, and follow-up periods to ensure that they were following the prescribed intervention, the level of skill between the student teachers in each of the classrooms varied. This could have had an impact on the study. The counterbalanced design, utilizing the two classrooms at two separate times of the day, should have helped account for this. It would also be interesting to conduct another study using hollow blocks instead of unit blocks to compare complexity when the size, shapes, and variety of blocks are limited. In the study, the scaffolding occurred in a condensed manner over a course of weeks. In natural practice, this strategy could be applied sporadically within the context of daily interaction. Verbal scaffolding during block play should be investigated over the course of an entire school year. Finally, as most play that occurs in block areas is cooperative building, a study designed to look at the complexity of group play and adult verbal scaffolding would be useful.

Observationally, it is interesting to note that it appeared that the scaffolding facilitated more dramatic play with the blocks for some children. For others, the scaffolding facilitated more constructive play. Even when very similar verbalizations were extended, the results toward dramatic or constructive play were quite varied. Further research to investigate this phenomenon is warranted.

Implications

These results have implications for early childhood classrooms. The mere act of placing an adult in the block area to facilitate play is not sufficient. Both the control group and the experimental groups had adults stationed in the block area. The demonstrated difference in overall complexity of structure and in the dimensionality complexity depended on whether or not the child experienced active verbal support (in the form of verbal scaffolding) that assisted in generating structures of increased complexity. This is a dynamic factor. It involves not only the adult's ability to recognize and identify the current level of complexity of block play by children but also his or her knowledge of the entire sequence of the components of block structure complexity as well as the ability to use this information in a verbal scaffolding process. While this is an intellectually complex task, this study demonstrates that it can be successfully accomplished.

To do this, adults working with young children must first be taught the three complexities of block play (stage, arches, and dimensionality) and their developmental progression. They must also be given opportunities to practice verbal scaffolding and receive feedback to gain skill with this practice.

In conclusion, if, in fact, block structures are our window into children's logical thinking processes and a direct view of children's developing representational thinking capacity, as Forman (1982a) suggests, then learning about the complexities of block structures and how to scaffold these could accomplish at least three important things. First, it could strengthen adults' abilities to effectively work with children. Second, it could help adults better understand individual children's levels of cognitive development. Third, as adults scaffold children up to the next level of complexity in their constructions, the potential exists that they can simultaneously increase the children's representational thinking abilities.

Blocks are a common material in early childhood programs. If teachers can facilitate children's development of skills without truly interfering with their play, as this study suggests, then the potential for children's development of spatial knowledge, cognition, and so much more can be realized. This needs to be investigated further in future research.

REFERENCES

Bailey, M. (1933). A scale of block constructions for young children. *Child Development, 4*, 121–139.

Beeson, B. S., & Williams, R. A. (1979). A study of sex stereotyping in child-selected play activities of preschool children. Muncie, IN: Ball State University. ED 186–102.

Berk, L., & Winsler, A. (1995). *Scaffolding children's learning: Vygotsky and early childhood education.* Washington, DC: National Association for the Education of Young Children.

Bodrova, E., & Leong, D. (1998). Scaffolding emergent writing in the zone of proximal development. *Literacy Teaching and Learning, 3*(2), 1–17.

Conrad, A. (1995). Content analysis of block play literature. Memphis, TN: University of Memphis. ED 382-357.

Cuffaro, H. K. (1995). Block building: Opportunities for learning. *Child Care Information Exchange* (May), 35–41.

Donnelly, G. F. (1985). *An analysis of language, thought and action during the block play of preschoolers: A gender difference perspective.* Unpublished doctoral dissertation, Bryn Mawr College.

Forman, G. (Ed.). (1982a). *Action and thought: From sensorimotor schemes to symbolic operations.* New York: Academic Press.

Forman, G. (1982b). A search for the origins of equivalence concepts through a microanalysis of block play. In G. Forman (Ed.), *Action and thought: From sensorimotor schemes to symbolic operations* (pp. 97–135). New York: Academic Press.

Franklin, M. B. (1973). Non-verbal representation in young children: A cognitive perspective. *Young Children, 29*, 33–53.

Goodson, M. (1982). The development of hierarchic organization: The reproduction, planning, and perception of multiarch block structures. In G. Forman (Ed.), *Action and thought: From sensorimotor schemes to symbolic operations* (pp. 165–201). New York: Academic Press.

Guanella, F. M. (1934). Block building activities of young children. *Archives of Psychology, 174*, 5–91.

Gura, P. (Ed.). (1992). *Exploring learning: Young children and blockplay*. London: The Froebel Blockplay Research Group.

Halliday, J., McNaughton, S., & Glynn, T. (1985). Influencing children's choice of play activities in kindergarten. *New Zealand Journal of Educational Studies, 20*(1), 48–58.

Hirsch, E. S. (Ed.). (1984). *The block book*. Washington, DC: National Association for the Education of Young Children.

Hulson, E. L. (1930). Block construction of four year old children. *Journal of Juvenile Research, 8*(2), 209–222.

Isbell, R. T., & Raines, S. C. (1991). Young children's oral language production in three types of play centers. *Journal of Research in Childhood Education, 5*(2), 140–146.

Johnson, H. M. (1933). The art of block building. In E. S. Hirsch (Ed.), *The Block Book* (pp. 8–23). Washington, DC: National Association for the Education of Young Children.

Jones, D. (1992). Toy with idea. In P. Gura (Ed.), *Exploring learning: Young children and blockplay*. London: Froebel Blockplay Research Group.

Meckley, A. M. (1994). *The social construction of young children's play*. Unpublished doctoral dissertation, University of Pennsylvania.

Reifel, S., & Greenfield, P. (1982). Structural development in a symbolic medium: The representational use of block constructions. In G. Forman (Ed.), *Action and thought: From sensorimotor schemes to symbolic operations* (pp. 203–232). New York: Academic Press.

Rogers, D. L. (1985). Relationships between block play and the social development of young children. *Early Child Development and Care, 20*, 245–261.

Stiles-Davis, J. (1988). Developmental change in young children's spatial grouping activity. *Developmental Psychology, 24*(4), 522–531.

Stone, C. A. (1993). What is missing in the metaphor of scaffolding? In E. A. Forman, N. Minick, & C. A. Stone (Eds.), *Contexts for learning: Sociocultural dynamics in children's development* (169–183). New York: Oxford University Press.

Varma, M. (1980). *Sex-stereotyping in block play of preschool children*. New Brunswick, NJ: Rutgers University. ED 197–832.

Vygotsky, L. (1962). *Thought and language*. Cambridge: Harvard University Press.

Wood, D. J. (1989). Social interaction as tutoring. In M. H. Bornsteing & J. S. Bruner (Eds.), *Interaction in human development* (pp. 59–80). Hillsdale, NJ: Erlbaum.

Wood, D. J., Bruner, J., & Ross, G. (1976). The role of tutoring in problem solving. *Journal of Child Psychology and Psychiatry, 17*, 89–100.

Part III

Children's Playfulness and Learning

Chapter 8

Levels of Analysis in Pretend Play Discourse: Metacommunication in Conversational Routines

R. Keith Sawyer

In many studies of children's play, both psychological variables and cultural variables have been shown to play important roles. There is a tension in this interdisciplinary field between methodological individualists, who assume that all social interaction can be reduced to individual-level variables, and more culturally and contextually oriented researchers, who explain social interaction with reference to cultural or interactional variables. Most developmental psychologists are individualists, whereas most anthropologists and conversation researchers are contextualists. Rarely does a single study simultaneously examine variables at both levels of analysis to determine the relative explanatory contributions of both individual and contextual factors.

The purpose of this study was to examine these two levels of analysis in children's play metacommunication. Speakers use metacommunication—"communication about communication"—to comment on a conversation, both reflexively, on the current conversation (Sawyer, 1997; Schiffrin, 1980; Silverstein, 1993), and reportively, on a past conversation (Lucy, 1993). In social pretend play, children use metacommunication to clarify, maintain, negotiate, and direct the emerging play frame (Bateson, 1971, 1972; Goffman, 1974). Before children can play together, a play frame must first be created and understood by the participants, containing specific transformations of specific objects, persons, time, space, action, and rules. As with adults, metacommunicative abilities help children to engage in coherent discourse (Andersen, 1986; Black & Hazen, 1990; Boggs, 1990; Hickmann, 1985; McTear, 1985; Sawyer, 1993, 1997; Silverstein, 1993); for example, metacommunicative skills in play have been linked to a child's ability to participate in intersubjective social interactions (Fogel & Branco, 1997; Goncu, 1993a; Sawyer, 1997).

My focus is on metacommunicative strategy in an ongoing stream of discourse. Two distinct bodies of prior research have resulted in apparently contradictory findings. Developmental psychologists, using controlled experimental methods to study individual children, have found that play metacommunication can be partially predicted by individual traits and developmental stages. At the same time, conversation researchers have found that many conversational behaviors can be explained with reference to the preceding discourse context. To examine this apparent contradiction, I examined variables at both the child level of analysis (the overall tendency of a child to use a strategy) and at the discourse level of analysis (the discourse context preceding the child's turn). This design allowed an evaluation of the relative roles of individual and context in explaining play metacommunication.

METACOMMUNICATION

Many studies of pretend play conversation have found that metacommunicative skills develop rapidly during the preschool years (Auwarter, 1986; Doyle & Connolly, 1989; Fein, Moorin, & Enslein, 1982; Garvey & Kramer, 1989; Sawyer, 1997; Trawick-Smith, 1998). These studies restricted the definition of metacommunication to explicit metacommunicative strategies—when a child steps out of the play frame and speaks in a narrator's or director's voice (e.g., Doyle & Connolly, 1989; Garvey & Berndt, 1977; Garvey & Kramer, 1989; Trawick-Smith, 1998). Nonetheless, researchers have often noted that children can also metacommunicate while remaining in-frame and enacting a play role (Doyle & Connolly, 1989; Doyle, Doehring, Tessier, & de Lorimier, 1992; Goncu, 1993a, 1993b; Sawyer, 1997). These researchers have proposed that metacommunicative negotiation and role enactment may be blended and interdependent during play. Despite these frequent observations of in-frame metacommunication, there have been very few empirical studies of implicit metacommunication (e.g., Giffin, 1984; Goldman, 1998; Sawyer, 1997).

For example, Sawyer (1997) extended these studies to include implicit and in-frame metacommunicative strategies and found that these strategies are also widely used in social pretend play. Likewise, when adults talk, metacommunication is often implicit and in-frame. For example, if a speaker is uncomfortable with the way that a conversation is heading, that speaker may simply change the topic abruptly—an implicit metacommunication—rather than choosing an explicit metacommunication such as, "I'd rather not talk about that; let's change the topic." Pretend play discourse may provide an important context for learning these conversational skills.

In Example 1, Jennifer and Muhammed are playing with a duck and a dinosaur in the sand table. Jennifer makes a proposal to change the play frame, using an explicit and out-of-frame metacommunicative strategy (all transcripts are from the author's data). This proposal is typical of those examined in prior studies of play metacommunication.

(1)	Jennifer	Pretend her name was Cera, OK?	(referring to the duck)
(2)		OK?	
(3)		Cera!	(enacting as the duck)
(4)	Muhammed	Pretend he was Redhead, OK?	(referring to his dinosaur)
(5)	Jennifer	Redhead!	(enacting as the duck)

Utterances (1) and (4) are both examples of explicit and out-of-character metacommunication. The children explicitly acknowledge the fact that they are pretending; and they speak as themselves, rather than as their play roles. In contrast, utterances (3) and (5) are in-frame, although neither proposes a new aspect of play. Utterance (5) is an example of an in-character response's being used to accept a proposal.

However, children often propose changes to the play frame without explicitly mentioning "play" or "pretend," and children often propose changes while speaking as a play character (Example 2).

Example 2: Implicit and in-frame metacommunication. Jennifer is enacting a big horse; Jennie is enacting as a zebra. They are playing on a block structure on the floor. They have already established that Jennifer's horse is the mother of Jennie's zebra.

(1)	Jennie	Momma! Help!	(Her toy zebra is on top of the blocks)
(2)		I can't get down!	(High-pitched voice)
(3)		Help!	
(4)		It's too scary!	
(5)	Jennifer	I'm not gonna get you down. (Angry voice)	

Jennie's sequence (1–4) maintains coherence with the existing play frame by addressing Jennifer's horse as "Momma" and by using a high-pitched prosody associated with young children, consistent with her established role assignment as the baby. By enacting a scared baby zebra, stuck on top of a wall, she is proposing that this new emergency situation be incorporated into the play frame, and she is indirectly proposing the act of "rescue" for Jennifer. Neither of these proposals is explicitly metacommunicated, nor does Jennie speak out-of-character to propose these frame changes. Jennifer's rejecting response is also in character, although it seems somewhat more explicit than Jennie's proposal.

A child can be more explicit than Example 2 even without mentioning "play," as in Example 1. Consequently, the explicitness of a metacommunication cannot be coded simply as a binary variable but requires additional levels to represent these differing degrees of explicitness. Example 3 shows a proposal that is more explicit than Example 2, although it is in-frame and in-character.

Example 3: Eddy, John, and Sam are playing with animals in the sand table. These utterances are spoken in a prosody indicating a play character's voice.

(1)   Eddy   And sometimes they would put us in jail.

(2)   John   No they wouldn't.

Eddy, speaking in character, explicitly proposes an event that sometimes happens to their animal characters. Although spoken using his play character's voice, this proposal's relative explicitness leads it to have the feel of a reflexive, narratological comment on the play.

Examples 1 through 3 demonstrate that there are several levels of explicitness of metacommunicative strategy. Likewise, a metacommunication cannot be coded as simply in-character or out-of-character because there are many metacommunications where a child steps out of character, but still voices within the play frame, using a dialogic narrator's voice (Bakhtin, 1981; Goldman, 1998). In example 4, Jennifer proposes in-frame but out-of-character.

Example 4: Jennifer and Kathy are playing with animals in the sand table. Kathy's animal is "Cera," and Jennifer's animal is "Little foot."

(1)   Jennifer   Little foot in the big valley

(2)   And there's

(3)   Know what else?

(4)   um Little foot goes to the great beast

(5)   Kathy   OK.

Jennifer speaks using a director's voice, rather than the character's voice. As in Example 3, she does not explicitly mention pretend or play. At the same time, by providing descriptions of the play frame using a present tense, continuative aspect, Jennifer is relatively indirect in proposing these play changes, more so than Eddy in Example 3.

In the face of this metacommunicative variety, it's not surprising that prior studies have each used quite different operationalizations of metacommunication. For example, several studies (e.g., the canonical Garvey & Berndt, 1977) code an utterance as metacommunication if the words "play" or "pretend" appear. In contrast, other studies (Giffin, 1984; Trawick-Smith, 1998) operationalize metacommunication as a child stepping out of the play frame—typically, speaking in an out-of-character voice—to take a directorial role. The present study builds on the two-variable model presented in Sawyer (1997), which incorporates both types of definition. On the first variable, a child's metacommunication can range from explicit to implicit; on the second variable, a child's metacommunication can range from in-frame to out-of-frame.

Metacommunication and Conversational Context

Metacommunication has typically been studied by developmental psychologists who focus on individual children's linguistic behavior. For example, studies often identify all of the conversational turns in which a child proposes a change to the play frame and then aggregate these data to calculate the child's *interactional profile*, including variables such as the proportion of the child's proposals that use explicit metacommunication or the number of meta-communications per given time unit. The interactional profile is then correlated with child variables like age, gender, and popularity (Black & Hazen, 1990; Putallaz & Wasserman, 1990; Sachs, 1982). However, several studies by developmental psychologists have shown that many properties of children's conversation vary with social context. For example, children modify their conversation to match their addressee—they speak differently to younger children than to same-age playmates (Brownell, 1990), differently in same-gender and mixed-gender dyads (Leaper, 1991), and differently to partners of different verbal skill levels (Masur, 1978).

In addition to these addressee-related differences, studies of adult and child conversation suggest that the conversational context itself may have an effect on the child's choice of metacommunicative strategy. The conversational context is the discourse situation established by the prior flow of the interaction—Silverstein's *entextualization* (1993) or Sawyer's *emergent* (1997). Elements of conversational context that have been documented to influence speakers include the discourse topic (Keenan & Schieffelin, 1983), the speech style (Andersen, 1990), and the perceived interactional frame (Tannen, 1993). In addition, conversation analysts have documented that children use conversational routines as scaffolds to structure play conversation (Boggs, 1990; Corsaro, 1985; McTear, 1985); the conversational routine functions as a context that then influences the language of each speaker participating in it. Likewise, research in the pragmatics of adult conversation has repeatedly shown that conversational context influences conversation (e.g., the essays in Ochs, Schegloff, and Thompson, 1996, and in Tannen, 1993). All of these studies point out an unanswered question in studies of play metacommunication: How is metacommunicative strategy influenced by conversational context?

To explore the influence of conversational context on metacommunicative strategy, Sawyer (1997) analyzed children's metacommunicative strategies within a two-turn negotiation sequence. Children create and modify the play frame using negotiation sequences, which begin with a proposal to change the play frame, followed by the response of the play partner, whether to adopt the proposal into the shared play frame or not. Some studies have emphasized the importance of proposal responses, by suggesting, for example, that affirmative yet extending responses are either associated with the greater intersubjectivity of older children (Goncu, 1993a), with popular children (Black & Hazen, 1990), or with girls rather than boys (Sheldon, 1992). However, these studies did not examine metacommunication and did not examine the sequential relationships across turns of discourse. In a study of metacommunication in two-turn negotiation sequences, Sawyer (1997) found that an in-frame proposal was more likely to receive an in-frame response than an out-of-frame one and that an implicit proposal was more likely to receive an implicit response than an explicit one. For example, in Example 2 Jennie's in-frame and implicit proposal—to enact a scene in which she is rescued—is rejected by Jennifer using an in-frame and implicit response.

Example 2 demonstrates a general feature of in-frame and implicit strategies: they can work effectively only when some elements of the shared frame have already been established. Without first sharing a play frame, the children would not be able to distinguish between a new metacommunicative proposal and a straightforward enactment of the already negotiated play activity. The implicit metacommunicative negotiation of Example 2 is effective only because both children have already established roles and a mother–daughter relationship, and both know that they are not already enacting a rescue scenario. With implicit and in-frame proposals, the addressee must rely in part on the context to determine the intent of the proposal.

The present study was designed to address a potential problem in Sawyer's study of metacommunication in conversational sequence, in that Sawyer did not examine the influence of child-level variables. Each of the above discourse-sequence findings could potentially be an artifact of child-level variables. For example, Sawyer found that an implicit proposal tends to be followed by an implicit response, and he concluded that this was a property of the discourse level of analysis. However, it could be the case that children with preferences for implicit metacommunication tend to play together and that children with preferences for explicit metacommunication likewise tend to play together. If so, the discourse-level finding could be explained with reference to properties of individual children; in other words, the discourse level explanation can be reduced to a psychological explanation. To evaluate this possibility, the present study considers both interactional-level and child-level variables, allowing a simultaneous comparison of the relative explanatory value of these two levels of analysis.

METHOD

Participants

Twenty-four children (12 boys and 12 girls) participated in this study. A research site was selected that contained children ranging in age from 39 months to 62 months, mean age 49.9, with age evenly distributed through the age range. This selection was based on previous research that suggested that children younger than 36 months do not engage in metacommunication (Fein et al., 1982; Garvey & Kramer, 1989) but that between 36 and 60 months there is a tremendous development of children's metacommunicative skills (Auwarter, 1986; Giffin, 1984). Previous research has also indicated the importance of familiarity and friendship to many aspects of pretend play, including metacommunication. Thus, the 24 children were students in a single preschool classroom, which was the subject of intensive observational research over an eight-month period. The class was predominantly upper-middle socioecomic status (SES), in an urban private preschool with an ethnically mixed population.

Procedure

Because of the high level of background noise in preschool classrooms, gathering naturally occurring discourse is problematic. The microphone has to be placed immediately next to the target play group, and the researcher has to sit only a few feet away to take down field notes. This requires the researcher to become a natural part of the preschool environment, so that children's play will continue as if the researcher were not present. The preschool was approached using a field entry strategy described in Corsaro (1985). This involved an initial four-month entry period, during which the researcher visited the classroom for two or three times each week and sat quietly on the floor in each of the main play locations. The researcher ignored the children's attempts to engage him in dialogue, to ensure that the children would continue playing with each other. After four months, the children were effectively ignoring the researcher, and a tape recorder and microphone were introduced.

Over a six-week period, the researcher entered the classroom each day and taped the 50-minute indoor play period. This was an unstructured time period, when the teachers allowed the children to choose their own activity; play was neither encouraged nor discouraged. Data were collected in all areas of the school where pretend play was frequent, with the majority of data collected from the sand table, the block area, and the doll corner. The observation locations for each day were selected in advance. Thus, the children appearing on each day's audiotape were those who self-selected both the location and their play partners. All locations where children engaged in social pretend play were represented, and each location was sampled in proportion to the frequency and amount of social play observed in that location during the initial four-month observational period. Because the audiotape data were sampled by classroom location, with the day's location determined in advance, the method did not favor any one type of play discourse or group membership over another. This resulted in a data set of 29 hours of audiotaped peer play discourse.

Table 8.1
Metacommunicative Strategies: Frame and Explicitness

Level	Frame	Explicitness
4	Out-of-character, out-of-frame	Explicitly mentions "play" or "pretend"
3	Out-of-character, blended frame	Second-person, commands, punctual aspect
2	In-character, blended frame	Progressive aspect, questions
1	In-frame	First-person singular

Data Analysis

The audiotapes were transcribed shortly after they were collected, using the corresponding field notes to disambiguate unclear speech. Ten hours of play discourse were selected from the data set, approximately one-third of the total data. The 10-hour subset was selected to be proportionally representative of the play locations and activities of the 29-hour data set. This sample size is larger than in most studies of children's conversation. Using a coding scheme of comparable complexity, Goncu (1993b) analyzed a total of 4 hours of conversation. In a study that required a similarly close analysis of all play discourse, Corsaro (1979) used less than 5 hours of data.

Interactional Data

A *negotiation sequence* was defined as two consecutive conversational turns, a proposal to modify the play frame by one child (the *proposer*) to another child or group of children and the response of a second child (the *responder*). The data set contained a total of 764 negotiation sequences. A response was coded as an *acceptance* if the proposal was adopted and incorporated into the shared play frame or as a *rejection* if the proposal was not adopted and did not become a part of the shared play frame. An acceptance was coded as an *extension* if the responder accepted the proposal and also made a new proposal that consistently elaborated on the original proposal. A rejection was coded as a *modification* if the responder combined the rejection with an alternative proposal.

For each negotiation sequence, both the proposal and the response were coded for two metacommunicative strategy variables, frame and explicitness (see Table 8.1).

Frame. The *frame* of a proposal or response was coded using a four-category coding scheme, ranging from out-of-frame and out-of-character to in-frame and in-character. Level 1 was the most in-frame, with the child voicing as his or her play character and with no references to the world outside the play frame:

"Watch out for the earthquake!" Levels 2 and 3 represented differing degrees of combination of the play frame and the everyday frame in a single turn. A turn was coded as Level 2 if the child was speaking in character but referenced some out-of-frame objects or events: "I need some more blocks!" spoken in a super-hero voice. A turn was coded as Level 3 if the child was speaking out of character, but with references to in-frame objects or events: "Let's say my guy was killed in the earthquake." Level 4 was the most out-of-frame, with the child using his or her own, everyday voice and with no references to the world within the play frame: "Let's play house now."

Explicitness. The *explicitness* of a proposal or response was coded using a four-category coding scheme, ranging from maximally explicit to minimally explicit. Explicitness roughly corresponds to the directness of the proposal in its implications for the play partner; a proposal that concerned the addressed child's character is more direct than a proposal that concerns the speaker only. Explicitness was operationalized in terms of deictic, syntactic, and lexical features of the language used in the child's turn. Level 4 turns included explicit mention of the fact of pretending, for example, "Let's pretend this is the earthquake." Level 3 turns did not mention play explicitly and included performatives such as commands or prompts, often in the second person, for example, "You're a good guy." Level 2 turns were often progressive aspect and were frequently first-person plural, for example, "We're burying him." Level 2 turns included warnings and announcements of events, phrased such that the event is taking place or has taken place. Level 1 turns were usually first-person singular, with the proposal concerning primarily the proposer's play character, for example, "I'll lock the door." Thus, they were maximally indirect, since the implications for the responder were not addressed.

Reliability. A coder was hired to calculate the reliability of the above coding scheme. The coder was a graduate student in developmental psychology who was unfamiliar with prior research in this area and was not aware of the hypotheses of the study. The coder was trained on transcripts from the original 29-hour data set that were not part of the 10-hour sample.

After training, a total of 44% of the 10-hour corpus, 2,944 utterances, was jointly coded for reliability measurement. The researcher's and the coder's agreement on the identification of negotiation sequences (as opposed to discourse exchanges that did not meet the above definition) was 86%. Discrepancies were reconciled before proceeding with the joint coding of this set of negotiation sequences. The reliability for the four different response types (acceptance, rejection, extension, and modification) was high, with Cohen's kappa of .75. Reliabilities for the two strategy variables, for both proposals and responses, was high, with the following kappas: proposal explicitness, .72; proposal frame, .86; response explicitness, .74, response frame, .82. These kappas are quite large; by comparison, Lampert and Ervin-Tripp (1993) suggest that kappas of .60 are high for such coding schemes.

Child Interactional Profile

For each child, 10 interactional profile variables were defined. The child's score on each variable was determined by aggregating all of the negotiation sequences in which that child participated.

Proposal Variables

• Total sequence proposals—Total sequences in which the child was the proposer
• Acceptance rate—Percentage of the child's proposals that were accepted by the responder
• Proposal explicitness—Average explicitness of the child's proposals
• Proposal frame—Average frame of the child's proposals

Response Variables

• Total sequence responses—Total sequences in which the child was the responder
• Response explicitness—Average explicitness of the child's responses
• Response frame—Average frame of the child's responses
• Positive response rate—Percentage of the child's responses that accepted the proposal
• Extending response rate—Percentage of the child's positive responses that were extensions
• Modifying response rate—Percentage of the child's negative responses that were modifications

The last three variables are measures of the tendency of the child's responses to contribute to connected play discourse (cf. Goncu, 1993a; Hazen & Black, 1989).

Of the 24 children, 3 did not participate in any negotiation sequences either as proposers or as responders. One other child did not participate at all as a responder, although that child did participate as a proposer; 3 additional children did not participate at all as proposers, although they did participate in some sequences as responders. Thus, a total of 17 children participated in at least one sequence as proposers and at least one sequence as responders. Consequently, in the analyses of the characteristics of a child's proposals, the 6 children who did not propose at all were excluded; in the analyses of the characteristics of a child's responses, the 4 children who did not respond at all were excluded; and in the analyses of relationships between proposal and response variables, only the 17 children who participated in both proposals and responses were included.

RESULTS: METACOMMUNICATIVE USAGE AND THE INTERACTIONAL PROFILE

The purpose of this study was to examine two levels of analysis in children's play metacommunication. Relationships at the child level of analysis are pre-

Table 8.2
Mean Values for Interactional Variables at the Two Levels of Analysis

Child Variables N = 18, 20, or 24[a]	M	SD	Sequence Variables N = 724	M
Proposal Explicitness	2.31	.30	Proposal Explicitness	2.42
Proposal Frame	2.25	.46	Proposal Frame	2.15
Response Explicitness	2.16	.42	Response Explicitness	2.26
Response Frame	2.36	.66	Response Frame	2.12
Total Proposals	31.83	42.60		
Total Responses	31.46	35.30		
Acceptance Rate	.70	.23	Acceptance Rate	.75
Positive Response Rate	.68	.27		
Extending Response Rate	.62	.30		
Modifying Response Rate	.65	.36		

[a]*N* for the child means vary as follows: for the proposal variables, children who did not propose at all were excluded, resulting in an *N* of 18. For the response variables, children who did not respond at all were excluded, resulting in an *N* of 20. For two variables, total proposals and total responses, all 24 children were included.

sented in this section, and these results are compared with findings at the discourse context level in the following section. Of particular interest, given the exclusive focus in prior studies on explicit and out-of-frame meta-communication, is the usage of implicit and in-frame strategies. Sawyer (1997) found that children use a wide range of metacommunicative strategies, not only the explicit and out-of-frame strategies that prior studies had emphasized. However, Sawyer did not conduct individual-level analyses; thus, it was not possible to identify developmental trends. To identify developmental trends, in this study I used the aggregated interactional profile data. Linear regression analyses were used to test the relationship of age and sex to the 10 child interactional profile variables. Mean values for these variables are reported in Table 8.2. Sex was not significantly related to metacommunicative strategy usage or to any other interactional profile variables. Age was related to the two variables for total participation in negotiation sequences: older children participated in more sequences both as proposers and as responders. However, age was not significantly related to metacommunicative strategy usage: older children were not more or less explicit or more or less in-frame.

For a more direct comparison with prior studies that contrasted proposal meta-communication in 3- and 5-year-olds, I calculated mean total sequence proposals for the children of these ages, excluding 4-year-olds. The mean total sequence proposals for 5-year-olds was 69.4 and for 3-year-olds, 14.4; 5-year-olds were proposers in almost five times as many sequences. However, age was not significantly related to the proportional use of any particular metacommunicative strategy.

To explore other potential patterns in metacommunicative strategy usage, I evaluated relationships among the interactional profile variables. To show the significance of the associations, I calculated correlations between the 10 profile variables (see Table 8.3).

Among the proposal variables, there were no significant relationships. However, many of the response variables were significantly related both to other response variables and to proposal variables. Three of the response variables were measures of the child's tendency to respond in ways that contributed to connected play discourse—with acceptances, extensions, and modifications rather than outright rejections. Two of the three possible correlations between these variables were significant, suggesting that they may be aspects of a single construct, a child's tendency to engage in connected play discourse. Children who accepted more also tended to accept with an extending elaboration, and children who had a high proportion of such extensions were more likely to reject a proposal by proposing an alternative.

Several other correlations among the response variables suggested that certain children tend to engage in intersubjective play. Children whose responses were more in-frame were also more likely to accept a proposal, to extend when accepting, and to modify when rejecting. These correlations suggest that children whose responses are more in-frame overall are more likely to provide responses that contribute to intersubjectively shared, connected play discourse.

Interactional Profile and Metacommunication

There are several relationships among the proposal and response variables, suggesting that each child has a distinct interactional profile. Children who were more explicit in proposals were also more explicit in responses, and children who were more out-of-frame in proposals were also more out-of-frame in responses.

I also found a fairly even distribution of participation in negotiation sequences. Children who participated in more total sequences as proposers also participated in more total sequences as responders. The children who tended to accept proposals were the same children whose proposals were also likely to be accepted. These two findings suggest that the classroom is not split between passive children who meekly accept proposals put to them and dominant children who propose more often, who are always accepted, and who reject proposals made to them.

In sum, the only significant relationships with the independent variables, age and sex, were that older children participated in more sequences as both pro-

Table 8.3
Correlations between Child Interactional Profile Variables

	proposal explicitness	proposal frame	total proposals	acceptance rate	response explicitness	response frame	total responses	positive response rate	extending response rate	modifying response rate
proposal explicitness	1.0									
proposal frame	.17 (18)	1.0								
total proposals	.38 (18)	-.24 (18)	1.0							
acceptance rate	-.47 (18)	-.36 (18)	.24 (18)	1.0						
response explicitness	.60* (17)	-.27 (17)	.37 (17)	-.12 (17)	1.0					
response frame	-.12 (17)	.90*** (17)	-.10 (17)	-.13 (17)	-.38 (20)	1.0				
total responses	.61** (17)	-.24 (17)	.97*** (17)	.09 (17)	.31 (20)	-.39 (20)	1.0			
positive response rate	-.20 (17)	-.12 (17)	.06 (17)	.77*** (17)	-.03 (20)	-.55* (20)	.27 (20)	1.0		
extending response rate	-.14 (17)	.53* (17)	.02 (17)	.24 (17)	.04 (20)	-.46 (20)	.36 (20)	.53* (20)	1.0	
modifying response rate	.44 (17)	-.40 (17)	.32 (17)	-.47 (17)	.34 (20)	-.69** (20)	.52* (20)	.32 (20)	.61** (20)	1.0

***p < .001, **p < .01, *p < .05.

posers and responders. This confirms prior findings that older children engage in more metacommunication than younger children. However, age was not associated with any changes in the relative use of metacommunicative strategies or with any changes in the child's tendency to contribute to connected play.

RESULTS: RELATIVE EFFECTS OF CHILD- AND SEQUENCE-LEVEL VARIABLES

The above results provide potential explanations of a child's metacommunicative strategy usage in terms of individual-level interactional profile variables. However, Sawyer (1997) explained metacommunicative strategy selection using the negotiation sequence level of analysis. For example, he found that in-frame proposals were more likely to receive in-frame responses, and implicit proposals were more likely to receive implicit responses. These sequence-level findings demonstrated several strong relationships between the proposal strategy and the response strategy; for example, the responder tended to use the same strategy as the preceding proposal. However, the above child-level findings demonstrate that individual children have distinct and identifiable styles of responding; for example, children who are more implicit in their proposals are also more implicit in their responses.

Thus, we have two potential explanations for response strategy selection, at two different levels of analysis, and these findings present us with a more complex question: Given an instance of a metacommunicative strategy selection, to what extent is that instance explained by the discourse context and to what extent by the child's interactional profile? For example, regarding the finding that the response tends to be the same strategy as the proposal, it remains a possibility that implicit responders simply tended to engage in play with implicit proposers, and thus the sequence-level findings might actually reflect properties of the responder's general style. This possibility is suggested by the strong correlation between a child's proposal strategy and response strategy; since implicit proposers also respond implicitly, if implicit children played together, this could result in a correlation at the negotiation sequence level.

To evaluate the relative effects of the child's interactional profile and the proposal–response sequence context, linear regression analyses were used. The results are reported in Table 8.4. In both cases, the first model in Table 8.4 used only the responding child's interactional profile variable (response frame or response explicitness), and the second model added the negotiation-sequence variable (proposal frame or proposal explicitness). The following discussion focuses on the proportion of variance explained by the overall equation (R^2) and the effect size of each independent variable in the equation (B).

With the sequence response frame as the outcome variable, the first model used the responding child's response frame as the single predictor variable (recall that this is the average frame of all of the child's responses). The effect size of the response frame was .353, and the proportion of variance explained

Table 8.4
Relative Influence of Child Response Profile and Sequence Context

	B[a]	R^2	p
Model 1: Responder Frame	.353	.124	.0001
Model 2: Responder Frame + Proposal Frame	.108 .752	.630	.0001
Model 1: Responder Explicitness	.216	.045	.0001
Model 2: Responder Explicitness + Proposal Explicitness	.182 .412	.215	.0001

[a]B is the regression coefficient of the independent variable and is a measure of effect size; R^2 represents the proportion of the outcome-variable variance explained by the complete model. Note that these results must be interpreted with caution, as the 764 negotiation sequences are not statistically independent.

was .124. The second model was added in the sequence proposal frame as a second predictor variable. The proportion of variance explained rose to .630, indicating that the discourse context provides additional explanatory power. Given my goal of contrasting the relative importance of the two levels of analysis, the most interesting findings are the effect sizes associated with the two independent variables. In this two-variable model, the effect size of the responding child's response frame was .108, and of the sequence proposal it's frame was .752. Thus, the discourse level of analysis had almost eight times the effect size of the individual level of analysis.

Similar regressions were conducted with the sequence's response explicitness as the outcome variable, and the pattern of findings was similar. The first model used the responding child's response explicitness as the single predictor variable (recall that this is the average explicitness of all of the child's responses). The effect size of the child's response explicitness was .216, and the proportion of variance explained was .045. The second model was added in the sequence proposal explicitness as a second predictor variable. Again, the proportion of variance explained rose, to .215, indicating that discourse context provides additional explanatory power. As with the frame variable, I was particularly interested in the relative effect sizes of the variables at the two levels of analysis. The effect size of the child-level variable was .182, and for the discourse level variable it was .412.

With both metacommunicative variables, adding in the negotiation sequence-level variable increased the predictive power of the regression equation beyond the predictive power of the child-level variable. When comparing the relative effect sizes of these two variables, the effect sizes of the negotiation-sequence variables were much larger than those of the child level.

CONCLUSION

The purpose of this study was to simultaneously consider both individual- and discourse-level variables as potential explanations of play behavior, to allow an evaluation of which type of explanation is most helpful in analyzing play metacommunication. Sawyer (1997) examined only the discourse level of analysis, whereas most prior studies of metacommunication considered only individual-level variables. This study extended Sawyer (1997) by aggregating these data to a child level of analysis, allowing the calculation of each child's interactional profile.

One problem with prior studies is that they have operationalized metacommunication solely in terms of denotational or referential properties of the utterance. There are several problems with this methodology, particularly when the object of study is extended to include implicit and in-frame metacommunicative strategies, which may or may not function as proposals depending on the discourse context. No obvious syntactic surface features of these utterances allow the analyst to code them as metacommunicative proposals. How can one be sure that a discourse turn is viewed by the children as a metacommunicative proposal? Even when the proposal is explicit—for example, with a child saying, "Pretend you were the Mom"—not all proposals are successful, nor are they even necessarily responded to. Utterance-based coding methods typically don't consider whether the proposal actually introduces a new play transformation; if the addressed child is already enacting the "Mom" character, the statement "You are the Mom" may not actually be a metacommunication but may carry a more subtle meaning. To be certain that a proposal is new, is heard, and is interpreted as a proposal by the other children, the analyst must consider both the context and the response of the other participants to that proposal. This study addressed these multiple concerns by coding only proposals that introduced new, previously unmentioned frame transformations and that were perceived by the children to be proposals, as indicated by their response to them.

Consistent with prior studies by developmental psychologists, I found statistically significant correlations at the child level. I found that each child tends to use a similar strategy in both proposals and responses. I also found that older children participate in more sequences as proposers and as responders; on average, the 5-year-olds participated in almost five times as many sequences as the 3-year-olds. However, older children were not found to be proportionally more explicit or out-of-frame than younger children; there were no significant relationships between a child's age and the metacommunicative strategy variables. Although prior studies found that explicit and out-of-frame proposals increased with age during the preschool years, they did not examine changes in the usage of implicit and in-frame strategies. These findings are consistent with past studies in that older children metacommunicate more overall, participating in more negotiation sequences—both more total proposals and more total responses. However, older children do not use proportionally more explicit and out-of-frame strategies than younger children.

I also found that the classroom does not split into two interactional types that we might think of as "proposers" and "responders"—into children who always propose and are always accepted and children who respond but never propose their own play frame transformations. At the child level, the correlation between total proposals and total responses was .97, indicating that each child responds almost exactly as many times as he or she proposes. Also, the children whose proposals were more often successful were the same children who were more likely to respond positively to another child's proposal—this correlation was .77. These high correlations suggest that active players contribute to play both by offering new ideas through proposals and by acknowledging others' proposals and responding positively to them.

The three connected play response variables—positive response rate, extending response rate, and modifying response rate—were interrelated, with two of the three possible cross-correlations being significant. These three variables may be interpreted as a measure of a child's intersubjectivity in play (Goncu, 1993a, 1993b). Of the four metacommunicative strategy variables, the response frame had the strongest relationships with connected play responses; children who tended to respond with more in-frame strategies also tended to accept proposals and to reject proposals by proposing a modification. Thus, a high number of in-frame responses seems to be the metacommunicative tendency most likely to result in intersubjective play.

Thus, we could speak of a child's "interactional profile," an overall tendency to use certain metacommunicative strategies, regardless of discourse context. Although age was not related to the interactional profile, future research could explore how a child's interactional profile changes in different play settings (e.g., contrasting domestic, constructive, or fantasy play) or with different play partners (friends vs. non-friends, large vs. small groups). For example, there is some evidence that friends are more implicit than non-friends (Sawyer, 1997, p. 137). Such contrasts may also display interaction effects with age; for example, older friends might tend to be even more implicit, relative to non-friends, than younger children.

Although the negotiation sequence patterns identified in Sawyer (1997) are large—for example, 84% of responses used the same Frame as the proposal— the above analyses of interactional profile variables suggested an alternative explanation, that the negotiation sequence effects may actually be reducible to the interactional profile of participating children. To determine to what extent these negotiation-sequence effects are independent of any characteristics of the participating children, I evaluated the relative effects of two potential predictors of response strategy, the child level of analysis and the discourse level of analysis. Several linear regression models were examined to evaluate these hypotheses, including variables representing two levels of analysis. In the two model comparisons—for explicitness and for frame—the results indicate that the discourse level has a strong effect above and beyond what could be predicted from the child level. In fact, in both equations, the discourse-level effect sizes are much greater than the child-level effect sizes. In other words, a child's overall linguistic behavior in this classroom is not the best predictor of how that child will speak in any specific situation.

These findings seem not to be reducible to explanations in terms of the participating children's interactional profiles. Because these conversational patterns are not reducible to the child level of analysis, these findings suggest that children's conversational behavior cannot be explained solely through psychological study of individual children. This suggests a problem with prior studies of metacommunication that should be addressed in future studies: because discourse context is a better predictor of metacommunicative behavior than child-level variables, future studies of metacommunication in children's play discourse must incorporate conversational context.

This focus on negotiation sequence falls in the tradition of conversation analysis, and these findings are consistent with discourse-analytic studies that demonstrate the influence of context on conversation. However, unlike most conversation analytic studies, I analyzed the data set not only at the discourse level of analysis but also at the child level of analysis. This hybrid method draws theoretical inspiration from sociocultural psychology, which emphasizes a joint focus on both individuals and social events as units of analysis (Rogoff, 1990; Wertsch, 1998). In this study, the negotiation sequence is an event level of analysis. By aggregating data for each child, I was able to provide additional information that was not available at the discourse level of analysis and to determine which aspects of discursive behavior were more appropriately analyzed as properties of individual participants. This is particularly important information when data are gathered using ethnographic or quasi-experimental methodologies, since individual participation in conversational events cannot be controlled or evenly distributed.

The discourse level of analysis allowed me also to examine the effect of conversational context on a child's strategy selection. Sawyer (1997) found that the response strategy was strongly related to the proposal strategy and to the goal of the responding child. These strong relationships—between proposal strategy, response strategy, and responder's goal—suggest that metacommunicative strategy selection is heavily influenced by the conversational context. These findings are consistent with past studies that found significant speech variation in different conversational contexts, for example, in different interactional routines. Combining the results from these two levels of analysis leads to a more complex, multileveled picture: children may have overall strategy preferences, but each specific use is heavily influenced by the conversational context.

This is particularly interesting considering that age was not related to a child's interactional profile. Although older children metacommunicate more, they do not use proportionally more explicit or out-of-frame strategies. Thus, if there are developmental changes in metacommunicative usage, they must be extremely sensitive to conversational context. For example, older children might develop an increasing ability to share intersubjective understandings of the play frame, to correctly evaluate exactly how intersubjective this play frame is, and to select the appropriate metacommunicative strategy, one that best matches both the conversational context and their interactional goal. Such topics could be a productive area for future research.

REFERENCES

Andersen, E. S. (1986). The acquisition of register variation by Anglo-American children. In B. Schieffelin & E. Ochs (Eds.), *Language socialization across cultures* (pp. 153–161). New York: Cambridge University Press.

Andersen, E. S. (1990). *Speaking with style: The sociolinguistic skills of children*. London: Routledge.

Auwarter, M. (1986). Development of communicative skills: The construction of fictional reality in children's play. In J. Cook-Gumperz, W. A. Corsaro, & J. Streeck (Eds.), *Children's worlds and children's language* (pp. 205–230). New York: Mouton de Gruyter.

Bakhtin, M. M. (1981). Discourse in the novel. In *The dialogic imagination* (pp. 259–422). Austin: University of Texas Press.

Bateson, G. (1971). The message "This is play." In R. E. Herron & B. Sutton-Smith (Eds.), *Child's play* (pp. 261–266). Malabar, FL: Robert E. Krieger Publishing Company. (Reprinted from *Group processes*, B. Schaffner [Ed.], New York: Josiah Macy Foundation, 1956, pp. 145–151).

Bateson, G. (1972). A theory of play and fantasy. In G. Bateson (Ed.), *Steps to an ecology of mind* (pp. 177–193). New York: Chandler. (Reprinted from *American Psychiatric Association Research Reports* 2, 1955, pp. 39–51).

Black, B., & Hazen, N. L. (1990). Social status and patterns of communication in acquainted and unacquainted preschool children. *Developmental Psychology, 26*(3), 379–387.

Boggs, S. T. (1990). The role of routines in the evolution of children's peer talk. In B. Dorval (Ed.), *Conversational organization and its development* (pp. 101–130). Norwood, NJ: Ablex.

Brownell, C. A. (1990). Peer social skills in toddlers: Competencies and constraints illustrated by same-age and mixed-age interaction. *Child Development, 61*, 838–848.

Corsaro, W. A. (1985). *Friendship and peer culture in the early years*. Norwood, NJ: Ablex.

Doyle, A. B., & Connolly, J. (1989). Negotiation and enactment in social pretend play: Relations to social acceptance and social cognition. *Early Childhood Research Quarterly, 4*, 289–302.

Doyle, A. B., Doehring, P., Tessier, O., & de Lorimier, S. (1992). Transitions in children's play: A sequential analysis of states preceding and following social pretense. *Developmental Psychology, 28*, 137–144.

Fein, G. G., Moorin, E. R., & Enslein, J. (1982). Pretense and peer behavior: An intersectoral analysis. *Human Development, 25*, 392–406.

Fogel, A., & Branco, A. U. (1997). Metacommunication as a source of indeterminism in relationship development. In A. Fogel, M.C.D.P. Lyra, & Jaan Valsiner (Eds.), *Dynamics and indeterminism in developmental and social processes* (pp. 65–92). Hillsdale, NJ: Erlbaum.

Garvey, C., & Berndt, R. (1977). *The organization of pretend play.* Corte Madera, CA: Select Press.

Garvey, C., & Kramer, T. L. (1989). The language of social pretend play. *Developmental Review, 9,* 364–382.

Giffin, H.L.N. (1984). The coordination of meaning in the creation of a shared make-believe reality. In I. Bretherton (Ed.), *Symbolic play: The development of social understanding* (pp. 73–100). Orlando, FL: Academic Press.

Goffman, E. (1974). *Frame analysis: An essay on the organization of experience.* New York: Harper & Row.

Goldman, L. R. (1998). *Child's play: Myth, mimesis and make-believe.* New York: Berg.

Goncu, A. (1993a). Development of intersubjectivity in social pretend play. *Human Development, 36,* 185–198.

Goncu, A. (1993b). Development of intersubjectivity in the dyadic play of preschoolers. *Early Childhood Research Quarterly, 8,* 99–116.

Hazen, N. L., & Black, B. (1989). Preschool peer communication skills: The role of social status and interaction context. *Child Development, 60,* 867–876.

Hickmann, M. (1985). Metapragmatics in child language. In E. Mertz & R. J. Parmentier (Eds.), *Semiotic mediation: Sociocultural and psychological perspectives* (pp. 177–201). Orlando, FL: Academic Press.

Keenan, E., & Schieffelin, B. B. (1983). Topic as a discourse notion: A study of topic in the conversations of children and adults. In E. Ochs & B. B. Schieffelin (Eds.), *Acquiring conversational competence* (pp. 66–113). London: Routledge & Kegan Paul. (Reprinted from *Subject and topic,* C. Li [Ed.], New York: Academic Press, 1976, pp. 337–384).

Lampert, M. D., & Ervin-Tripp, S. M. (1993). Structured coding for the study of language and social interaction. In J. A. Edwards & M. D. Lampert (Eds.), *Talking data: Transcription and coding in discourse research* (pp. 169–206). Mahwah, NJ: Erlbaum.

Leaper, C. (1991). Influence and involvement in children's discourse: Age, gender, and partner effects. *Child Development, 62,* 797–811.

Lucy, J. A. (Ed.). (1993). *Reflexive language: Reported speech and metapragmatics.* New York: Cambridge University Press.

Masur, E. F. (1978). Preschool boys' speech modifications: The effect of listeners' linguistic levels and conversational responsiveness. *Child Development, 49,* 924–927.

McTear, M. (1985). *Children's conversation.* London: Basil Blackwell.

Ochs, E., Schegloff, E. A., & Thompson, S. A. (Eds.). (1996). *Interaction and grammar.* New York: Cambridge University Press.

Putallaz, M., & Gottman, J. M. (1981). An interactional model of children's entry into peer groups. *Child Development, 52,* 986–994.

Putallaz, M., & Wasserman, A. (1990). Children's entry behavior. In S. R. Asher & J. D. Coie (Eds.), *Peer rejection in childhood* (pp. 60–89). New York: Cambridge University Press.

Rogoff, B. (1990). *Apprenticeship in thinking: Cognitive development in social context.* New York: Oxford University Press.

Sachs, J. (1982). "Don't interrupt!": Preschoolers' entry into ongoing conversations. In C. E. Johnson & C. L. Thew (Eds.), *Proceedings of the 2nd international congress for the study of child language, Volume 1* (pp. 344–356). Washington, DC: University Press of America. (Conference held in Vancouver, BC, August 9–14, 1981).

Sawyer, R. K. (1993). The pragmatics of play: Interactional strategies during children's pretend play. *Pragmatics, 3*(3), 259–282.

Sawyer, R. K. (1997). *Pretend play as improvisation: Conversation in the preschool classroom.* Norwood, NJ: Erlbaum.

Schiffrin, D. (1980). Meta-talk: Organizational and evaluative brackets in discourse. *Sociological Inquiry, 50*(3–4), 199–236.

Sheldon, A. (1992). Conflict talk: Sociolinguistic challenges to self-assertion and how young girls meet them. *Merrill-Palmer Quarterly, 38*(1), 95–117.

Silverstein, M. (1993). Metapragmatic discourse and metapragmatic function. In J. A. Lucy (Ed.), *Reflexive language* (pp. 33–58). New York: Cambridge University Press.

Tannen, D. (Ed.). (1993). *Framing in discourse.* New York: Oxford University Press.

Trawick-Smith, J. (1998). A qualitative analysis of metaplay in the preschool years. *Early Childhood Research Quarterly, 13*(3), 433–452.

Wertsch, J. V. (1998). *Mind as action.* New York: Oxford University Press.

Chapter 9

Symbolic Play through the Eyes and Words of Children

Janet K. Sawyers and Nathalie Carrick

INTRODUCTION

Previous research on children's symbolic play has relied almost exclusively on adults' (parents, teachers, researchers) interpretations of children's play. The purpose of this study was to expand our understanding of symbolic play through the eyes and words of children.

In their comprehensive review of the research on play, Rubin, Fein, and Vandenberg (1983) noted the lack of knowledge about children's interpretations of symbolic play. In identifying questions concerning both content and methodology needed to advance our understanding of play, they suggested providing children with videotaped samples of children engaged in "make-believe" play to determine their "conceptions" of pretense. This methodology provided a different and insightful way to examine children's play.

Fantuzzo, Coolahan, Mendez, McDermott, and Sutton-Smith (1998) recently developed the Penn Interactive Peer Play-Scale. It was created in response to the need to "identify quality practices that are informed by valid assessment of the developmental needs and capabilities of young children" (p. 411) noted by the National Association for the Education of Young Children. They join a growing number of researchers concerned with the development of a contextually relevant understanding of children's behaviors (Pelligrini, 1992, as cited in Fantuzzo et al., 1998). Thus, the concept of a contextually relevant understanding of play was another focus of this study.

Following the lead of Rubin et al. (1983) and Fantuzzo et al. (1998), children were directly asked questions regarding their symbolic play. Children were interviewed while watching previously videotaped segments of their symbolic play from their classroom. The parents and teachers were subsequently interviewed to gain further insight into the children's symbolic play. The interview questions were based on developmental aspects of symbolic play found in the literature.

LITERATURE REVIEW: ELEMENTS OF PLAY

The elements of pretend play include themes, roles, object substitutions, and differentiation between fantasy and reality. An awareness of previous studies on these elements is necessary to set the stage for interpreting data in the present study.

Themes

The theme of a play scenario is defined by the events of the play, including children's actions and what they announce the play to be. Within the theme of the play is a script. A script is the action plan for the theme (Garvey, 1977).

Two theories explain scripts, script theory and emotive theory. In script theory (Shank & Abelson, 1977) it is thought that children's intentions during group pretend play are to imitate events that they have experienced. To do this successfully, children must share a common knowledge base about the script for dialogue with the play partner (Corasaro, 1983; Nelson & Gruendel, 1979; Nelson & Seidman, 1984; Short-Meyerson & Abbeduto, 1997; Snow, Shonkoff, Lee, and Levin, 1986). Emotive theory claims that during pretend play, children focus more on enacting events that allow them to express emotions (Fein, 1986, 1987, 1989, 1991). Fein's emotive theory suggests that children know that pretend play is not real; therefore, they are allowed to enact events that either have occurred but become distorted or are simply imagined. Children enact these events because there is a strong affective power to them. Consequently, in play they are able to play with the emotion of the event without actually feeling the emotion directly. Children can adjust the intensity of the emotion by either playing the event longer and in more detail or ending the play.

Roles

During the enactment of a theme, children engage in role-play. "Role" has been defined as a "behavior in which the child simulates the identity or characteristics of another person" (Fein, 1981 p. 101). Garvey (1977) identified four types of role-play: functional, relational, stereotype, and fictional. Functional, the first type, is determined by the script. The player performs the given function like serving food or driving a car. The second type is the relational role representing a family member, a friend, or a pet. Garvey labeled the third type stereotype because it is highly predictable and based on an occupation (cowboy or policeman). Roles taken from a story or television are labeled fictional. The third and fourth roles are both character roles. Garvey also noted an additional role that the children did not enact but rather talked about. She called this the "absent" role (imaginary person on the phone). With development in perspective-taking skills (Creasey, Jarvis, & Berk, 1998; Rubin & Pepler, 1980) and decentration (Fein, 1981), children are able to negotiate changes in the type of roles enacted from familiar and domestic to more fictional ones (Fein, 1981).

Object Substitution

Object substitution follows a developmental sequence (Copple, Cocking, & Matthews, 1984; Lillard, 1993a; Trawick-Smith, 1990; Ungerer, Zelazo, Kearsely, & O'Leary, 1981; Vygotsky, 1978). By 12 months of age, children can symbolically transform a common object from its original purpose to a pretend purpose. At this age, children need an object that highly resembles the object of pretense. For example, they can pretend to drink from a real cup. The complexity of their substitution skills matures, and after the age of 3, children begin to decrease their reliance on the realism of the object for pretense. By school age, children are able to represent an object through gestures (Fein, 1975, 1981; Lillard, 1993a).

Fein (1975) and Mathews (1977) researched different levels of object substitution. By combining Fein's (1975) and Matthews' (1977) results, it appears that there are four levels of substitution: functional, high-level prototypical, low-level prototypical, and insubstantial. Functional substitution occurs when the child uses the object in the way that it is intended (a stick as a stick). High prototypical-level substitution occurs when the pretend object closely resembles the real object (a stick as a spoon). A low prototypical-level substitution occurs when the pretend object does not resemble the real object at all (a stick as a baby). Insubstantial substitutions occur when there is no object present, but the child pretends that there is something there (announces that there is a stick or moves hand to represent a stick). The use of these levels increases with age. However, once a new level has been attained, the lower-level substitutions may still be present in the child's play.

Fantasy and Reality

The literature on children's understanding of fantasy and reality is extensive. Since the concept of children's understanding of fantasy and reality is extremely complex, blanket statements regarding children's ability to distinguish between the two can be misleading (Taylor, 1997). One reason is that the tasks utilized in the studies reveal only a fraction of the complete picture. For example, children are able to distinguish between mental images and real objects (Flavell, Flavell, & Green, 1987; Harris, Brown, Marriot, Whittal, & Harmer, 1991; Wellman & Estes, 1986); however, in Taylor and Howell's (1973) study, children had difficulty saying that a cartoon image in a picture was part of fantasy.

Johnson and Harris (1994) asked children to imagine an item in a box and nothing in a control box. Children opened the box with the imagined item more often than the control box. On the other hand, Wooley and Phellps (as cited in Wooley, 1997) used a similar technique but added a consequential behavioral test at the end. After children were asked to imagine a pencil in a box, a stranger entered the test room and asked if there was a pencil that she could use. In this situation only a few children actually looked inside the box to give her the imagined pencil.

It appears that any emotions related to the items being used must also be considered in the children's performance on such tasks. In Samuels and Taylor's (1994) study, older children could differentiate between pictures depicting neutral, real, and fantasy situations as possibly occurring in real life, but younger children could not. However, when the photographs elicited frightening emotions, children were not able to make correct distinctions. Samuels and Taylor interpreted the children's statement that the frightening photographs representing real events could not happen in real life as a strategy for coping with their fear. The children in Harris' et al. (1991) study who had just imagined a scary object in a box did not want to be left alone in the room with that box. See Wooley (1997) for an extensive review of the literature on children's understanding of fantasy and reality.

Although children may have performed differently during experiments, their typical behavior during pretend play indicates that they do not confuse fantasy with reality (Lillard, 1993a). During pretend play, children can layer the pretend world onto the real world without losing the properties of the real world (Lillard, 1993a). For example, a child pretending that a block is a cookie will not attempt to eat the block. They are able to act among the layers of pretense and reality.

Children's Understanding of Pretense

Lillard (1993b, 1994, 1996) has researched an interesting side to children's understanding of pretense. She suggests that children see pretense as more of an action than a mental representation. During pretense, one creates an image of an object (a telephone) and places it on a real object (a block). The real object is then treated like the image of the desired object (telephone); a child puts the block to ear and speaks into it. Lillard makes the distinction that the major requirement for pretense to exist is the mental image of the telephone, not the action of putting it to the child's ear and speaking (Lillard, 1993b).

Lillard (1996) had children categorize different concepts as either mental (thinking, imaging, pretending etc.) or physical (falling over, etc.) as requiring the mind, body, or both. Children between the ages of 3 and 6 said that mental acts required the mind more often than the body. However, there was a difference among the mental acts. Pretense received the lowest number of responses for needing a mind. This shows that some of the children had not yet made the link between needing mental representations during pretense. In follow-up questions, a few young children explained that pretense required "one's own body, an outfit, or a friend" (p. 1720), all of which are physical items.

In another study by Lillard (1993a), 4- and 5-year-olds were presented with a troll doll and were told that the troll did not know what a rabbit is and had never seen a rabbit. The experimenter made the troll move up and down, said the troll was hopping like a rabbit, and then asked the children if the troll was pretending to be a rabbit. Only 37% of 4-year-olds and 68% of 5-year-olds correctly answered that the troll was not pretending. The other children, who incorrectly answered the question, ignored the need for the troll to make a mental representation of a rabbit hopping in order to be actually pretending to be a rabbit.

In a later experiment in the study, the children were shown a picture of a child either thinking or not thinking about an action followed by another picture of the child enacting or not enacting the same action. Most children said that the child was pretending in the second picture, even when they were presented with the first picture of a child not thinking about the action and a second picture of the child enacting the same action. Both experiments show how children do not view pretending as primarily requiring mental representation.

METHODOLOGY

This study was conducted in a university laboratory preschool in Virginia. The selected children were in a morning program that operates for three and a half hours, five days a week. The school was equipped with video cameras in each classroom. The cameras, mounted on the walls, were operated from a location outside the classrooms. This placement of the cameras allowed the first author to see, record, and follow the selected children as they moved about the classroom in a non-intrusive manner.

Selection of Participants

Teachers of a classroom with 4- and 5-year-olds were asked to nominate children who were frequently observed engaging in symbolic play and who had the verbal skills and propensity to respond to questions about their play. After conducting informal observations of the four children nominated, the first author chose two children for inclusion.

Participants

Hannah, a loquacious 5 year, 1 month old girl, frequently engaged in symbolic play with her friends or by herself with stuffed animals that she brought from home. She was a dominant figure in her group of friends, but not overly directive. She was able to initiate and follow different symbolic play episodes. Her play revolved around nurturing themes of play, including taking care of dolls, building homes for stuffed animals, and pretending to be mother or baby with her friends.

Skeeter was an active 5 year, 6 month old boy who appeared to prefer symbolic play to all other activities in the classroom. Skeeter had a large vocabulary and is very articulate. He rarely engaged in the art-based activities. He used the constructive play activities such as making an airport out of blocks to support his symbolic play. He was observed playing different themes with a diverse group of children. The two most frequent themes in Skeeter's play were emergency/recovery play and play involving "chemicals" in a "laboratory."

Procedures

Videotaping

The first author spent one week in the classroom of the target children interacting with all the children. This allowed time for her to build rapport with Hannah and Skeeter before videotaping their play. This rapport was believed necessary for the children to feel comfortable during the interview sessions.

The naturally occurring symbolic play of both Hannah and Skeeter was videotaped daily for four weeks. Excerpts of each child's symbolic play during a week were edited onto another videotape and given to the parents of each child at the end of the week. Edited segments ranged from one to three different episodes of symbolic play. The segments were representative of the important structural properties of symbolic play identified in the research literature on play: enacting a theme, taking on a role, or making an object substitution (Rubin et al., 1983). Segments were edited to last no longer than 10 minutes. Immediately following each child's interview session, the next series of videotaping commenced, repeating the above procedure. Due to scheduling conflicts, only three child interviews were conducted. The entire four weeks of unedited video were analyzed.

Child Interview Sessions

The edited videotapes were given to the parents the day before the child interview session. They were asked to have the children watch the videotape at least once before the interview session in an effort to make the children feel comfortable and to familiarize them with the content of the video. The interview sessions took place in the child's home. Each child participated in one interview at the end of the week for three consecutive weeks.

Interview Questions. The interview questions used in the semi-structured interviews were drawn from the research literature and theories on symbolic play and were designed to uncover children's thoughts on themes' roles, object substitutions, and reality/fantasy.

A semi-structured interview was chosen because it allowed the interviewer the possibility of having set questions to begin a dialogue with the child and also the opportunity of following up on individual comments made by the child. This format allowed the researcher to distribute the questions systematically and strategically across the interviews rather than overwhelming the child with too many questions in any one interview or posing questions out of context. The first author audiotaped and transcribed each interview. The transcriptions were read and questions were noted to follow up on in subsequent interview/reflection sessions.

The questions related to themes were grounded in the prior research on the use of themes in symbolic play (Corasaro, 1983; Fein, 1986, 1987, 1989, 1991; Nelson & Gruendel, 1979; Nelson & Seidman, 1984; Shank & Abelson, 1977; Short-Meyerson & Abbeduto, 1997; Snow et al., 1986). The questions were designed to elicit children's responses to preference in themes of emotions related to themes of negotiation and repetition of themes.

1. "Tell me about what you are playing here." (in relation to the video)

2. "Why did you choose that?"

3. "You were [smiling, frowning] in that play. Tell me what you were feeling while you were playing that."

4. "What kind of things do you like to pretend to do or play? Why? Which is your favorite? Why?"

5. "Are there things you don't like to pretend? Why?"

6. "If you could play [name of favorite theme of play] however you wanted, would you play it over and over again the same way or change it? Why?"

7. "If you could choose anybody to play [name of favorite theme of play] with you, who would it be? Mom, Dad, sister/brother, friend? Why?"

8. "Tell me about how you and your friends decided to play something."

9. "Are there things you like to pretend just by yourself? Why?"

10. "Tell me what it means to you to 'pretend' something."

The literature (Bretherton, 1989; Garvey, 1977, 1982; Miller & Garvey, 1984; Stockinger Forys & McCune-Nicolich, 1984) provided the basis for questions related to roles. The questions were designed to elicit responses regarding preference and choice of roles and restrictions of roles according to gender and age.

1. "Tell me about who you are pretending to be here." (in relation to the video)

2. "How did you choose that?"

3. "Tell me about your favorite thing to pretend to be."

4. "How does it make you feel to be that?"

5. "If you were playing house, would you ever be the mom (for a boy)/dad (for a girl)? Why?"

The questions about object substitution were drawn from previous research (Fein, 1975; Matthews, 1977; Vygotsky, 1978). The questions were intended to elicit information about choice of objects for substitutions and any limitations of specific objects for substitution.

1. "I see you are using a [name of object] here to [action]. What else could you use to do that? Could you use a [name of object with higher level of realism]? How about a [name of object with lower level of realism]?"

2. "Another child told me I could not use a block to pretend to brush my hair. What do you think? What else could I use?"

3. "If you could play this over again, what would you like to see the teacher put out for you to play with? Why?" (in relation to the video)

Teacher and Parent Interviews

The teachers and mothers were interviewed at the completion of videotaping and interviews with the children. This allowed the researcher the opportunity to discuss emerging findings (e.g., "Hannah [Skeeter] said that she [he] was not pretending in [a specific scene]. How do you see that?" Other questions were designed to gather background information on each child's symbolic play (e.g., "Tell me about Hannah's [Skeeter's] pretend play"), exposure to watching videotapes of themselves, and any reaction that their child had to watching the edited videotapes of their play. These interviews were also audiotaped and transcribed.

RESULTS AND DISCUSSION

"Cup or a Cone": How Themes Are Explained

The children elaborated more in answering questions about the theme of their play through the script theory (Shank & Abelson, 1977) perspective than emotive theory (Fein, 1986, 1987, 1989, 1991) perspective. Script theorists claim that children imitate the world around them in their play, while emotive theory sees play as more of an emotional expression.

Script Theory

During one of the sessions, Hannah watched an episode of herself playing "ice cream." This play consisted of Hannah and her friends at the media table filled with sand. During the play she would ask a friend or teacher if the person wanted some ice cream by saying, "Do you want some ice cream, in a cup or a cone?" During the session, Hannah was asked what she was doing in the play episode. She described her play as an imitation of what actual people do who work in ice cream stores.

N (interviewer): What are you doing here?

H (Hannah): Well, we were saying "cups and cones" because we had these little things for the cups. And we were pretending like we said for real stuff, we said "in a cup or a cone" and like real people say, and all the people say cup and cone and that stuff.

N: You mean when you go to an ice cream shop that's what they say?

H: Yeah, they usually say "Do you want a cup or a cone?" and I say "Cup, or cone?"

N: So you were pretending to say just what the people say in the store.

H: Yeah.

To demonstrate, she then enacted this same script while watching the video-tape. To better explain her "ice cream" play, she walked to the cabinet next to the television and pulled out different puzzle boxes. Each puzzle box represented the different flavors of ice cream.

Skeeter watched an episode of his play at the media table filled with shaving cream where he pretended to play "ice cream." While watching the videotape, he got out a book about an ice cream factory. The book showed cartoon illus-trations of the progression of manufacturing ice cream with cartoon people at each stage of the manufacturing process.

While watching this episode of his play, Skeeter indicated which parts that the children playing with him were enacting (Skeeter points to each cartoon person in the book and labels each one as someone from his classroom play scenario: teacher, Hannah, himself).

N: So you in your play are pretending to be someone in a test lab [what the book calls where a person examines the ice cream].

S (Skeeter): Yeah.

N: And Rachel [teachers] is [are] pretending to be someone at the taste lab [what the book calls where a person tastes the ice cream].

S: And, Hannah is, works right here [points at book] because she puts the chunks in to make sure they are stinky chunks.

Since Skeeter was imitating a book from home that he did not bring to school, the other children in the classroom were not playing with the same knowledge base as Skeeter. A shared knowledge base is reportedly needed for playing out a script (Corasaro, 1983). However, the children did not act in a way that vio-lated Skeeter's interpretation of the script, so the play continued. One reason may be that the script of "every child makes a different part of the ice cream" was general enough to allow for variations. For example, Hannah making the ice cream "stinky" was not in the ice cream book but was an acceptable pro-cedure to the children for making ice cream in their play. This appears to support Fein's (1991) idea that children are not as concerned with the details of play as the script theory literature claims. This slot filler (Nelson & Gruendel, 1979) of making ice cream "stinky" was appealing to the children because they liked the idea of people eating stinky ice cream.

Both children referred to having "parts" to their play as if following a script, without the interviewer's previously using that word. Hannah described how she negotiated a play scenario of making ice cream with a friend.

H: Me and Suzy we each have different parts and Suzy gives out the cakes because we have agreed which part is what. And Suzy agrees, see I say she makes cakes and she jumps up and down and says "I want to make cakes" and I jump up and down and say "I'll make the ice cream" and so we both agree on it and then we do it.

Skeeter explained what each child's part is in his "laboratory" play at the sink area.

N: What about Hannah and Emily [in the tape they are playing on the other side of the classroom sink from Skeeter and are not pretending the same thing as Skeeter]?

S: Well, they are down there because the part is when they are down there they aren't making something bad like us so usually the fire starts over on the sand table.

Skeeter spoke of what "usually" is done in a play episode of laboratory, even though he had played it only once.

S: Well, what we usually do if we don't is we don't come down, we watch there in the lab to know when.

(Said in another part of the interview)

S: Well, he usually does, what I usually do is I tap on him [Kenny] like this and if I can, hear his heart beating.

Hannah and Skeeter's use of the word "part" and Skeeter's use of the word "usually" made their play appear to follow a set flow of events similar to a script (Shank & Abelson, 1977). By following a script, the children were able to predict events and know how to act (Nelson & Gruendel, 1979). For example, Hannah knew that by imitating the people at the ice cream store, she could convey the intent of her play (serving ice cream), her role (employee), and her friend's role (customers). Since the other players knew what to do, this resulted in one of her longest episodes of sociodramatic play.

Emotive Theory

During the interviews, the first author asked the children questions to explore their understanding of the emotional side of their play. Generally, their responses were short, and occasionally they did not respond at all. Hannah was able to express her favorite and least favorite roles (mermaid, tree), what a sad theme would be (the prince that she marries drowns), and why she liked to enact the role of mother (changing diapers) and baby (can ask to have diapers changed and take a nap). However, when asked to name a scary theme to play, she stared and was silent for the only time in all the sessions. When the first author told her that a scary theme that she played was going to the doctor to get a shot, Hannah seemed curious at first but then switched the subject.

Even though Hannah answered all but one question describing the emotional side of her play, she did not elaborate on the answers the way she did with other questions.

Skeeter's responses to what would be a happy or scary play were concrete. He said that a happy type of play would be when a fellow classmate who tends to hit other children apologizes for hitting them. A scary type of play would be playing hide-and-seek because someone must say, "Boo." When asked why he does not like to play a father role, he said, "I don't know." After further probing to find an answer, he was silent. He was able to tell the first author that his favorite pretend play is being an inventor.

While watching the scene of Skeeter pretending to be a baby and play-fighting with David, the first author asked him what he was doing in the scene. He quickly replied, "Fighting," but then later when she asked if he was fighting, he lowered his voice and said, "No." He kept looking to the other room where his parents were present. He appeared to have been embarrassed that he was "fighting," even though he knew that he was only pretending. He then tried to justify his fighting by saying that the children playing with him knew that he was pretending.

N: What are you two doing there?

S: We're fighting there. (giggling)

N: You're fighting? (giggling)

N: So Suzy is the mom. So when you were playing with David, what were you doing?

S: Uh huh.

N: Were you fighting?

S: No. (He lowered his voice and appeared embarrassed. He looked into the kitchen.)

N: Were you just playing pretend fighting? (Said to show interviewer understood that he was only pretending so that he would not upset his parents.)

S: Uh huh. They [other children] know because of what we were doing.

N: Yeah, it looked like you were smiling (in the play scenario). Like you were just pretending.

During another time in a session, Skeeter looked to the room where his parents were when asked a question about emotions. During his play in the classroom, he pretended to be a baby a few times. When the first author asked, "And you like to play the baby?" he responded, "Sorta, yeah" while looking in the other room. This may have been due to the arrival of a baby sister two months prior. He may have been working through emotions regarding his new sibling that he does not yet understand, so he was uncomfortable with the question.

The children's inability to elaborate or even answer the questions regarding emotions supports Fein's (1989) explanation that there is a subconscious aspect to symbolic play. Fein explained that as children develop their ability to create symbols, the tie between that which is signified and that which signifies becomes looser and even unclear. Children may not always understand why the emotional arousal is present in pretense, but it still exists and can be very strong for children. Skeeter associated emotions to enacting the role of baby, but he did not have the emotional or cognitive developmental ability to retrace the steps of why he associated good feelings to playing baby. Hannah was able to say that she liked playing baby because she can have her diapers changed, but this response was still very concrete. Changing diapers had associations with emotions that she did not or could not describe (being taking care of).

"To Tell the Truth, I'm a Real Chemist": Distinctions in Pretense of Role Play

While watching the videotapes, the children were repeatedly asked the question, "Who are you pretending to be here?" or "Are you pretending to be someone?" Surprisingly, the children most often replied that they were not pretending to be someone. For example, when Skeeter and the first author watched the segment of videotape in which he was pretending to make ice cream in the media table filled with shaving cream he was asked to tell when he was pretending to be someone. His very quick response was that he was not pretending to be somebody. The quickness in his reply and the directive tone in his voice indicated that he was shocked that the first author would ask him such a question.

N: Let me know when you are pretending to be somebody.

S: Well, I'm not pretending to be somebody at all.

N: The whole time you are not?

S: Uh huh.

N: So then who are you here?

S: Skeeter. (said very quickly)

After listing the instances when the children said that they were pretending and not pretending to be someone, a distinction between the types of roles being enacted became apparent.

Scenes in which the children said that they were not pretending to be someone included Hannah making cookies, Hannah caring for a doll, Skeeter making experiments in the laboratory, and both Hannah and Skeeter playing "ice cream." These roles were defined by Garvey (1977) as functional roles. A functional role is used to enact the script, like a server of food. Interestingly, the children did not think that they had to pretend to be someone to enact these roles. On the other hand, Skeeter and Hannah said that they were pretending when they were taking the role of babies in their play. This role is, according to Garvey (1977), relational. Also, when asked, "What are some roles you could pretend to be?" they responded an airplane pilot, spy, chef, firefighter, nurse, mermaid, and inventor. These are what Garvey (1977) defines as character roles, either stereotypic or fictional.

Unlike adults who see all role-playing as pretense, Skeeter and Hannah appear to be making a distinction depending on the type of role. Also, as seen in a latter example, the same rules for when it is pretending for them do not apply to their playmates. During the first session, the first author asked Hannah if she ever pretended to be someone, and she immediately referred to the dress-up clothes in her closet.

N: Do you ever pretend to be somebody else?

H: Well, I have dressing stuff in my room and I pretend to be somebody.

(Later in conversation)

H: And sometimes we pretend to be other things too.

N: Like what?

H: Like, all sorts of things, I can't explain every single thing cause my dresser is filled to the top.

In the last session, after Hannah said that she was not pretending to be the mother of her doll when she played with it, the first author asked her if she could give an example of when she was pretending to be someone with her doll. She first described going to the hospital with a big belly and giving birth and then being a nurse to the baby.

N: So let's say you took Shelline [doll] to the, at the hospital still, let's say she was sick. Could you pretend something then, could you pretend to be someone then?

H: I could well I could pretend she had an invisible mom, there was someone else her mom and I was the hospital girl, and the baby would lay down and I would (does pretend motion like fixing the doll).

N: So that's pretending?

H: Yeah, that's pretending.

Although Hannah said she did not have to pretend to be the mother of her doll, she did describe similar play with the doll by her friend Suzy.

N: I have a question, Shelline is your baby, so when Suzy holds it and takes care of it, she has to pretend to be somebody?

H: She pretends.

Skeeter explained that if the first author wanted to be a detective, she had to acquire certain props (credit card, license plate, and jet fuel). It appears that for the children to see a role as pretend, there must be a change in the appearance or capability of the person, including costumes, props, or doing something that is not possible (giving birth or being a nurse). When the children were making cookies or an experiment, they did not have to change themselves to engage in the play. They were not playing as if they were someone else (Bretherton, 1989). They saw themselves as Hannah and Skeeter playing, not Hannah and Skeeter, a baker or chemist, playing. When they were babies, there was a change in their behavior. They cried and sucked their thumbs. They were acting as if they were babies. They also referred to themselves as other people. Here are their descriptions while watching themselves playing "babies."

H: I was so mad at her [other friend playing with her].

N: You were mad at her? Why?

H: Cause she hit Hannah the baby.

N: She hit Hannah the baby?

H: Yes.

N: Emily the baby hit Hannah the baby?

H: Yes.

N: So here you are still playing babies. Oh did you see who came by? Who is that? [referring to a child dressed as a tiger going by to where Skeeter, Randy, Suzy, and David were on the couch]

S: That's the tiger. Randy has to go after that because we pretend that that scares the babies so the dad has to go fight it off.

N: Oh the dad went to go fight off the tiger. So to protect the babies.

S: Uh huh, while the mom stays with us the babies.

The idea that the children must change themselves to pretend may be the reason that Hannah said that she was not pretending to be the mother to her doll. When asked if she was pretending to be a mom to her doll, she responded, "No, no, no way!" Garvey (1977) stated that some functional roles, like mother, can also be relational roles. Hannah treated being a "mother" as if it was a functional role. Hannah may not think that she is pretending to be the mother because she does not have to change herself to be a mother. She only needs to carry out the function of caring for a baby. Perhaps the type of doll that Hannah was caring for was responsible for this. This doll was highly realistic; it cried, ate, and even urinated. Hannah may not have felt the need to pretend with this doll because it was so realistic. Hannah may have said that Suzy was pretending when she played with Hannah's doll because the doll did not belong to Suzy. Suzy has to somehow change herself to have ownership of the doll.

Along this line, Skeeter was also engaged in a functional role during his "experiment" play. Since Skeeter is actually using materials during his experimenting, he may not think that he needs to pretend. His mother and teacher also agreed that since the materials are similar to what real experimenters use (baking soda, vinegar), he was actually a 5-year-old experimenter.

In both instances, they are performing actions with props and do not need to make a mental representation of the character (mother, experimenter). They are not changing anything about themselves to play. Hannah is pretending that the doll is real and that the food is real, but she herself is still the same. Skeeter is pretending that baking soda makes an explosion, but he himself is an actual experimenter.

Requiring a change to consider themselves, pretending shows pretense as a physical act. This supports Lillard's (1993b) suggestion that children understand their pretense as an action before they understand it as a mental representation. When asked about pretense, Skeeter and Hannah did not emphasize the importance of a mental image but focused more on the action made during pretense. For example, they made references to needing props and changing their behaviors in order to pretend.

The children's mothers offered interesting interpretations of why the children did not think that they were pretending. Greta reported that while trying to encourage Hannah's self-esteem, she tells Hannah to "just be yourself" and "you don't have to look at other people and wish that you could be who they are." Greta proposed that this might have an effect on Hannah's role-play. Greta also stated that Hannah does most of her play in her room with her brother, so Greta did not exactly know what kind of play she engaged in. Greta did report that she had never heard Hannah say that she was someone else.

Alice confirmed the finding that Skeeter did not say that he pretends to be someone when playing. When in his laboratory at home (behind a chair and under a table), Skeeter pretends that there are people there with him (Charles Lindbergh), but Skeeter never pretended to be someone else. She said that when Skeeter is alone, he does not engage in the type of symbolic play where he takes on a role, like an animal or other person. Occasionally, when playing with a younger female neighbor, Skeeter will be the father in the play at the neighbor's request.

"Only Boys Can be Pilots and Only Girls Can Be Flight Attendants": How Gender Affects Role-Play

Both Hannah and Skeeter agreed that females could not pretend to take on male roles, and vice versa. However, children could take on adult and baby roles. Their ability to cross the generation line but not the gender line follows Garvey's (1977) and Miller and Garvey's (1984) findings. Skeeter explained that a girl could take on a male role if she was not imitating reality. Skeeter's response that girls could not be pilots is interesting because his mother said that Skeeter says Amelia Earhart lives in their house. Although he has extensive knowledge of a female pilot, he still said that girls could not be pilots.

Here, the interviewer asks Skeeter if she could pretend to play pilot with him:

S: Yeah, but only boys can be pilots only girls can be flight attendants.

N: Oh, ok. So if I wanted to pretend to play airplane with you . . .

S: You would be a flight attendant.

N: And you would be . . .

S: A pilot.

N: A pilot I see.

S: Or the co-pilot. Of course, I think co-pilots can be a girl.

N: Oh, co-pilots can be a girl. I wonder why we [girls] can be a co-pilot and not pilot, hmm. That's interesting, so even if it's just for pretend they can't be it.

S: Well you know what, you can but if you want to play like real life, that's how it goes.

During the second session, Hannah was asked if Skeeter could be the mother in their play, and she quickly laughed in disapproval. At the end of the third session, without prompting, Hannah stated that Skeeter had asked to be the mother in their play in the classroom and that she now thought that he could be the mother.

H: Do you remember that question one time you said "Can Skeeter be a mom?" And Skeeter said "Can I be a mom?" in class one time. [Laughs as if she's amazed]

N: Oh, and what happened?

H: And one time he wanted to be a sister and one time he wanted to be the baby girl baby.

N: And what did you do?

H: Well, we didn't do anything [said as if I should know that].

N: Was he the mom, did he pretend to be the mom?

H: Yes, and the baby and the sister.

N: That's so interesting.

H: Baby girl, a girl baby, a girl sister, and the mom.

N: So he could be all those things [said like a realization].

H: Yeah, if he wanted to, and Suzy could be the brother or the dad or the baby boy.

Ants, Scorpions, and Dolls: Descriptions of Object Substitutions

During the sessions, the first author asked questions that would evoke what the children thought about each level of object substitution (Fein, 1975; Matthews, 1977). Most questions were, "Could you use a [blank] for a [blank]?" or "If you did not have that [blank] object, what else could you use?" However, the most intriguing remarks came spontaneously. The children demonstrated many levels of object substitution in their symbolic play on the videotapes; however, these questions were designed to understand what they thought about object substitution.

One result was that Hannah did not consider objects that had a functional level of substitution (a plastic cup as a cup) (Matthews, 1977) to require pretense. Hannah does not have to pretend with her baby doll because it is so highly realistic (eats and cries) and has accessories that are really lifelike.

H: I don't pretend she's real, cause she's like a real baby because she goes, does all the stuff that real babies do.

This quote is not interpreted as Hannah's thinking the baby is actually real, but more as her stressing the point that the baby doll is like a real baby. This observation provides interesting support for Olszewki and Fuson's (1982) findings that highly prototypical objects can limit 5-year-old children's play. If Hannah does not think that she has to pretend with functional objects, then she may not extend her play in pretense. Actually, during the time that Hannah played with this doll in the classroom, she did not extend her play past caring for the baby. When it was suggested that she could make Play-doh food for the doll, she replied that she did not need to because the doll already had real packaged food. When asked what other objects the children could use in substitution for the objects that they had used in their play, they both suggested highly prototypical object substitutions. Hannah said a rolled-up piece of paper could become an ice cream cone, and Skeeter said the loft area could be used for a house. Hannah did not think that a pencil could be used to represent an ice cream cone because it would not be able to hold the ice cream, in this case, sand. Her inability to accept a low prototypical substitution is not typical of her age, since 5-year-old children are known to use low prototypical substitutions (Cole & La Voie, 1985; Fein, 1981).

The children were given an opportunity in the interviews to describe an insubstantial substitution (Matthews, 1977). In play, an insubstantial substitution occurs when the child either gestures or says that something is there when it is not. Hannah was asked, If she was in an empty room playing "ice cream shop," what could she do if she wanted to pretend a cone was there? Hannah was not able to say that she could just pretend the cone was there. Instead, she gave the following examples of what she could use.

H: If we were bored, and we had extra shirts on, just take our shirts off and use it as games [motions rolling up the shirts] [laughs]

N: What happens if you didn't even have that on?

H: We would be naked.

N: And what happens then if you wanted to play ice cream?

H: Take our nose off to pretend they were cups and we would take, actually our ears off to pretend they were cups and we would take our hands off to pretend they were cones.

Even though Hannah could not describe an insubstantial substitution for a cone, she continually made such substitutions while talking. She moved her hands to suggest rolling up a shirt and even holding an ice cream cone. She appeared to need what Vygotsky (1978) called a pivot in object substitution. She had to describe an actual object for the substitution, almost as a reference point for her understanding of the substitution. Vygotsky claimed that with age, children lessen this reliance on pivots during object substitution and eventually can make substitutions where the object used in pretense does not at all resemble the represented object. Hannah demonstrated this again when discussing her ice cream play in the classroom. On the videotape, her teacher asked for Chunky Monkey flavor ice cream, and Hannah scooped up sand and gave it to her. Another child later asked for bug and scorpion ice cream, and Hannah scooped the same sand and gave it to him. When asked to explain how she knew where which flavor was in a table with such a large amount of sand, her response was a description of what the flavor looked like.

H: For the bugs [bug ice cream] it's chocolate chips cause it's called bug ice cream because there are ants in it and it's really crazy cause there's ants, like ice cream they eat, and we call it bug ice cream cause ants are black and chocolate chips are black so we call it.

There really are no chocolate chips in the sand. However, instead of saying that she just pretends there are ants in the ice cream, she had to describe an in-between object (chocolate chips) that looked like ants. Interestingly, by saying that there were chocolate chips, she made an insubstantial substitution. However, it may have been too foreign for her to make a substitution for "ant ice cream," so she needed the chocolate chips as a reference point or pivot.

In the next description, she explained how Skeeter, who was also playing "ice cream shop" with her, knew that the sand represented scorpion ice cream. Again she used a pivot to describe the scorpions.

H: And like the chocolate ants are chocolate chips, well scorpion, do you know why we call it scorpion ice cream they have these red kind of bubble gum in it and you chew it all up and it looks like scorpion. They are shaped like scorpion and the chocolate chips are shaped like ants.

N: Oh, so that's why he [Skeeter], he's pretending that those little red things are scorpions. [On the videotape, Skeeter said there were scorpions in the sandbox.]

H: Yeah.

N: But are there little red things in the sand box?

H: Well, no, we are just pretending.

N: So, Hannah, you are pretending that there are red things in the ice cream and Skeeter is pretending that the red things are scorpions. I get it.

When Skeeter was asked how he could play ice cream if there was nothing there, he simply said he would get a bucket and pretend there was ice cream inside it.

N: If you are playing in a room and you wanted to play ice cream like you were at school that day, and you didn't have those toys to play with, what else do you think you could pretend to be ice cream? What kinds of things could you use to be ice cream?

S: Well, I'd just imagine there was ice cream.

N: Just imagine, like what?

S: Take a box full of nothing and then just pretend fill it with stuff and stir it (gestures with hands).

N: So you can just take a bucket and pretend there's ice cream in it?

S: Uh huh.

N: And what could you use for the cone?

S: Pretend you go [gestures holding a cone and eating from it].

Since children's ability to make object substitutions develops with age (Fein, 1981), it is not surprising that Hannah was unable to describe an insubstantial substitution. It may also stem from Hannah's interpretation of the question. She may have thought that she was being asked for another object that she could use.

For Real-Real? Fantasy versus Reality

The children were asked questions to elicit their thoughts on the distinction between fantasy and reality in their play. Since the interviews were conversational in their structure, the children did not have force-choice answers as in more structured experiments like Samuel and Taylor (1994) or Flavell et al. (1987).

Therefore, the children's responses did not reveal as much of their actual understanding of the difference between fantasy and reality as expected, but the responses did demonstrate an interesting side to the children's view on fantasy and reality. During the four weeks of videotaping and during the interview sessions, the children did not appear to confuse fantasy with reality in their behavior. For example, the children did not eat plastic food or run out of the room while pretending that there was a fire.

It appeared that the children were able to understand the different layers of pretense and act within those layers (Lillard, 1993a). However, when questioned if something was "real or not real," they reacted in a way that suggests they wanted to keep the illusion of pretense present (Giffin, 1984). This conclusion comes from not only their verbal responses but also their non-verbal cues, such as whispering or smiling as in jest.

Both Hannah and Skeeter's responses below indicated more of a desire to believe and act imaginatively than confusion in distinguishing between fantasy and reality.

N: Now can I ask you something, is it really going to burn you those experiments?

S: Particularly, at least if you put a lot a lot of mixture, yes.

N: But when you are playing here, is that a real experiment or just a pretend experiment?

S: Actually they can be real if you put enough bad stuff in.

N: Then you really have to put your gloves on.

S: And then the more and more you experiment with the same experiment it will turn into a real explosion.

While watching a videotape segment of Skeeter and Kenny playing in the laboratory, Skeeter told me that Kenny died because the chemicals (sand, water, and soap) that he was mixing together killed him. He was then asked if his chemical was real.

N: Is it a real chemical?

S: I try not to breathe mine [chemical] because I try to make mine real. I try not to breathe it.

It appeared that Skeeter wanted to believe that his pretend scenarios of chemicals and death of his friend were real. This desire to believe in fantasy was also present in Hannah's answers. In the following example she spoke in a quiet voice when proclaiming that the oven that she had made to cook Play-doh cookies was real.

N: Hannah can I ask you something? Is it a real oven?

H: [in a quiet, soft voice] It's a pretend oven.

When Hannah wanted to demonstrate the "ice cream" episode that she had played in the classroom during our interview at her home, she took out puzzle boxes to represent the ice cream flavors. When the first author said the word "box" in reference to the pretend ice cream flavors, she was upset that the illusion of fantasy was broken.

The interviewer asked what Hannah was doing in a play episode:

H: I'll show what we are doing [goes to cabinet]. Say this is the ice cream [takes out puzzle box].

N: The box is the ice cream.

H: Well, don't say the box.

During the conversations about pretense and reality, the difficulty in questioning children about their understanding became apparent. As Taylor (1997) explained, when children are asked questions about play, they must step outside the play scenario to answer them. The child may then still continue to act "playful" in the response. Hannah and Skeeter demonstrated a "playfulness" with their desire to act imaginatively. Another obstacle was found in the use of the word "real." Whereas fantasy and reality are usually thought of as two opposing concepts, the children showed that during the act of pretense, an item may be and people may act "for real." In this example the first author asked Hannah if the oven that she drew on a piece of paper was real.

H: Well, no, it's a real oven.

N: It's a real oven.

H: Yeah, for us, we're just pretending.

N: So it's real when you pretend.

H: Yes, well, the cookies are not pretend either.

N: The cookies are not pretend?

H: No.

N: Can you eat those cookies?

H: [Nods yes]

N: You can eat those cookies right there that we are looking at right now.

H: [strange voice with a smile] Yes.

N: All the time?

H: [Nods no with an embarrassed look]

N: Just for pretend you can eat them. I get it.

People may also act "for real" during pretend. Hannah described her teacher pretending to eat ice cream made out of sand as being real within the terms of pretend.

N: So here she [teacher] is eating it [ice cream].

H: Yes.

N: Is she really eating it?

H: No, just for pretend.

N: She's pretend eating it.

H: But for pretend she's really eating it.

N: For pretend she really eats it, there's a difference.

IMPLICATIONS

This methodology opens avenues for both learning more about children's understanding of play and using videotapes as a methodology to study play. Through their responses and behaviors, the children shared their ideas about a number of important aspects of play. They were better able to discuss the script of their play than any emotions that they attached to their play. This observation supports Fein's research that children do not always understand their emotions during play (Fein, 1989). In keeping with Lillard's (1993b, 1994, 1996) work on pretense, it appeared that the children did not yet understand that pretense requires mental representation. Gender affected their choice of role-play, as seen in Garvey's work (1977). Finally they demonstrated that while they understood the difference between fantasy and reality, they preferred to sustain the playfulness of fantasy in their responses (Taylor, 1997).

The edited videotaped segments of the children's play served as a wonderful catalyst to spark conversation between the children and researcher. Having a tangible illustration of abstract concepts such as object substitution or roles depicted in the videotaped play segments, the interviewer was able to ask specific questions about complex concepts that otherwise may not have been possible. For example, the interviewer and children were able to pause the video and refer to actual images of the children's play. This was a common occurrence during all the interviews. The videotapes also provided a distance between the children and their actual play. This distance allowed the children to look at their play and answer questions about it without being disrupted in their play. The use of clips of their own play appeared to maintain a meaningful context for the children to reflect. Further, the multiple interview sessions allowed the researcher to spread out the questioning about themes, roles, object substitution, and the distinction between fantasy and reality.

Due to the small number of participants, the findings of this study are better cast in the form of possible avenues for future research rather than as specific conclusions. The children were excited to view the tapes and discuss their play with an interested adult. Seeing play from the eyes of children and in their words may help researchers reclaim their sense of wonder about symbolic play.

REFERENCES

Bretherton, I. (1989). Pretense: Acting "as if." In J. J. Lockman & N. L. Hazen (Eds.), *Action in social context* (pp. 239–274). New York: Plenum Press.

Cole, D., & La Voie, J. (1985). Fantasy play and related cognitive development in 2- to 6-year olds. *Developmental Psychology, 21*, 233–240.

Copple, C., Cocking, R., & Matthews, W. (1984). Objects, symbols, and substitutes: The nature of the cognitive activity during symbolic play. In T. D. Yawkey & A. D. Pelligrini (Eds.), *Child's play: Developmental and applied* (pp. 105–124). Hillsdale, NJ: Erlbaum.

Corasaro, W. (1983). Script recognition, articulation and expansion in children's role-play. *Discourse Processes, 6*, 1–19.

Creasey, G., Jarvis, P., & Berk, L. (1998). Play and social competence. In O. N. Saracho & B. Spodek (Eds.), *Multiple perspectives on play in early childhood education* (pp. 116–143). Albany: State University of New York Press.

Fantuzzo, J., Coolahan, K., Mendez, J., McDermott, P., & Sutton-Smith, B. (1998). Contextually-relevant validation of peer play constructs with African American Head Start children: Penn interactive peer play scale. *Early Childhood Research Quarterly, 13*, 411–431.

Fein, G. (1975). A transformational analysis of pretending. *Developmental Psychology, 11*, 291–296.

Fein, G. (1981). Pretend play in childhood: An integrated review. *Child Development, 52*, 1095–1118.

Fein, G. (1986). The affective psychology of play. In A. W. Gottfried & C. C. Brown (Eds.), *Play interactions* (pp. 31–50). Lexington, MA: Lexington Books.

Fein, G. (1987). Pretend play: Creativity and consciousness. In D. Gorlitz & J. Wohlwill (Eds.), *Curiosity, imagination, and play* (pp. 283–305). Hillsdale, NJ: Erlbaum.

Fein, G. (1989). Mind, meaning, and affect: Proposals for a theory of pretense. *Developmental Review, 9*, 345–363.

Fein, G. (1991). Bloodsuckers, blisters, cooked babies, and other curiosities: Affective themes in pretense. In F. S. Kessel, M. H. Bornstein, & A. J. Sameroff (Eds.), *Contemporary constructions of the child* (pp. 143–158). Hillsdale, NJ: Erlbaum.

Flavell, J. H., Flavell, E. R., & Green, F. L. (1987). Young children's knowledge about the apparent-real and pretend-real distinctions. *Developmental Psychology, 23*, 16–22.

Garvey, C. (1977). *Play*. Cambridge, MA: Harvard University Press.

Garvey, C. (1982). Communication and the development of social role play. In D. L. Forbes & M. T. Greenberg (Eds.), *Children's planning strategies* (pp. 81–102). San Francisco: Jossey-Bass.

Giffin, H. (1984). The coordination of meaning in the creation of a shared make believe reality. In I. Bretherton (Ed.), *Symbolic play: The development of social understanding* (pp. 73–100). New York: Academic Press.

Harris, P. L., Brown, E., Marriot, C., Whittal, S., & Harmer, S. (1991). Monsters, ghosts, and witches: Testing the limits of the fantasy-reality distinction in young children. *British Journal of Developmental Psychology, 9*, 105–123.

Johnson, C., & Harris, P. L. (1994). Magic: Special but not excluded. *British Journal of Developmental Psychology, 12*, 35–51.

Lillard, A. (1993a). Pretend play skills and the child's theory of mind. *Child Development, 64*, 348–371.

Lillard, A. (1993b). Young children's conceptualization of pretense: Action or parental representation state? *Child Development, 64*, 372–386.

Lillard, A. (1994). Making sense of pretense. In C. Lewis & P. Mitchell (Eds.), *Children's early understanding of mind: Origins and development* (pp. 211–234). Hove, U.K.: Earlbaum.

Lillard, A. (1996). Body or mind: Children's categorizing of pretense. *Child Development, 67*, 1717–1734.

Matthews, W. (1977). Modes of transformation in the initiation of fantasy play. *Developmental Psychology, 13*, 212–216.

Miller, P., & Garvey, C. (1984). Mother–baby role play: Its origins in social support. In I. Bretherton (Ed.), *Symbolic play: The development of social understanding* (pp. 101–130). New York: Academic Press.

Nelson, K., & Gruendel, J. (1979). At morning it's lunchtime: A scriptal view of children's dialogues. *Discourse Processes, 2*, 73–94.

Nelson, K., & Seidman, S. (1984). Playing with scripts. In I. Bretherton (Ed.), *Symbolic play: The development of social understanding* (pp. 45–72). New York: Academic Press.

Olszewski, P., & Fuson, K. (1982). Verbally expressed fantasy play of preschoolers as a function of toy structure. *Developmental Psychology, 18*, 57–61.

Rubin, K., Fein, G., & Vandenberg, B. (1983). Play. In P. H. Mussen (Series Ed.) & E. M. Hetherington (Vol. Ed.), *Handbook of child psychology: Vol. 4. Socialization, personality, and social development* (pp. 693–774). New York: Wiley.

Rubin, K., & Pepler, D. (1980). The relationship of child's play to social cognitive growth and development. In F. C. Foot, A. J. Chapman, & J. R. Smith (Eds.), *Friendship and social relationships in children* (pp. 209–234). New York: Wiley.

Samuels, A., & Taylor, M. (1994). Children's ability to distinguish fantasy events from real-life events. *British Journal of Developmental Psychology, 12*, 417–427.

Shank, R., & Abelson, R. (1977). *Scripts, plans, goals and understanding.* Hillsdale, NJ: Erlbaum.

Short-Meyerson, K., & Abbeduto, L. (1997). Preschoolers' communications during scripted interactions. *Journal of Child Language, 24*, 469–493.

Snow, C., Shonkoff, F., Lee, K., & Levin, H. (1986). Learning to play doctor: Effects of sex, age, and experience in hospital. *Discourse Processes, 9*, 461–473.

Stockinger Forys, S., & McCunce-Nicolich, L. (1984). Shared pretend: Sociodramatic play at 3 years of age. In I. Bretherton (Ed.), *Symbolic play: The development of social understanding* (pp. 159–194). New York: Academic Press.

Taylor, B. J., & Howell, R. J. (1973). The ability of three-, four-, and five-year-old children to distinguish fantasy from reality. *Journal of Genetic Psychology, 122*, 315–318.

Taylor, M. (1997). The role of creative control and culture in children's fantasy/reality judgments. *Child Development, 68*, 1015–1017.

Trawick-Smith, J. (1990). The effects of realistic versus non-realistic play materials on young children's symbolic transformation of objects. *Journal of Research in Childhood Education, 5*, 27–35.

Ungerer, J., Zelazo, P., Kearsely, R., & O'Leary, K. (1981). Developmental changes in the representation of objects in symbolic play from 18 to 34 months of age. *Child Development, 52*, 186–195.

Vygotsky, L. (1978). *Mind in society.* Cambridge, MA: Harvard University Press.

Wellman, H. M., & Estes, D. (1986). Early understanding of mental entities: A reexamination of childhood realism. *Child Development, 57*, 910–923.

Wooley, J. (1997). Thinking about fantasy: Are children fundamentally different thinkers and believers from adults? *Child Development, 68*, 991–1011.

Chapter 10

Rural Children's Play in the Natural Environment

Betty A. Beach

INTRODUCTION

The farm pond across the road became the site of an imaginary kingdom for a group of 1950s-era rural children. In constructing their private world, they built a simple raft to navigate around the pond, created a geography and a map for their kingdom (including an island, which they named), wrote a constitution to govern it, learned how to sew and made a flag for it, and listed punishments, which included dunking recalcitrant members in the pond. For several years, this multi-aged, mixed-gender group invented play scripts around this special place, inserting variations and new directions as inspired. The big boys even walked up to the local cemetery as reconstruction was being carried out and, spotting an ancient coffin with remains containing only handles and a skull, asked politely for the latter as a prop for ongoing pirate play in their kingdom.

This 50-year old recollection, from an ongoing study of rural children's play past and present, illustrates the persistent hold of childhood play experiences in the human consciousness. Memoirists, ecological psychologists, oral historians, and play researchers all recognize the deep-rootedness of early play experiences in the human memory, impressed by their tenacity and clarity even after half a century or more has passed. Although interpretation of such play varies according to the researcher's disciplinary background, the sheer commonality of such memory evidences a widely shared bond of human experience. Analyses of these retrospectives (principally collected from eminent, creative figures rather than ordinary people) have insightfully explored the role of such play in human development, identifying common themes that appear to contribute to the individual's psychological growth (Cobb, 1977).

Regularly, one prominent theme threads through such recollections: the significance of the natural environment as the setting for such memories. Just as in the farm pond example depicted above, research consistently finds that adults recall the outdoors as central to their childhood experiences, affectionately remembering favorite outdoor places "out of all proportion to the actual amount of time spent there" (Chawla, 1992, p. 76). Looking back, adults cherished these outdoor places as sources of refuge, peace, and ecstasy (Chawla, 1990; Dovey, 1990; Schiavo, 1988). Trees, forts, hideout holes, ditches, rocks, and other natural sites were examples of specially remembered places, starkly eloquent reminders of the significant role played by the natural environment in children's development. The disproportionate pervasiveness of natural sites in adult memories and their connection with treasured play spaces engender thought-provoking questions about the role of play in the human experience. Why is this such a compelling memory? How do the natural world and play reciprocally influence each other? How does the social context in which children develop affect the availability and practice of outdoor play? Although adult memories testify to the spell cast by early outdoor experiences, regrettably few studies have focused on children's concurrent experiences of play. In the absence of substantial direct evidence from children's lives, some of the answers to these important questions can be only fragmentary.

CHILDREN, PLAY, AND THE NATURAL ENVIRONMENT

These powerful outdoor play recollections do not surprise one group of researchers interested in children's developing concepts of the natural environment. Writing from an evolutionary perspective, Nabhan and Trimble (1994) argue that children need experience with wild places, reflecting a recognition that, as biological beings, we have an affinity for the natural environment around us. Such biophilia is innate, and interaction with nature is a fundamental necessity for healthy human development (Wilson, 1993). Young children commonly manifest this evolutionary concern in their fascination not with the big picture and grand sweep of nature but with the tiny and seemingly inconsequential. Unlike adults, children prefer the intimate and cloistered environments of the cozy den in the bushes rather than the cliffside panorama, responding to the "ancient animal notion encoded within us: the simple comfort of the nest" (Nabhan and Trimble, 1994, p. 7). Thus, children's play, the natural world, and cherished spaces are inevitably connected, a necessary, fundamental core of the human experience. Indeed, writers from this perspective worry that as children are increasingly cut off from the opportunity to roam, confined instead to adult-designed and -constructed play areas that are barren of the natural materials so vital to their development, fewer occasions for productive childhood will exist (Rivkin, 1995). Such constriction would be disastrous not only for individual children but also for our collective ecological well-being since, proponents argue, direct contact with nature is a necessary precondition for developing an ecological consciousness. Children who encounter the natural world through play in their young lives are far more likely to become adults who value and understand nature's role in human ecology; children who lack this direct, daily experience (as in the case of perhaps most non-rural children) are less inclined to appreciate the natural world and more prone to seek solutions through technological domination (Chawla & Hart, 1995).

Child development researchers offer a second vantage point for examining outdoor play. Although play researchers recognize a number of different categories of children's play, many acknowledge that the free-flowing, imaginative play recollected by memoirists is the quintessence of childhood. Labels may vary—imaginative play, pretend play, sociodramatic play, make-believe—propelled by more elaborate schemes for analyzing play, but these researchers share an interest in children's unfettered play because of both its relevance to healthy child development and its role as a singular bellwether regarding children's place in contemporary society. Thus, their observations extend beyond issues of individual psychological development to the conditions of contemporary childhood as they seek to understand play's place in the child's world and in the larger society.

Consistent with previous findings, play researchers suggest that children's imaginative play is fostered by a "sacred space," unencumbered time, and simple, minimally structured objects (Singer & Singer, 1990, pp. 11–18). Although such sacred spaces dedicated to pretend play can occur anywhere, they are frequently outdoors, allowing the child to capitalize on a natural setting and to employ natural objects (sticks, stones, dirt) in creating elaborative imaginative play. Thus, an accessible natural environment would seem to provide conditions that permit and enhance children's imaginative play; some observers would consider such accessibility a fundamental requirement of childhood, while others might argue for more attention to how urban children access these needs for sacred space, time, and simple objects. Most would concur that unfettered space, time, and objects are indispensable to children's imaginary play.

Against this backdrop, prominent play observers like Brian Sutton-Smith bemoan the encroachment of adults on children's imaginative play. They see play as increasingly regimented, dominated, and "domesticated" by adults. As children's free play becomes roped in by adults, confined to institutions such as schools, child-care programs, organized recreation, and play groups, its quintessentially child-centered characteristics diminish. Thus, one would expect to see fewer examples of children at play in the natural environment, fewer future memories of sacred spaces, time, and objects, and presumably fewer corresponding benefits to healthy human development. Sutton-Smith (1986) argues that such a sea change in children's play epitomizes a pervasive social change as we move from a culture that once valued communal sociability to extreme individualism. Play must now prepare the child for the solitary endeavor as "success in the modern world is generally a relatively lonely pursuit" (p. 23). In this evolution, children's play must be reined in and commodified to prepare children to become consumers, reliant on the commercial toy industry for direction. This removal from the imaginative possibilities of the natural environment helps the "growing persons learn to abstract themselves from the world around" (p. 24).

Nostalgic images of rural children at play in fields, woods, and village neighborhoods provide an implicit backdrop for contemporary concerns about the erosion of children's play. Enduring American cultural beliefs still honor the notion of the countryside as a fount of simple virtues, a more unsullied, less complicated habitat for child development, creating

in the United States an adult's perception of the child's world . . . colored by the myth of the boyhood enshrined in such literary creations as Huckleberry Finn and Tom Sawyer . . . [a child who is] an undomesticated being who thrives in open spaces, close to nature. (Tuan, 1978, p. 26).

This image of the unfettered child at play in the natural environment is sharpened by its contrast with the more widely documented commentary on non-rural children's play. Observers of urban and, increasingly, suburban life note that children have essentially been removed from public spaces and public life, segregated into age cohorts dominated by adult-organized environments and cocooned into a car that "functions as a protective capsule from which the child observes the world but does not experience it directly through encounters with others" (Sibley, 1995, p. 51). The juxtaposition between the free-roaming, unsupervised rural child and the unaccompanied urban child who is perceived as out of place and endangered geographically represents this contrast (James, Jenks, & Prout, 1998, pp. 47–52).

As children's play becomes increasingly domesticated and regimented by adults, limited to boundaries established and overseen by adults, pressured by commercial interests, and subject to intensifying demands for academic achievement, it is reasonable to inquire whether unfettered play still exists. Pessimistically, Hart (1992, p. 23) notes the decline in the industrialized world of "free (unprogrammed) play with peers in resource-rich outdoor settings" due to "fear for children's outdoor safety, parents' work patterns, and growing pressures for academic achievement." Similarly, Rivkin (1995) examines multiple factors that have eroded children's outdoor play as she describes "vanishing habitats and access" (pp. 1–14) in urging a restoration of outdoor play possibilities.

If any contemporary setting can still offer children the sacred spaces, time, and outdoor materials of play, one would assume that a rural community might do so. Unfortunately, compared with the enormous amount of research effort expended on the twin foci of adult life—work and love—children's play, although an intimate and central piece of their development, garners minimal attention from social scientists. Tinier still is the amount devoted to rural children. Even the increasing interest in ecological studies of childhood among child development researchers has produced few studies examining the rural environments of play. The direct evidence that does exist is primarily non-rural and institutional; that is, it examines children in the institutions created for them by adults. Rather than analyzing children's unfettered play in its natural habitat, most studies focus on children in child-care centers, schools, recreation programs, and other places where "the boundaries of children's experiences are patrolled by adults" (Graue & Walsh, 1995, p. 144). Consequently, we have very limited knowledge of rural children's encounters with their natural habitat.

PROCEDURE

For the past several years, I have been studying children's play in two rural communities, trying to assess the status of outdoor play. Pieces of the study reported here address some of the issues raised about children's encounters with play in the natural environment. Through interview, naturalistic observation, and document analysis (historical documents and newspapers), I examined play in outdoor places, trying to determine whether children still experience rich outdoor play or whether, in Tuan's (1978) words, "only in the poorer parts of rural America do children still grow up with nature woven into the texture of their lives" (p. 27).

Two rural Maine towns, both with populations under 2,500, were the sites of the study. Both have traditional natural resource-based economies now declining and evolving toward tourism, both contain comparably proportionate percentages of children in their population, and neither is on the fringe of a larger urbanized center that might dominate their economy or social structure. One town, which I call Eastbay, is a traditional fishing community located on the Atlantic coast; the second town, which I call Westmount, is located in the western Maine mountains, a traditional logging and farming community. Results reported here are part of a larger study of child development in rural communities that utilized interview, document analysis, and naturalistic observation.

This report on children's play is based on 100 hours of naturalistic observation of children under the age of 12 at play in the two communities, semi-structured interviews with 15 adults, and analysis of local historical and municipal documents. Data collection and analysis were rooted in a qualitative approach. Qualitative research can be especially fruitful in situations where phenomena have been minimally explored, where the ecological context is a crucial component, where participants may be non-verbal or otherwise susceptible to adult influence, and where a non-interventionist stance on the researcher's part is vital (Goodwin & Goodwin, 1996, pp. 107–113). Consistent with a qualitative approach, data analysis in this study followed data collection by "half a step" (Goodwin & Goodwin, 1996, p. 119).

Naturalistic observations of children's play were collected systematically in one-hour walks around each town conducted at varying times of the day and differing seasons of the year. Event sampling consisted of every appearance of children in publicly visible areas; sites included streets, sidewalks, open spaces, parks, commercial areas, woods, beaches, and yards. Each observation was coded for number of children involved, apparent ages, genders, activity, and material of play. Observations were initiated in the summer of 1997 and continued through fall, winter, spring, and summer of 1998 in order to capture the effect of seasonality on children's play.

I then contrasted what I found from 100 hours of naturalistic observation of children's play with what I learned from interviewing 15 adults who had grown up in the same communities in an effort to identify subtle changes that may have affected and continue to affect children's experience of outdoor play. Each semi-structured interview took place in the adult's home or workplace, lasting 1.5 to 2 hours. Questions and conversation focused on the adults' own experiences of play, their comments on play activities and spaces in the towns, and their observations on the current context of play in their community.

Finally, historical and municipal documents (e.g., historical society records, town newspapers, census, and planning documents) were analyzed to create a more complete understanding of the conditions and changing context of play in the two communities.

RESULTS: HABITATS OF PLAY, THEN AND NOW

First, rural children are indeed still visibly roaming their communities in a free-ranging manner, generally unaccompanied by adults. Via foot or the ubiquitous bike, they have ready access to local terrain in backyards, streetscapes, streams, undeveloped areas, the seashore, and common play gathering spaces. Children utilized these spaces for play ranging from building snow forts to digging in sand, kicking stones, and staging dramatic play. Their ready presence throughout the town kept them in the public eye but not under adult vigilance, as fewer than one-third of the observations involved adult presence, and these, principally, revolved around toddler-aged and preschool children. Curiously, children were *not* to be found in an environment built for them by adults: the school playground. The school playground in each town was usually devoid of children after school hours, echoing Hart's (1979, p. 430) observations that "even very well equipped playgrounds attract children for only a small part of their time outdoors." It would appear that children who have a choice of constructed or natural environments of play still prefer the latter.

What were children doing in their observed play? Analysis of their activities produced 60 distinct categories, ranging from carving, climbing, fishing, playing ball, and games such as hopscotch and hide-and-seek through quieter activities like reading, sitting under trees, and talking or watching. Children effortlessly utilized their natural environment for these activities—a grassy hill for rolling down, a wharf for jumping off into the sea, gardens and mud piles or sandpiles for digging—evidencing a familiarity and a casual accessibility to such a habitat. In contrast with urban children who may experience the natural outdoor habitat only through organized ventures like field trips, adult-chaperoned activities, or adult-determined play dates, children in these two rural towns easily entered and exited such environments throughout the day.

Children's play also incorporated the environment in a second way, one that is barely mentioned in research on children's play: the weather. People living in a climate with dramatic changes in season must attend to and attune themselves to changes in the environment. Despite such an obvious aspect of the natural world's influence on human life, it is surprisingly difficult to locate research addressing how children respond to these seasonal changes. Children's outdoor activities in these two towns were patently affected by seasonal change as children's clothing, play activities, and play materials metamorphosed in response to the weather. In winter, children skated on the town pond, ice-fished, built snow forts and snow people, skied, sledded, engaged in snowball fights and, despite bulkier clothing, moved more quickly around the town en route to warmth indoors. Spring and summer found them fishing, playing ball, climbing rocks, dawdling and pausing in their walks, jumping in puddles, and catching tadpoles, all activities clearly responsive to changes in the natural world around them. Although not formally trained ecologists, they certainly have a sense of how their play is fostered and confined by the outdoor setting.

Despite the pressures of commercialization from the toy industry, children were still employing natural objects in their play. Tuan (1978, p. 18) argued that "nature may indeed be prodigal of play objects, but it is not inevitable that children become aware of them and know what to do with them"; nonetheless, children were observed playing primarily with either objects from nature or tools linking them to the natural world (e.g., shovels for digging or hoes for gardening, fishing poles, snow-play related items such as shovels or sleds). Certainly and unsurprisingly, commercial items of play were present: the abundant, ubiquitous bikes, balls, swings, and, for toddlers, strollers. However, children were also observed playing with rocks and pebbles, leaf piles, sandpiles, dogs, seaweed, crabs, water, and sticks, among other similar objects. Such nature-related play objects outnumbered exclusively commercial items in both communities; of the stereotypically commercially popular toys, only one skateboard, one pair of rollerblades, and one outdoor trampoline were observed. These findings indicate that children have not abandoned objects from nature and indeed continue to incorporate their natural surroundings in their play. Favored sites of play, activities, and implements continue to connect children to their outdoor habitat.

Interviews with local adults two or three generations beyond these present-day children confirmed some of the continuities in rural children's play; outdoor play, roaming neighborhoods, and picking up and playing with scavenged items were common. Some of the activities and locations of play crossed generational boundaries. For example, some of the sacred spaces (the boulder on the town green, the woods behind a particular neighborhood, low water tidal flats, a dead end street) were remembered by 70-year olds and still used by 5-year olds. However, these interviews also revealed some of the changes in the context of that play that are subtly altering children's contemporary experiences, gradually bounding but by no means eliminating free-flowing play. Through examining these spaces at the intersection of nostalgic memory and contemporary empirical use, a play researcher can begin to piece together some tentative observations on the evolution of children's play.

Three principal themes contrasted interview memories with contemporary observations. Prompted principally by economic changes, each of these themes of difference suggests a limiting of the boundaries of unfettered play. Narrowing of common areas, shifts in housing patterns, and loss of adult support describe these categories of change. Although abundant opportunities for these rural children to encounter and utilize the natural environment in their daily play continue to exist, especially compared with the average non-rural child, incremental limitations suggest that future opportunities may be less assured.

Most apparent from interview data was a narrowing of common areas for play. A local pasture that served older generations as an amateur hillside ski area is now filled with a residential development. The same is true of a once-vacant wooded lot where boys acted out World War II battles of fantasies and younger children looked for monsters and of an extensive piece of wooded shore land where children played hide-and-seek in the moonlight. Such an obvious narrowing of children's outdoor play spaces is familiar to any observer living in a community under pressure for development and the presumed economic advantages that it engenders. Less apparent are some of the other means by which children's outdoor play spaces are reduced or confined: a whole network of shortcuts ("secret pathways," in one interviewee's words) throughout the town is gone now, replaced by parking lots or a new bank building or, in some cases, "no trespassing" signs by recent in-migrants to the towns. The loss of shortcuts, probably invisible to the adult community, fractured a child-centered universe fondly remembered by more than one interviewee.

Changes in schools also led to a limiting of children's spaces. The consolidation of schools in the late 1950s in one community closed a scattering of small, one- and two-room schoolhouses in favor of busing children to a central, in-town school building. Busing cut children off from a prime connection to their ecology—the walk to school. One interviewee remembered his leisurely, half-hour walks to school past interesting natural sites where he often lingered to catch frogs at the pond, chase snakes, or bury and hold funerals for dead animals encountered along the way. Similar recollections of the walk to school revealed a shared attentiveness to the environment as well as the collecting of interesting objects en route brought into the schoolroom for discussion.

Changes in patterns of schooling also affected school-yard play. A once unfenced school yard offered adjacent pine woods where one woman recalled utilizing many little natural spaces as playhouses. Pebbles, nuts, pinecones, and pine needles served as the materials for endless tea parties, while other children climbed trees and played hide-and-seek amid the wooded setting. Now, the school playground fences off these woods, and children are overseen by teachers who restrict their play to manufactured play structures. Thus, as schooling has come increasingly to dominate children's lives, it has also narrowed their opportunities for encounters with the natural environment, ironically perhaps replacing this once everyday element with structured curriculum about ecology.

A final influence on the narrowing of children's play spaces appears with the onset of traffic. Once quiet rural towns have become increasingly subjected to heavier traffic flows as train travel disappeared in favor of heavy trucking, as tourism and general mobility increased, and as families became wealthier and able to afford not just the "family car" but also multiple cars. Better roads, faster cars, even school busing all conspired to eliminate some favored play spaces. One small-town green, surrounded on four sides by roads, once collected children from the neighborhood who engaged in free-form, ongoing dramatic play that involved not only children of all ages and genders but also numerous pets that, in pre–leash law days, were part of the gang. Most interviewees remembered this as a special place for child-initiated games, plays, circuses, and just climbing the boulder to think. However, as traffic has increased, children's access to this green has been curtailed, and rarely were present-day children observed there.

A second principal change in children's play, prompted also by changing economic conditions, lies in housing shifts, especially the loss of farms. Older interviewees, growing up on farms, recalled myriad treasured spaces for play: the farm pond cited in the opening example, stone walls, woodlots, pastures, and farm buildings that offered attics, storage chambers, sheds, and workshops to explore. "The barns had a system of tunnels through the haymows with 'secret meeting places,' " recalled one woman, while ells and shed chambers provided secluded spots for imaginative play. The potato cellars offered overhangs for deep snowdrifts in which to dig snow forts and caves, roofs for sliding off, and, throughout the farm, real tools for digging, constructing, creating, and imagining. Farm children also recalled the thrill of daredevil play, building physical adventures into imaginative play through jumping and swinging off high beams into haymows, careening down icy hillsides in homemade sleds, or felling trees to build forts. Consequently, it was not unusual for interviewees to recall injuries and scars from their early years, evidence of a physical adventurousness now probably less widespread among children for whom safety has become a societal concern.

Now, in one town that was once a farming community, only two working farms remain, evidence of economic changes initiated in the post–World War II era. On former farms, once treasured play sites disappear with collapsing barns and torn-down work sheds, although houses themselves are often restored and maintained by in-migrants who value antique homes. Families with young children are increasingly likely to live in more affordable, small modular homes or trailers that contain correspondingly fewer play spaces, especially those with the imaginative potential offered by farm buildings. Such paring down of children's play spaces has been a century-long effort, reflected in early designs of urban and suburban family rooms, dens, and backyards equipped with play structures designed to keep children close to home and visible in non-rural communities. Such indicators of adult failure to appreciate children's need to play widely and creatively have limited children's opportunities to seek out sacred spaces for play in the natural environment.

Finally and seemingly ironically, interview data point to a withdrawal of adults from children's creative play lives. This seems to be a contradiction in a modern era in which adults have intensified their involvement in children's organized play, initiating sports leagues, developing town recreation programs, and providing an array of specialized lessons (art, music, computer, etc.) or other adult-guided opportunities. Compared with interview data, contemporary adults seem to be *very* involved in children's play lives, but the fine distinction lies in what type of play is being fostered. Formalized, structured opportunities for children were rare in both towns prior to the 1980s. The unfettered play still visible in both towns predominated; however, adults still had an important role to play as facilitators and supporters but not directors of play. Interviewees recalled a freedom from adult vigilance while simultaneously acknowledging that their parents knew what children were up to. Parents were ready sources of materials—cookie cutters for packing snow, dress-up clothes for a circus, "jewels" (old beads) from grandmother's special box—but did not participate in, organize, or supervise play directly. Parents set some rules—don't get stuck in the sawdust pile, don't bring the barn cats into the house, don't get in the pigpen, don't get too near the riverbank—but generally left children up to their own devices. Finally, parents expected children to play but also expected chores to be completed on time, allowing children both autonomy and responsibility.

Adults supported children's independent play in a second way through the interest of non-family members. Children's escapades through town were observed by many eyes (just as they are today), and parents seemed comfortable with the idea that someone would contact them if their child misbehaved. Such joint, unobtrusive supervision permitted children's free-ranging play and also drew multiple other adults into the role of supplying and fostering imaginative play, as well as serving as neighborhood audiences for the plays, circuses, animal shows, and other productions that interviewees remembered putting on.

Finally, interviewees remember adults' allowing them time and space to play in simple and profound ways. While all were expected to complete certain chores, none felt pressured for time. One woman recalled that despite hard work required on the farm, there was also plenty of unstructured time; she recalled "just flopping on the ground, doing nothing, watching clouds . . . you could sit and think, or practice something you had learned that day," having more time to reflect. Now, as a teacher, she says that "kids have to learn so much more at school," and everyone (children and parents) is in a "frazzle." She wondered if growing up rural and isolated was better for facilitating thoughtfulness, if somehow isolation breeds a reflectiveness and imaginativeness no longer available to busily programmed children.

Her comments return full circle to the vital contribution that time, space, and natural objects offer children's imaginative play, paralleling Singer & Singer's (1990, pp. 11–18) comments that sacred spaces, unencumbered time, and minimally structured objects are essential components of such play. It may be impossible to disentangle the three as they thread together to provide the foundation for children's playfulness. Adult incursions into that delicate balance, even well-intentioned ones, may disrupt the conditions so necessary for that playfulness to develop. A massive toy industry communicates that the good parent provides his or her child with commercial objects of play, not simple, natural ones. Unstructured time is a rarity for adults and, consequently, for their children, whose lives they seek to fill with organized activity. Sacred spaces can be only identified by children, not constructed artificially for them. In perhaps the ultimate irony, adults may be busily circumscribing children's play while simultaneously remembering their own unrestrained childhoods with nostalgia.

REFERENCES

Chawla, L. (1990). Ecstatic places. *Children's Environments Quarterly, 7*(4), 18–23.

Chawla, L. (1992). Childhood place attachments. In I. Altman & S. Low (Eds.), *Place attachment* (pp. 63–84). New York: Plenum Press.

Chawla, L., & Hart, R. (1995). Roots of environmental concern. *The NAMTA Journal, 20*(1), 148–157.

Cobb, D. (1977). *Ecology of imagination in childhood.* New York: Columbia University Press.

Dovey, K. (1990). Refuge and imagination: Places of peace in childhood. *Children's Environments Quarterly, 7*(4), 13–17.

Goodwin, W., & Goodwin, L. (1996). *Understanding quantitative and qualitative research in early childhood education.* New York: Teachers College Press.

Graue, M. E., & Walsh, D. (1995). Children in context: Interpreting the here and now of children's lives. In J. A. Hatch (Ed.), *Qualitative research in early childhood settings* (pp. 135–154). Westport, CT: Praeger.

Hart, R. (1979). *Children's experience of place.* New York: Irvington.

Hart, R. (1992). *Children's participation: From tokenism to citizenship.* Florence, Italy: UNICEF International Child Development Centre.

James, A., Jenks, C., & Prout, A. (1998). *Theorizing childhood.* New York: Teachers College Press.

Nabhan, G., & Trimble, S. (1994). *Geography of childhood: Why children need wild places.* Boston: Beacon.

Rivkin, M. (1995). *The great outdoors: Restoring children's right to play outside.* Washington, DC: National Association for the Education of Young Children.

Schiavo, R. S. (1988). Age differences in assessment and use of a suburban neighborhood among children and adolescents. *Children's Environments Quarterly, 5*(2), 4–9.

Sibley, D. (1995). Families and domestic routines: Constructing the boundaries of childhood. In S. Pile & N. Thrift (Eds.), *Mapping the subject: Geographies of cultural transformation* (pp. 123–142). London: Routledge.

Singer, D., & Singer, J. (1990). *House of make-believe: Children's play and the developing imagination.* Cambridge: Harvard University Press.

Sutton-Smith, B. (1986). *Toys as culture*. New York: Gardner.

Tuan, Y. (1978). Children and the natural environment. In I. Altman & J. Wohlwill (Eds.), *Children and the environment* (pp. 5–32). New York: Plenum Press.

Wilson, E. O. (1993). Biophilia and the conservation ethic. In S. R. Kellert & E. O. Wilson (Eds.), *The biophilia hypothesis* (pp. 31–44). Washington, DC: Island Press.

Part IV

Children's Play, Humor, and Education

Chapter 11

Play on Words: Humor as the Means of Developing Authentic Learning

Phil Fitzsimmons and Barbra McKenzie

FINDING THE UNEXPECTED: LANGUAGE USE AS PLAY

This chapter began with a lunchtime chat where the authors began to share data. This initial chat focused on a particular teacher with whom we had both been working as a respondent on a fourth grade classroom management project, but focusing on different issues. I had been using Terry as an emic lens to view his highly personalized classroom management skills, while Barbra had been looking at his use of non-verbal communication approaches in classroom management. As we talked, we realized that we had stumbled into a "research rose garden" (Guba & Lincoln, 1989, p. 183) because our data were telling us something very different from the actual focus of our study. Terry's success as a classroom teacher was not due to the way that he managed his class or the way that he used kinesic or proxemic approaches (Ikeda & Beebe, 1992; Robinson, 1995; Woolfolk & Galloway, 1985); rather, these were simply a secondary manifestation of his "theory in action." The actual driving and binding force in his room was his use of language. As soon as we realized this, the "cascading approach" that we believed in took over, which led to the mind mapping of a new course of analysis, viewing Terry as developing a "living educational theory" (Whitehead, 1989).

As we revisited our interviews and applied the tools of looking for "recurring regularities" (Merriam, 1985) and then overlaying these themes over the video data and field notes, two dominant themes began to surface. The first was his continual use of humor as play, and the second was the nature of the interaction that ensued once he began to introduce his jokes, sarcasm, and cutting humor.

These classroom themes had emerged because from the moment that he had begun his teaching career he had constantly been asking himself, "What has not worked for me at school?" and "How do I improve my practice?" Here was a perfect example of a teacher practicing a "living educational theory" (Whitehead, 1989) developed through tension, realized through personal reflection, and refined and integrated through personal beliefs free from other theoretical perspectives.

For Terry, humor was the means through which he engaged children in challenging dialogue and simultaneously began to draw individuals and the whole class into highly personal relationships with him and each other. We had inadvertently stumbled into a situation in which there was congruence between ideology and practice, the first indicator of a highly skilled teacher (Cambourne, 1991).

We also realized that here was a perfect opportunity to begin a reflective practice cycle (Frid & Reid, 1998) in which student teachers could explore and discuss an expert's practice. Thus, we began what we thought would be a two-phase program of investigation whereby our students could share and critique our data.

Phase One—Understanding Terry's Ideology in Action: An Ideology of Humor as Play

While we knew that there was a vast difference between Terry's approach and that of other teachers whom we have used as respondents, it wasn't until we began to revisit our data that the features that distinguish his room from all the others became glaringly different. In this particular room there was a very different set of norms in operation. There was a different power structure, a different communication structure, and a different set of relationships. This room and all the events that occurred in it were almost in complete contrast to all that we had experienced beforehand. While, just like the other rooms that we had visited, there were tremendous learning experiences, in Terry's room there were two significant differences. Here there were spontaneity and a completely different "feel."

Terry's personal philosophy is extremely simple. As far as he is concerned,

Kids are the best judges of everything that happens in the classroom. You have to be real and everything you do has to be real. You have a product to sell, and it's got to be real to turn the kids onto it!

But for this practitioner, the term "environment" means much more than the physical elements of the classroom. Terry views this term to mean the interaction between pupils and teacher and the subsequent relationship that is formed. He believes that developing this interaction, of which humor is the key component, is the means by which a classroom atmosphere of empathy and inclusion is formed. To achieve this, he instigates several distinct strategies. Herein lies an apparent anomaly. While he aims to deliberately set up instances where he can develop humorous interactions, he is also completely spontaneous. His pupils, in fact, have come to realize that they can always expect the unexpected. They eagerly look forward to the times in which they can enjoy each other's sense of humor.

Terry believes that when he "aims humour at the class" a channel of communication is begun in which the children will reciprocate and open up to him as well.

I think kids almost eliminate teachers from their experience if they don't open up. Kids like it. You get much more from them: They start to open up to you as well. Enjoying a laugh is the best way to do this.

Terry believes that as the year progresses and the children see firsthand the openness of the teacher and the gradual unfolding of the relationships formed through the humor, each individual and the class as a whole open up more and more. Thus, a culture of mutual respect is developed instead of a climate based on "Do as you're told, or there will be consequences." Although instituting a broad variety of classroom management strategies, Terry believes that all are funneled through the use of humor and the development of an atmosphere and classroom climate that engender this opening up. Motivation for both the individual and the class to engage in a relationship is thus formed and enhanced through an intrinsic rather than an imposed philosophy of control. "Motivation is being with the kids and being for the kids, and enjoying the language and interaction that naturally flows from this kind of viewpoint."

Further pursuing this aim of establishing a harmonious working atmosphere through the developing of relationships based on this notion of "self-divulgence" is a set of language strategies that are both deliberate and aimed at further recruiting the child to be a part of the collective whole.

Having reached this point and given the overwhelming volume of research that suggests that communicating with children and classroom management have concerned beginning teachers for decades (Lazovsky, Shrift, & Harel, 1997), we began to wonder what our own students would make of our findings and what they believed the role of humor as play would be in the classroom. Thus, with little inkling of what was to follow, we embarked on the second phase.

Phase Two—Understanding the Student Teachers' Ideology: The Surprise

As stated in the opening section, we had originally intended to begin sharing our research with the students, and so to begin with, we decided to gain an idea of what they believed about humor and its place in the classroom. During the first semester of 2000 we surveyed both first- and third-year pre-service primary teachers. The aim of the survey was to collect data regarding the prior knowledge of pre-service teachers with respect to using humor as a classroom strategy. This survey was part of a pre-test, intervention, post-test action-research design and so a precursor to undertaking a range of planned interventions within tutorial sessions.

As we began the research and as the sharing program began, we realized that we would never fully complete this facet!

The data were collected from tutorial sessions in both a third- and first-year language and literacy subject. All groups were convenience samples.

The survey itself was small, consisting of responses to six statements. These were:

- Humor can play an important role in the learning environment.
- Humor can be used as a tool to create a positive learning environment.
- A sense of humor is an important component in a teacher's repertoire.
- I learn more easily in an atmosphere where humor is present.
- I view teachers who display their sense of humor in class as more caring and approachable.
- Teachers who create classroom environments that include an element of humor assist with the development of positive interpersonal relationships.

Asking participants to respond to these statements on a five-point Likert scale generated the data. The five-point scale ranged from "Strongly Agree," "Agree," and "Neutral" to "Disagree" and "Strongly Agree." Each response was scored between 1 and 5, where 1 = Strongly Agree, and 5 = Strongly Disagree. The lower the mean score, the more strongly the group agrees with the statement, and vice versa.

In addition to the collection of data via a Likert scale, students were encouraged to write an explanatory comment for each of the statements. A series of semi-structured interviews was also conducted and then transcribed and analyzed by means of the constant comparative method. The interviews and open-ended question responses were then analyzed and categorized in order to triangulate with the Likert scale data.

The results of this simple survey shocked us, as both groups of students knew a great deal about the value of humor as a classroom strategy. Their responses to the open-ended questions fell into six categories. These students believed that humor was a vital component of any classroom, as it:

- promoted a positive classroom environment;
- increased learning;
- was a tool for engagement;
- promoted enjoyable learning;

Table 11.1
Mean Scores of Cohorts

Statements	Year One Mean Score	Year Three Mean Score
1. Humor can play an important role in the learning environment.	1.6	1.2
2. Humor can be used as a tool to create a positive learning environment.	1.4	1.2
3. A sense of humor is an important component in a teacher's repertoire.	1.7	1.2
4. I learn more easily in an atmosphere where humor is present.	1.6	1.4
5. I view teachers who display their sense of humor in class as more caring and approachable.	1.6	1.5
6. Teachers who create classroom environments that include an element of humor assist with the development of positive interpersonal relationships.	1.5	1.3

• was a tool for conflict resolution; and

• developed interpersonal relationships.

Here, embedded in the responses of these pre-service teachers was a summary of Terry's belief system. But of even more importance was the consistent notion among these students that teachers needed to use various types of humor in their room.

The follow-up interviews triangulated and expanded upon these areas. Table 11.1 and Figure 11.1 show that the third-year group was more confident and sure of their responses, as demonstrated by their lower mean score on each of the questions. The first-year group was not as adamant, as demonstrated by their higher mean score.

These responses were expanded upon during interview and demonstrated that both groups had a wide-ranging knowledge and understanding about the value of humor as a classroom strategy. Their responses included:

• "Humor is an important tool for putting people at ease" (subject a).

• "It can relax students and make them feel comfortable with the teacher and with other students" (subject b).

• "I believe humor can play an important role as it can be a tool for engagement" (subject c).

• "I think it's important to realize that humor has a place in teaching . . ." (subject d).

Figure 11.1
Comparison of First- and Third-Year Student Teachers' Responses

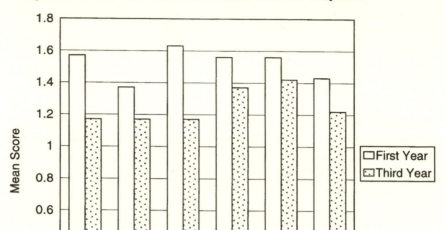

- "A teacher that has a sense of humor and lets the class laugh, you just feel they care more about how the class feels. I guess humor helps create a warmth as well" (subject e).

The follow-up interviews also revealed some interesting connections between research and the knowledge about humor that exists in the public domain (Galloway & Cropley, 1999; Nevo, Keinan, & Teshimovsky-Arditi, 1993). Some of the student teacher comments included the following:

- "There also seems to be a lot in the media, movies like *Patch Adams* and that sort of thing are teaching us all how important humor is in our lives" (subject f).
- "I think there is even some research that indicates that it [humor] released endorphins in the brains of students who are relaxed" (subject d).
- "If people are sick, from my own experience, I have a son with a chronic illness and he and the family use humour to help him manage his pain. Sometimes this is the only way to distract him from the pain" (subject e).

Obviously, we had tapped into a vein of tacit knowledge. These student teachers did not need to be involved in a program of reflection and critique but rather a program of cognitive consolidation and affirmation of their beliefs. Hence, our original cycle of critique became a third cycle of delineation of sharing beliefs concerning Terry's practice and simply sharing our data. The following is where we started in this third phase of the cycle, sharing Terry's "personal story and organising metaphor" (Kupferberg & Green, 1998).

Phase Three—A Personal Vignette of Learning: Language

Play as the Curriculum

In order to fully understand this teacher's current ideology and practice, it's necessary to realize its conception. After completing high school, Terry had initially decided to undertake a law degree but decided on teaching instead, believing that it would be more personally rewarding. While he believes that this most certainly proved to be the case, when he finally graduated with a diploma of education, he found that the course that he had undertaken was virtually of no use in developing his classroom practice or the refinement of his own personal ideology. He found this particularly frustrating, but this lack of substantive help was the catalyst that he needed to begin to search for the optimum mode of teaching. Thus, he embarked on a private crusade of profes-sional development. Having no other starting point, he decided to simply be himself, using principles that he had not been taught. The elements of school life that he craved and thought would be a natural part of any classroom were the development of a relationship between student and teacher, the ability to question things that he didn't agree with, and simply having fun. For Terry, these conditions form part of what he believes the ideal family should put into place.

It wasn't until I got into the real classroom that I learnt anything. All I could do was start enjoying myself. This meant just starting to throw in 'one liners' to ease the kids in. I keep on remembering what my own family had been like.

These familial beliefs and the instigation of throwing "one-liners" at the chil-dren apparently produced results. "The classroom environment is the key for me. By that I mean more than the physical environment. I mean the total struc-tures the teacher sets up, most of which involves the language used."

Terry believed that not only was he more at ease but he did not "fall into the trap of simply playing teacher." He believes that this is perhaps the reason that many children either do not engage with learning or fail to reach their potential. As he sees it, children want a meaningful relationship with their teacher, but too many "chalkies" (teachers) are either afraid that they will lose class control or unable or unwilling to reveal their true self. As a student, this has been an obvious lack in his own relationship with his teachers. "You had your lessons with the chalk and talk, and half the teachers wouldn't know you by the end of the year. I don't ever remember sharing a joke with any of my teachers."

Upon leaving the university and becoming responsible for his own classroom, Terry was determined to chart a very different course. This course of action was not without trauma, because most of the transition from theory into practice came through trial-and-error learning.

College gave me no help in the dynamics of doing it; only a small bit of the process and product of curriculum. I simply had to do it myself. I had to come up with the goods. I made lots of mistakes, but you know I had fun doing it. It was just me that was the secret, just being me. I can't help myself, I just have to blurt it all out.

In the initial stages, as Terry developed his practice of deliberately throwing humor at individual children and the class in general, he noticed that the children began to "throw humour back." Although apprehensive at first, rather than discourage the children, he believed that his classroom needed to be founded on mutual respect.

And so, after 20 years of teaching, Terry has developed a unique approach to teaching that is not always fully appreciated by parents or other staff members. In both the classroom and staff room he delivers jibes and jokes at the most unexpected times. His quips carry not only a laugh but also, more often than not, a strange mixture of wit, social comment, and a pungent sense of self-evaluation. Always ready with a gag, he has a powerful vocabulary and turn of phrase. His comments often contain traces of a sense of anticipation that leaves all recipients, both children and peers, with a smile and an apparent aftertaste of personal reflection written on their faces. As one staff member said, "Terry can always relieve the tension in any situation. He has the gift of genuine comic relief."

This was particularly evident in the staff room immediately following a morning observation in his class. A female staff member was discussing a very personal problem concerning her daughter's morals. Terry was fiddling with a clarinet that he had been showing the class and at a very emotive moment piped up with, "I practise safe sax!"

"Humor" in Practice: A Negotiated Explanation

As we sat with Terry in front of the television screen and reviewed the videotape of his classroom practice, several layers of ideology were revealed.

College stressed correct steps to take, cycles and all sorts of stuff; there was a "correctness" about it. It always seemed to me that as long as you looked good in the classroom, kept the kids quiet, you were seen to be an ok teacher. The reality in that kind of classroom isn't pretty! Nothing happens! The stuff that happens in my room isn't correct; we laugh and dig at each other. But there's a reality to it. We all enjoy being there, and the kids just want to come, even when they're on death's door, they'll front up [show up].

Through this constant review process, a "sophisticated level of consensus" (Guba & Lincoln, 1989, p. 149) was reached. This emergent and as yet incom-

Figure 11.2
Humor as Engagement Model

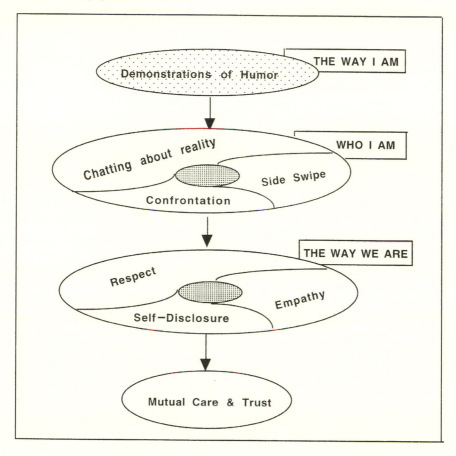

plete "grounded theory" is described in the ensuing paragraphs followed by the schematic diagram, Figure 11.2, that evolved through the debriefing sessions. The terms used in this section are those negotiated between the emic and etic perspectives, with the total process of interaction having been represented as a typical day. As seen in the following interaction with fictitious student names, Terry begins to aim the use of humor immediately as the class begins to move into the classroom.

Terry: Do you know what I'm talking about?

Roy: An oasis?

Terry: This is not even an intellectual oasis. (Class members burst into laughter). Not even a modicum of intellect. I'm not sure what a modicum is but I like it. (Whole class giggles)

Naomi: Isn't an oasis a computer program?

Terry: Oh no!

Naomi: Rats!

Terry: Thank you Naomi for stating the obvious. Up you go; we might get some sensible answers upstairs. Roy before all this I thought you were intelligent. (Whole class giggles)

Naomi: You've taught us everything we know.

Although many educators would deem Terry to be using sarcasm, this interaction begins the thrust and parry of humor that will carry over through the rest of the day. Both teacher and pupil will be constantly on the lookout for opportunities to lampoon and "have a go at each other." Rather than being a derogatory precursor to the day, this interaction sets the tone of positive interaction that would occur for the remainder of the day. Rather than being sarcasm, Terry views this as the means of developing trust. Both teacher and pupil interact in order to maintain the relationship. However, Terry carefully prepares his class so that both parties never step over the line in which wit becomes sarcasm, and both strive to enjoy the closeness of the interaction.

In each of the ensuing teaching sessions, Terry uses several forms of humor. All could be considered as part of what he came to call the "language of genuine care and openness." Consisting of three interlocked forms, each is connected through a genuine concern for the children's well-being and the need for them to feel safe and comfortable. Terry actually believes that children are very conscious of what he terms "genuine involvement." Teachers who have this trait are "willing to get their hands dirty, reach out and touch the kids, meeting them at their level." Conversely, he feels very strongly that if children cannot detect this air of involvement, they often deliberately choose not to develop any lasting or true relationship with either the teacher or the class as a whole.

As seen in the brief excerpt below, a common type of humor that Terry uses is a form that is very casual and relaxed, what he also terms "chatting about reality."

Terry: Yeah, Keith, writing the first draft is simply the beginning. It's not like when I was at school. You had to knock the teacher's socks off first time. It was very difficult because the nuns all wore stockings.

Keith: So you were the only boy at an all girls' school?

Another conscious form of humor is the type that occurs between lessons. During the various lesson stages or segments, Terry consciously takes a break from the more formal requirements of the classroom by deliberately introducing a more relaxed atmosphere that in a cultural sense could be termed "the side-swipe." During these episodes humor plays a large role in what Terry calls "focussing on another to draw the whole in." The focus is placed on a third party in this example:

Erin: Hi Mr. Fitz.

Phil: Hi Erin, what's that you've got?

Terry: She's making a balloon out of duck's intestine. It's the sort of thing that Mr. Fitz gives his kids every Christmas. [Whole class laughs]. Ok, kids pack up please.

A third form used is on the surface extremely confrontational, and yet neither the teacher nor children took offense. The interaction below, surrounded by uproarious laughter from the rest of the class, is characteristic of this form.

Terry: Kay, you're a dag. You know what that means?

Kay: A sheep's bottom.

Terry: No.

Kay: Tail?

Terry: It's, we'll talk in scientific terms. It's a poo ball that sticks to the wool.

Kay: Mr. M, I now know what planet you're from.

Terry: Oh yeah?

Kay: Yep, Uranus!

While often lasting only a few moments, for Terry these are the most important aspects of his day. During these sessions he believes that both teacher and pupil open up. As far as Terry is concerned, these instances tie the whole classroom experience into a cohesive whole, by totally loosening the formality. The aim of this personal approach is to break down the barriers that may exist, forcing the student to take steps toward the conclusion that Terry is totally approachable and that each student is also free to open up and reveal himself or herself to him as well. In his opinion, anything less than such a commitment leads the children to view the teacher as being totally removed from their sphere, which leads to the setting up of communication barriers and the ultimate rejection of the teacher by the pupil.

In Terry's case, humor as play interludes allows his students to become co-directors in the power structure, co-learners through the interactions, and co-sharers in the entire learning process. Rather than setting up instances where discipline becomes a problem, the humor as play interactions provides a stability and platform in which the teacher gains more respect from the children who do not wish to damage the relationship that has been created.

A Summary of Terry's "Living Educational Theory"

The ideology in practice was not a passive underlying structure; rather, it was viewed by the teacher as a "communicable being" in its own right. Similar to an iceberg with a small visible and tangible tip, resting on a large semiotic submerged base, Barthes (1985) describes language as "a stereophony . . . by that I mean it is a space, it puts thoughts and feelings into place according to different volumes and distances" (p. 104).

Similar to the suggestion made by Hampes (1999) that there is a strong link between humor and the development of trust, the data in this study demonstrate that the relationship could be likened to a magnetic mirror. The following schematic diagram shows the working of this metaphor of humor in action, as the teacher draws children into a symbiotic relationship through his demonstrations of humor through the revelation of the "way he is" and "who he is."

This model is also similar to Pearl's (1981) description of the optimal climate of psychological security, for adolescents often seek a climate free from psychological and physical harm as opposed to the creation of a "feudal estate with a landlord," writes White (1988, p. 317).

In a time when classroom management in Australia is receiving greater scrutiny than ever before, could it be that the psychology-based models currently, being purported to be "best practice," actually omit the most important elements of quality teaching and optimal classroom management? Has the criticism leveled at managerial models a decade ago by researchers such as Tattum (1989) and Slee (1992), decrying their narrowness and lack of dynamic adaptability, been ignored? This study would suggest that educators and administrators need to seriously rethink their positions and policies.

Rather than the development of a power structure in which the teacher was dominant and the students submissive, the actions of this teacher suggest that a more empowering structure can be developed. This is possible when the teacher and pupils share an environment in which the teacher was a directing element, and humor is used to "reduce tension, motivate students, aid instruction, strengthen teacher–pupil relationships, and help the teacher stay interested and relaxed" (Rareshide, 1993, p. 26).

In essence, this study suggests that a highly specific cooperative classroom culture can be created in which the students become an integral part of the norms, roles, and social fabric as opposed to one in which they are coerced or forced to comply with the teacher's demands. The result of this shared belief system is that the children are drawn into a genuine relationship based on empathy, self-disclosure, and respect. The structure set up by the teacher could possibly produce harmonious benefits, drawing both teacher and pupils into deeper levels of learning as co-learners.

There is, thus, a way of looking at socialization from what one might call a "policeman's point of view"; that is, socialization can be viewed primarily as the imposition of control from without, supported by a system of rewards and punishments. There is another, more benign way of looking at the same phenomenon; namely, one can perceive socialization as a process of initiation in which the child is permitted to develop and expand into a world available to him or her (Berger & Berger, 1981, p. 63).

What Does This All Mean?

The findings of this study show very clearly that "language as play" has the potential to be a powerful tool for teaching. While many teachers may use it, they may not understand its power, and for beginning teachers it may be a desired facet, but because of a lack of emphasis in tertiary institutions, it becomes sublimated by other more mechanical approaches of ordering classrooms. In essence this study reveals that "humor as play":

• can have a positive affect on the atmosphere, the classroom climate, and interpersonal relationships and promotes engagement in learning: "Language is a major cultural tool that enables us to think logically and to learn new behaviours. It influences more than just the content that we know; it also impacts thinking and the acquisition of new knowledge" (Bodrova & Leong, 1996, p. 37);

• can provide instances in which students feel supported as they attempt to analyze, synthesize, and challenge the range of information provided for them: "Humour is a basic ingredient of binding in society; it provides an effective means of communicating a wide range of ideas, feelings, opinions" (Brownwell & Gardner, 1988, p. 17);

• can develop a classroom culture that is warm, empathic and supportive: "Play can indeed serve developmental, socialization, enculturation, therapeutic, remedial and educational purposes. But play is also a time-honored expression of being human and should be cherished in its own right" (Johnson, Christie, & Yawkey, 1999, p. xi);

• can develop a broad range of learning possibilities: "Play gives children opportunities to understand the world, interact with others in social ways, express and control emotions and develop their symbolic capabilities" (Bredekamp & Copple, 1997, p. 14); and

• needs to be a fundamental aspect of the tertiary curriculum: "Barriers to play are considerably more daunting in the elementary grades. American elementary schools have a long tradition of being work orientated. Elementary schools are viewed as agencies, the main duty of which is to prepare children for their roles in adult society, with goals focussing almost exclusively on academic skills and work habits" (Johnson, Christie, & Yawkey, 1999, p. 333).

On a professional level, it seems that teacher education institutions could benefit by including humor play or play in general into their curricula. It would seem that this is a neglected or forgotten aspect that has been relegated to the early child sphere, if even there. Children do not suddenly drop play from their psyche when they enter the upper grades of elementary school. Rather, it seems that they enjoy its use within the classroom as well as out.

While more research needs to be undertaken, it would also appear that beginning teachers can see the potential of using language in innovative ways, which are not tapped into by tertiary institutions. More importantly, teachers must realize that successful teaching comes out of a close relationship and close emotional ties with students. Waller (1932) stated this well many years ago in that to the natural distance between adult and child is added a greater distance when the adult is a teacher and the child is a student, and this distance arises mainly from the fact that the teacher must give orders to the child. They can not know each other, for we can never know a person when we only peer through institutional bars. (p. 279)

REFERENCES

Barthes, R. (1985). *The grain of the voice*. London: Jonathan Cape.

Berger, P., & Berger, B. (1981). *Sociology: A biographical approach*. Middlesex: Penguin.

Bodrova, E., & Leong, D. (1996). *Tools of the mind: The Vygotskian approach to early childhood*. Columbus, OH: Prentice-Hall.

Bredekamp, S., & Copple, C. (1997). *Developmentally appropriate practice in early childhood programs*. Washington, DC: National Association for the Education of Young Children.

Brownwell, H., & Gardner, H. (1988). Neuropsychological insights into humor. In J. Durant & J. Miller (Eds.), *Laughing matters: A serious look at humour* (pp. 71–89). New York: Wiley.

Cambourne, B. (1991). *Ideology and the literacy curriculum: The teaching of phonics*. Paper for Centre for Studies in Literacy, University of Wollongong.

Frid, S., & Reid, J. (1998). Professional portfolios in teacher education: Compiling the subject in teaching. In S. Schuick, L. Brady, C. Deer, & G. Segal (Eds.), *Challenge of change in education* (pp. 36–49). Sydney: Education Research Group, UTS.

Galloway, G., & Cropley, A. (1999). Benefits of humor for mental health: Empirical findings and directions for further research. *Humor: International Journal for Humor Research, 12*(3), 301–314.

Guba, E., & Lincoln, Y. (1989). *Fourth generation evaluation*. Newbury Park, CA: Sage.

Hampes, W. P. (1999). The relationship between humor and trust. *Humor: International Journal for Humor Research 12*(3), 253–260.

Ikeda, T., & Beebe, A. (1992). *A review of teacher non-verbal immediacy: Implications for intercultural research*. Paper presented at the annual meeting of the International Communications Association, Miami, FL, May.

Johnson, J., Christie, J., & Yawkey, T. (1999). *Play and early childhood development*. New York: Longman.

Kupferberg, I., & Green, D. (1998). Metaphors enhance radio problem-discussion. *Metaphor and Symbol, 13*, 103–123.

Lazovsky, R., Shrift, R., & Harel, Y. (1997). *Professional development of preservice education students: Early entry into the education system*. Beit Berl College: Research and Evaluation Unit, Kfar Saba, Israel.

Merriam, S. (1985). The case study in educational research: A review of selected literature. *The Journal of Educational Thought, 19*(3), 204–217.

Nevo, O., Keinan, G., & Teshimovsky-Arditi, M. (1993). Humor and pain tolerance. *Humor: International Journal of Humor Research, 16*(1), 71–88.

Pearl, A. (1981). *A phenomenological cost benefit analysis approach to adolescence: Parent child interaction*. Sydney: Academic Press.

Rareshide, S. W. (1993). *Implications for teacher's use of humor in the classroom*. Charlottesville: University of Virginia Press.

Robinson, R. (1995). *Affiliative communication behaviours: A comparative analysis of the interrelationships among teacher nonverbal immediacy, responsiveness and verbal receptivity on the prediction of student learning.* Paper presented at the annual meeting of the International Communication Association, Albuquerque, NM, May.

Slee, R. (1992). *Discipline in Australian public education, changing policy and practice.* Melbourne: Australian Council for Educational Research.

Tattum, D. (1989). Alternative approaches to disruptive behaviour. In N. Jones (Ed.), *School management and pupil behaviour* (pp. 46–61). London: Falmer Press.

Waller, W. (1932). *The sociology of teaching.* New York: Russell and Russell.

White, R. J. (1988). Questionable assumptions underlying secondary school classrooms. *American Journal of Education, 32*(3), 311–338.

Whitehead, A. J. (1989). Creating a living educational theory from questions of the kind, "How do I improve my practice?" *Cambridge Journal of Education, 19*(1), 41–52.

Woolfolk, A., & Galloway, C. (1985). Nonverbal communication and the study of teaching. *Theory into Practice, 24*(1), 77–84.

Chapter 12

"When I Play Funny It Makes Me Laugh": Implications for Early Childhood Educators in Developing Humor through Play

Grace Masselos

INTRODUCTION

An observer of preschool children's play can relate to the spontaneous nature of their activities. Through play children can express their understanding of the world around them. Each developmental area can be helped and enhanced through play as children test themselves against the spontaneous happenings that occur during their interactions with peers, props, and the environment as a whole.

One area that has appealed to the present writer relates to the development of humor in young children. This interest arose from a previous in-depth, qualitative study of conflict and acceptance within the peer culture of 3- and 4-year-old children during block play. One of the features that was noted in this study relates to one particular child who used humor to gain entry into a much desired spaceman block play dominated by a group of older boys. An important factor eventually emerged in that although this child's earlier attempts to gain entry were negative and immature, he eventually discovered, over a period of time, that a humorous approach would be more acceptable. Even though this was not entirely satisfactory from this little boy's point of view, his continual rejection by the older boys was not as aggressive, and there was some positive reaction by one of the children. Thus, the function of humor was to gain a more positive acceptance by his peers. This was a dynamic finding for a young child to work out for himself. Even though he was not fully accepted into the block play, this child had worked out a strategy for himself that had a more positive reaction than his other endeavors. Keeping this in mind, this chapter looks at humor within play of the peer culture of 4-year-old children in early childhood centers in the Illawara area of New South Wales, Australia. More specifically, this chapter discusses the types and functions of humor within play and the peer culture of preschool children and some implications for early childhood educators.

Play and the Peer Culture of Preschool Children

Within the context of play in early childhood centers, young children can have the freedom of choice to play according to their whim or need of the moment. They can use a wide range of props or merely rely on basic equipment such as that found in the block area. Children can extend the theme of their play for weeks or suddenly change direction and even terminate without any reason that may be obvious to adults. As noted by McGhee (1979): "In their fantasy world, children create experiences that they know cannot take place in reality. They love self-made incongruities and exaggerations because they offer endless strings of new ideas and events to explore" (p. 55).

The peer culture that a child may belong to at any moment of play provides the structure that binds the children together. Peer culture gives a rationale for the group to formulate its own rules and a means to be in control of its play rather than other children or adults. Peer culture can be defined as "[a] stable set of activities or routines, artefacts, values, and concerns that children produce and share in interactions with peers" (Corsaro, 1997, p. 95).

An important aspect of peer culture within the parameters of this phenomenon indicates that play has great meaning to the children concerned. The direction of play depends on the definitive rules formulated by a collaborative effort of each member. Sometimes a dominant member of the group can manipulate these rules. In play within peer culture, adult control is definitely not part of this decision-making process. Thus, compatibility would be an important aspect of the group. That each member can contribute, share, and enjoy the play would be deemed an essential part of the whole experience.

One aspect of this experience would be to enjoy any humorous situation that may arise. This humor may not be planned or structured into the play. Rather than planning for humorous situations, they tend to happen spontaneously according to whatever happens at the time. For example, in one of the observations as noted by the present researcher, three 4-year-old children were building a house. They spent a great deal of time working hard carrying blocks from the shelves and stacking them to make four walls for a house. It was serious business as they worked cooperatively at a steady pace until the final block was put into the correct place. As the leader of the group accidentally knocked over one of the walls, the children in this group all laughed when the blocks fell down. Despite the destruction of all their hard work, this display of humor was quite spontaneous as these children shared a moment that was funny to them. It could have been a devastating moment, especially for the leader; however, the collapse of the wall was met with group laughter, possibly to relieve tension.

The following section discusses some of the important features of the development of humor in young children.

Humor in Preschool Children's Play

In terms of types and the functions of humor, a great deal of study was carried out in the 1970s and 1980s. According to these early researchers, the development of humor, incongruity, and cognitive skills is closely related, as the stages that young children go through correspond to the Piagetian perspective of cognitive development (McGhee, 1979; Tamashiro, 1979; Zigler, Levine, & Gould, 1967). McGhee (1979) claims that incongruity is an important prerequisite for all occurrences of humor, even though this alone is not a sufficient condition. He notes that a child could react to an incongruous situation with curiosity, anxiety, or amusement. The function of *play signals* is regarded by McGhee as important by helping a child know how to react to others if a situation should be perceived as being *funny* or not to be taken seriously. These play signals relate to others' behavior or environmental cues and can indicate to a child as to whether an incongruous situation can be regarded as funny or interesting or to be avoided.

The development of humor and incongruity can be viewed as a cognitive function and progresses further by means of socializing experiences and the increasing maturity of expressive language. For this reason young children need to have many opportunities to listen to and observe others react to humorous situations. This helps them to appreciate incongruity and humor when confronted by such occurrences. McGhee (1979) draws attention to the fact that the peak of spontaneous laughter reaches at about three years of age and declines from then on and that the type of situations that induce laughter increases as children grow older.

In the present study, the observed situations that the children experienced indicated that they were valuable ones for the development of social as well as cognitive areas. For example, in one anecdote, a boy and a girl were sitting together looking at a book. The girl pointed out something to the boy, and he threw back his head and laughed. In this instance, the children gained valuable experience in sharing a spontaneous humorous moment; they also shared companionship and gained practice in communication—verbal and comprehension skills.

During play, children can laugh with sheer enjoyment and excitement of playing with others without needing to have a specific stimulus of a humorous nature. McGhee (1979) tends to regard this exuberant laughter during energetic motor play as a means of relieving built-up tension. This observation supports the psychoanalytical perspective that regards humor primarily as a means of providing a coping mechanism for the individual. Scatological humor is evident in young children, especially when overcoming anxieties about toileting activities. Humor about gender differences also reflects tension fears as well as confusion (Wolfenstein, 1954). Early childhood educators could help children by using quality children's literature in order to allay such fears. For those children who are ready to cope with such literature, *The Story of the Little Mole Who Knew It Was None of His Business* (Holzwarth & Erlbruck, 1989) can be great fun as well as a way of introducing children to different types of animals.

Incongruity in Young Children

One important aspect of humor is incongruity. McGhee (1979) views incongruous relationships as forming the basis of humor development. He interprets incongruity as a mismatch of concepts that are known to be correct or a form of distortion of reality from a child's point of view. He states, "Humour in the young child then results from the playful contemplation of incongruity, exaggeration, absurdity, or nonsense only when the child realises that the events exist in fantasy" (McGhee, 1979, p. 61).

McGhee (1979) also claims that fantasy assimilation is a necessary prerequisite for humor, although it is not sufficient to produce humor. He suggests three ways in which children may make sense out of incongruity. They are as follows:

• Where a child has to stretch already learned concepts to fit in with incongruous situations. This can create humorous situations.

• Where a child is involved in fantasy assimilation of incongruous situations. In order for this to take place, the child must first be in a playful mood. There needs to be a recognition that there is a distortion of reality when it actually takes place.

• Where the characteristics of play can influence appreciation of humor.

Further, McGhee (1979, p. 60) draws attention to the notion that there are two basic categories of play—object and social play:

Object play is regarded as an important aspect of creative play as a new object motivates curiosity and exploratory behaviour. After the novelty of the object has been exhausted, it then encourages the child to expand further understanding of the toy and incidental learning may take place. Once a child has explored all possibilities he/she could use fantasy to attribute functions that are beyond the normal aspects of the object. This is where the child deliberately introduces incongruity and in a sense, humour to the play activity.

Social play is important in terms of maintaining playful moods and learning from others. Although humour can be viewed in children's solitary play, it is the verbal and non-verbal interaction with others that can encourage and stimulate social relationships. The need to share humour with others is another important social influence. (McGhee, 1979, p. 60)

Following this further, Burt & Sugawara (1988, p. 21) note that important aspects of cognition and playful experimentation influence novel and incongruous events. These researchers claim that there are three requirements for humorous play:

1. A sense of playfulness—where children are able to explore new relationships using laughter to reduce tension, and to gain influence of a social nature;

2. Experimentation—where incongruity plays an important part in the development of humour. Given the opportunity, young children can use and experiment with props, peers and situations of all kinds in order to create a world of their own. These situations in themselves however, may not be humorous, even if the children concerned perceive them as so. The important factor is that there is a realisation of distorted reality. In one instance, it was noted that humour was evident when several boys were playing on a spacecraft made from blocks. The situation was precipitated when one of the smaller blocks fell. It was right in the front where the *space men* sat. The leader of the game laughed as he replaced the block that was an essential part of the construction. This particular block helped the spacecraft to *blast off*. In other words, when the block fell out of its rightful place, there was a distortion of reality or some incongruity within their fantasy world that was very true for these boys at this point in time. The humour factor is evident where there is recognition of the fact that a comparison has been made between the pretend object and the real one and a subsequent judgement made as to how funny it may be.

3. Incongruous comparisons—when young children, reflecting cognitive development, are able to recognize that there is an incompatible relationship in a situation and react humorously. For example, young children are highly amused when looking at a picture of a baby wearing an adult's hat. They are well aware that babies do not wear an adult's hat.

Another important aspect of humor incorporates the study of laughter. In his search for the structure of laughter, Provine (1996), using a sound spectrograph, found that adult laughter has a distinctive and identifiable character. The spectrograph is an apparatus that converts a sound into an image that over time shows the changes in frequency and intensity of a particular sound. Even though there are individual differences in the production of laughter, Provine found that there is a basic structure. For example, he noted that laughter is composed of a series of short syllables approximately 75 milliseconds long, which are repeated at regular intervals of about 210 milliseconds. Another feature of laughter is that it has a harmonic structure; female laughter has a fundamental frequency at approximately 503 hertz, whereas males have a lower rate of about 276 hertz.

In the context of this chapter, the phenomenon of "group glee" must be mentioned. In group glee a group of preschool children laugh loudly or scream together in a joyful nature (Sherman, 1975). An interesting feature of group glee is that it tends to be "contagious" or create a "ripple effect" among any particular group. For example, in a group situation, one child may react by laughing loudly to a humorous stimulus, and then this response can carry over to the other children without each individual's knowing what may have been funny in the first place. In a study of preschool children covering 596 formal lessons over a period of two years, Sherman (1975) found that "group glee" can be precipitated by several factors. These include children's responses to volunteering or answering teacher's requests, the mass movement of a group of children from a passive activity to a more active one (release of tension), and responding to cognitive incongruities that may have been apparent during the group experience. Sherman (1975) also noted that "group glee" was more likely to occur in small boy/girl groups of seven to nine children, rather than groups of one gender. In the present writer's study, "group glee" was observed when a group of children were seesawing on equipment that was not made for that function. One boy who was watching nearby came over and pushed up one end, causing the children to fall off. Everyone laughed loudly and excitedly, yelling, "Oh, oh, oh!" When the teacher came over, the laughing stopped very quickly.

Another interesting phenomenon that warrants mention has been coined by Corsaro (1997) as "cantilena" or "children's chanting." During his study of Italian preschool children, Corsaro observed children carrying out a singsong chant that occurred during their play and was usually accompanied by rhythmic movements. The present writer during observations of the children also noted this. For example, one 4-year-old boy was playing with small figures of a family. He picked up one figure and lightly touched the others, chanting in a minor third tonal mode, "Hello, Daddy, Hello, Daddy." He was soon joined by another boy of a similar age sitting next to him, and this child was able to keep up with the first boy with the same pitch, tonal interval, and timing. In another observation, a group of children were carrying pails of water from the tap to a large container in the sandbox. One boy started a chant of two tonal intervals of "beef-stew." The other children joined in as they traipsed from the tap to the sandbox and back again. Then with a giggle, the leader changed the chant to "bum-stew." After a short while the chant was changed to "wee-wee-stew, wee-wee-stew." The tonal interval became a minor third, possibly to accommodate the three syllables rather than the two as with the earlier chant of "beef-stew." Of course, all the children joined in, and this activity continued for some time without any adult intervention.

SUMMARY OF ONGOING RESEARCH

The 4-year-old children were videotaped during free play in both the indoor and outdoor play. Any evidences of humor as such had to be decided on review of the videotapes. Each humorous situation was written as a complete anecdote. None of the situations regarded as humorous were contrived. The researcher had to wait for the humorous situation to occur during the children's play. The main criterion for the identification of a humorous situation was evidence of a child's or children's laughter, a smile, or some verbalization or behavior that evoked a humorous response from the child or other children.

Table 12.1
A Taxonomy of Observed Humor during the Play of 4-Year-Old Children in Preschool Settings

Observed evidences of humor (n = 9)	Anecdotes (n = 101)	Instances (n = 139)
Smiles	27	44
Laughing	21	41
Vocals	21	22
Body movements	15	15
Group glee	6	6
Giggles	5	5
Chuckles	4	4
Chortles	1	1
Clowning	1	1

Table 12.2
A Taxonomy of the Functions of Smiles of 4-Year-Old Children during Humorous Play in Preschool Settings

Function (n = 8)	Quantity (n = 43)
Pleasure	19
Group glee	6
Relieving tension	5
Negative	5
Compatibility	3
Being in control	2
Teasing	2
Incongruity	1

To date, a total of 116 anecdotes have been compiled with 167 instances of observed evidences of humor during play. The children observed were 77 boys and 47 girls. The same children were observed in more than one anecdotal situation. A taxonomy of the various types and functions of observed humor has been noted in the following six tables. Table 12.1 provides an overall picture of the nine types of observed humor as evident during the play of these 4-year-old children during play.

The next five tables list the functions of each of the above. Table 12.2 provides a summary of the instances of the observed functions of smiling. In this

Table 12.3
A Taxonomy of Examples of the Types of Laughter of 4-Year-Old Children during Humorous Play in Preschool Settings

Belly laugh	Ho, ho, ho
Chortle	Hysterical
Chuckle	Imitative
Group glee	Raucous
Ha! (single but expressive sound)	Repetitive
Hee hee	Squeals, Tee hee, Titter

Table 12.4
A Taxonomy of the Functions of Laughter of 4-Year-Old Children during Humorous Play in Preschool Settings (n = 41)

Group glee	13	Compatibility	2
Pleasure	9	Relieving tension	2
Negative situations	6	Being in control	1
Teasing	3	Incongruity	1

context, the most prevalent function of smiling indicated pleasure in relation to the children's actions during play. For example, in one anecdote (pleasure/satisfaction of a job well done) a boy stands up as he places the last block on top of the wall of the house made of long blocks and smiles broadly as he does so.

Group glee was included as a category as it was a group function. For example, it was when there was collective squealing as demonstrated in an anecdote in which children responded by smiling when the teacher took a photo of their block construction.

Table 12.3 shows the laughter sounds that were observed during various aspects of the children's play. They were spontaneous sounds that occurred during their play and provoked according to the situation.

Table 12.4 shows that 13 instances of *group glee* were the most frequent occurrence in laughter situations. *Negative situations* related specifically when one child was deliberately being nasty to another, whereas *teasing* in this category was carried out in fun.

Table 12.5 indicates the type of body movements that the children displayed when they found a situation amusing. For example, whole body movement was illustrated when the child moved all of his or her body either on the spot or away from the original position to return again, leaning back, moving forward, or when he or she fell down with laughter. Arm and hand movements included pointing to the source of amusement, hand over mouth, and hands on head as

Table 12.5
A Taxonomy of the Functions of Body Movements of 4-Year-Old Children during Humorous Play in Preschool Settings (n = 15)

Whole body	6
Hand movements	5
Head	2
Hips	1
Arms and/or legs	1

Table 12.6
A Taxonomy of the Types of Vocalizations of 4-Year-Old Children during Humorous Play in Preschool Settings (n = 22)

Rhythmic	11
Expressive	7
Chanting	4

expressions of amazement. Head movements included being thrown back as the child laughed with mouth open wide, head moved sideways or hunched into shoulders. Eye movements were also noted as either being opened wide or closed when laughing.

Table 12.6 shows the three types of vocalizations of these children during their expressive humor. All were in the context of their play. A breakdown of the three observed vocalization types is as follows:

Rhythmic
- What's the poo soup?
- Oww, wow
- Ooh, oh, ah
- Woops ee doo
- I put my name up
- Arghh, there you are
- I feel, I feel, I feel
- Look what I've found
- Chuff, chuff, chuff
- Hawh, hawh, aaah
- Oh ah, haw, haw, haw, ah hah

Expressive

• I can kill people too!—giggles—tee hee
• That's funny!
• Don't make it tooooo biiig this time!
• No, not yet!
• What's the poo soup?
• Shush!
• Hey, look how wet my dress is!

Chanting

• Beef stew, beef stew, beef stew
• Wee stew, wee stew
• Bum stew, bum stew, bum stew
• Hello Daddy, Hello Daddy, Hello Daddy

THE ROLE OF THE EARLY CHILDHOOD EDUCATOR

In the context of the development of humor in early childhood, the above information has important implications for learning and teaching. Humor can be a positive source of social experience for young children. Early childhood educators need to be aware that by having humorous interactions with adults and other children, the development in areas such as language, cognitive, socialization, and emotional skills can be further reinforced and extended. In the present study, the information gathered to date indicates that by playing with others or with adults, children can learn from their interactions with others. For example, in one anecdote, a boy was rebuilding a block construction after a wall fell down. He stated quite emphatically, "This time, I'm going to make it strong," smiling as he says this. Another boy who was watching him replies, "Right, don't make it too-oo, biiig THIS time," also smiling as they talk to each other. This is an example of how children can support and help each other as they learn how to handle play materials as well as scientific facts. They both found the situation amusing, yet together they learned several important principles involving mathematical concepts, the consequences of cause and effect, trial and error, and not to get upset if all does not go as planned. The teacher, who was watching nearby, reinforced the boys' efforts with humorous comments, all of which supported their statements.

McGhee (1979) regards the development of humor and incongruity in the same light. He not only associates the development of humor as a cognitive function but also delegates importance toward the social and psychodynamic functions as well. Groch (1974) points out that communication is another important aspect of humor. As noted in the above anecdote where the teacher shared a humorous moment without intrusion on the boy's play, such a situation can be a valuable experience as it requires verbalization and expressive speech, as well as the cognitive ability to comprehend verbal exchange and, if necessary, to respond.

Early childhood educators also need to be aware of the wide range of ability of 4- and 5-year-old children in being able to participate in conceptual language play activities. Varga (2000) in her research of young children, found that they were capable of initiating, organizing, and maintaining language play interactions that included exaggerated incongruity in order to produce a humorous response. Her study encourages early childhood educators to understand this aspect of children's development and to encourage those children who have yet to develop this ability.

Another important point that early childhood educators need to remember relates to the fact that there is a difference between the humor of young children and that of adults. Due to the cognitive maturity of adults, the interpretation of humorous incidents can vary in many ways. For example, the use of sarcasm can be lost on young children, even though the adult's tone of voice and facial expressions could indicate a negative attitude. Young children's humor is influenced by the individual's level of cognitive and incongruity development. Types of humor as noted from the present writer's observation of children in naturalistic settings indicated that children use a variety of forms of humor according to the situation. These expressions of humor came naturally within the context of the play situation. Smiles seemed to be more prevalent than laughter as such.

These particular children had the opportunity to engage in play where they could freely experiment with language, use their imagination, and test these out on their peers. Non-verbal and verbal interactions were equally important; however, the children in the present study were mainly non-verbal.

The use of humor in play can be evidenced in many ways. In an early study of 30 preschool children's humor carried out by Groch (1974), findings indicated that three distinct types of humor could be categorized during children's play as responsive, productive, and hostile. *Responsive humor* has been identified in situations where a child may react with a smile or a laugh. *Productive humor* relates to behaviors such as teasing, joking, and evidence of the ability to recognize incongruity. *Hostile and non-hostile humor* have been categorized as productive humor, which depended on the motivational intent, even though, according to Groch, the structure was similar.

Thus, an important point for early childhood educators to be aware of relates to Groch's (1974) findings that these three types of humor were influenced by the activities as set up in the preschool. For example, productive humor was more evident during unstructured play, such as free and block play, in comparison to activities that were set up by staff such as cooking experiences or during story time where responsive humor was more predominant. The researcher indicated that these activities allowed for more unexpected events to take place. Hostile humor was more evident among the boys' play, which in this study occurred in the block area and appeared to be related to evidences of hostile joking, ridicule, and defiant behaviors. Groch (1974) did not dwell on this aspect of her study; however, she did note that since the "type of humour is related to activity, the differential participation which typifies each sex may additionally affect the pattern of humour found" (p. 1101).

In relation to Groch's work, it would be pertinent for early childhood educators to carefully observe children's behavior in each of the above-mentioned types of play for evidences of humor. In order to provide situations where humor can be appreciated throughout the whole program, early childhood educators could include opportunities for the unexpected and for children to respond to open-ended situations. There would also be a need for adults to be aware of situations where hostile humor takes place and to analyze these events accordingly and to see what can be done to help children resolve their own conflict. As noted earlier, young children are capable of using humor to gain entry into much desired block play. Thus, early childhood educators can help children to use humor to defuse conflict. Although this may be a difficult strategy for some children to use when emotions run high, adults can certainly help children to use such an approach by modeling this principle.

Other recommendations that would be useful for early childhood educators are noted as follows:

• To show that they enjoy working with children and their families. This encourages compatibility among all, including fellow staff members;

• To make the most of an amusing moment—taking care that it is not at the expense of another person. By doing this, tension can be eased, thus helping children to be more motivated on their tasks;

• To help children use humor as a mnemonic function. Children who favor this form of learning may be able to retain information more efficiently due to the amusing association;

• To help children share an amusing incident, as this can make life more interesting. This can add fun to life as well as help children to develop their expressive and comprehension skills;

• To use quality children's literature, as a great deal can be learned about others and their emotions. Humorous experiences as noted in these stories can be shared and discussed, thus helping to develop communication skills;

• To recognize and appreciate incongruity versus novelty. Incongruity involves a cognitive process that matures with the child when given the opportunity to do so. Novelty situations, on the other hand, can be fleeting and provide only limited intellectual challenge after the event; and

• To provide opportunities for children to have the freedom to appreciate, experience, enjoy, and engage in, as well as take *risks* in humorous situations and playful behaviors. This would, of course, involve helping children to be sensitive to the feelings of others.

Finally, Tamashiro (1979) reinforces the notion that teachers should understand the developmental aspects of children's humor in order to be able to accommodate their behavior particularly in relation to situations requiring discipline. Tamashiro claims that if teachers have knowledge of the developmental stages of humor, they would be better prepared in the handling of behavior problems. He suggests that disciplinary action should be "in harmony with the children's developmental stage, and to make the learning environment more delightful and developmentally meaningful to students by including humour in the class activities" (Tamashiro, 1979, p. 750).

CONCLUSION

In terms of types of humor in young children, research has indicated that the development of humor is a progressive function related to cognitive processes. With positive experiences with others and opportunities to fine-tune their skills, young children should be able to appreciate and be creative in their own expression of humor. The functions of humor are many. The most important can be viewed as providing enjoyment of life and as a means for relieving tension. Early childhood educators have an important role when working with young children and their families by helping them to appreciate humor and recognize the pleasure and companionship that humorous situations can bring. Also, as noted from this study to date, teachers need to recognize the importance of young children's peer culture and the influence that each member has on each other.

By watching how children make each other laugh and what things they joke about in their spontaneous play, we can begin to discover the process by which humour is socialised and the ways in which the child develops his (her) own individualised sense of humour. (Groch, 1974, p. 1101)

REFERENCES

Burt, L. M., & Sugawara, A. I. (1988). Children's humour: Implications for teaching. *Early Child Development and Care, 37*, 13–25.

Corsaro, W. A. (1997). *The sociology of childhood*. Thousand Oaks, CA: Pine Forge.

Groch, A. (1974). Joking and appreciation of humor in nursery school children. *Child Development, 45*, 1098–1102.

Holzwarth, W., & Erlbruck, W. (Illustrator) (1989). The story of the little mole who knew it was none of his business. Pymble, Australia: HarperCollins.

McGhee, P. E. (1979). *Humour: Its origin and development*. San Francisco: W. H. Freeman.

Provine, R. R. (1996). Laughter. *American Scientist, 84*(1), 38–48.

Sherman, L. W. (1975). An ecological study of glee in small groups of preschool children. *Child Development, 46*, 53–61.

Tamashiro, R. T. (1979). *Children's humour: A developmental point of view*. Glencoe, IL: Free Press.

Varga, D. (2000). Hyperbole and humour in children's language play. *Journal of Research in Childhood Education, 14*(2), 142–151.

Wolfenstein, M. (1954). *Children's humour*. Glencoe, IL: Free Press.

Zigler, E., Levine, J., & Gould, L. (1966). Cognitive processes in the development of children's appreciation of humour. *Child Development, 37*(3), 507–518.

Chapter 13

Recess in a Middle School: What Do the Students *Do?*

Olga S. Jarrett and Michelle Duckett-Hedgebeth

The extreme rarity of recess in middle school may be the reason for the lack of research on informal play behaviors of middle school students in school settings. Research findings on the importance of recess for younger children suggest the need for such research with the middle school age group as well as the testing of methods appropriate for such research.

ELEMENTARY SCHOOL RECESS

In most elementary schools, the need for schoolchildren to move around, to socialize, and to play has been recognized in the scheduling of recess periods. Traditionally, school recess is a time in which children can go outdoors with considerable choice as to how they play or otherwise interact with their peers. Research suggests that recess, as a break in the day, time for free choice, opportunity for physical activity, and time for social interaction, can have many advantages both for the children and for the teachers (Jarrett & Maxwell, 2000). For example, breaks improve cognitive functioning (Pellegrini & Bjorklund, 1997) and on-task behavior (Jarrett, Maxwell, Dickerson, Hoge, Davies, & Yetley, 1998). Children appear to need a time in the day when they can make choices (Maxwell, Jarrett, & Roetger, 1999). According to Jambor (1994, p. 19), "the playground during recess is one of the few places where children can confront, interpret, and learn from meaningful social experiences."

Social experiences on the playground can be either positive or negative. Jarrett, Farokhi, Young, and Davies (2001) observed leadership qualities as children organized their own games, problem solving as children determined who was "it," and very little negative behavior between children. However, Olweus (1993) noted that the playground is a place where bullying is more likely to occur. Boulton (1993) found considerable fighting on English playgrounds, especially toward the end of the long play break at lunch. However, the playground may also be one of the places where teachers can note and intervene in bullying and other negative situations. As one of the few times in the day when one can observe spontaneous peer interaction (Pellegrini, 1995), recess provides teachers with good opportunities to observe positive behaviors such as leadership, turn-taking, and prosocial behavior as well as negative behaviors such as social isolation, aggression, and bullying (Jarrett & Young, 2000; Pelligrini & Bjorklund, 1996). One study found that play interventions by adults during recess could enhance social skills, decreasing negative behavior (Butcher, 1999).

An obvious advantage of recess is that it affords the opportunity for physical activity. According to Werner, Timms, and Almond (1996), research indicates that children engage in insufficient physical activity. They report that 6- and 7-year-olds are engaged in exercise, sufficiently intense as to have health benefits, only 4–8% of the time and that children who lead sedentary lifestyles have increased health risks. Also supporting the need for physical activity are (1) studies with rats and cats showing relationships between enriched environments, active participation, and development of brain connections (Sprenger, 1999); and (2) research with humans that shows connections between exercise and motor fitness, high academic performance, stress reduction, and positive attitude (Jensen, 1998; Pellegrini & Smith, 1998).

How active are children during recess? Research has examined both amount of time spent in active play and numbers of children who tend to be active on the playground. Pellegrini and Smith's (1998) review of the literature on active play included one study in which vigorous active play accounted for 13% of all outdoor behavior during recess and another study reporting that 60% of the children engaged in some type of active play during recess. Although not all children are active during recess, children's tendency to choose physical activity on the playground when they need it the most is expressed in higher levels of activity on the playground after recess deprivation (Pellegrini & Davis, 1993; Pellegrini, Huberty, & Jones, 1995), higher activity levels by children who tend to be inattentive in the classroom (Pellegrini & Smith, 1993), and high initial activity levels, decreasing after the first six to seven minutes on the playground (Pellegrini & Davis, 1993). In spite of the advantages of recess, an increasing number of school systems have abolished recess, even in elementary school, in favor of structured physical education classes and/or more instructional time (Chmelynski, 1998).

MIDDLE SCHOOL RECESS

Recess in middle school is very rare, in spite of concerns about the level of physical activity of adolescent students (McKenzie, Simon, Sallis, & Conway,

2000; Savage & Scott, 1998; Wechsler, Devereaux, Davis, & Collins, 2000) and the need for adolescents to have supervised places where boys and girls can interact appropriately.

Even more rare than recess in middle school is research on what students do when given an outdoor play break. Assumptions drawn from gender research or from playground observations of elementary school children may or may not be supported by observations of middle school students. Of question is research on gender differences that indicates the following: (1) cross-gender contacts follow a U-shaped curvilinear pattern, increasing during adolescence after a dip during the elementary school years (Ramsey, 1998), (2) much cross-gender interaction takes the form of "borderwork" (Thorne, 1993) involving chasing and teasing, (3) boys dominate competitive games and large play spaces while girls are relegated to the fringes (Sadker & Sadker, 1994), (4) boys narrow their activities with age to fewer games and sports while girls continue to be involved in a wide range of play activities, not necessarily games (Dahmes, 1993), and (5) considerable cross-gender game playing and rough-and-tumble play occurred in an inner-city elementary school (Jarrett et al., 2001).

The original purpose of this research was to study how a sample of middle school students spends its time during recess. Of specific interest was how adolescent boys and girls interact, how much of the playground behavior can be considered physically active, to what extent recess behaviors can be considered "play," and how much negative behavior occurred. These questions were explored by systematically observing the play area during recess.

A secondary interest emerged while conducting the observational research: Why do some students not go out for recess? How do students view recess, and what suggestions do they have for improving it? These questions were explored through a student survey.

METHOD

The school studied in this research is a Georgia charter school, established in 1999 with a focus on the arts as a way to reach students who might not excel in a traditional school. According to Ghezzi (2001, p. B6), "The approach weaves art into academic courses and devotes a third of the school day to arts education." Some of the arts classes, specifically "drama," "African dance," "African drumming," and the "athletic and movement group," involve physical activity. However, there is no physical education teacher, and there are no scheduled physical education classes. Because of the freedom that charter status brings, this school has recess, although the county in which the school is located abolished recess even in the elementary schools over a decade ago.

During the 1999–2000 school year, the school had fifth through eighth grades. During the 2000–2001 school year, ninth grade was added. There are 9 students in grade 5, 45 students in grade 6, 37 students in grade 7, 43 students in grade 8, and 16 students in grade 9. Approximately 95% of the students are African

American, and the other 5% are white. Most of the students come from middle-income families; 40% of the students receive free and reduced-price lunch. Because the county school system in which this charter school is located has a policy against recess, the students who attended elementary school in the county had not experienced recess before coming to this school.

Observations during Recess

The observational study was conducted during two different school years and during two seasons. The first set of data was collected in May and June 2000. The second set was collected in January and February 2001. Each year, recess was held around lunchtime with one to three teachers supervising. During the 1999–2000 school year, there were three lunch periods and three recess periods, approximately 20 minutes each. During the 2000–2001 school year, there were two lunch periods and two recess periods with recess lasting approximately 30 minutes. Half of the students had recess before lunch. The other half ate first. This latter group occasionally had "extended recess," in which they were allowed to stay outside longer. Another difference between the two years was that the assistant principal, who played football with the students during the first set of observations, tore a ligament in his knee and was not seen on the playground during the winter 2001 observations. Students were not required to go outside, and on each day some students chose to stay inside.

The school is located in a former Drug Emporium in a strip mall. All of the observations for this study were done on the school play area behind the mall. This area consists of a flat parking lot with dumpsters, bordered by a 20–30-foot-wide strip of weeds and trees at the back, separated from the properties behind it by a chain-link fence. The asphalt play area is approximately 340 feet long with an irregular width, averaging approximately 80 feet. There are no distinctive boundaries on the sides of the play area. Several times, play was interrupted by large delivery trucks making deliveries to stores that are located in the strip mall. There are no benches or other seats in the play area, and students wishing to sit used walls, curbs, or the asphalt surface. During spring 2000, a portable basketball hoop was available during most recess periods. However, the hoop fell victim to vandalism and was not available during the winter 2001 observations.

The co-authors of this study observed the students using an observation system adapted from Jarrett et al. (2001). The adaptations involved changing some categories of behavior to better coincide with common behaviors of this age group. For example, "rough-and-tumble play" became "roughhousing," and "group talk" became "hanging out/group talking." A copy of the coding sheet is shown in Figure 13.1. The observational scheme involves noting whether the listed behaviors (described below) occurred during two-minute periods and whether boys, girls, or both engaged in the behavior. The end of each two-minute period was marked by a tone on a specially prepared audiotape, played

Figure 13.1
Observational Coding Sheet

	1	2	3	4	5	6	7	8	9	10
Chasing										
Roughhousing										
Hanging out/ group talking										
Teasing/ bullying										
Fighting										
Jumprope										
Children's games										
Sports: basketball										
Sports: football										
Toys/dolls										
Solitary behavior										

Observe the children at 2-minute intervals and enter a **b** if you see boys engaged in the behavior, a **g** if you see girls and a **b&g** if they are engaged together. If possible, note names of children fighting, teasing, or solitary and note type of game played.

Date_____Observer_____

Classroom/grade level_____

on a small tape recorder. During the first year, the observer(s) stood in a spot where she (they) could see the area where the students played, though occasionally students moved from view around one side of the mall. During the last few sessions of the second year, one observer moved about the playing area in order to hear the students' conversations. The behaviors of the teachers in charge of supervising recess were not systematically coded, although the observers noticed that sometimes the teachers (especially the assistant principal during the first year) played with the students but that more often the teachers remained in one spot on the playground talking with other teachers or conversing briefly with students.

At the end of each two-minute period, one observer quickly counted the number of students who were moving, sitting, or standing. The purpose of this "quick count" was to capture in a general way how physically active students were. Those students tallied as "moving" were either walking, jumping, running, or actively moving their arms. For example, students jumping rope or turning the rope were considered "moving." Those waiting their turns were generally "standing." Those playing football could be either "moving" if physically active in the play or "standing" while waiting for something to happen.

In order to achieve inter-observer agreement on the coding system, consensus had to be obtained on the categories of play and other behaviors. Behaviors were defined and generally fit the descriptions below:

1. Chasing: running one after another. Any group or individual running from or after another group or individual was considered chasing if the chasing was not part of an organized game.

2. Roughhousing: tackling, wrestling, kicking, hitting, dragging in a manner that seemed to be fun for all children involved. The distinction between roughhousing and fighting was often determined by the attitude displayed by the students involved. If there were no negative responses—attempts to retaliate in a more aggressive manner, reporting to the teacher, and so on—it was deemed roughhousing. Tackling in the play of the football game was not recorded as roughhousing.

3. Hanging out/group talking: standing around in shifting groups and talking and laughing or watching other games that were being played. If a student was alone throughout the entire two-minute segment, she or he was considered to be solitary and not coded as hanging out/group talking.

4. Teasing/bullying: any behavior that was verbally aggressive or taunting. If the behaviors were overheard as one-sided taunting or dominatingly aggressive, they were coded as teasing/bullying. Since whether a student is teased or bullied may be an issue of degree, duration, and interpretation by the victim, it was not possible to separate the behaviors in the coding.

5. Fighting: any violent verbal and physical contact between two or more students in a dispute that is obviously confrontational and not fun for those involved.

6. Jumprope: usually loosely organized group of children taking turns turning the rope and jumping double-Dutch style.

7. Children's games: defined rather freely as physical play involving some organized

behaviors among children. The games could have precise rules—checkers, four-square, and so on—or could have some kind of loose guidelines—catch, group cheer-leading, defense basketball.

8. Basketball: a loosely structured game involving dribbling and shooting a ball at a hoop.

9. Football: a loosely organized game of throwing a football and placing a two-hand touch on the player who received the ball. Distinct teams emerged. However, some switching of sides occurred during game play.

10. Toys/dolls: any teddy bear or doll or other electronic or physical toy, usually brought from home.

11. Solitary behavior: self-imposed sitting or standing alone for a considerable time with no attempts to interact with other students.

Inter-rater reliability, calculated as the percentage of agreement on whether particular behaviors occurred within the two-minute intervals, averaged 85.6% in the spring and 91.8% in the winter. On some specific behaviors, however, reliability was lower during one season or the other. This may have occurred because of the size of the play area and the focus of the observers. There were times when diverse activities were occurring and the raters were looking in opposite directions and therefore unable to observe all occurrences of some of the more brief behaviors. The quick count of the number of children moving, standing, and sitting was made by the same observer during the entire observation period. Usable data were collected on five days in spring 2000 and five days in winter 2001. The observers made note of the general weather conditions on the coding sheets each day.

Student Survey on Recess

Because observations during recess raised additional questions, the researchers decided to survey the students concerning their views on recess and their suggestions for making recess better. The survey, which took approximately 10–15 minutes to complete, is shown in Figure 13.2. The students filled out the survey during an early morning homeroom period in mid-February 2001. All but one homeroom (20–25 students) returned the surveys. That homeroom was taking a test and did not have time to complete the survey. The survey was answered by 43 boys and 40 girls: 20 sixth graders, 28 seventh graders, 19 eighth graders, and 15 ninth graders. Only one fifth grader completed the survey; the others were probably taking the test. The other students who did not complete surveys were presumably late or absent the day the survey was administered.

RESULTS

Observations during Recess

The number of two-minute intervals during which at least one student participated in each category of play or other behavior was tallied to describe, in a

Figure 13.2
Student Recess Survey

Gender: ___Male; ___Female **Grade level**: ___5th; ___6th; ___7th; ___8th; ___9th

1. How often do you usually go outside for recess when the weather is nice?
___never; ___once a week; ___twice a week; ___3–4 times a week; ___every day

2. When it is very cold:
    Do you go out about the same? ___ OR Are you more likely to stay in? ___

3. When it is very hot:
    Do you go out about the same? ___ OR Are you more likely to stay in? ___

4. If you often stay inside during recess, why do you stay in?

    What do you do inside during recess time?

    What would make you want to go outside during recess?

5 If you generally go outside during recess, what do you usually like to do?

6. What might make recess time better? Check any you agree with.
___ I like it the way it is
___ more organized games
___ more shade
___ playground equipment suitable for middle school
___ basketball hoop
___ more balls, jumpropes, or other equipment;
    list things you wish you had: _____
___ other _____

7. Do you think there is a problem during recess with teasing, fighting, or leaving people out?
___ often;   ___ sometimes;   ___ none or almost none
    If you think there is a problem, what do you think should be done?

8. How long do you think recess should last?
___ 20 minutes;   ___ 30 minutes;   ___ more than 30 minutes

9. What do you think the people supervising recess ought to do during recess?
___stand/watch;   ___organize games/sports/activities;
___play sports/games with students;   ___talk with students

---

broad sense, how middle school students spend their time during recess. This number of time intervals in which the behavior occurred was divided by the total number of two-minute observations in order to determine the percentage of time during which one or more students participated in various recess activities. Table 13.1 shows the percentages obtained, calculated by year and recess period.

These percentages give a general indication of the types of behaviors in which middle school students engaged during recess but do not indicate specific numbers of students and the duration of their involvement in those activities.

Table 13.1
Percentages of Intervals in Which the Various Play and Other Behaviors Occurred

	Spring 2000			Winter 2001	
Type of Behavior	**Period 1**	**Period 2**	**Period 3**	**Period 1**	**Period 2**
	5 & 6	**5, 6, 7, 8**	**7 & 8**	**5, 6, 7**	**8 & 9**
Chasing	30%	39%	38%	40%	40%
Roughhousing	33%	32%	15%	55%	36%
Group talking/hanging out	100%	86%	65%	86%	100%
Teasing/ bullying	2.7%	7%	0%	36%	30%
Fighting	0%	0%	0%	4%	4%
Jumprope	25%	90%	73%	29%	48%
Children's games	39%	75%	47%	20%	44%
Basketball	39%	91%	76%	0%	0%
Football	39%	95%	100%	100%	72%
Toys/dolls	22%	18%	44%	30%	6%
Solitary behavior	83%	54%	79%	9%	18%

Table 13.2
Percentage of Chasing, Roughhousing, and Teasing of Males and Females Based on the Gender of the Dominant Person in the Activity

Type of Activity	**Boy to Girl**	**Girl to Boy**	**All Boy**	**All Girl**
Chasing	34%	26%	25%	15%
Roughhousing	30%	22%	28%	21%
Teasing/Bullying	11%	43%	37%	8%

Table 13.2 indicates ways in which boys and girls interacted in terms of some of the behaviors.

General observations are as follows:

• The students had very little to play with. Generally, 2 jump ropes and 2–3 balls of various types were taken outside. Occasionally, students brought their own play materials, such as dolls, teddy bears, or electronic toys.

• Hanging out/group talking and football were the most consistent activities observed across grade levels.

• Fighting was the least frequently observed behavior across grade levels. No fighting was observed during the spring, and only 4% of the time intervals involved fighting

Table 13.3
Average Percentage of Students Who Were Moving, Standing, and Sitting during Recess (by week)

Recess Period	Moving	Standing	Sitting
1st week, Spring 2000	16.3%	77.7%	6%
2nd week, Spring 2000	45%	47.7%	7.3 %
3rd week, Spring 2000	48%	34.3%	17.7%
1st week, Winter 2001	38.5%	54.8%	6.8%
2nd week, Winter 2001	50.6%	41.4%	8%

during the winter observations. The few fights were limited to angry talk and shoving rather than hitting.

- During the first year, five students were repeatedly solitary. However, in the second year almost no solitary behavior was observed. Sixty-two percent of the solitary behavior was by male students. A number of children were solitary during a single interval, and the observers determined that these students were generally taking a short break before rejoining the football game.

- The observers developed a new symbol for the coding sheet: a heart with "bg" inside suggesting a romantically involved couple. A small number of repeat couples were observed.

- The boys dominated the play area with the football games. However, in 29% of the intervals there were between one and three girls actively participating in football.

- More behaviors were coded as teasing/bullying during the 2001 observations, after the observer began moving around the play area to better detect what children were saying.

- In 43% of all teasing, girls initiated the teasing toward boys. The boys' initiation of teasing of girls was a mere 11%.

- In single-gender teasing, boys were much more apt to tease boys (37% of all teasing) than girls were to tease other girls (8% of all teasing).

- Sixty percent of the chasing was mixed-gender. Boys chasing girls was the predominant form of mixed-gender chasing.

- Fifty-two percent of the roughhousing was mixed-gender. Boys were the primary initiators of roughhousing toward girls.

- Jump rope was dominated by the girls. More of the jump rope time was spent in talking and deciding what to do than in actually jumping.

- Solitary behavior was observed primarily among males. Sixty-two percent of the solitary students were boys, and 38% were girls.

- With the exception of play with toys and dolls, there was a generally equal engagement in activities across the grade levels as represented by different recess periods.

Table 13.3 was developed from the tally of how many students were moving, standing, and sitting at the end of each two-minute interval. The percentages of students who were moving varied greatly from week to week, with a mean of 40% of the children moving during the quick count. Those identified as "standing" were either in a game waiting for something to happen or hanging out with their friends. Those sitting were resting from activity, playing with toys/games, or watching the play or appeared socially isolated.

Student Survey on Recess

The analysis of student responses on the survey was done primarily by hand tallies. Seven girls and only two boys said that they rarely went outside (never or once a week). Overall, 67% of the students said that they went out every day. Boys and girls did not differ significantly in how often they said that they went out, using a chi-square test of independence. However, boys thought that there was less "teasing/ fighting/ leaving people out" occurring, $X^2(1) = 5.54$, $p < .05$. Nineteen boys and 8 girls said there was none, whereas 23 boys and 31 girls thought such negative behaviors occurred sometimes or often. Of the 5 girls who never went outside, 3 said that there was often teasing/fighting/leaving people out during recess. One girl said that she never went outside "because I have bad memories of being outside." She said that there were sometimes problems with teasing/fighting and suggested that "people just need to learn how to treat people decently." The other students, however, seemed to prefer to stay in not because they felt excluded but because their friends stayed in, and they liked to sit and talk, play with the computer, or play games with their friends. One boy said that he "would go out maybe if they made it more fun."

According to many students, weather had an effect on their decision to go outside. Forty-four percent said that they would be more likely to stay in if it were very cold, and 11% said that they would be more likely to stay in if it were very hot.

Students had many suggestions for improving the play area. Of the 81 students who answered this question, 14% said, "I like it the way it is," though most of those students also made suggestions. Thirty percent said they would like more organized games, 28% wanted more shade, 52% wanted playground equipment, 58% requested a basketball hoop, and 65% wanted more equipment or "other." "Other" ranged from the easy-to-provide "air for balls" or more balls and jump ropes, through activities that could be provided with a little money and planning such as volleyball nets and four-square courts to the "dream requests" of a gymnasium, grassy field, football field, and basketball court.

In response to the question on what the supervisors should be doing during recess, 36% of students checked only "stand/watch," basically what supervisors were doing during the winter 2001 observations. Another 10% checked "stand/watch" as well as one of the other options. Forty percent wanted the supervisors to play sports/games with students, 32% thought they should organize games/sports/activities, and 16% would like the supervisors to talk with students during recess.

CONCLUSIONS AND DISCUSSION

Most of the students chose to go outside during recess period, but those who wished to stay inside also had a type of recess break. Whether they stayed inside or went out during recess, the students seemed to appreciate the opportunity to socialize with their friends. The results of the survey as well as spot checks on what was going on inside indicated that many of the students who stayed inside played board games or computer games while interacting with their friends. Although outdoor recess offers the added advantage of promoting physical activity, indoor recess could be given as an option, especially during inclement weather. Indoor recess appears to offer some of the benefits of traditional recess, a break from work, time for social interaction, and the opportunity for choice.

The large percentage of intervals in which students were hanging out rather than involved in activities that could be described as play may reflect the needs of this age group. However, this may also be an artifact of the scarcity of play equipment available, especially equipment appealing to the girls. The quick count done every two minutes and summarized by the week found that from 16.3% to 48% of the students were actively moving during the spring 2000 observations and that 38.5% to 50.6% of the students were actively moving during the winter 2001 observations. These findings suggest that many students take advantage of the opportunity to play actively but also that many students, at any given time, are not physically active. Any interpretation should be made with caution since the counts were made by one observer only, precluding estimates of inter-rater reliability. However, the quick count appears to be an easy and fruitful way to gather general information on physical activity level. Future research should include the measurement of inter-rater reliability. Since one argument against recess has rested on the assumption that children fulfill their need for activity during physical education classes, research using the quick count could be useful for comparing the physical activity levels of students during recess and during physical education, especially during different types of games and motor skill instruction.

More negative behavior was observed during winter 2001 than during the previous spring (2000), though the teasing/bullying and fighting observed appeared to be mild, and very few students registered it as a concern on the survey. However, the girl who said that she never went outside "because I have bad memories of being outside" reminds us that behaviors that may look mild to observers may be devastating to students who are repeatedly victimized. The increase in negative behavior may be due to one or more of the following: (1) a change in supervision, since the assistant principal did not play with the students during the winter observations, (2) the length of recess (see Boulton, 1993), since the winter recess periods tended to be longer, or (3) the method of observation. One observer noticed more teasing/bullying when she left her usual coding location and moved about the play area. It is very difficult, if not impossible, for a supervisor who remains in one location to be aware of cruel verbal behavior that occurs across the playground. More research is needed on factors promoting negative behavior and ways in which playground supervisors can better detect teasing and bullying.

Especially during the winter 2001 observations, the play space was dominated by football games with very few female participants. This finding is similar to previous research that indicated that boys dominate the playing fields with their more competitive games (Sadker & Sadker, 1994). Cross-gender interactions were common and included what Thorne (1993) termed "borderwork," chasing, teasing, and roughhousing. In what was coded as teasing, girls tended to instigate the teasing of boys, though some of the cross-gender roughhousing and chasing that boys tended to instigate may also have been a form of teasing. However, most of the roughhousing and chasing did not appear to be negative and may provide a bridge to more romantic behavior, also seen during recess, especially among the older students.

The scarcity of play materials, often only two footballs and two jump ropes, meant that the students had very little choice in playing games requiring even simple equipment. However, students could also have made up games that required no equipment (e.g., relay races, capture games, or clapping games). Very few such games were seen. Perhaps middle school students consider such games babyish. However, another explanation is possible. The fact that students who attended elementary school in the county school system did not have recess throughout their elementary school years may mean that they do not know the kinds of games generally learned on the playground or how to organize such games. The rich range of game playing found by Jarrett et al. (2001) may be lost in school systems that have abolished recess.

The surveys indicated that the students had good ideas for ways to improve recess, especially the provision of more balls, ropes, and other inexpensive items. Consulting with students is an appropriate way to plan school improvements that will affect students. The next step for this research involves painting a four-square court and hopscotch area on the asphalt and providing more balls, hula hoops, and ropes. The observations will then be repeated to see whether the new materials promote more activity and play.

The findings of this study suggest that recess provides valuable opportunities for middle school students to interact with their peers, engage in physical activity, and play games. The observational coding system and the quick count used in this study can be employed by other researchers, teachers, or parents to gather data on what behaviors occur during recess. This study suggests that recess is important to students and allows for play and other social behaviors that would not occur in structured physical education classes. Any school system considering the substitution of physical education for recess should learn what actually occurs during recess and consult with students before making a decision.

REFERENCES

Boulton, M. J. (1993). Aggressive fighting in British middle school children. *Educational Studies, 19*(1), 19–39.

Butcher, D. A. (1999). Enhancing social skills through school social work interventions during recess: Gender differences. *Social Work in Education, 21*(4), 249–262.

Chmelynski, C. (1998). Is recess needed? *Education Digest, 64*(4), 27–28.

Dahmes, V. M. (1993). *A descriptive study of multicultural elementary student playground behaviors and their relationship to gender, age, race and socioeconomic status.* Paper presented at the annual meeting of the Mid-South Educational Research Association, New Orleans (ERIC Document Reproduction Service No. ED 369 521).

Ghezzi, P. (2001). Low scores may close DeKalb charter school. *Atlanta Journal*, February 12, pp. B1, B6.

Jambor, T. (1994). School recess and social development. *Dimensions of Early Childhood, 23*, pp. 17–20.

Jarrett, O. S., Farokhi, B., Young, C., & Davies, G. (2001). Boys and girls at play: Games and recess at a southern urban elementary school. In Stuart Reifel (Ed.), *Play and culture studies* (vol. 3, pp. 147–170). Westport, CT: Greenwood Press.

Jarrett, O. S., & Maxwell, D. M. (2000). What research says about the need for recess. In R. Clements (Ed.), *Elementary school recess: Selected readings, games, and activities for teachers and parents* (pp. 12–23). Boston: American Press.

Jarrett, O. S., Maxwell, D. M., Dickerson, C., Hoge, P., Davies, G., & Yetley, A. (1998). The impact of recess on classroom behavior: Group effects and individual differences. *The Journal of Educational Research, 92*(2), 121–126.

Jarrett, O. S., & Young, C. (2000). School playground supervision: Distinguishing between rough and tumble play, fighting, and bullying. In M. L. Christiansen (Ed.), *Playground safety: Proceedings of the 1999 International Conference.* University Park, PA: Penn State University.

Jensen, E. (1998). *Teaching with the brain in mind.* Alexandria, VA: Association for Supervision and Curriculum Development.

Maxwell, D. M., Jarrett, O. S., & Roetger, C. D. (1999). *Recess through the children's eyes.* Paper presented at the Conference on Qualitative Research in Education, University of Georgia, Athens, January.

McKenzie, T. L., Simon, J., Sallis, J. F., & Conway, T. L. (2000). Leisure-time physical activity in school environments: An observational study using SOPLAY. *Preventive Medicine: An International Journal Devoted to Practice & Theory, 30*(1), 70–77.

Olweus, D. (1993). Bullies on the playground: The role of victimization. In C. H. Hart (Ed.), *Children on playgrounds: Research perspectives and applications* (pp. 85–128). Albany: State University of New York Press.

Pellegrini, A. D. (1995). *School recess and playground behavior: Educational & developmental roles.* Albany: State University of New York Press.

Pellegrini, A. D., & Bjorklund, D. F. (1996). The place of recess in school. Issues in the role of recess in children's education and development: An introduction to the special issue. *Journal of Research in Childhood Education, 11*(1), 5–13.

Pellegrini, A. D., & Bjorklund, D. F. (1997). The role of recess in children's cognitive performance. *Educational Psychologist, 32*(1), 35–40.

Pellegrini, A. D., & Davis, P. L. (1993). Relations between children's playground and classroom behaviour. *British Journal of Educational Psychological Society, 63*, 88–95.

Pellegrini, A. D., Huberty, P. D., & Jones, I. (1995). The effects of recess timing on children's classroom and playground behavior. *American Educational Research Journal, 32*, 845–864.

Pellegrini, A. D., & Smith, P. K. (1993). School recess: Implications for education and development. *Review of Educational Research, 63*(1), 51–67.

Pellegrini, A. D., & Smith, P. K. (1998). Physical activity play: The nature and function of a neglected aspect of play. *Child Development, 69*(3), 577–598.

Ramsey, P. G. (1998). Diversity and play: Influences of race, culture, class, and gender. In D. P. Fromberg & D. Bergen (Eds.), *Play from birth to twelve and beyond: Contexts, perspectives, and meanings* (pp. 23–33). New York: Garland Publishing.

Sadker, M., & Sadker, D. (1994). *Failing at fairness: How our schools cheat girls.* New York: Touchstone.

Savage, M. P., & Scott, L. B. (1998). Physical activity and rural middle school adolescents. *Journal of Youth and Adolescence, 27*(2), 245–253. [Abstract from SocialSciAbs, ISSN: 0047-2891]

Sprenger, M. (1999). *Learning and memory: The brain in action.* Alexandria, VA: Association for Supervision and Curriculum Development.

Thorne, B. (1993). *Gender play: Girls and boys in school.* New Brunswick, NJ: Rutgers University Press.

Wechsler, H., Devereaux, R. S., Davis, M., & Collins, J. (2000). Using the school environment to promote physical activity and healthy eating. *Preventive Medicine: An International Journal Devoted to Practice and Theory, 31* (2, Pt. 2), S121-S137. [Abstract from PsycFIRST, ASSN: 0091-7435]

Werner, P., Timms, S., & Almond, L. (1996). Health stops: Practical ideas for health-related exercise in preschool and primary classrooms. *Young Children, 51*(6), September, 48–55.

Chapter 14

Questioning Play and Work, Early Childhood, and Pedagogy

Jeanette Rhedding-Jones

INTRODUCTION

Work and play have been seen as two opposing practices. Traditionally, schools have been seen as places of work, and kindergartens and preschools (day-care centers, in Norway) as places of play. Changing these views requires a shift in the practices of teachers and learners. It also requires a shift in theory. For work and play to come together, working at play and playing at work develop pedagogical praxis differently. In Northern Europe, this may be seen as *didaktik* (Gundem & Hopmann, 1998), a term not translatable into English but carrying meanings regarding the actions of a teacher and the learning of a discipline. For children aged 0–8 the notions of play and work are, in any case, blurred. This chapter suggests a blurring for the adults who work and play with children. If this happens, teachers of 6–8-year-olds at school present learning as play. Conversely, teachers of preschoolers acknowledge that play is sometimes work. Being able to play and to know about the work of play is the *didaktik* of preschool education. Extending this to schooling requests a change in what is valued, a change in adult role, and a change in the organization of time and physical settings.

The chapter's theoretical assumption is that the "naturally playing child" can be seen as a cultural construct, made up under patriarchal conditions. Similarly, the naturally work-oriented schoolteacher can also be seen as a historic construction following gendered patterns of competence. Given a critical theory, then, play as child-directed learning and schoolwork as teacher-directed learning must both be read as cultural constructs. Obviously, this reading is a simplistic one, as no situation, person, or idea can ever be so firmly located. I offer it now as a springboard to a reconstructing of pedagogy/*didaktik*, within the dichotomized institutions that we now have for early childhood learning and professional care. Without critique, teachers are in danger of complacency. Without awareness of today's changing cultural contexts, they reproduce worn-out practices. The chapter thus has implications for the practical development of play in early schooling. Further, it has implications for the theoretical development of work in preschool day care. Beyond this, the chapter is a call for future critical interrogations of the notion of play and its normalized practice in institutions caring for and educating the very young.

WORK AND PLAY

Although play is considered the basis of preschool pedagogy and the natural media of children, as well as the art of the teacher/carer, it rates little mention in some recently published texts on early childhood, such as Creaser and Dau's (1996) *The Anti-Bias Approach in Early Childhood* and Dahlberg, Moss, and Pence's (1999) *Beyond Quality in Early Childhood Education and Care*. This is in contrast to early childhood texts a few decades earlier such as Bjorklund's (1978) *Planning for Play: A Developmental Approach* and Cohen and Rudolph's (1977) *Kindergarten and Early Schooling*. While isolated examples prove nothing, it is possible that such texts, each set for study by students of its relevant decade, are reflecting something else. This could be that experienced teachers are no longer seen as "the experts." The new experts may be "highly qualified" in terms of academe, but not necessarily in terms of praxis with young children. Without firsthand experience of play, perhaps inexperienced intellectuals are focusing on other things. But there may be other forces causing these texts' shifts away from play. Such forces could include the increasing challenge from discourses of power (Foucault, 1979) and with the role of an adult with a child now constantly under surveillance. Another possibility is simply that fashions in education come and go, and now there are more sophisticated words than "the meaning" or "promoting development" (Bjorklund, 1978; Cohen & Rudolph, 1977).

This chapter deals with what is happening with theorizations of "play" and its supposed opposite, "work." From a young child's point of view, play may be what one does before one goes to school, and work is the real stuff that one does after one grows up a bit. Though many young children see the business of their play as work, not many beginners at school see schoolwork as play. What matters is the ownership of the work and the play. Is it the school's work? Is it the child's play? (A school play is something quite different. So is the person working at the preschool at the end of the day doing the cleaning.)

I present the view that work and play may at all times be blurred, even when play and work are enacted by adults. For example, I play with my computer to see what I am able to write, by cutting and pasting, deleting, going onto the

Internet. These activities are a kind of experimentation, not taken too seriously until I require a product ready for evaluation by others. Similarly, when I teach on campus, I play around with the group of students, to see what engages them, to find out what works as a classroom strategy, what their substantive concepts and problems are, what they have read, and what kinds of sense they are making of what they have experienced.

In the same ways, when I visit a preschool or day-care center, I sit on the floor with the children, to be guided by them in what I do with the blocks or the puzzles, to wait till they make linguistic or embodied contact, to see and to hear what happens, to try out some imaginative intitiatives. All of these are both play and work. In preschool education the pedagogical hypotheses are that work via play is socially communicative interaction, cultural construction, a world of individual make-believe, a means of conceptualization, a learning of language, an engagement with objects, a production of subjectivities.

In contrast, in schooling the equipment costs less, the space is smaller, and the importance of play diminishes. Yet in schooling the ratio of adults to children and the status of the job are both higher. Looked at historically, this is not surprising, as schoolteacher training derives from other ideologies, other forms of child management, other sets of readings, other kinds of professionals. In particular, the preschool arena has been dominated by women, with the exception of the men who wrote the founding doctrines (Bruner, Jolly, & Sylva 1976; Dewey, 1938; Erikson, 1963; Piaget, 1952; Vygotsky, 1962). Women writers have provided additional local and understandable knowledge (Bae, 1996; Butler, 1980; Cohen & Rudolph, 1977; Os & Aamild, 1995). Like the men's knowledge, the women's knowledge is culturally specific. This is because it regards the contemporary present of particular places (Rhedding-Jones, 2001a, 2001b). Here the interests of the women writers are to combine pedagogical practices with theories and with their own working knowledge and experience of play. In thus dividing the two genders, I have presented a generalized picture. There are, of course, exceptions, as there are also exceptions with my time-related categorizations of books about and not about play.

SCHOOLS AND PRESCHOOLS

The age of beginning school is seen as the determinant of what pedagogical practices are appropriate. Thus, when the official age of starting is altered (for Norwegian documentation, see L-97, 1996), the normalized practices of schooling become problematic. Hence, new pedagogies for teachers of 6-year-olds in Norway become an issue with the lowering of the traditional beginning school age of 7. In Australia, where children begin school somewhere between 4.5 and 5.5 (Rhedding-Jones, 1997, 2000b), the age-related practice of play in early schooling is not new, although teacher-directed activities dominate, often unintentionally.

From the point of view of teachers, usually the younger the children with whom one works, the less valued the job is perceived to be, at least by the public, and also in terms of financial remuneration and employment opportunities. Relatedly, many who get to teach/lecture in teacher education have no practical pedagogical experiences to match the theories that they take up regarding early childhood. Further, many excellent teachers simply "burn out" or become disenchanted and leave the practical fields of early childhood teaching and care. In many ways this situation is related to the status of play as not quite professional and as something that anyone can do.

For English speakers, the Northern European term *didaktik* is useful here, although it is not without its problems. I introduce it because I don't want this chapter to address only Anglophones, who see didactics (here the English word does not match *didaktik*) as probably the furthest removed from freedom. We are didactic with our dogs, when we point a finger at them and tell them to sit. But this is not, even metaphorically, what Northern Europeans are advocating for young children, though many teachers around the world revert to such practices in overcrowded classrooms or when all creativity is gone or when no one is looking. To use the English word, the preschool teacher/carer is never didactic, but the schoolteacher may be, and (sadly) the higher education teacher often is. The European spelling of *didaktik* means "radical pedagogy" or the praxis of pedagogy, with *pedagogikk* as the more traditional and less specific way of working for learning.

So in preschools *didaktik* means play. In early schooling play may be defined differently, as in "playtime," when all the children go outside to do whatever they like while the teachers have their cup of coffee. Or when they "play with" the play dough (Garrison, 1997). Hence, private and artistic experiences (with the play dough) are confused linguistically with the sociocultural aspects of shared play. Here the agenda of the art curriculum becomes the means of working, as children shape the dough for representation, develop the skills of manual dexterity, manipulate a medium. In this case the English word "play" causes the confusion. Playing music, for example, may be just turning on the compact disc (CD). Here the Norwegian words *lek* and *spill* appropriately vary the verb and allocate play to its differing semantics. (Å *leke* is to play as children do. Å *spille* is to play the piano.)

TEACHERS AND LEARNERS

In preschools, there are histories of teachers working at play: refining it, studying it, recording it, discussing it, and developing it. For teachers in early schooling, the work of refining, studying, discussing, and developing has often been about process writing, where children work at consequent drafts of text production or at small group projects. Here what counts are the interaction of the group and their ways of gathering and presenting information or ideas (L-97, 1996; Board of Studies, 1995). Though teachers call process writing and thematic multicurricula projects "work" (because of their earlier views of play as unprofessional), I would argue that these are play with texts and contexts. Here the school emphasis is on what gets done, who experiments, how decisions are arrived at, where the initiatives are, how creative the project and its process become. The teacher questions occasionally, intervenes sometimes, shows by demonstration, and points people in particular directions regarding content or social cooperation. In fact, the location for the processing of the product may even be the floor, a usual place for play. Project work and writing in schools are not play, though, as students are not free do what they like. They must produce a product by using the allocated time in the manner deemed appropriate.

Searching for similarities, the noun "play" would indicate that drama may be the curriculum equivalent of what happens in preschools. On investigation, it is not the production of "a play" that relates to the spirit of preschool play. Rather it is improvised drama that is the near relation (Board of Studies, 1995; L-97, 1996; R-96, 1995). Here language and bodies, sounds and silence, movement and stillness, objects and subjects interact, imaginatively converge, momentarily exist for the experience itself, for the brief gaze of others. But such drama is not the usual practice of classrooms. Few teachers develop the skills, and even fewer schedule it into a busy week or let it happen spontaneously. If they do, they are not likely to be in a dramatic role themselves, needing instead a distance from the fantasy, a position from which to command if necessary.

In summary, valuing children's thoughts and experiences more than timetables, conservative furniture arrangements, and the teacher's own voice has not been the hallmark of traditional primary schooling. This is because losing control of the class is a fear for many teachers in schools. Voluntarily giving up traditional control (Bae, 1988) because of a desire for children's autonomy, however, is a driving force behind preschool pedagogy and its practices of play.

THEORIES AND PRACTICES

I have been presenting the case that early childhood is constructed differently within the differing discourses of preschooling and schooling. These constructions occur across continents and languages, in the "Western" locations that I have experienced. (But Australia and Norway are, in fact, north and south.) It can be seen that in undoing some of the binaries of thought regarding play and work, I am also undoing other binaries (Spivak, 1999), such as learning and teaching, schools and preschools, adult and child, professional and personal, practices and theories.

In summary, usual theories of learning are that the teacher role needs to change according to the age of students and that play is appropriate for the very young but not for the not-so-young. Other theories are that the work of learning is a kind of play and that teachers need particular skills to see learning as playing, rather than teaching as working. Moreover, as metatheory, I am working/playing with the idea that binary thought be broken down. This follows philosophical directions from postmodernity, with consequent practices of deconstruction, critique, and reconstruction (Cannella, 1999; Rhedding-Jones, 1996, 2000a). Deconstruction is not destruction. Rather, it is the tracing of the old and the reworking or reconstructing of the new. In short, submitting that schools work more practically with play and that preschools work more theoretically with work stems from the same philosophical position.

EXEMPLIFICATION THROUGH TEACHING A FOREIGN LANGUAGE

Presented with the problem of 6-year-olds (in Norway) supposed to be learning English in early schooling and knowing that most of them were already picking up quite a bit of the language anyway (via travel and television), I began to query some of the pedagogical differences between early schooling and preschooling. Teaching a foreign language (in this case English) has historically been constructed as teacher-directed, not as the learner playing with the language. Hence, singing a few songs known by the teacher and "taught" to the children serves as a repetition of this pedagogical practice. Questioning the nature of learning, however, and of language learning in particular leads us to other practices. Of course, playing with a language is not the same as playing with a doll or a truck. Or is it?

Further, if the learning of (English/foreign) language can be a site for learning through play, then maybe the problematics of the development of home languages for ethnic minority children and their emergent reading and writing of both the dominant language and their home languages could also be reduced. Here extended practices of play offer new possibilities for language and literacy developments in multilingual contexts. It is, after all, through linguistic play, not through work, that we all learned our own language in the first place. As babies we said what we needed to say, without anyone instructing us. All we needed were reasons for wanting to talk, people showing us what talk sounded like, success along with our incorrect attempts, ways of linking up what we were beginning to think with what we heard ourselves say. In these ways and in a relaxed atmosphere of play with language, learning happened.

There is no reason that the learning of another language cannot proceed in the same ways. Here the learning of a language used outside the home gives the learner access to wider audiences and new contexts. As an international language that is both foreign yet slightly familiar to children in Europe, Africa, Asia, South America, and other non-English-speaking places, English is heard and seen in everyday situations, in advertisements, on television. By playfully extending these situations in schools and in a variety of situations inside and outside, beginners would become used to hearing and using English in informal and enjoyable situations, occasionally. But for this to eventuate, teachers would need to know not only how to play but how to play with language.

DILEMMAS

The dilemmas here regard the differences between theories and practices of literacy/language and pedagogy/*didaktik*. Will we take up a natural learning model or beg for an active role for the teacher? Here what is at stake are the professional skills and the related need for a reputation for expertise. Given the differences also in the histories of preschool education and early schooling, the problem divides, with preschool teachers as opposites to primary school teachers. On the one hand, preschool teachers are skilled and experienced in the functions and organization of play as a way of learning. Primary school teachers, on the other hand, may let the children get on with playing by themselves, without documenting what happens, building on the play experiences, or joining in. Yet recent radical changes in curricula require the elimination of categorized learning and the development of new technical skills and other ways of being professional.

These question the role of the teacher, the place of advance planning and organizing, the allocations of space and time, the institutional setting and its physical locations. Presuming that new practices are driven by theories, not just by exigencies, a primary school teacher will believe in the inherent ability of children to learn, in the importance of freedom and differentiation and of social interactions with peers (Johannessen, 1987). These qualities also represent the long-held qualities of preschooling.

A dilemma here is what to do as the teacher and how to unlearn the habits of a profession. Of course, not all primary school teachers can be labeled as anti-play. Generations of successful teachers have pioneered their own ways of working, with love and with tact. The institution of schooling is the problem, with its organizational rules, its society of expecting parents, its eager-to-become-encultured students. A step in the direction of blurring preschool knowhow with schooled expertise is course work offered to teacher education students combining preschooling and schooling to provide new perspectives. Among the central themes of such course work is an emphasis on learning through play and the resultant changes to adult roles.

NEW PRACTICES FOR SCHOOLS AND NEW THEORIES FOR PRESCHOOLS

If we widen the narrow confines of preschooling and early schooling so that each becomes loosened from its historically constructed practices, new pedagogies emerge. Doing away with the binary division of play in preschool and schoolwork in school requests other ways of relating to the young people who are the students and the cared for. I am not alone in suggesting that schoolwork be differently practiced in early schooling. What I suggest at the end of this chapter may be more challenging, for I suggest that pedagogy be differently theorized in preschooling. What follows leads toward this theorization.

For early childhood pedagogies, the two suggestions (of different practices for schooling and different theories for preschooling) represent a change in line with postmodernity, where borders are blurred and where more than one meaning can operate at once. Working within the cultural shifts of postmodernity, new truths are not espoused. Rather, other ways of seeing the world(s) can be realized. Seeing differently involves becoming critical of pedagogical practices, of hidden and overt tasks, of curriculum documentations, of the roles and the expertise of the adults employed. In traditional schooling situations, adults set tasks for children and gave instruction. Even now, children working on a thematic project know that projects are work, that the teacher and the system of schooling require it, even if the teacher is a caring one (Noddings, 1992). Selecting their own topic, working at their own pace, producing a finished product, retelling or performance are the task of the group. For less directed activities in school, such as the so-called free play with materials (clay, water, blocks, carpentry, dressing up, paints), the qualities of the classroom, the time-based schedules, and the ratio of adults to children all contribute to the understanding that this is preparation for work or that it is light relief from the more difficult things done earlier in the day.

Thus, an appearance of play in these contexts, given the teacher's agenda of work (toward curriculum competence and differentiations between children) is not at all the same as the play that takes place, without the teacher, in the playground. Learning through this kind of play is outside the range of the teacher, who desires certain measures of control, the organization of the objects of play, the power to say when the play will begin and end. More radical teachers and those themselves disliking physical confines will take the children outside, work with what is found, teach through what happens, take a minor role in determining outcomes, and talk less.

In preschooling and day care, play has long been the focus. Because of Piaget and the "consequent constructivist programs and the creation and marketing of developmentally appropriate practice" (Cannella, 1997, p. 165), teacher-directed activities are institutionally disguised as play. Here the paid adult takes the role of a friend, someone who gets down to the level of the child, on the floor if need be, to share, communicate, nurture, and demonstrate. Following critical theory, at this point our white, educated, middle-class values shine through. This is because in preschool pedagogy the teacher shows the child how to play, suggests changes to the play, rearranges the playthings, sends everyone outside or inside. Again following critical theory (Giroux, 1983; Popkewitz, 1994), play may be an inappropriate activity for children whose home cultures value something else, for example, daylong body contact with parents, sharing of family responsibilities such as baby care by very young children, play with language rather than play with objects, apprenticing to real tasks rather than the playing out of approved fantasy situations. When play is seen as a cultural construct, then monoculturalism presents major problems for play-based pedagogy. Following this reasoning, only the culturally dominant can succeed, and only the dominant classes, races, and ethnicities will want to enter the profession of preschool education. (Here it can be seen that I am not at all following Vygotsky's cultural-historical theory, where culture implies creativity and aesthetics. I am theorizing from cultural diversity, which implies ethnicity, race, social class, gender, religion, sexual preference, and color.)

I suggest that what underlies an ideology of play for preschool pedagogy is a firm fixation on particular cultural values, namely, those deriving from the Germanic tradition built up following Froebel (1887). Times have changed since then, and today's cultural diversities are quite different from what was happening yesterday. For Froebel's "construction of group education for young children" (Cannella, 1997, p. 97), monocultural groups provided a useful context for theories of preschool teaching as extended mothering. Although Froebel began by training men to work with young children, he admitted women when the men showed little interest in the training. From this he developed his view of women as "those who ultimately submit their will for the good of the child" (Canella, 1997, p. 141). This view represents the split between the pedagogies historically developed by schoolteachers (men) and preschool teachers (women). Play became the pedagogy appropriate for the women, who would submit to children's desires so that children could learn through play. Work became the pedagogy appropriate for the men who would lead children to learning via set tasks and mastery. Today's changing gender roles are not unrelated to the changes in the pedagogies of schooling. With play the driving force of preschooling and women the ones employed to see that the play happened, the activities of schooling became constructed as age-appropriate. Hence, the gendered history of the development of practices became veiled by ideas of small children playing and older children playing only outside at lunchtime. For teachers, parents, and children this became acceptable as "the truth" of education. In fact, we adults also play our own games; and in some cultures very young children take responsibility for the work of their families.

What I say next goes against the theories circulating in preschool education, where play is constructed as a child-centeredness theorized from psychological discourses of human development. If psychology itself is seen as a construct of its times and its culture (Piaget, 1964), then its location as master discipline in early childhood education is open to question. To take a feminist position again, both Piaget and Froebel can be read as male experts informing women non-experts. The questions are: Who is the expert when it comes to child care and teaching, those with the experience or those with the experiments and positivist research paradigms? Why want a discursively constructed expert anyway? Here it can be seen that I am playing with the modernist binary of logic. However, the work of this chapter is not only to deconstruct the locations and the dislocations of play but also to assist in reconceptualizing early childhood education, to take positive steps toward something useful for all children, not just for those with the advantages of class and cultural dominance.

I am now working at critiquing power relations producing regulation and injustice (Foucault, 1979). Through a critical theory, play and work are differently construed. In the case of early schooling, groups of adults have power over children, although this power takes different forms. This depends on the gendered history of the teaching professions, though such difference is usually construed as appropriately age-related to those being taught. Further, because discourses of cultural diversity were unheard of at the time of the making up of the master theories of play, an unquestioned monoculturalism pervades all such practices. These are only now being questioned as culturally specific and hence inappropriate for many children from minority groups (de Wal Pastoor, 1998). If we are to reconceptualize early childhood education, then we must take into consideration the children who are being disadvantaged by the perpetuation of play as usual in preschooling and by teachers setting work (even if they call it play) in early schooling.

If we manage to get rid of the dichotomies that we currently have, between the structures of work and play, between school and preschool, between the teacher and those taught, then we could be said to be working/playing post-structurally. As a way of practicing and theorizing, this is useful if it helps us to reconsider our professional values and their relation to the diverse groups of children attending schools and preschools. The challenge of culturally diverse children "taught by" teachers of monocultural backgrounds is a major problem. I suggest that we can begin to deal with the problem by considering the specifically cultural locations of work and play.

When play is seen as a cultural artifact (Cannella, 1997) and games with rules, competitions between participants, and the keeping of marks or scores as dependent on cultural contexts, then it is not surprising that children coming from cultures not stressing these values but stressing others will be seen as underachieving. When professionals label play and work as good or bad, appropriate or inappropriate, then they themselves construct the disadvantage that many children suffer. Forms of learning are not universal. Verbalized and demonstrated knowledges and skills cannot be read in the same ways for all (young) people. Not all children from all cultures find it natural to explore, to question, to imagine together with others, to build up constructions, to produce products, to talk as they do so.

I believe that it is a useful start to begin to theorize preschool play differently. Seen as the discursive work of particular cultures, the activities the children are engaged in, under the surveillance of professional adults, come under critique. This critique regards who the categories of people are: the adults who are culturally located, the children who are seen to be playing well and showing various competencies, and the children who are not. Theorizing play not as Piaget would have it, with the child as a developing (Western) scientist systematically examining problems and solving them (Burman, 1994), but as the work of enculturation produces another praxis. So does a reassessment of play theories following Froebel, where curriculum development models of planning, supervision, and evaluation (Cannella, 1997) link to who is playing what and with whom. Leaving out the cultural aspects of pedagogy assumes that all children are similar regarding race, ethnicity, religion, and class. This links to the related histories of play and non-play, to parental desires for children, to ways of conduct and uses of space and time. Knowing about cultural differences, yet continuing with pedagogically organized play as it was, is today's problem.

REFERENCES

Bae, B. (1988). Voksnes definisjonsmakt—barns selvopplevelse (Adults' power to define—and children's experiences of self). *Norsk pedagogisk tidskrift.* (Norwegian Journal of Pedagogy), *4,* 213–227.

Bae, B. (1996). *Det interessante i det alminnelige* (The interesting within the ordinary). Oslo, Norway: Pedagogisk Forum.

Bjorklund, G. (1978). *Planning for play: A developmental approach.* Columbus, OH: Charles Merrill Publishing Company.

Board of Studies. (1995). *Curriculum and standards framework.* Carlton, Victoria, Australia: Victorian Curriculum and Assessment Authority.

Bruner, J. Jolly, A., & Sylva, K. (1976). *Play: Its role in development and evolution.* New York: Basic Books.

Burman, E. (1994). *Deconstructing developmental psychology.* New York: Routledge.

Butler, D. (1980). *Babies need books.* London: Penguin Books.

Cannella, G. (1997). *Deconstructing early childhood education: Social justice and revolution.* New York: Peter Lang.

Cannella, G. (1999). The scientific discourse of education: Predetermining the lives of others—Foucault, education, and children. *Contemporary Issues in Early Childhood, 1*(1), 36–44.

Cohen, D., & Rudolph, M. (1977). *Kindergarten and early schooling.* Englewood Cliffs, NJ: Prentice-Hall.

Creaser, B., & Dau, E. (Eds.). (1996). *The anti-bias approach in early childhood.* Pymble Sydney, Australia: HarperEducational.

Dahlberg, G., Moss, P., & Pence, A. (1999). *Beyond quality in early childhood education and care: Postmodern perspectives.* London: Falmer Press.

deWal Pastoor, L. (1998). "De leker sÂ merkelig. Mangfold samspill i et flerkulturelt skolemilj" ("They play so strangely." Diverse social interaction in a multicultural school environment). Master's thesis in social anthropology, University of Oslo, Norway.

Dewey, J. (1938; 1963). *Experience and education.* New York: Crowell-Collier-Macmillan.

Erikson, E. (1963). *Childhood and society.* New York: Norton.

Foucault, M. (1979). *Discipline and punish: The birth of the prison.* A. Sheridan, Trans. New York: Random House.

Froebel, F. (1887). *The education of man.* M. W. Hailman, Trans. New York: D. Appleton and Company.

Garrison, J. (1997). *Dewey and eros: Wisdom and desire in the art of teaching.* New York: Teachers College Press.

Giroux, H. (1983). *Critical theory and educational practice.* Geelong, Australia: Deakin University Press.

Gundem, B., & Hopmann, S. (Eds.). (1998). *Didaktik and/or curriculum.* New York: Peter Lang.

Johannessen, E. (1987). Hvordan kan barn lúre Â bli mer populúre lekekamerater? (How can children learn to be more popular playmates?) *Debattserien for Barnehagefolk* (Debate series for preschool and day-care professionals) 2, pp. 38–49.

L-97. (1996). *Lúreplanverket for den 10-rige grunnskolen. (L-97)* (Curriculum frameworks documents for years 1–10 in schools.) Oslo, Norway: Det Kongelige kirke-, utdannings- og forskningsdepartement.

Noddings, N. (1992). *The challenge to care in schools: An alternative approach to education.* New York: Teachers College Press.

Os, E., & Aamild, K. (1995). Vi ere en nasjon vi med . . . (We are also a nation . . .). *Debattserien for barnehagefolk* (Debate series for preschool and day-care professionals), *3*, 25–35.

Piaget, J. (1952). *The origins of intelligence in children.* New York: International Universities Press.

Piaget, J. (1964). *The early growth of logic in the child.* New York: Harper.

Popkewitz, T. (1994). Professionalisation in teaching and teacher education: Some notes on its history, ideology and potential. *Teaching and Teacher Education, 10*(1), 1–14.

R-96. (1995). *Rammeplan for barnehagen* (National curriculum frameworks for preschools and day-care centers). Oslo, Norway: Barne- og familiedepartementet.

Rhedding-Jones, J. (1996). Researching early schooling: Poststructural practices and academic writing in an ethnography. *British Journal of Sociology of Education, 17*(1), 21–37.

Rhedding-Jones, J. (1997). Changing the subject of literacy. *Literacy: Secondary Thoughts, 5*(1), 58–63.

Rhedding-Jones, J. (2000a). Fakultetsopponenten sammanfattar. (Examiner's report and discussion of doctoral dissertation.) *Emancipation och motstnd: Dokumentation och kooperativa laroprocesser i forskolan* (Emancipation and resistance: Documentation and cooperative learning processes in preschooling) by Hillevi Lenz Taguchi. Stockholm University, Sweden. In *Pedagogisk Forskning i Sverige* (Research in Education in Sweden), *5*(4), 320–327.

Rhedding-Jones, J. (2000b). The other girls: Culture, psychoanalytic theories and writing. *International Journal of Qualitative Studies in Education, 13*(3), 263–279.

Rhedding-Jones, J. (2001a). *"Child development," learning and culture: Decentering Anglo-American power in early childhood education.* Paper presented at Reconceptualizing Early Childhood Education Conference, Columbia University, New York, October.

Rhedding-Jones, J. (2001b). Shifting ethnicities: "Native informants" and other theories from/for early childhood education. *Contemporary Issues in Early Childhood, 2*(2), 135–156. (www.triangle.co.uk/ciec)

Spivak, G. C. (1999). *A critique of postcolonial reason: Toward a history of the vanishing present.* Cambridge, MA: Harvard University Press.

Vygotsky, L. (1962). *Language and thought: The problem and the approach.* Cambridge, MA: MIT Press.

Part V

Asian Play Dynamics

Chapter 15

Play, Racial Attitudes, and Self-Concept in Taiwan

Li-Chun Chang and Stuart Reifel

Research conducted over the past 60 years has demonstrated that young children's views of the social status of various ethnic groups are congruent with the views held by the dominant ethnic group of the society, (Clark & Clark, 1947, 1950; Fox & Jordan, 1973; Horowitz, 1939; Katz, 1987; Lasker, 1929; Spencer, 1982, 1984). Minority children, especially black children, usually showed a preference for the color white or white persons (Goodman, 1952; Porter, 1971; Wemer & Evans, 1986; Williams and Roberson, 1967), and often demonstrated that the color brown or brown persons were perceived as inferior in living status and social roles (Radke & Trager, 1950). These white-biased or Eurocentric preferences and attitudes by minority group children were referred to as race dissonance (Spencer, 1984). Researchers also suggested that children became aware of racial differences at a very early age (Porter, 1971).

Researchers have been looking for answers to explain why children develop color and racial bias at an early age. Several factors that contribute to the development of color and racial bias have been identified. Williams and Morland (1976) presented a developmental theory of color and race bias. They identified three general classes of determinants contributing to the development of color and race bias:

the biologically based early learning experiences of the child with light and darkness; a message regarding color and race which the child received from the general culture; and the amplification or suppression of the general cultural messages as a result of subculture and family membership. (p. 260)

Studies across cultures have demonstrated that pro-white and pro-light-skinned biases were found not only in American and Western children (Adams & Osgood, 1973; Best, Field, & Williams, 1976; Best, Naylor, & Williams, 1975; Neto & Williams, 1997; Skinto, 1969; Williams & Edwards, 1969; Williams & Roberson, 1967), but also in Japanese preschoolers (Iwawaki, Sonoo, Williams, & Best, 1978). The first part of the present study investigated the racial attitude of Taiwanese preschoolers, and was similar to Iwawaki et. al's (1978) study to see if Taiwanese children also develop a pro-white bias. Japanese society is similar to Taiwanese society in that both societies are highly homogeneous racial group societies that consist of one racial group, Asian. All the leading role models are Asian, and Asian is the dominant race group in Japanese society. However the pro-white bias was still found in Iwawaki et al.'s study. They found that pro-white biases were more highly correlated with age; therefore, they believed that racial biases were more likely to be attributable to cultural learning. If the pro-white bias of subjects in Iwawaki et al.'s study was attributed to cultural learning, then mass media may be a very important factor for conveying this message to young Japanese children.

Cultural imperialism studies have indicated that increased exposure to a foreign culture leads to a more favorable affect toward that culture (Berkowitz & Roger, 1986; Tan, Li, & Simpson, 1986). Also, Read (1976) discussed the American media's influence on developing nations and proposed that developing nations would lose their cultural autonomy. He also asserted that their cultures would be homogenized with the West partly through the influence of foreign mass media. Taiwan is a developing country with a highly homogeneous Asian race group. However, Taiwanese children are constantly exposed to Western culture, especially American culture, through the influence of media and toys. According to a survey in 1986, 33% of television programs in Asia and the Pacific were imported from the United States (Tan et al., 1986). The influence of the American media in Taiwan has increased since Taiwan opened the cable market in the early 1990s. CNN, HBO, Disney, and other major cable companies in the United States have channels in Taiwan. Therefore, Taiwanese children growing up in the 1990s were influenced by American culture via the media.

As for toys, Fleming (1996) pointed out that the content of the Southeast Asian toy industry is Western popular culture. Since the 1980s, multinational companies have completely dominated the toy industry. Distinctly national markets and manufactures have had to adapt or disappear. When Southeast Asian toy manufacturers design their own prototypes, they consistently imitate Western popular culture (Fleming, 1996). Likewise, Taiwan, which is in Southeast Asia, is also selling toys imbued with Western popular culture. For instance, Caucasian dolls with beach accessories, looking as if they have just left the set of television's *Baywatch*, are sold everywhere in Taiwan. Furthermore, major cities in Taiwan have Toys R Us franchises, and the toys sold there are similar to those found in American stores.

A special phenomenon that caught the first author's attention was the dolls with which Taiwanese girls play. Most dolls in the toy market are white dolls with blue eyes and blond hair. A doll in Chinese is called *Yang-wa-wa*, which literally means "foreign doll." *Yang* means foreign, and *wa-wa* means doll. Ever since the first blond doll was imported to Taiwan and named *Yang-wa-wa*, most people have had the misconception that dolls must be white with blond hair and blue eyes. This is a very prevalent view in Taiwanese society even today. A recent report (Su, 1998) in Taiwan's newspaper supports this observation. The report was about a charity event for the funding of children in wheelchairs held in one Toys R Us store in Taiwan. Barbie dolls in wheelchairs were sold to raise funds for children with disabilities. All the dolls sold were blond. Furthermore, a disabled Taiwanese teenage girl who was helping to promote the charity was dressed like Barbie and was wearing a blond wig. The sponsor of this charity also hoped that by playing with wheelchair Barbie, Taiwanese children would learn to respect and know how to get along with children with disabilities. Since blond Barbie dolls were used, I wonder if Taiwanese children would learn to identify themselves with blond girls. Children may be misled by the cultural message conveyed, that only blond children with disabilities should be respected.

Considering the strong influence from media and toys, we believe that Taiwanese children might develop a white-biased attitude. Furthermore, the racial attitude of Taiwanese children living in different regions of Taiwan may vary. Previous studies conducted in the United States have indicated that children living in more integrated areas report more positive attitudes toward black dolls and pictures (Fox & Jordan, 1973; Hraba & Grant, 1970; Katz, 1982) while negative attitudes appeared to be more prevalent in the segregated areas (Clark & Clark, 1947; Katz, 1982; Stevenson & Stewart, 1958). With regard to geographical variations found in previous studies, the present study selected two regions in Taiwan for comparison. One region has been exposed to a significant amount of Western culture, and the other region has not been exposed to as much Western culture.

As for the relationship between racial attitude and self-concept, current research and theory have cast considerable doubt on the idea that African American children who express a preference for whiteness have self-concept problems and low self-esteem and harbor self-hate. This was a popular view from the 1940s through the 1970s (Clark & Clark, 1940, 1947, 1950; Horowitz, 1939; Kardiner & Ovesey, 1962; Pettigrew, 1964; Trager & Yarrow, 1952). Recent research and theory have indicated that personal identity and group identity were separate phenomena and that minority children could express a bias toward whiteness and white people and yet have high self-esteem and positive self-concepts (Banks, 1984; Clark, 1982; Spencer, 1982, 1984). However, a more recent study conducted by Corenblum and Annis (1992) did find significant relationships between racial attitude and self-concept. In light of these new findings, it is necessary to assess the self-concept of Taiwanese children to determine the relationship between racial attitude and self-concept.

Modification studies of racial attitudes concluded that racial attitudes could be modified through reinforcement and modeling (Edwards & Williams, 1970; Powell-Hopson, 1985; Spencer & Horowitz, 1973; Williams & Edwards, 1969; Williams & Morland, 1976). These studies indicated that young children's bias toward the color white could be changed by interventions that reinforced the color black. In addition, when color bias in young children was reduced, this reduction of bias was generalized to people. Research also indicated that intervention with children was much more hopeful than the intervention with adults (Katz, 1976). Pilot research indicated that most Taiwanese girls thought that a Caucasian doll was prettier than an Asian doll, while Taiwanese boys did not express such opinions. This result indicated that young girls' play experience with a Caucasian doll might serve as a reinforcer in their selections of answers. In Taiwanese culture, most parents will not buy dolls for boys. Therefore, the present study proposed giving Asian dolls to children with pro-white attitudes to play with to see whether playing with ethnic-identifiable dolls would modify children's racial attitudes.

The purpose of the present study was to investigate the development of racial attitude and self-concept of Taiwanese preschoolers and the influence of ethnic-identifiable dolls in their racial attitudes. The present study used dolls to assess racial identification, racial preference, and racial attitudes of Taiwanese pre-schoolers and then as an intervention for the modification of young children's racial attitudes. Additionally, a self-concept instrument, Pictorial Scale of Perceived Competence and Social Acceptance for Young Children (Harter & Pike, 1984), was used to assess Taiwanese preschoolers' self-concept. A number of questions were answered from the analysis of collected data.

What evidence was there that Taiwanese children had a white-biased racial identification, preference, and attitudes at an early age? What kind of ethnic-identifiable doll was most played with by Taiwanese children? What were the differences in racial identification, racial preference, and racial attitudes between young Taiwanese girls and boys? What were the differences in racial identification, racial preference, and racial attitudes between Taiwanese children who lived in a metropolitan area with more Western cultural influences and those who lived in a rural area with less Western cultural influences? What was the relationship between Taiwanese boys and girls who developed white-biased attitudes and their self-concept, including children who lived in a metropolitan area and those who lived in a rural area? How did playing with an ethnic-identifiable doll impact a child's racial attitudes? What were the differences in racial attitudes and self-concept between different age groups of Taiwanese children?

METHOD

Research Design

The research design included three parts. The first part was an interview. Each subject was administered a 16-item questionnaire to assess racial identification, racial preference, and racial attitudes. One pair of dolls, one Caucasian and one Asian, was shown to the subject at the time of the interview. Female dolls were used while asking questions of female subjects, whereas male dolls were used with the male subjects. The second part of the design was a self-concept assessment, the Pictorial Scale of Perceived Competence and Social Acceptance (adapted from Harter & Pike, 1984). The self-concept instrument was administered to each subject individually one or two days after the doll test. The third part of the design was an experiment. After the interview, children with pro-white attitudes were identified. In each city, one experimental group and one control group were randomly assigned. In the experimental groups, each child was given an Asian doll to play with for a two-week period. Each child actually owned that doll and brought it home with him or her. Each child in the control groups received another toy. After the two weeks, all subjects were administered the racial attitude questions again.

Participants

One hundred and 95 preschool children, 97 from metropolitan Taipei areas (47 males and 50 females) and 98 from rural Chaiyi areas (54 males and 44 females), were selected to participate in this study. All subjects were between the ages of 54 months and 82 months with a mean age of 69.61 months (SD = 7.09). All subjects were from four kindergarten programs. Two programs were in metropolitan Taipei, one in Taipei County and the other in Taipei city. Two other programs were from two different communities in the rural areas of Chaiyi County. Taipei was selected because it is the capital city of Taiwan. Taipei is the home of major world-class multinational giants and many foreign residents. Therefore, it is internationalized and has a lot of Western cultural influences. It is the most Westernized city in Taiwan, whereas the rural Chaiyi County has less Western cultural influences. Most residents in this area are workers and farmers. The opportunities to interact with people from Western culture are rare. Subjects in rural Chaiyi were from the lower to middle socioeconomic class, and subjects in metro Taipei were from the middle to upper socioeconomic class.

The subsample of children subsequently administered the self-concept instrument procedure consisted of 163 subjects. There were 83 boys and 80 girls in this group, ranging in age from 54 months to 82 months with a mean age of 69.79 months (SD = 7.15). The reduction in number of subjects for the self-concept testing was not intended and was due to conflicts of schedule. No bias was involved in the participation of the subsample of children who were measured.

Based on the test result of the racial attitude measure in the first stage, 113 children with strong pro-white racial attitudes were recruited to participate in the subsequent experiment. After the treatment, five subjects (all boys) indicated that they did not play with the dolls, and four subjects were absent on the day of testing; therefore, they were dropped from the study. Consequently, a total of 104 children, 41 boys and 63 girls, ranging in age from 56 months to 80 months with a mean age of 70.41 months (SD = 6.51), were administered the racial attitude questionnaire. There were 60 subjects (25 males, 35 females) in the experimental group and 44 subjects (16 males, 28 females) in the control group.

In sum, the initial pool of subjects consisted of 210 children coming from seven classrooms of kindergarten programs. One hundred and 97 subjects agreed to participate in the study. Data from two children were missing. One hundred and four subjects participated in all phases of the study.

Setting

The first author administered the tests to each subject individually in a private room in the kindergartens in Taipei and Chaiyi. Taipei is a city where people of different color are commonly seen, whereas Chaiyi is a small city where people of different color are virtually never seen, although children may see such persons in commercials and Western shows on television. The classroom settings of the kindergartens from the two cities were different. The two kindergarten programs in Chaiyi were very academically oriented. There were no learning centers in the classrooms. No dramatic centers and dolls were found in the classrooms in either kindergarten. The two kindergarten programs in metro Taipei were more child-centered. Both programs had learning centers. However, the dolls found in the dramatic play centers were Caucasian dolls.

Materials

Four dolls were used in the study, two Caucasian dolls and two Asian dolls. The Caucasian dolls, one male and one female, had the blue eyes, blond hair, and white skin that were commonly seen in stores. The Asian dolls, also one male and one female, had the black eyes, black hair, and yellow skin that were unfamiliar to Taiwanese children but represented their identities. Dolls of the same gender were identical in every aspect except skin, eyes, and hair color. The dolls used in the present study were specially ordered from a factory in Taiwan, as Asian dolls were unavailable in markets. A special request to manufacture Asian dolls was granted by a doll factory owner to make this study possible.

Instruments

Racial identification/preference/attitude assessment questions were selected from the Preschool Racial Attitude Measure (Williams, Best, Boswell, Mattson, & Graves, 1975) and Gopaul-McNicol (1995). Question 1 was used to assess racial identification, and questions 2–3 racial preference. Questions 4–15 assessed racial attitudes for a racial attitude score. Question 16 surveyed the popularity of the blond doll in Taiwan. English translations of the items appear in Figure 15.1.

A shortened version of the Racial Attitude Measure consisting of questions 4–15 was used in the experimental phase to measure the change in racial attitudes. For scoring of racial identification/preference/attitude measure, chi-square tests were conducted on question 1 to compare frequency for racial identification. Chi-square tests were also conducted on questions 2 and 3 to compare frequency for racial preference. For questions 4–15 a racial attitude score was computed. One point was given to each pro-Euro response and each anti-Asian response. For instance, one point was given to the Caucasian doll response for questions containing a positive adjective and one to the Asian doll response for a negative adjective. Upon completion, each subject was given a racial attitude score ranging from 0 to 12, with a high score indicating a pro-Euro/anti-Asian attitude (E+/A−), a low score indicating a pro-Asian/anti-Euro attitude (A+/ E−), and a score in the midrange, around 6, indicating no racial bias. Statistically speaking, whenever a child obtained a score of 9 or higher, he or she was showing evidence of significant E+/A− bias, while a score of 3 or lower was indicative of a significant A+/E− bias.

Self-Concept Assessment

The measure employed was the Pictorial Scale of Perceived Competence and Social Acceptance for Young Children (Harter & Pike, 1984). This instrument was selected because it used graphic presentation of actions and activities to facilitate the young child's understanding of the task. Therefore, these forms of self-description are developmentally appropriate.

This instrument includes four separate subscales: Cognitive Competence, Physical Competence, Peer Acceptance, and Maternal Acceptance. There are two versions of this instrument, one for preschoolers and kindergartners and a second for first and second graders. There are 24 items, and each subscale comprises six items. Each item has brief statements accompanied by pictures. The child's first task was to indicate, for example, which of the two girls she was most like. After making that decision, the child was then asked to think only about the picture on that side and indicate whether she was a lot like that girl or just a little bit like the girl. Item scores were averaged across six items for a given subscale, and these four means provided the child's profile of perceived competence and social acceptance. For the purpose of the present study, a total score was calculated across all subscales to assess a child's global self-concept. Item 6 (stay overnight at friend's) in peer acceptance was eliminated because it is not relevant in the Taiwanese culture. The first author did the initial translation into Chinese. Kindergarten teachers examined translated materials in order to ensure that the vocabulary employed would be comprehensible to young children. The test was administered either in Mandarin or in Taiwanese.

Figure 15.1
Items from the Racial Identification/Preference/Attitude Assessment

---

1. Which doll looks like you?

2. Which doll do you like to play with?

3. Which doll would you like to take home?

4. Which doll is the clean doll?

5. Which doll is the bad doll?

6. Which doll is the dirty doll?

7. Which doll is the healthy doll?

8. Which doll is the pretty doll?

9. Which doll is the sick doll?

10. Which doll is the poor doll?

11. Which doll is the smart doll?

12. Which doll is the good doll?

13. Which doll is the ugly doll?

14. Which doll is the stupid doll?

15. Which doll is the rich doll?

16. Do you have a doll at home? What kind of doll do you have?

Scoring of Self-Concept Measure

Each item was scored on a four-point scale. Item scores were averaged across six items for a given subscale, and a total score was added up from the four subscales.

Reliability

In this study, the translated Chinese version of the Pictorial Scale of Perceived Competence and Social Acceptance for Young Children was administered twice to the same small sample of Taiwanese preschoolers to establish the reliability of the instrument. The tests were administered about two weeks apart. Test–retest reliability was .86 for the total test. Test–retest reliability for subcales was .85 for Cognitive Competence, .79 for Physical Competence, .77 for Peer Acceptance, and .81 for Maternal Acceptance. In this study, Cronbach's alpha correlation coefficient for the total test was .88. For the subcales, Cronbach's alphas were .59 for Cognitive Competence, .64 for Physical Competence, .73 for Peer Acceptance, and .75 for Maternal Acceptance. These values are satisfactory and acceptable compared with the original sample on which the manual was developed and tested and the other studies cited in the literature review section that used this measure.

Table 15.1
Taiwanese Children's Responses to Racial Identification and Racial Preference

	Caucasian Doll (%)	Asian Doll (%)	Chi-Square	P
Which doll looks like you?	42.3	57.7	4.630	.031
Which doll do you like to play with?	63.1	39.9	13.338	.000
Which doll would you like to take home?	63.1	33.3	17.894	.000

Procedure

The Racial Identification/Preference/Attitude Measures and the Self-concept Measures were administered individually to subjects in a school area immediately outside their classrooms. Two or three weeks later, the shortened version of the measure containing only questions 4–15 was administered individually to a subsample of 103 children who were readministered because of their pro-Euro/anti-Asian racial attitudes. The first author administered all the assessments and experiments. The data collection time was two to three months.

Data Analysis

Chi-square was conducted to test frequency of racial identification and racial preference questions. Cross-tab was conducted to test gender and geographical difference on racial identification and racial preference. Type I errors were controlled by using the Bonferroni method. Descriptive frequencies were reported for the survey of ethnic-identifiable dolls. Multiple t tests were conducted to compare group means of pre-racial attitudes. Pearson correlation coefficients were computed between racial attitude score and age, racial attitude score and self-concept score, and self-concept score and age to determine whether these pairs of variables are correlated. T tests were conducted to compare group means of post-racial attitude scores. Factorial analysis was conducted to test the interaction of gender, geographical locations, and treatment.

Results

Data analysis of racial identification indicated that a majority of Taiwanese children (57.7%) identified with their own race, Asian. However, this result was not statistically significant when Type I error was controlled. The finding of racial preference indicated that Taiwanese children demonstrated significantly less own-race preference (Table 15.1). The finding of racial attitude indicated that most Taiwanese children developed a white-biased attitude at an early age

Table 15.2
Proportion of Subjects in Racial Attitude Categories

	Pro-Euro/ Anti-Asian (%)	No Bias (%)	Pro-Asian/ Anti-Euro (%)
Taiwanese Children	57.9	30.3	11.8

Table 15.3
Percentage of Taiwanese Preschoolers Choosing Caucasian Dolls in Response to Positive Adjectives and Choosing Asian Dolls in Response to Negative Adjectives

		Caucasian Doll (%)	Asian Doll (%)
Positive Adjectives	Clean	70.8	29.2
	Healthy	75.9	24.1
	Pretty	73.3	26.7
	Smart	67.2	32.2
	Good	72.8	27.2
	Rich	70.3	29.7
Negative Adjectives	Bad	28.2	71.8
	Dirty	24.1	75.9
	Sick	29.7	70.3
	Poor	37.9	62.1
	Ugly	25.2	74.4
	Stupid	27.7	72.3

(Tables 15.2–3). Survey of ethnic-identifiable dolls indicated that only a small portion (39%) of children had dolls at home. Most of them (82%) were girls, and most of them (84%) had Caucasian dolls at home.

Significant gender differences were found on all race question inquiries. The results indicated that most boys identified with their own race, while most girls identified with the white race. Most girls expressed a white preference and attitude, while the racial preferences and attitudes of boys were not biased (see Table 15.4).

Inconsistent results were found on the geographical difference regarding race questions. No significant geographical differences were found regarding racial identification and racial preference. However, significant geographical differences were found regarding racial attitudes. Children living in the metropolitan

Table 15.4
Mean Racial Attitude Scores for Male and Female

	M	M	t	P
	Female	Male		
	n = 94	n = 98		
Gender Comparison	9.56	7.6	3.874	.000

Table 15.5
Mean Racial Attitude Scores for Taipei and Chaiyi

	M	M	t	P
	Taipei	Chaiyi		
	n = 97	n = 98		
Gender Comparison	9.39	7.71	3.226	.001

Table 15.6
Mean Self-concept Scores for Gender Groups

	M	M	t	p
Gender Groups	Female	Male		
	14.65	13.99	2.704	.008

area expressed a pro-white bias, while children living in the rural area indicated no racial bias (see Table 15.5).

Results indicated that racial attitude was not correlated with self-concept among Taiwanese children. A significant gender difference was found on the self-concept score. The result indicated that Taiwanese girls had higher self-concept than boys (see Table 15.6). No significant geographical difference was found on the self-concept scores.

A comparison, via t-test, revealed that the post-racial attitude mean of the experimental group was significantly lower (t [df 102] = 2.228, p < .05) than the mean of the control group. The mean racial attitude scores of the experimental group and the control group in the pre-test were about the same. After the treatment, the mean racial attitude of the experimental group fell into the no-bias racial attitude category, while the mean of the control group still remained in the pro-Euro/anti-Asian category (see Table 15.7). The present study provided evidence that playing with ethnic-identifiable dolls for only two weeks could modify a child's racial attitudes. Factorial analysis revealed no significant

Table 15.7
Effect of Treatment on Racial Attitude Scores

	Experimental Group	Control Group		
	M	**M**	t	p
Post–Racial Attitude Score	8.63	10.16	−2.228	.028*
Pre–Racial Attitude Score	11.23	11.40	.494	.632

*p ≤ .05.

results on the interaction of treatment, gender, and geographical locations. The results indicated that age was not related to either racial attitudes or self-concept.

DISCUSSION

The results raise several general issues worth discussing. This section discusses some general issues that emerged from the data analysis, including age, geographical location, gender, self-concept, and cultural influences.

Age Issues

The present study did not find age a significant factor relating to the development of Taiwanese children's racial attitudes. In contrast, most studies have found age to be a significant factor related to affecting the development of racial attitudes (Banks, 1993; Katz, 1982; McAdoo, 1977; Miel & Keister, 1967; Morland, 1958). For instance, Morland (1958), and Miel and Keister (1967) found that the ability to recognize racial differences increased with age. McAdoo (1977) found that in-group preferences increased with age among minority black children. Banks' review (1993) also indicated that out-group preferences decreased with age. Conversely, cross-cultural studies found that pro-white racial bias increased with age among Japanese children (Iwawaki et al., 1978) and Portuguese children (Neto & Williams, 1997). Collectively, in the American multiracial society and Portuguese monoracial society (white), in-group preference increased with age, and in the Japanese monoracial society (Asian), pro-white bias increased with age. These studies indicated that every culture is unique in the ways in which it shapes the development of children's racial attitudes.

Although the present study did not find that a relationship between age and racial attitudes existed, this does not imply that such a relationship does not exist. The age range of the present sample was perhaps too small to find significant results. We suggest that more racial attitude studies with children of various age groups in Taiwan should be conducted. Considering the uniqueness of cultural differences, early childhood educators and researchers in Taiwan should apply results found in other cultures with discretion.

Geographical Issues

The present study found significant geographical differences regarding Taiwanese children's racial preferences and racial attitudes. The data indicated that Taiwanese children who lived in the rural areas did not express pro-white bias, whereas Taiwanese children living in the metropolitan areas had developed a white-bias preference and attitude. The atmospheres of the two geographical locations that the present study investigated were very different; Taipei is a modernized and international city, with multinational giant companies and many foreign residents. McDonalds restaurants, considered to be a symbol of U.S. imperialism (Kincheloe, 1997; Watson, 1997), are everywhere in Taipei city and Taipei County. Other fast-food chains that represent American culture, like Wendy's, Burger King, Pizza Hut, and KFC, also have franchises in Taiwan and are scattered throughout the metro Taipei area. Therefore, children living in the Taipei metropolitan area have greater opportunities to experience Western culture than do their rural peers.

Furthermore, we believe that children living in metropolitan Taipei may be receiving more Western cultural influences from television than children in the rural areas. Taipei is a very crowded city. Most children living in metro Taipei live in apartments where outdoor activities are restricted. Conversely, children living in rural areas usually live in a house, allowing more outdoor activities. Therefore, children living in Taipei might spend a lot of time watching television. Hence, they might receive more Western cultural influence from television than their rural peers. This may explain why children living in the metropolitan area expressed a white bias while children living in the rural area did not indicate such a bias.

This finding was also different from Katz's (1982) review reporting that more positive attitudes toward black dolls and pictures had occurred at large American urban centers, whereas negative attitudes appeared to be more prevalent in the South and in smaller towns. Katz's review indicated that in a multiracial society, children would develop a more positive attitude toward the minority racial group when living in an integrated setting. Evidence from the present study did not support this view. Instead, the finding from the present study suggested that children living in a monoracial society should not be exposed to other cultures too early in order to develop a positive attitude toward their own racial group and culture.

Gender Issues

The present study found gender to be an important factor in all the inquiries investigated. Data analysis indicated that Taiwanese boys had a clarified self-identification and did not express white-biased racial preference and racial attitudes at an early age. However, young girls in Taiwan did not have a clarified self-identification and expressed strong pro-white racial preference and racial attitudes. We believe that Taiwanese girls are capable of identifying with their own race as their male peers do. The reason for the non-significant result in the self-identification question was actually a reflection of cultural influences and playing experiences with dolls. Blond dolls were considered to be more beautiful than Asian dolls in Taiwanese culture. From a survey of dolls, we know that most parents in Taiwan bought only blond dolls for their girls. When parents bought blond dolls for their girls, they might be implicitly guiding their children's experience and passing on pro-white values to them. In addition, the present study proved that playing with ethnic-identifiable dolls could change a child's racial attitudes. Under such a socialization process, it is not hard to understand why Taiwanese girls developed such an out-group preference. Therefore, the pattern of answers that Taiwanese girls revealed indicated that they were quite aware of the cultural message conveyed to them that "blond is superior," and some of them just expressed a wish for wanting to identify with the preferred race.

The finding of the present study regarding gender differences was also very different from findings of previous studies. Studies that have explored this variable did not find sex a significant factor whether in a multiracial setting (Gopaul-McNicol, 1995; Miel & Keister, 1967; Morland, 1958) or a monoracial setting (Neto & Williams, 1997). The unique finding of the present study indicates that, unlike other children in the world, Taiwanese girls and boys are socialized differently with respect to their racial development.

Self-Concept Issues

The present study did not find that a relationship existed between racial attitudes and self-concept of Taiwanese preschoolers. This finding was consistent with that of most studies investigating the relationship between these two variables (Banks, 1984; Clark, 1982; Spencer, 1982, 1984). However, Corenblum and Annis' (1992) study using the same self-concept measure found a substantial relationship between racial attitudes and self-concept with white and Indian children.

Spencer's studies (1982, 1984) and Banks' review (1993) have indicated that personal identity and group identity are separate phenomena and that young children can express a bias toward whiteness and white people and yet have high self-esteem and positive self-concepts. Although similar results were found from previous studies conducted in the United States, we think that we should apply the same conclusion with caution for the following reasons. First, inconsistent results were found from previous studies on different ethnic groups in different contexts. In studies investigating self-concept of black children in the United States, no relationship was found between racial attitude and self-concept

(Banks, 1984; Clark, 1982; Spencer, 1982, 1984). However, Corenblum and Annis (1992) found that such a relationship existed among white and Indian children in Canada. Second, no other empirical data were found among Asian subjects whether in a multiracial society or in a monoracial society like Taiwan. Finally, the attrition of subjects in the self-concept measure that the present study encountered might have influenced the results. Therefore, more studies exploring these two variables should be conducted in Taiwan to clarify conclusions regarding Taiwanese children's pro-white racial attitudes and self-concept.

Cultural Influence

The white preference results of the present study suggest that the atmosphere in which children live and the values passed on to them from toys and the media are powerful influences in spite of the racial demographic makeup of a country. The results and the social context of the present study were very similar to those of Gopaul and McNicol's studies conducted in Trinidad (1986) and in the West Indies (1995). In both studies white-bias attitudes were found among black children from a culture where the majority of the people were black and where leading role models were black. The research identified two sources explaining why the children evidenced such a strong white preference. One came from the perception of white supremacy fostered by an English-colonial education system; the other came from the media, as the same programs that were shown in North America and Europe were shown in the West Indies, resulting in the same white bias.

Although the results and the social context of the present study were similar to Gopaul-McNicol's (1986, 1995) study, a different theory is postulated. Integrating results from previous studies and findings from the present study, we believe that three factors contributed to the white preference in Taiwanese preschoolers. First, the diurnal nature of Homo sapiens results in a learned preference for light over darkness, and this tendency was transferred to the human race as a pancultural tendency for a preference toward white human figures over dark human figures. The series of cross-culture research conducted by Williams, Best, and their associates (Best et al., 1975, 1976; Iwawaki et al., 1978; Neto & Williams, 1997) provides strong support for this theory. Although the present study did not investigate the relationship between color meaning and racial attitudes among Taiwanese children, the finding about the racial attitudes of Taiwanese preschoolers revealed the tendency to prefer white color. The present study used ethnic-identifiable dolls instead of drawings of human figures to assess Asian children's racial attitudes to avoid the confusion that was found in Iwawaki et al.'s (1978) study. The visual stimuli to Taiwanese subjects were very clear that the Asian doll was a representation of themselves. However, only a very small portion (11.8%) of subjects expressed a pro-Asian/anti-Euro preference, even though in the school settings all teachers were Asian and the experimenter bias (Asian tester) favored a pro-Asian preference. In addition, some of the inadvertent comments made by the children could support the white color bias theory. Many children referred to the blond doll as the "white color doll." They called the blond color hair "white hair." A child told the first author, "I like the white color one better, because the white color is more beautiful."

Second, white preference was, in part, attributed to the prevalence of blond dolls in Taiwan's toy market. The present study proved that playing with ethnic-identifiable dolls can change a child's racial attitude. However, the survey of the present study indicated that playing experiences with dolls might account for only a small portion of white preference. The survey of ethnic-identifiable dolls indicated that only 39% of children had dolls at home, and 84% of these children indicated that they had Caucasian dolls at home. Therefore, 32.76% of all children had Caucasian dolls at home. However, the results of racial attitude data indicated that 57.9% of all children expressed pro-Euro/anti-Asian bias. Thus, playing with Caucasian dolls cannot account for all children's white preference.

Finally, we believe that the major reason that Taiwanese children expressed white preference at an early age is the "systematic" influences of Western cultural imperialism from the joint power of media and toys. According to Fleming (1996), through new total marketing strategies, toys are typically related to television animation series, videos, books, fast-food chains, and cinema. He also pointed out that toys are popular culture and that multinational capitalism has made Western toys a global culture. As was pointed out above, the content of Taiwanese toys is Western popular culture. According to Cross (1997), "play is the work of children and toys are their tools" (p. v). Cultural messages are transmitted through playthings. Therefore, white hegemony might be passed on to the younger generation of Taiwanese children through their play with Western toys and from the commercials of mass media. The results of the present study support this observation. Data analysis indicated that children living in metro Taipei had greater Western cultural influence and expressed strong pro-white attitudes, while children living in the rural areas with few Western cultural influences did not have pro-white biases.

Based on the knowledge gained from the present study, several considerations for future research can be made. The age groups of the present study were restricted to preschool children. It would be desirable in future studies to examine the racial attitude of Taiwanese elementary children to find out if formal education leads to more in-group preference.

Despite the fact that the majority of children in this study evidenced a white preference, a small group of Taiwanese children made Asian choices and stuck to them. It would be desirable in future studies to examine the backgrounds and sociocultural experience of the children who did not respond the same as the majority. Also, qualitative studies can be conducted to investigate whether the play patterns of these children are different from those of the majority.

Recent studies (Corenblum & Annis, 1992; Spencer, 1982, 1984) have explored the relationship between racial attitudes and cognitive development. Future studies conducted on Taiwanese subjects can investigate these two variables. Also, racial attitudes of Taiwanese parents can be investigated to discover whether the white-biased attitudes of Taiwanese children are passed on from the parents.

A series of cross-culture studies can be conducted to investigate the racial attitudes and identification of children growing up in countries where Western culture influences are rare (e.g., Middle Eastern countries), and the leading role models are non-white to see if white preference is really a pancultural phenomenon.

Finally, this study has important implications for manufacturers and local Taiwanese media. Toy manufacturers can improve young Taiwanese girls' attitude toward their own race by producing Asian ethnic-identifiable dolls. Taiwanese media companies can also positively influence Taiwanese children's attitude about their own race by broadcasting more programs and commercials featuring Taiwanese actors, characters, and personalities.

REFERENCES

Adams, F. M., & Osgood, C. E. (1973). A cross-cultural study of the affective meaning of color. *Journal of Cross-Cultural Psycholgy, 4*, 135–156.

Banks, J. A. (1984). Black youths in predominantly white suburbs: An exploratory study of their attitude and self-concepts. *The Journal of Negro Education, 53*, 3–17.

Banks, J. A. (1993). Multicultural education for young children: Racial and ethnic attitudes and their modification. In E. Spodek (Ed.), *Handbook of research on the education of young children* (pp. 236–250). New York: Macmillan Publishing Company.

Berkowitz, L., & Rogers, K. (1986). A priming effect analysis of media influences. In Jennings Byrant and Dolf Zillmarm (Eds.), *Perspective on media effects* (pp. 78–97). Hillsdale, NJ: Erlbaum.

Best, D. L., Field, J. T., & Williams, J. E. (1976). Color bias in a sample of young German children. *Psychological Reports, 38*(3), 1145–1146.

Best, D. L., Naylor, C. E., & Williams, J. E. (1975). Extension of color bias research to young French and Italian children. *Journal of Cross-Cultural Psychology, 6*, 390–405.

Clark, K. B., & Clark, M. P. (1940). Skin color as a factor in racial identification and preference in Negro children. *Journal of Social Psychology, 1*, 156–169.

Clark, K. B., & Clark, M. P. (1947). Racial identification and preference in Negro children. In T. M. Newcomb & E. L. Hartley (Eds.), *Readings in social psychology* (pp. 169–178). New York: Holt, Rinehart, & Winston.

Clark, K. B., & Clark, M. P. (1950). Emotional factors in racial identification and preference in Negro children. *Journal of Negro Education, 19*, 341–350.

Clark, M. L. (1982). Racial group concepts and self-esteem in black children. *Journal of Black Psychology, 1*(2), 75–88.

Corenblum, B., & Annis, B. C. (1992). Development of racial identity in minority and majority children: An affect discrepancy model. *Canadian Journal of Behavioral Science, 25*, 449–521.

Cross, G. (1997). *Kid's stuff: Toys and the changing world of American childhood.* Cambridge, MA: Harvard University Press.

Edwards, C. D., & Williams, J. E. (1970). Generalization between evaluative words associated with racial figures in preschool children. *Journal of Experimental Research in Personality, 4,* 144–155.

Fleming, D. (1996). *Powerplay: Toys as popular culture.* New York: Manchester University Press.

Fox, D. J., & Jordan, V. B. (1973). Racial preference and identification of black, American Chinese, and white children. *Genetic Psychology Monographs, 88,* 229–286.

Goodman, M. E. (1952). *Race awareness in young children.* Cambridge, MA: Addison-Wesley.

Gopaul-McNicol, S. (1986). *The effects of modeling, reinforcement, and color meaning word association of black preschool children and white preschool children in New York and Trinidad.* Unpublished doctoral dissertation, Hofstra University.

Gopaul-McNicol, S. (1995). A cross-cultural examination of racial identity and racial preference of preschool children in the West Indies. *Journal of Cross-Cultural Psychology, 26*(2), 141–152.

Harter, S., & Pike R. (1984). The pictorial perceived competence scale for young children. *Child Development, 55,* 1969–1982.

Horowitz, R. E. (1939). Racial aspects of self-identification in nursery school children. *Journal of Psychology, 7.* 91–99.

Hraba, J., & Grant, G. (1970). Black is beautiful: A reexamination of racial preference and identification. *Journal of Personality and Social Psychology, 16,* 398–402.

Iwawaki, S., Sonoo, K., Williams, J. E., & Best, D. (1978). Color bias among young Japanese children. *Journal of Cross-Cultural Psycholgy, 2,* 61–73.

Kardiner, A., & Ovesey, A. (1962). *The mark of oppression: Explorations in the personality of the American Negro.* New York: World.

Katz, P. A. (1976). Attitude change in children: Can the twig be straightened? In P. A. Katz (Ed.), *Towards the elimination of racism.* New York: Pergamon.

Katz, P. A. (1982). A review of recent research in children's attitude acquisition. In L. Katz (Ed.), *Current topics in early childhood education, Vol. 4* (pp. 17–54). Norwood, NJ: Ablex.

Katz, P. A. (1987). Developmental and social processes in ethnic attitudes and self-identification. In J. S. Phinney & M. J. Rotheram (Eds.), *Children's ethnic socialization: Pluralism and development* (pp. 92–99). Beverly Hills, CA: Sage Publications.

Kincheloe, J. L. (1997). McDonald's, power and children: Ronald McDonald (aka Ray Kroc) does it all for you. In S. R. Steinberg & J. L. Kincheloe (Eds.), *Kinderculture: The corporate construction of childhood.* Boulder, CO: Westview Press.

Lasker, B. (1929). *Race attitudes in children.* New York: Holt, Rinehart, & Winston.

McAdoo, H. P. (1977). *The development of self-concept and race attitudes in black children: A longitudinal study.* ERIC Document Reproduction Service No. ED 148 944.

Miel, A., & Keister, E., Jr. (1967). *The shortchanged children of suburbia: What schools don't teach about human differences and what can be done about it.* New York: Institute of Human Relations Press, the American Jewish Committee.

Morland, J. K. (1958). Racial recognition by nursery school children in Lynchburg. *Virginia. Social Forces, 32,* 132–137.

Neto, F., & Williams, J. E. (1997). Color bias in children revisited: Findings from Portugal. *Social Behavior and Personality, 25,* 115–122.

Pettigrew, T. F. (1964). *A profile of the Negro American.* Princeton, NJ: Van Nostrand.

Porter, J.D.R. (1971). *Black child, white child: The development of racial attitudes.* Cambridge, MA: Harvard University Press.

Powell-Hopson, D. (1985). *Effects of modeling, reinforcement, and color word meaning association on black preschool and white preschool children in New York.* Unpublished doctoral dissertation. Hofstra University.

Radke, M., & Trager, H. G. (1950). Children's perceptions of the social roles of Negroes and whites. *Journal of Psychology, 29,* 3–33.

Read, W. H. (1976). *American mass media merchants.* Baltimore: Johns Hopkins University Press.

Skinto, S. M. (1969). *Racial Awareness in Negro and Caucasian Elementary School Children.* Master's thesis, West Virginia University, Morgantown.

Spencer, M. B. (1982). Personal and group identity of black children: An alternative synthesis. *Genetic Psychology Monographs, 106,* 59–84.

Spencer, M. B., (1984). Black children's race awareness, racial attitudes, and self-concept: A reinterpretation. *Journal of Child Psychology and Psychiatry, 25,* 433–441.

Spencer, M. B., & Horowitz, F. D. (1973). Effects of systematic social and token reinforcement on the modification of racial and color concept attitudes in black and in white preschool children. *Developmental Psychology, 9*(2), 246–254.

Stevenson, H. W., & Steward, E. C. (1958). A developmental study of race awareness in young children. *Child Development, 29,* 399–410.

Su, F. (1998). Lun i "Becky Wa Wa," teng tai i mat (Wheel Chair Becky, charity sale in Taiwan). *Tzu Yu Shih Pao* (Freedom Times), April 4, p. A19.

Tan, A. S., Li, S., & Simpson, C. (1986). American TV and social stereotypes of Americans in Taiwan and Mexico. *Journal Quarterly, 6*(3), 809–814.

Trager, H. G., & Yarrow, M. R. (1952). *They learn what they live: Prejudice in young children.* New York: Harper & Brothers.

Watson, J. L. (1997). *Golden arches east: McDonald's in East Asia.* Stanford, CA: Stanford University Press.

Wemer, N. E., & Evans, I. M. (1986). Perception of prejudice in Mexican-American preschool children. *Perceptual and Motor Skills, 27,* 1039–1046.

Williams, J. E., Best, D. L., Boswell, D. A., Mattson, L. A., & Graves, D. J. (1975). Preschool racial attitude measures II. *Educational and Psychological Measurement, 35,* 3–18.

Williams, J. E., & Edwards, C. D. (1969). An exploratory study of the modification of color and racial concept attitudes in preschool children. *Child Development, 40,* 737–750.

Williams, J. E., & Morland, J. K. (1976). *Race, color and the young child.* Chapel Hill: University of North Carolina Press.

Williams, J. E., & Roberson, J. K. (1967). A method of assessing racial attitudes in preschool children. *Educational Psychology and Measurement, 27,* 671–689.

Chapter 16

Contextual Understanding of Children's Play in Taiwanese Kindergartens

Pei-Yu Chang

Play is an important vehicle for children to learn and to develop. Play-based curriculum is a highly recommended practice in early childhood education (Bredekamp & Copple, 1997). However, the idea of play as the center of early childhood education is challenged when the idea is introduced to countries with different educational systems, where people have different cultural values. A clear example is in Taiwan with its long history of mimetic teaching and its contemporary exam-oriented system of education.

During the past decade, many Taiwanese teacher educators have acquired their graduate degrees in Western universities and have introduced Western theory of early education to Taiwan, especially seen in the promotion of the value of play for young children. Even though the importance of play has been accepted by professors in early childhood education in Taiwan, the pedagogy of learning through play is still not widely accepted by parents or adopted in early childhood programs. Instead, didactic instruction and "reading-writing-arithmetic" (3Rs) approaches are still commonly used, and play is not a sanctioned school activity.

Here I compare children's behavior in an academically oriented kindergarten and in a play-based kindergarten in Taiwan. I seek to understand the influences of classroom contexts on children's learning through play in Taiwan. As you will see, differences between the classrooms are closely related to factors outside the classrooms. Contextual factors appear to be influential on parents' decision making, on children's learning, and on children's play.

CONCEPTUAL FRAMEWORK

King (1992) proposes that the understanding of human interactions cannot do without investigating context variables. Recently, the concept of seeing "children in context" has been recognized by researchers as an important perspective taken for achieving a thorough understanding of children because this idea suggests that making interpretations of children's learning should go beyond the surface meaning and recognize multiple factors embedded within the environment where children live that affect their development. Taking this contextual view not only allows us to see the dynamic interaction between children and the environment but also helps us understand the interactions of factors at the biological, psychological, physical, and sociocultural levels that influence children's development (Kagitcibasi, 1996). Bronfenbrenner's (1979) "ecological theory" and Super and Harkness' (1986) "developmental niche" notion are two conceptual frameworks undergirding the present study.

Ecological View of Human Development

Bronfenbrenner (1979) perceives development as the product of the interaction between a growing person and the environment. The environment is viewed as a set of nested structures consisting of four levels—microsystem, mesosystem, exosystem, and macrosystem. Microsystem is the innermost level and refers to the immediate environment (e.g., family environment, schools, out-of-school activities, etc.). Mesosystem refers to the interactions among two or more settings (e.g., communication between parents and school). The exosystem refers to the settings in which children do not actively participate but that are very influential (e.g., information or suggestions given by family's friends or relatives, mass media, parents' workplaces, etc.). The outermost level of this model is the macrosystem, which includes attitudes, values, laws, regulations, ideologies, customs, and so forth (Berk, 1989).

The Developmental Niche

Super and Harkness (1986) proposed the notion of "developmental niche" for understanding the cultural structuring of child development. The developmental niche framework posits three subsystems that shape children's lives. The first is physical and social settings where children live, including the size of households, the number of siblings, the family structures, the schools that children attend, the interaction between parents or teachers and children or among peers, and so forth. The second component of this framework is the customs of child care used by members of a culture without any conscious awareness or rationalization. The appropriate practices of child care are closely related to the cultural milieu (Tobin, Wu, & Davidson, 1989). For instance, children are told and expected to receive objects from others with two hands in some Asian countries but this is not emphasized by adults in Western countries. The third element of the developmental niche framework is the inner psychology of the caregiver that refers to the beliefs, expectations, or goals of the caregiver in taking care of children or their understanding about children and their needs. This framework supplies a good lens for perceiving mutual interactions between children and cultural factors.

Influences of Contexts on Children's Play

According to King (1992), the meaning of human behavior derives from the context where the behavior occurs. She claims that contexts are the essential source for understanding children's play because play behavior is shaped by different contexts. Understanding children's play cannot be limited to the setting where play occurs because children's play behavior has different meanings in different cultural, social, and physical contexts. Four kinds of contexts that affect children's play are the classroom contexts, the societal contexts, the historical contexts, and the cultural contexts.

Classroom Contexts

Classroom contexts include physical, personal, social, and curricular factors. Factors in classroom contexts that influence children's play behavior are types of materials available to children, length of play periods, arrangement of play space, each individual child's personal histories, interests, and aptitudes, relationships among people in the classroom, curriculum foci, the way that activities are organized, and teachers' perceptions of and their involvement in play. Several studies demonstrated how elements in classroom settings influence children's play, elements such as the structures of play materials provided (Johnson, 1983), the availability of materials and the teachers' expectations for their use (Christie & Johnsen, 1989), the physical arrangement of play areas (Petrakos & Howe, 1996), the themes introduced and the design of equipment (Howe, Moller, Chabers, & Petrakos, 1993), the classroom structures (Huston-Stein, Friedrich-Cofer, & Susman, 1977), the educational orientation (Tizard, Philps, & Plewis, 1976), the theoretical foundation upon which a program is based (Johnson & Ershler, 1981; Johnson, Ershler, & Bell, 1980), and finally the types of teacher talk (Wilcox-Herzog & Kontos, 1998).

Societal Contexts

Societal forces also profoundly influence children's play. The implementation of curriculum affecting the role of play in learning is determined by adults whose decision making is a response to societal demands. Children's play content reflects societal influences as well. For example, before the last Taiwanese presidential election, "election" became a theme for children's dramatic play with stages set up for pretend presidential debates. Many other examples reflect the influence of popular culture on children's play (King, 1992). Roles that children take in pretend play, for instance, are often derived from favorite television cartoon shows or movies.

Historical Contexts

Historical contexts refer to past attitudes held by people who were influenced by the social and the economic forces at the time. These have indirect impacts on children's play. A clear example can be found in the general attitudes toward play held by Chinese people. During the Sung dynasty, play was "depreciated in favor of a strict curriculum that valued a rigorous examination system" (Pan, 1994, p. 36). This attitude toward play reveals the incompatible relationship between play and curriculum. To this day, emphasizing hard work over play is still the operative principle for most Chinese parents, who generally do not think of childhood as a time for children to enjoy playing and exploring in the world around them (Fielding, 1997).

Cultural Contexts

Children's play varies in certain ways across cultures because of differing beliefs, customs, and materials (Frost, Wortham, & Reifel, 2001). Traditional values of a specific culture can influence adults' beliefs and involvement in children's play. For example, parents in some countries are more comfortable being playmates than are parents in other countries; some are more used to being play facilitators (Frost et al., 2001).

A major cultural influence on children's play is the customs of a culture. A collection of old Chinese paintings of children's play exhibited in the National Palace Museum in Taipei depicts children's play endowed with cultural features, such as playing with lanterns during the Lantern Festival or playing with toads in the dragon boat festival (because toads were used in curing diseases during that season). Chinese children's play in Taiwan today still shows the influences of cultural customs. A good example is provided by Lin and Reifel (1999), who saw in children's pretend play the Taiwanese social custom of worshiping ancestors during the wedding ceremony. Play material also reflects culture, as seen when Chinese children use chopsticks as a prop in various play episodes.

METHODS

The purpose of the study is to understand the influence of contexts on children's play in Taiwan. The interest is to present and compare children's play and parents' and teachers' beliefs and attitudes toward play and learning at two kindergartens.

Research Design

Comparative, multiple-case inquiry was used to maximize our understanding of the influences of contexts on Taiwanese children's play (Stake, 1995). Extreme case sampling that recruits participants with very different characteristics was employed to yield rich information about contrasting contexts useful to this study's purpose.

Selection of Schools

Two kindergarten settings were selected with contrasting philosophy, curriculum arrangement, and teacher–child relationship based on observations using the Classroom Practice Inventory (CPI) (Hyson, Hirsh-Pasek, & Rescoria, 1990). The kindergarten with a higher level of developmental appropriateness (score = 114) was labeled the Exploratory Learning School, with the other classroom called the Efficient Learning School, with a score of only 28.

Both kindergarten classes are located in a northwestern city of Taiwan. The Exploratory Learning School, a national kindergarten located in an elementary school affiliated with a Teachers College, was in session from 7:40 A.M. until 3:40 P.M. Monday through Friday except Wednesday, when school ended at 11:50 A.M. The kindergarten director (called kindergarten department head) was designated by the faculty members of the Teachers College. Teachers who planned the curriculum adopted the project approach that involved discussing experiences related to the topic chosen and jotting down children's questions, interests, or suggestions. Information was used in the forthcoming curriculum.

The classroom environment was furnished with a variety of resources for children to construct their knowledge. Children's learning was not limited to the indoor environment but extended to community parks, local stores or institutes, and children's houses. Parents were encouraged to participate in field trips, collect or provide resources for the curriculum, and work as classroom volunteers (e.g., helping with serving lunch).

The Efficient Learning School was a private kindergarten enrolling more than 300 children from 2 to 6 years old. The director did not have a degree in early childhood education but had taken some classes at Teachers College and at a community college. The school had a special policy of waiving the registration fee. Parents had to pay only the monthly fee of NT $5,500 (equal to U.S. $170), which was cheaper than for most of the private kindergartens in Taiwan (the fee for some affluent kindergartens could be as much as U.S. $880 per month).

The daily activity began at 8:45 A.M. and ended at 3:40 P.M., but parents could send children to the school as early as 7:15 A.M. and pick them up as late as 5:30 P.M. Monday through Friday. Children went to school every day with a school bag the same size as those used by elementary school children in Taiwan. The curriculum was divided into different subjects of learning. The regular teacher (one teacher per classroom, each with more than 30 children) taught lessons in basic math, use of the abacus, mental math, use of computers, and lessons in recognizing and writing both Chinese characters and phonics.

The school had signed contracts with companies that provided workbooks and textbooks for lessons in computers, mental math, and abacus lessons. These companies sent an instructor every month to teach the regular teachers how to teach these lessons. Textbooks for the learning of basic math and Chinese reading and writing were chosen by the director. The total number of the textbooks and worksheets used was 28. Each regular teacher divided the text contents evenly for each month to make sure that children could finish all the work by the end of the semester. Children were assigned written homework every day. During each semester, three tests administered in the paper-pencil format evaluate children's mastery in academic subjects. In this school, other areas of the curriculum were English, physical education, and the arts (music, dance, visual art). All these were taught by itinerant teachers who came once or twice each week.

Participants

There were 30, 5- and 6-year-old children enrolled in the class of the Exploratory Learning School with two formal teachers and one in-service teacher. The two formal teachers had teacher certifications from the Teachers College and had worked as kindergarten teachers for eight years. The in-service teacher had just graduated from the Teachers College and worked in this school as her internship for three months when the study was conducted.

The class of the Efficient Learning School recruited in this study had 35 children with only one teacher who did not have a background in early childhood education and who had worked in this school for three years. In the first one and one-half years, she was still a student in a five-year night college.

Nine parents from each school were interviewed. Parents from the Exploratory Learning School all had college-level education, but only two from the Efficient Learning School had college-level education, with the remaining having a high school diploma. In addition, parents from the Exploratory Learning School had higher income compared to those from the Efficient Learning School.

Gaming Entry, Establishing Rapport, and Researcher's Role

The researcher worked as a participant observer for six weeks in each kindergarten. During the first week building a good relationship with teachers and children, helping children become acclimated to the presence of the researcher, and gaining trust were important goals (Marshall & Rossman, 1995). The key to establishing rapport with children was being a competent player and maintaining friendship with them. Frequent smiling by the researcher was attractive to the children and made it easier for them to talk to the researcher. Being a playful researcher in the two schools was consistent throughout the study, although the behaviors exhibited varied due to different classroom rules and climate. In the Exploratory Learning School, the researcher was able to play as much as she could with the children; in contrast, in the Efficient Learning School she was quite careful talking with children because they were expected to sit well and be quiet all the time under the teacher's rigorous supervision.

Data Collection

Developing baseline data with detailed description of the two classes began during the first week. Descriptive field notes were taken during observations of classroom practices to record what was happening. The content included the descriptions of the physical classroom settings, types of materials and nature of activities supplied by the teachers, the way that teachers interacted with children, and the children's behavior. In addition to the field notes, classroom activities, routines, environment, special events, and children's work were videotaped and photographed. Furthermore, school documents such as sent-home notes (called family–school contact booklets in Taiwan), school brochures, materials used by schools (e.g., textbooks, work sheets, play materials, children's work) were collected for purpose of comparing the classroom practices.

From the second week on, the researcher began recording each individual's play behavior during free playtime. On-site observations and recordings of child's play were made during free playtime at the Exploratory Learning School. A regular free playtime was not sanctioned in the Efficient Learning School. The researcher overall recorded only two short free playtimes (about 15 minutes each) in a nearby park; children were allowed to play because extra time was left from structured lessons. In addition, some play behavior was recorded when teachers were busy preparing materials for subsequent classes or working on checking work sheets and were not attentive to the children.

From the fourth week on, the researcher began interviewing parents and teachers. Eighteen parents (nine from each school) and four teachers (three from the Exploratory Learning School and one from the Efficient Learning School) were interviewed. Seven of the parents were interviewed at their houses, with the remainder interviewed by phone. All the face-to-face interviews were audio-taped, but phone interviews were not; the researcher jotted down notes during the interview. Generally, questions were the same across participants; some were specifically framed to elicit parents' or teachers' opinions. The interview schedule covered many areas beyond the topics suggested by the items in the appendix. The average time for each interview was about one and a half hours.

Data Analysis

Data from interview transcripts, observations, and artifact collections inspection were treated in the same way. The first step was transcribing into the computer the word-for-word creation of data records made during observations, interviews, and artifact inspections. Since labeling data is necessary for retrieving data, code numbers were assigned to lines. With codes assigned to the raw data, the researcher began reading through the data line by line to develop categories, a process that is called "open coding," which purports to reveal concepts or to identify themes. Indeed, from reading through the data twice, a couple of categories did emerge. Then, a step called "axial coding" was taken to relate categories to subcategories to make sense of the phenomenon under study (Strauss & Corbin, 1998). These categories were abbreviated for convenient coding. For instance, BP was used to represent "beliefs about play." Finally, I read through the data again and used markers of different colors to highlight data belonging to different categories.

Three copies of all the data were made. One was stored in a safe place, the other was for cutting up, and the third was for examining when checking that right interpretations were made from the cut-up data. Observational records and interview transcripts from both schools were copied onto different colored papers to reduce confusion. During data processing, having different colors of papers and markers to sort the data into different categories saved much time when separating and pasting data to index cards. Each index card had names of the categories and was numbered. A clip was used to put all of the index cards that belonged together into the same category. Finally, all the index cards were put into different boxes based on the type of data for easy access.

Methods for Verification

The first method for verification was triangulation of data sources (people, space, and time) and methods (observations, interviews, videotapes, photographs, and artifacts). Triangulations were used to lessen bias and to seek truthful propositions (Mathison, 1988). The second technique was prolonged engagement for preventing distortion caused by the researcher's presence at the sites (Creswell, 1998). The six weeks spent at each school allowed the researcher to build trust and rapport with the teachers and the children and to learn the school culture (Erlandson, Harris, Skipper, & Allen, 1993). Peer debriefing was another strategy. James E. Johnson and Brent G. Wilson, who were professors at Pennsylvania State University, understood this study and listened to the researcher's ideas and concerns and provided alternative explanations and suggestions (Erlandson et al., 1993). Johnson, who was in Taiwan during data collection, was able to visit both sites with the researcher. Finally, member checking was the last method for ensuring the credibility of this study. This method involves soliciting participants' views about the researcher's interpretations. This technique was employed at the end of the interviews by summarizing what was interpreted and allowing corrections.

RESULTS

In general, children's play behavior and rights were deeply influenced by classroom contexts, which, in turn were related to the forces outside the classrooms. That is, children's play seems to be clearly affected by the immediate classroom environment, but the influences of different contexts beyond the classrooms also were viewed as affecting play behavior and learning experiences.

Children's rights to play and their play behavior varied across classrooms. However, children were enrolled by parents in different classrooms because of the interactions of factors embedded in larger contexts that affected parents' selections of schools for their children. Play in kindergarten classrooms seems closely related to the values of education and the goals of early learning. According to the conceptual diagram shown in Figure 16.1, parents have their concerns, expectations, and personal experiences that affect their selections of schools and how they arrange activities for their children. In turn, parental beliefs and actions are influenced by cultural, historical, and societal contexts. Viewed from a cultural and historical perspective, the role of education in traditional Chinese culture is one of the factors that produce a narrow definition of success and an emphasis on hard work over play. Moreover, a long history of didactic instruction as the effective way of learning hinders understanding the benefits of play in learning. The traditional image of children as clay (the belief of malleability) is another force that triggers this emphasis of work over play and the practice of didactic instruction. The most influential current force within the societal context is the exam-oriented educational system in Taiwan. This force directly influences parents' beliefs about schooling and about practices in kindergartens. Contextual influences on children's learning and play are multi-layered and interactive.

The Influence of Classroom Contexts on Children's Play

Children's rights to play and their play behaviors were quite different between the two classrooms. Within classrooms, physical, social, curricular, and personal contexts interacted with each other, profoundly impacting children's play. How children's play differed in the two classrooms is examined with respect to the understanding of the influences of classroom settings on children's play.

Physical Context

The two-classroom environment differed in the arrangement of space (see Figures 16.2a and 16.2b), the play materials available to children, and sanctioned playtime (see Figure 16.3 for the comparison of the timetables of the two schools).

As can be seen in Figures 16.2a and 16.2b, the arrangement of the classroom spaces of the two classrooms conveyed different images of children and meanings of learning. The classroom of the Exploratory Learning School was about 830 square meters in size and was divided into different learning areas with a variety of materials for children to access. Children did not sit at their own seats all day; instead, they could stay at any table close to the center for the convenient use of materials. In contrast, children in the Efficient Learning School were

Figure 16.1
Contextual Understanding of Children's Play in Taiwanese Kindergartens

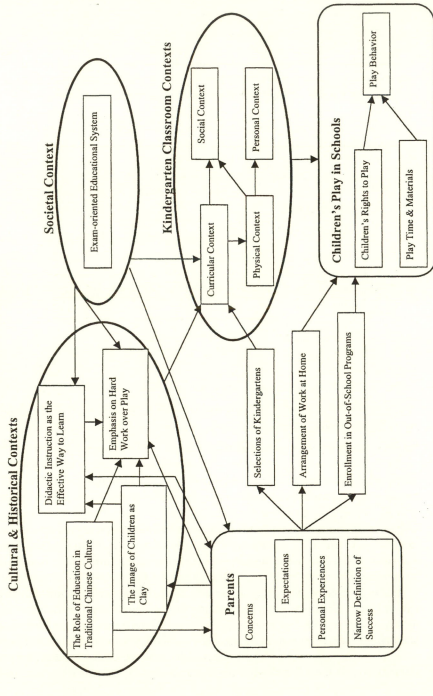

Figure 16.2a
The Floor Plan of the Exploratory Learning School

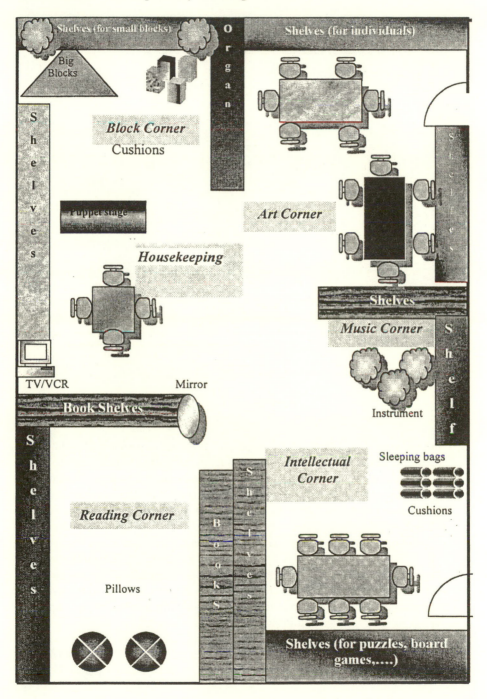

287

Figure 16.2b
The Floor Plan of the Efficient Learning School

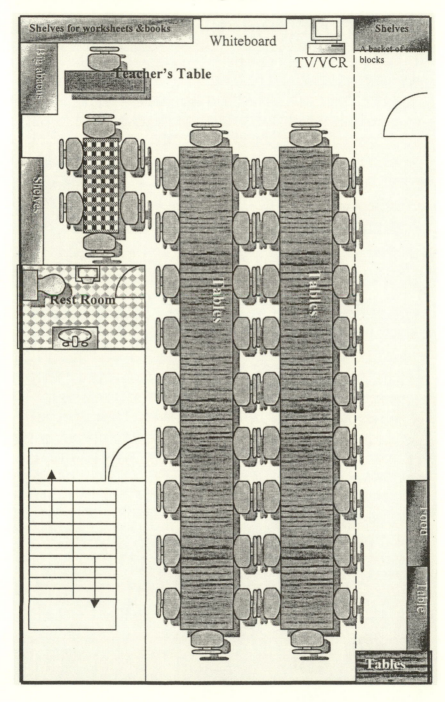

Figure 16.3
Comparison of the School Timetables at the Two Kindergartens

The Exploratory Learning School		*The Efficient Learning School*	
7:40	Free indoor play	*7:40*	Watch TV (children were required to sit quietly)
8:30	Morning ceremony and dancing		
8:45	Free outdoor play	*8:40*	Life education and dancing
9:10	Preparation for the day	*9:00*	Early snack
9:15	Circle time	*9:10*	The first class
9:30	Singing, dancing, story-telling	*9:50*	The second class
10:00	Snack time	*10:30*	The third class
10:35	Clean up		
10:40	Group project (free choice)	*11:10*	Lunch time
11:30	Lunch time	*11:55*	Nap time
12:30	Watch TV, have fruit, brush teeth	*1:55*	Get up
1:00	Nap time	*2:00*	The fourth class
2:20	Get up	*2:40*	The fifth class
2:30	Snack time	*3:20*	Snack time
3:00	Outdoor play and afternoon ceremony		
3:30	Wait for parents/picked up	*3:35*	Wait for parents/take school bus
5:30		*5:30*	

required to sit in their seats all day and were not allowed to move from one place to another. They sat close to each other, which impeded walking between rows within the limited classroom space of 345 square meters.

As shown in Figure 16.3, children in the Exploratory Learning School were provided with free playtime both indoors and outdoors, circle time, group project time, singing, dancing, and storytelling time, which constituted 42.7% of a school day. In contrast, in the Efficient Learning School, the five 45-minute classes in structured academic lessons with some arts classes occupied 41.6% of an entire school day.

Another difference was the play equipment and space. Children in the Exploratory Learning School had indoor and outdoor playgrounds equipped with a variety of facilities that included seesaws, slides, swings, tricycles, jumping ponies, a sandbox, balls, and so forth. However, children in the Efficient Learning School did not have a playground. The only play equipment that could be seen was two slides and some tricycles. The spaces where the slides stayed were quite small, so that it was difficult for children to have physical play. Children were not given time to play with the slides or the tricycles.

Daily in the Exploratory Learning School, children had about 90 minutes of free playtime in the morning and about 50 minutes in the afternoon. They were allowed to choose where and what to play. Provided with rich materials, children could explore and construct their knowledge. Constructive play was linked to social interactions because children tended to compare their constructive products. For instance, boys liked to compare their guns constructed with blocks. Social comparison fostered creative ideas (e.g., to make a more unique style after comparing with peers) and constructive competency (e.g., peers taught each other how to make things). When play materials did not meet children's needs, children spontaneously used raw materials to make things that they needed, thereby enriching their play. Since the use of materials was not tied to a specific area, play occurred from one corner to another. In sum, the physical environment allowed for a rich variety of spontaneous play across the classroom.

In the Efficient Learning School, play was not sanctioned. Children were given the chance to play only when the teacher finished scheduled lessons or as a reward when the children behaved quite well on a certain day. Toys were limited to a basket of small blocks. Given the paucity of play materials, toys served well as bait to draw children's attention or maintain their interests on the academic content. For instance, the teacher would throw a small ball to a child and require him or her to answer a question or to repeat a phrase after her. Children expected and were very excited to get the ball, even though some did not know the answer.

Social Context

The Exploratory Learning children were free to interact with peers. Interactions among peers helped children refine their skills (children discussed whose constructions were more unique and delicate), to generate creative ideas, and to develop friendships. The social context produced chances for interactions through which children learned and developed. Teachers were supporters of learning through play. They frequently interacted with children in playful ways, such as pretending to be someone else by using mimed voices or gestures.

In contrast, the Efficient Learning children did not have much freedom to interact with each other. When they talked to each other, their voices were usually quite low in order to prevent being called on for time-out. As a result, sustained social interactions among peers were rare in this classroom. With the teacher in control, children did not have opportunities to express ideas. The tone that the teacher used to speak to the children revealed a hierarchical relationship. The teacher's commanding or blaming was commonplace.

Curricular Context

The curriculum in the Exploratory Learning School was quite flexible because it evolved from children's interests and concerns. The teachers believed that it was important for children to learn from real-life experiences. All three teachers in this class believed that play was helpful to children and that the curriculum should be playful. As a result, the curriculum proceeded in a play-oriented way.

One of the formal teachers claimed that children should learn things in playful ways under conditions similar to real-life situations. The example that she gave was having children pretend to buy meatballs in a store to learn how much to pay and how much change to get back. Teachers also engaged in children's play when invited:

"[O]nce they said that I was seriously hurt and needed an operation. I lay down in the bed waiting for their preparation of materials for the operation. They even used some small plastic bottles substituted as props. (Formal teacher)

I pretended eating when they served me food and told them how delicious it was. I also gave them some suggestions about the food and praised their contribution. (In-service teacher)

Children learned not only from self-initiated activities but also from teacher-arranged play. Curriculum-generated play was provided for children to learn concepts of shapes, colors, and sizes and to develop skills of differentiation and classification.

In contrast, play had no relationship to children's learning in the Efficient Learning School. Children rarely learned through self-exploration. They often stayed in their seats and received direct instruction from teachers. Because play was not a sanctioned activity in the Efficient Learning School, some children seemed to interpret other children's play as misbehavior. For instance, once when the teacher was busy making marks on children's workbooks, a group of children took the chance to play by reciting some rhymes accompanied by body movement and gestures. A girl approached them and said, "I want to report to the teacher that you are playing here" (Observation #3, line 40, February 17, 2000). After she did so, the group of children suddenly stopped their play and returned to their seats with running steps to escape the teacher's sight.

Personal Context

Similar to Lin and Reifel (1999), boys tended to use materials to initiate pretend play, while girls were more focused on the relationship, role enactment, and appropriate role behavior in the Exploratory Learning School. Since the teachers did not intervene in children's selections of play, boys tended to engage in constructing guns, airplanes, and so forth; in contrast, girls occupied the housekeeping area. Although gender difference was found in preference for the play area, boys did not engage in more constructive play and girls in dramatic play. Many exceptions were found suggesting that differences can be traced to personal style as well as gender. For instance, one boy was found to spend more time in the housekeeping area. He usually went to teachers to ask them what they wanted to eat. After getting the answers, he returned to the housekeeping area and began preparing food. He was always busy preparing food for his customers.

Observing children's play in the Efficient Learning School led to the discovery of resilient children in this school. Some children's playfulness was not beaten down by the authoritarian teachers or restricted by the regimented classroom structures. These children took the risk of being called for a time-out by making use of available materials to initiate their pretend play.

The music teacher was helping children to make outlines of both hands on the whiteboard to help them differentiate their left hand from the right hand. Some children took advantage of the time and pretended themselves to be horsemen by imagining the straps of schoolbags as the horsewhip and raising the straps up and down as if they were controlling horses (the classmates sitting next to the ones who pretended themselves to be the horsemen were imagined as horses). (Observation notes)

The personal feature of resilience allowed children to adjust to the regimented classroom structures and find loopholes to create their imaginary worlds through which they exercised their playfulness. What about those children who were not resilient? It was impossible to picture them in play in this school. They usually sat quietly on their own seats and waited for the next commands given by teachers.

In sum, children's play behavior did differ, and the meaning of play differed in the two kindergarten classroom contexts. Children enrolled in schools chosen by parents. Parents were influenced by forces in two larger contexts. These two contexts were the cultural-historical and the societal.

Cultural and Historical Context

Culture influences beliefs about children's learning. In the traditional Chinese society, people are classified into four classes: scholars, farmers, laborers, and merchants. Among the four levels, scholars are regarded as the highest level and are most respected (Stevenson & Lee, 1996). The emphasis on education is based on the Confucian belief that "all things are beneath contempt, only education is to be esteemed" (Chen & Teng, 1995, p. 9). This sentiment profoundly influences Chinese people. Education has an important place in the traditional Chinese value system and is regarded as the ladder to the achievement of higher social status and economic advancement (Gow, Balla, Kember, & Hau, 1996).

Parents today in Taiwan still believe that without a good education, children would not have a bright future (Liou, 1997). Parents tend to judge children's success or failure based upon their performance and achievement on school-related tasks. This phenomenon (narrow definition of success) appears as early as children are in the preschool years (Barclay, 1989). Academic excellence is highly valued and is a distinguishing cultural facet (Liu & Chien, 1998). With the powerful value of *Wan tsu chen lung* (wishing the son to become a dragon or the daughter to be a phoenix), parents are very concerned about their children's education. From generation to generation every child is instilled with the idea that nothing is more important than obtaining a good education and achieving a diploma (Gow et al., 1996).

The image of children as moldable clay was another ideology that influenced parents' beliefs about education. Children can work hard to acquire higher education and achieve higher social status in the future. Thereby, every child is believed to be educable, and training and didactic instruction were valued as effective methods in education (Barclay, 1989; Stevenson & Lee, 1996). In the traditional Chinese culture, children learned from being told what to do or showed how to do something by skilled models (e.g., adults). Parents who learned in the more didactic way tend to believe that it was the best way for their children to learn; they fail to understand the benefit of learning through exploration or play.

Given the high value of education and the belief of malleability in traditional Chinese culture, parents do their best to provide all kinds of learning experiences. According to Chen and Teng (1995), Taiwanese parents never seem to have any complaints about the amount of financial support or energy that they spend on their children's education. Parents believe that providing education is one of the most important parental responsibilities (Liou, 1997). Many parents today can afford arranging extracurricular activities for their children to achieve educational goals.

Data from parent interviews (labeled as P1, P2, etc.) showed that children's play time was deprived due to such activities arranged by parents. Parents at both schools had similar ways of preparing children either to perform successfully in academics or to master artistic competence. After the school hours, children were sent to the out-of-school programs to take lessons in the arts, math, abacus, computer, composition, and English. Some parents who did not send their children to the out-of-school programs still had a tight schedule set for their children. One mother's statement reveals the importance of work over play:

He spends too much time on play thus he needs to return to his work as soon as possible . . . it is important to finish daily routine (writing assignment, playing the piano, reviewing Chinese phonics, reading storybooks, memorizing nine multiplication tables) before play. (P1)

Societal Contexts

With the high value of education in traditional Chinese culture, parents do their best to support children's acquisition of higher education. Under the exam-oriented educational system in Taiwan, equipping children with academic skills needed for academic tasks at the next grade level is the implicit goal at each grade level (Sun, 1993). This phenomenon is similar to the utilitarian view of education held by Malaysian parents (Hewitt & Maloney, 2000). Without question, this phenomenon occurs in Taiwan parent's stance toward kindergarten education. Quite a number of kindergartens in Taiwan focus on the learning of the 3Rs and use a traditional approach to teach because parents expect children to excel in the 3Rs. According to research conducted by the Hsin-Yi Early Childhood Education Foundation, 75% of the private kindergartens in Taipei city emphasize the learning of the 3Rs (Hsin-Yi, 1987). The Efficient Learning School aimed to help children learn academic skills but ignored the value of play in children's learning. Pan (1994) also asserted that play as a vehicle for children to learn is not common with Taiwanese kindergarten teachers.

In the present study parents' beliefs about the purpose of kindergarten education differed between the two schools. Six of the parents from the Exploratory Learning School believed that experiencing social life was the purpose of kindergarten. In contrast, the same number of parents from the Efficient Learning School indicated that the purpose of kindergarten education was to prepare children for elementary school. These parents' statements illustrate this:

Preparing for elementary school or it would be hard for her to catch up with others when entering the elementary school. (P7)

Early inspiration. The main purpose is to prepare for the elementary school. That's why it is called pre-education. (P3)

For the needs of connecting to the education of elementary school. (P5)

If kindergarten teachers do not teach anything, children might not be able to catch up with others when they get into elementary schools. (P6)

Children in kindergarten should play. However, because of the connection to elementary, they need to learn some basic knowledge. (PI)

The last statement suggested that play is separate from learning. For some parents, learning means only acquiring knowledge and skills from structured lessons and textbooks. The mimetic approach and didactic instruction are the effective ways to prepare children for examinations. Play has no role in the learning process. Some parents who expressed negative attitudes toward public kindergartens did so because they heard from friends that children attending these public kindergartens with play-based curriculum did not learn much and would fall behind others in elementary school: "I cannot send my child to the public kindergarten because children in the neighborhood who attended public kindergarten were falling behind others in first grade" (P7).

One father said that he did not choose the public kindergarten because he did not believe that children could learn from free play: "Semi-structured play is better than leaving children solely to play all day long" (P2).

Most of the parents from the Efficient Learning School also believed that children should finish their homework prior to playing. Some parents worked with children every evening on homework. One mother even scheduled her interview for Friday evening because it was the only time during the week that she would be free from supervising her children's doing homework assignments. Children's playtime in school or at home decreased, and their rights to play were deprived because adults were concerned about academics and educational competition among students under the national examination system in Taiwan.

FINAL REMARKS

The two classroom structures and cultures created different images of play and shaped children's play and their rights to play. Some children in the Efficient Learning School were found to interpret play as "not good" behavior and to believe that to be a good child meant to follow adults' commands. Fortunately, some resilient children in this school remained playful and were not beaten down by the regimented classroom structure or the authoritarian teacher. But what about those children who were not resilient? Their play behavior was not seen, and their voices were too weak to be heard.

The results are consistent with King's (1992) contention that children's play is the product of the interactions of multiple factors embedded in different contexts. Children's play behavior and their rights to play were affected by different curricular foci, the social context, the physical environment, and the personal context across the two kindergarten classrooms. Children usually do not have input to the selection of which school they will attend. Parents make this decision. Parents select the children's extracurricular activities. Parents' beliefs about education related to culture influence these decisions. In this sense, children's learning is profoundly influenced by historical cultural values and by contemporary societal forces in Taiwan. My analysis suggests a relationship between parents' beliefs or actions and the broader sociocultural context. Parents' perceptions and beliefs leading to educational arrangements for their children are a response to the demands of the sociocultural context. Perhaps parents are helping their children meet the needs of society or their culture, even as these educational arrangements are not necessarily developmentally appropriate practice or consistent with the latest theories in early childhood education.

REFERENCES

Barclay, L. K. (1989). Early childhood education in Taiwan. *Dimensions, 75*(1), 8–10.

Berk, L. E. (1989). *Child development*. Boston: Allyn & Bacon.

Bredekamp, S., & Copple, C. (1997). *Developmentally appropriate practice in early childhood programs*. Washington, DC: National Association for the Education of Young People.

Bronfenbrenner, U. (1979). *The ecology of human development*. Cambridge: Harvard University Press.

Chen, H.-M., & Teng, H. F. (1995). No longer just an academic question: Educational alternatives come to Taiwan. *Sinorama, 20*(3), 8–20.

Christie, J. F., & Johnsen, E. P. (1989). The constraints of settings on children's play. *Play and Culture, 2*, 317–327.

Creswell, J. W. (1998). *Qualitative inquiry and research design: Choosing among five traditions*. Thousand Oaks, CA: Sage.

Erlandson, D. V., Harris, E. L., Skipper, B. L., & Allen, S. D. (1993). Quality criteria for a naturalistic study. In *Doing naturalistic inquiry* (pp. 131–161). Newbury Park, CA: Sage.

Fielding, R. M. (1997). A socio-cognitive perspective on cross-cultural attitudes and practices in creativity development. *Australian Art Education, 20*(1–2), 27–33.

Frost, J. L., Wortham, S., & Reifel, S. (2001). Play and child development. Upper Saddle River, NJ: Prentice-Hall.

Gow, L., Balla, J., Kember, D., & Hau, K. T. (1996). The learning approaches of Chinese people: A function of socialization processes and the context of learning. In M. H. Bond (Ed.), *The handbook of Chinese psychology* (pp. 109–123). New York: Oxford University Press.

Hewitt, B., & Maloney, C. (2000). Malaysian parents' ideal and actual perceptions of pre-school education. *International Journal of Early Years Education, 8*(5), 83–92.

Howe, N., Moller, L, Chabers, B., & Petrakos, H. (1993). The ecology of dramatic play centers and children's social and cognitive play. *Early Childhood Research Quarterly, 5*, 235–251.

Hsin-Yi Early Childhood Education Foundation. (1987). *An analysis of the investigation of kindergartens and day care centers in Taipei city*. Taipei, Taiwan: Hsin-Yi Early Childhood Development Center.

Huston-Stein, A., Friedrich-Cofer, L., & Susman, E. J. (1977). The relation of classroom structure to social behavior, imaginative play, and self-regulation of economically disadvantaged children. *Child Development, 48*, 908–916.

Hyson, M. C., Hirsh-Pasek, K., & Rescoria, L. (1990). The classroom practices inventory: An observation instrument based on NAEYC's guidelines for developmentally appropriate practices for 4- and 5-year-old children. *Early Childhood Research Quarterly, 5*, 475–494.

Johnson, J. E. (1983). Context effects on preschool children's symbolic behavior. *The Journal of Genetic Psychology, 143*, 259–268.

Johnson, J. E., & Ershler, J. (1981). Developmental trends in preschool play as a function of classroom program and child gender. *Child Development, 52*, 995–1004.

Johnson, J. E., Ershler, J., & Bell, C. (1980). Play behavior in a discovery-based and a formal education preschool program. *Child Development, 57*, 271–274.

Kagitcibasi, C. (1996). *Family and human development across cultures: A view from the other side*. Mahwah, NJ: Lawrence Erlbaum Associates.

King, N. R. (1992). The impact of context on the play of young children. In S. A. Kessler & B. B. Swadener (Eds.), *Reconceptualizing the early childhood curriculum: Bringing the dialogue* (pp. 43–61). New York: Teachers College Press.

Lin, S. H., & Reifel, S. (1999). Context and meaning in Taiwanese kindergarten play. In S. Reifel (Ed.), *Play and culture studies: Play contexts revisited* (vol. 2, pp. 151–176). Stamford, CT: Ablex.

Liou, Y. F. (1997). Ideas of college-educated mothers in contemporary Taiwan about rearing young children. Unpublished doctoral dissertation, University of Wisconsin, Madison.

Liu, K.C.Y., & Chien, C. (1998). Project approach and parent involvement in Taiwan. *Childhood Education, 74*(4), 213–219.

Marshall, C., & Rossman, G. B. (1995). *Designing qualitative research* (2nd ed.). Thousand Oaks, CA: Sage.

Mathison, S. (1988). Why triangulate? *Educational Researcher, 17*(2), 13–17.

Pan, H.-W. (1994). Children's play in Taiwan. In J. L. Roopnarine, J. E. Johnson, & F. H. Hooper (Eds.), *Children's play in diverse cultures* (pp. 31–50). Albany, NY: SUNY Press.

Petrakos, H., & Howe, N. (1996). The influence of the physical design of the dramatic play center on children's play. *Early Childhood Research Quarterly, 11*, 63–77.

Stake, R. E. (1995). *The art of case study research*. Thousand Oaks, CA: Sage.

Stevenson, H. W., & Lee, S. (1996). The academic achievement of Chinese students. In M. H. Bond (Ed.), *The handbook of Chinese psychology* (pp. 124–142). New York: Oxford University Press.

Strauss, A., & Corbin, J. (1998). *Basics of qualitative research: Techniques and procedures for developing grounded theory*. Thousand Oaks, CA: Sage.

Sun, L. (1993). *Universal public kindergarten program implementation in the Republic of China, Taiwan*. Unpublished doctoral dissertation, Teacher College, Columbia University, New York.

Super, C. M., & Harkness, S. (1986). The developmental niche: A conceptualization at the interface of child and culture. *International Journal of Behavioral Development, 9*, 545–569.

Tizard, B., Philps, J., & Plewis, I. (1976). Play in pre-school centers—II. Effects on play of the child's social class and of the educational orientation of the center. *Child Psychology Psychiatry, 17*, 265–274.

Tobin, J. J., Wu, D.H.Y., & Davidson, D. H. (1989). *Preschoolers in three cultures: Japan, China, and the United States*. New Haven, CT: Yale University Press.

Wilcox-Herzog, A., & Kontos, S. (1998). The nature of teacher talk in early childhood classrooms and its relationship to children's play with objects and peers. *The Journal of Genetic Psychology, 159*(1), 30–44.

Chapter 17

Contextual Differences in Korean Mother–Child Interactions: A Study of Scaffolding Behaviors

Seunghwa Jwa and Joe L. Frost

Children encounter intellectual challenges through social interactions influenced by family members, teachers, and peers (Rogoff, 1990). In most families, children interact with their mothers, the natural caregivers, from early infancy through early childhood. In social contexts children begin to use and understand words in conversation. Parents' speech and interaction with their children provide an important context in which children learn shared meanings and language in a specific culture (Vygotsky, 1978; Wertsch, 1985). The Vygotskian approach, documented by the sociocultural view of human development, focuses explicitly on the role of adult–child interaction (Cole, 1985; Rogoff & Gardner, 1984; Wertsch, 1985). More skilled social partners, such as adults, provide rich opportunities for learning because they scaffold or guide children into more mature forms of problem solving than they could develop independently (Beilin, 1994; Bodrova & Leong, 1996; Rogoff, 1990). In mother–child dyadic interactions, the mother scaffolds or supports the child beyond the child's current abilities.

The Vygotskian paradigm implies that the choice of an appropriate teaching strategy is dependent on understanding both the abilities of the child and the requirements of the task (Wood, Bruner, & Ross, 1976). Regarding social interactions as physical and mental supports, each type of collaborative activity supports a different facet of development.

Contexts are described in terms of the extent to which a given environment or situation provides the child with resources that enhance or support the child's developmental progress (Pianta, 1997). Resources include materials as well as the people who mediate the child's experience with these materials. Erikson and

Schultz (1981) stated that "contexts are constituted by what people are doing and where and when they are doing it" (p. 148). Thus, there is a distribution of cognitive work not only among people but also between people and materials (Resnick, 1994). However, context, whether defined as variations in specific features of an experimental setting or more broadly in terms of general cultural and social practices, is no longer regarded as a controlled variable (Renshaw, 1992).

Context has become both the object of investigation and the preferred explanation for observed differences between subjects. Therefore, context is an object of investigation in studies of dyadic interactions to see how more capable partners scaffold less capable partners. In the matter of scaffolding strategies, are there important individual differences in mothers' use of scaffolding for children's cognitive development? Are the differences among contexts of pretend play different from the ways in which mothers help children to solve puzzle problems and retell a story? Although studies have provided information about maternal scaffolding behaviors separately in each of these activities, most of the data have been restricted to maternal behaviors in a certain context (Beizer & Howes, 1992; Fiese, 1990; McNamee, 1987; Wood & Middleton, 1975).

Play, a dominant activity of children, is influenced by cultural and social factors as well as parental beliefs (Roopnarine & Johnson, 1994). Contextual factors such as materials encountered, ideas, or reactions all contribute to play (Reifel & Yeatman, 1993). In this sense, Vygotsky's (1978) ideas of social interaction with others and using objects can be seen as contextual factors to aid children's mental transformation from action to meaning.

In contrast with puzzle games and story retelling, pretend play is relatively unstructured. Play activity is rarely intended to achieve one particular goal. Instead, these play situations allow an unlimited number of correct or at least acceptable outcomes (Beizer & Howes, 1992). It is likely that various adult interactions with children during pretend play differ from other ways in which adults help children to solve problems.

By looking at the ways in which mothers interact with their children, the present study described contextual differences in maternal scaffolding strategies within three contexts: pretend play, puzzle games, and story retelling. This report focuses on the effect of context suggesting maternal scaffolding behaviors in the Korean cultural setting.

RELATED LITERATURE

Maternal roles in children's play are receiving increasing attention. Young children's pretend play originates during early interaction with parents (Haight & Miller, 1993), and children's play activities are to a greater or lesser extent structured by adults (Dunn & Dale, 1984; Fiese, 1990; Garvey, 1990; Haight & Miller, 1992, 1993). For example, O'Connell and Bretherton (1984) found that the frequency of maternal suggestions was related to the types of play exhibited by the child. They observed that the diversity of the child's play increased beyond independent play levels when mother and child played together and concluded that collaborative play settings with mothers enhanced the play behavior of their children. Further analysis revealed that mothers' presence alone was not sufficient to change children's play behavior. Mothers' active guidance accounted for observed differences in children's play behavior.

Wemer and Kaplan (1963) claimed that the child's initial desire to share the object world with the mother motivates the earliest attempts at communication. Furthermore, they asserted that symbolic activity originated in an intimate interpersonal context of mother–child interaction. After three years of observations, Haight and Miller (1993) concluded that the American mother as the primary caregiver in the family was the most consistently available person in children's pretend play. As mothers provide suggestions and communicate the rules of playing pretend, children coordinate maternal guidance into their actions and can perform beyond their existing level of competence (Haight & Miller, 1993; Miller & Garvey, 1984; O'Connell & Bretherton, 1984; Slade, 1987). Mothers may structure or scaffold children's pretend play using literal and nonliteral coaching strategies (Dunn & Dale, 1984; Fiese, 1990; Haight & Miller, 1993; Miller & Garvey, 1984). For example, Miller and Garvey (1984) observed mothers and their 2- to 3-year-old children playing together with dolls. They provided an elaborate description of how mothers guide 2-year-old children in pretend play. Observation data showed that mothers facilitated mothering play by advising, encouraging, and directing the children to engage in more detailed and realistic mothering procedures.

In keeping with Vygotsky's views, children's solitary activities are transformed through parental facilitation, which enables children to engage in more advanced and culturally appropriate levels of play and helps them use objects in more conventional ways (Uzgiris & Raeff, 1995). Factors influencing parent–child play include different kinds of toys (Lewis & Gregory, 1987), adult behavior and attitudes (Christie, 1985), and the ability of play partners (Garvey, 1990). These contextual factors are interrelated and are influenced by culture. For example, cross-cultural studies with American, Mexican, and Indonesian young children have shown that mothers who valued play for its educational and cognitive benefits were more likely to provide props and suggestions than were mothers who viewed children's play as amusement or imitation of adult models (Faver & Howes, 1993; Faver & Wimbarti, 1995).

According to the cultural-context model of child development, all social environments, situations, and activities are culturally bound and, therefore, are always determined by the meanings inherent in the culture of the participants (Rogoff, 1990). Some researchers claim that children's social and play behaviors are closely linked to the environment in which they occur (Faver, Kim, & Lee, 1995). Research with Korean- and Anglo-American preschoolers found that adult beliefs about the value of play and developmental goals for children were associated with children's play behavior (Faver et al., 1995). Tudge, Putnam, and Sidden (1993) concluded that development occurs differently in different cultural contexts and that these differences are at least as important as similarities that exist across cultural contexts. With reference to cross-cultural comparisons, some aspects of children's play were examined in cultural contexts in Korea and the United States (Tudge, Lee, & Putnam, 1998). The findings of the study showed that children in Korean communities were more likely to play with academic objects than were their counterparts in the United States. By contrast, children in the U.S. communities were more likely to engage in pretend play. This research confirms that both children's play and the ways in which parents play with children reflect cultural and contextual differences and serve to re-create them.

Compared to pretend play, problem solving involves interpersonal and practical goals. It is purposeful, involving flexible improvisation toward goals. Thinking is functional, active, and grounded in goal-directed action (Rogoff, 1990). In this sense, Rogoff defines cognition and thinking as problem solving. Recent empirical work on the Vygotskian framework has shown that adults provide children with certain patterns of assistance based on their current capabilities toward a given task (Bruner, 1983; McNamee, 1980; Mervis & Mervis, 1988; Perez-Granados & Callanan, 1997). Parents monitor children's learning in ways that enable their reach to exceed their grasp (Moll & Greenberg, 1990; Rogoff, 1990).

In a series of studies with preschool children on problem-solving tasks, Wood and his colleagues found that adults sensitively tailor their support of children's efforts according to their skill and age (Wood et al., 1976). With 3-year-olds, the mother's efforts focused on maintaining the children's attention to the task. With 4-year-olds, the mothers concentrated on pointing out the nature of mistakes. With 5-year-olds, the mothers were needed only to check outcomes or to help with critical difficulties.

As in problem-solving tasks, parents play important roles in children's language development. Children learn how to tell stories as they give narrative accounts of events in dialogues with others. The social interaction inherent in such dialogues is the basis for how they understand narrative tasks and eventually carry them out on their own (McNamee, 1980). McNamee (1980, 1987) showed that adults structured children's developing narration skills by asking appropriate questions to organize the children's stories or accounts. Such questions implicitly provide children with which cues they may structure their developing narration skills. Based on observations, four levels of question strategies for maintaining child story retelling were identified: (1) repetition of the last comment, (2) general questioning, (3) "wh" questions (questions with interrogatives such as what, where, who, why, and how), and (4) tag questions or yes/no questions.

It is evident that maternal scaffolding contributes to the development of the child's cognitive development in various contexts. Mothers tend to provide positive support, elaborate story lines, and demonstrate pretend acts in mother–child interaction during pretend. When children work collaboratively with mothers in a task of problem solving, mothers provide children with a pattern of assistance so that children's future independent performance is enhanced.

The findings described above contribute to our understanding of maternal scaffolding behaviors in a given situation. However, mothers may not necessarily engage in one context in the same way that they do in another context. How mothers teach may well be influenced in significant ways by their judgments of contextual differences. Most studies have focused on American middle-class mothers participating in children's activities. The present study explored contextual differences in scaffolding interactions of Korean mothers and children engaged in pretend play, puzzle games, and story retelling.

METHODS

Settings

Observations took place at the home of the subjects during a predetermined convenient time for the parents. Mothers selected observation times that were optimal in terms of acting level and mood for the children. Home observation was selected for the study so that both mothers and children would have a familiar setting, allowing them to interact naturally with each other. It was assumed that the mothers guided their children's activities in typical everyday social contexts. Two home visits were conducted to separately observe mother–child dyadic interactions during pretend play and problem-solving activities. The different settings for these tasks were as follows:

Pretend Play: A toy doctor's kit was provided to each mother–child dyad. They were asked to play with the given toys in any way that they wanted to. Neither time limits nor any other specific direction to play was given. Consequently, mothers and children could freely play and terminate their play with few constraints.

Puzzle Game: Two sets of the same 25 piece-puzzle game were provided. One puzzle was already put together as a model, and the other was loose. Children engaging in this task were asked to put the 25 pieces together. The puzzle game provided mothers with opportunities to help the children with a task that is structured with a specific, definable outcome. Therefore, mothers were encouraged to help in any way that they liked.

Story Retelling: The researcher read a Korean storybook to the children. After that, children were asked to retell the story to their mothers (mothers were aware of the story since they were allowed to read the book prior to this task). While explaining this whole procedure, the researcher refrained from providing mothers with any information on how to help the children retell the story. Like the puzzle games, mothers were encouraged to help the children's narration in any way. However, compared to the puzzle games, the story retelling had fewer inherent structures or goals.

A toy doctor's kit was chosen because doctor equipment toys have the potential to activate children's pretense and are common toys in pretend play. In problem-solving activities, puzzle games and story retelling were selected because they are different in task demands. The puzzle game elicits object-mediated mother–child interaction whereas story retelling requires language-mediated social interaction between mother and child. Although different in their activities and mediations, these tasks require mothers to use scaffolding behaviors. Accordingly, the various kinds of materials create contextual differences and allow comparisons of scaffolding interactions between mother and child across tasks in children's cognitive process.

Participants

Ten Korean mother–child dyads participated in this study. The target age of the child subjects was 4 years. The ages of the children ranged from 42 to 53 months with a mean age of 47.3 months. All of the subjects were recruited in Austin, Texas, from intact Korean families with mother and father residing in the home.

Each mother–child dyadic interaction was observed once in each setting of pretend play, puzzle games, and story retelling. A total of 30 mother–child dyadic interaction sessions were observed.

Materials

To observe mother–child interactions in three different settings, three kinds of materials were presented to the mother–child dyads. A toy doctor's kit (manufactured by Fisher-Price) was used to observe mother–child interactions during pretend play. The doctor's kit contained a stethoscope, plastic bandages, a plastic injector, a sphygmomanometer, a thermometer, a hammer, a flashlight, and real bandages. One set of loose puzzle pieces with a completed puzzle and one Korean storybook containing nine story episodes were used to provide contextual difference in problem-solving tasks.

On the day of distributing the mother's consent forms, the mothers were asked about the appropriateness of the materials in terms of children's problem-solving abilities of puzzle games and their language preference between Korean and English. A Korean storybook was prepared because the 4-year-old preschoolers were less exposed to English than elementary school children, and the dominant language spoken in the Korean intact family homes is Korean. The equipment used as data-gathering instruments included a tape recorder and a video camera.

Data Collection

Mother–child interactions at the participants' homes were observed, audiotaped, and videotaped in order to learn how mothers scaffold their child while engaging in pretend play, puzzle games, and story retelling. An informal interview with each participating mother was conducted immediately after the last observation. The purpose of this informal interview was to obtain information on her perspectives about what she had done during pretend play, puzzle games, and story retelling activities. In addition, informal talk was intended to get her impression about interactions with her child during observations. An informal interview was utilized in this study because securing feedback from the participants serves to increase corroboration and confirmability of findings (Miles & Huberman, 1994).

The general questions used in the informal interview included (1) Were there any differences in your interactional style with your child between your daily behavior and your behavior during observation? (2) How often do you play, do puzzles, and read to your child? (3) Did you feel any difference in your interactions with your child during pretend play, puzzle games, or story retelling? (4) Tell me about how the tasks were different and how they influenced your interactional processes, and (5) How do you play with your child in daily life, and who does your child play with mostly? The contextual factors of maternal behaviors and each participant's perspectives toward child's play and academic activities were reflected in maternal responses.

Two home visits for each mother–child dyad were planned. One visit was for the puzzle games and story retelling problem-solving activities, and the other home visit was for pretend play. Mostly, pretend play was observed on the first home visit, and the puzzle games and story retelling were observed on the second visit. However, three families insisted on only one home visit due to personal concerns. In these instances, all three sessions (pretend play, puzzle games, and story retelling) were observed with a brief break after each task.

Data Analysis

Data were analyzed quantitatively. The transcripts of mother–child interactions in pretend play, puzzle games, and story retelling were analyzed using coding categories for maternal scaffolding levels, children's responses, and control of interactional processes.

Pettit, Raab, and Harrist (1988) defined a social event as the smallest possible social interactive episode having a meaning. The data analyses began with deciding where the episode was identified. Each episode was coded into three different coding schema: scaffolding levels, status of successful/unsuccessful, and status of mother-control, mother–child joint control, and child-control. Scaffolding levels were ranked from Level 0, which means no intervention, to Level 4, a high level of scaffolding.

After each episode had been coded with three of the coding categories, we counted the frequencies of scaffolding levels, successful children's responses, and interactional control of mother, mother–child, and child. The percentages of scaffolding behavior at each level were computed as a function of the total number of scaffolding behaviors.

To investigate the types and percentages of Korean mothers' scaffolding strategies, the percentages of each scaffolding level during mother–child interactions in all three contexts were tabulated to determine the level and percentages of Korean mothers' scaffolding strategies. To examine contextual differences between scaffolding strategies, we aggregated mothers' proportional scores at each context to compare mothers' scaffolding strategies in three different contexts. After examining the contextual differences among scaffolding levels, repeated measures of one-way analysis of variance were used to compare mean scaffolding levels in each context. Mean percentage differences between scaffolding levels within each context were also compared using an analysis of variance (ANOVA) test with repeated measures to examine the contextual difference between maternal scaffolding behaviors.

Mothers' proportional scores of contingent shifting rule use were counted to examine in which context mothers use scaffolding strategies more effectively than others. Mother-control, mother–child joint control, and child-control were counted to analyze external regulatory processes.

Measures of Maternal Scaffolding Levels

The different qualities of maternal input into the flow of pretend play and problem solving were classified into the levels of maternal scaffolding in each task. The utterances and actions of the mothers during the dyadic interactions with the children were rated according to five levels of scaffolding behaviors. The levels of scaffolding began with Level 0 (no maternal intervention). Utterances and actions of mothers that did not match any level of scaffolding were defined as "no maternal intervention." Mostly, Level 0 occurred when the child's behaviors were not thematically relevant to the play frame. In other words, children were distracted from the task parameters. In many cases, the mother interrupted the task by either following the child's request or by redirecting the child into the task. Although it appeared in all three contexts, it did not occur very often.

Level 0 was integrated into the scaffolding level system to separate maternal non-scaffolding behaviors from scaffolding behaviors. Therefore, Level 0 was excluded from statistical analysis.

Pretend Play

Mothers' behaviors during pretend play were clustered to form five levels of maternal scaffolding. Codes for mothers' scaffolding of play behaviors were modified from previous studies (Beizer & Howes, 1992; Faver & Howes, 1993; Kermani & Brenner, 1996). Most studies in mother–child play identified and categorized maternal play behaviors as the partner's contribution to the emergence and development of pretend play rather than sequencing supporting levels. Based on maternal behavior categories from implicit to explicit in previous studies, mothers' supporting levels were used to code maternal play behaviors as follows:

Level 0: No maternal intervention.

Level 1: General positive support—Mother praises and encourages independence for the child's symbolic play such as nodding, smiling, or positive comments. ("I'm sure you could play a doctor's role. Right?")

Level 2: General verbal instruction—Mother verbalizes the child's pretend intent, narrating the child's symbolic play activity, suggesting symbolic play, or labeling play objects to animate as the child uses them in pretend. In addition, mothers respond to play themes by taking into account children's invitation in play frame (Roskos & Neuman, 1993).

Level 3: Indirect guidance—Mother provides interpretive commentary, keeping her child informed about progress, or follows the child's lead in play such as requesting help, adding to or describing new elements for the child's pretend theme, joining child's play to enact a pretend role similar to or complementary to the role the child is playing, describing child's behavior and describing own behavior, incorporating children's input, and elaborating play along with play frame.

Level 4: Direct guidance—Mother explicitly organizes and directs play activity, and the child follows mother's lead. Examples include directing play, modeling specific pretend acts, labeling objects, correcting child, and making invitations to engage in particular play acts.

Puzzle Games

The five levels of this coding system were adapted from a synthesis of a previous analysis of maternal teaching behaviors (Pratt, Kerig, Cowan, & Cowan, 1988; Pratt, Green, MacVicar, & Bountrogianni, 1992; Wood, 1980):

Level 0: No maternal intervention.

Level 1: General verbal instruction—Mother praises and encourages the child to perform on his or her own or attempts to activate the child toward some generally specified goal. ("You do one." "Okay, good job. Next.")

Level 2: Specific verbal instruction—Mother lays down some clues by providing verbal hints for search or operation. ("Check the shape of the piece." "Why don't you go ahead and see if it fits." "Needs another green one.")

Level 3: Identifies material or placement—Mother intervenes directly in the process of placement or shows the child what material should be used or combines any of these strategies. ("This one [points] will fit." "You need that one over there." "Get that yellow one and put it here [points].")

Level 4: Mother demonstrates an operation—Mother selects and assembles material while the child looks on.

Story Retelling

Different mother elicitation techniques were grouped into five levels of increasing mother probe support for maintaining child story retelling. Codes for mothers' scaffolding behaviors of story retelling were modified from McNamee's studies (McNamee, 1980, 1987) as follows:

Level 0: No maternal intervention.

Level 1: Repetition of the last comment that the child said—Instead of giving any story questions, mother repeated child's last comment to remind her or him where she or he is or provides general positive support or encouragement.

Level 2: Nonspecific general story questioning—These probes served to remind the child of where she was, to help her or him focus on the consequences of the information just reported. ("So what happened next?")

Level 3: Specific information through "wh"-questions—A "wh"- question is used to frame the next piece of information that the child needed to report in recounting the story. ("What was the cow doing?")

Level 4: Provided information through tag-questions or yes/no questions—Mother provides the information for the child in the form of a tag question. ("The baby cow followed his mom, didn't he?" or "Was she tired or not?")

Coding Process

Episodes of mother intervention–child responses were established based on the occurrence of an identifiable child response, attempt, or pause with signs of noncomprehension that specified the end of each episode. Each separate episode was then characterized by its most structured level in the five-level coding scheme for each task.

Each episode was scored as either successful or unsuccessful based on the child's response to the mother's scaffolding. If children carried out the mothers' guidance appropriately as intended, it was coded as successful. If children failed to follow the mothers' suggestions or did nothing, it was coded as unsuccessful. In the context of pretend play, mothers' pretend suggestions were coded as unsuccessful when the child's play behavior was not relevant to the preceding maternal input. On the other hand, when the child immediately engaged in symbolic play that was relevant to the suggestion, the episode was coded as successful (Beizer & Howes, 1992).

Each episode was also coded in terms of control—mother-control, child-control, or mother–child joint control—based on the extent to which either mother or child took responsibility in each episode.

Based on this coding system, the percentages of contingent shifting by the mother (Pratt et al., 1988, 1992; Wood & Middleton, 1975) were derived. Appropriate or contingent shifts are those that followed the principle of providing more support after the child failed and less support after success. The criterion measure was the right placement for the puzzle games and successful story

Table 17.1
Inter-rater Agreement for Dividing Episodes, Coding Scaffolding Level, Child's Response, and Control Status in Three Contexts

Context	Episode	Scaffolding Level	Child's Response	Control
Pretend Play	88%	90%	89%	90%
Puzzle Game	96%	96%	97%	93%
Story Retelling	93%	97%	94%	92%
Total	92%	94%	93%	92%

Table 17.2
Summary of Mean Percentages of Interactions at Each Scaffolding Level in 10 Mother–Child Dyads Regardless of the Nature of Contexts

Scaffolding Levels	0	1	2	3	4
Mean	4.17	25.26	26.48	28.14	15.94
(SD)	(4.90)	(20.66)	(15.53)	(20.01)	(14.24)

information for the story retelling. The criterion measure for the pretend play was the reciprocal response of children to the mothers' pretense. However, staying at Level 1 after the child's successful response was considered a contingent shift, as no further shift toward less supportive intervention was possible. Also, mothers' scaffolding strategies that were at the same level as the previous one were coded as contingent if they followed a child's unsuccessful response (Pratt et al., 1992).

Inter-rater reliability was computed for episode determination, maternal scaffolding levels, children's responses, and control status. Table 17.1 shows the exact agreement scores.

RESULTS

Data analysis focused on describing and comparing Korean mothers' scaffolding strategies at five levels in three different contexts.

The Pattern of Scaffolding Behaviors

The overall pattern of mothers' use of scaffolding strategies regardless of the nature of contexts revealed that mothers used all five levels of scaffolding behaviors when interacting with their children. Table 17.2 presents the overall extent to which the dyads engaged in each level of scaffolding.

Table 17.3
Proportion Means, Standard Deviations, and Analysis of Variance with Repeated Measures for Contextual Differences in Scaffolding Levels

Scaffolding Levels Mean (SD)	Pretend Play	Puzzle Game	Story Retelling	F	p
1	8.71 (4.47)	50.25 (16.40)	21.85 (19.11)	20.87	.000*
2	26.84 (12.14)	42.64 (14.66)	13.55 (6.36)	16.03	.000*
3	40.94 (9.52)	4.63 (7.17)	41.27 (15.07)	34.12	.000*
4	23.51 (15.73)	2.48 (5.11)	23.33 (8.74)	12.05	.000*

*$p \le .001$.

There is a striking similarity of findings in scaffolding Levels 1, 2, and 3. All three levels were used in similar proportions. The highest level of scaffolding strategy, Level 4, was least used—an average of 15.94%. The results indicate that, regardless of context, the dominant use of maternal scaffolding strategies occurred at low (Level 1) and medium levels (Level 2 and Level 3). Compared to those three levels of scaffolding behaviors, mothers did not use the highest and most directive scaffolding behaviors at Level 4 very often in any context. As shown in Table 17.2, the standard deviations at each scaffolding level were high. Thus, the overall pattern of mothers' scaffolding strategies shows that there were wide variations in using scaffolding strategies across the dyads or the contexts.

Contextual Influences on Scaffolding Interactions

Mother–child interactions during pretend play, puzzle games, and story retelling were analyzed in light of changes in levels of maternal scaffolding strategies. The levels of scaffolding strategies were determined by the qualitative coding system in scaffolding episodes with the exception of Level 0. Then, the proportion of each level of scaffolding to the total scaffolding episodes in each context was obtained. Due to the various lengths of observations in each context, all original frequency data of scaffolding behaviors were transformed into proportion scores for statistical analysis (Table 17.3).

The data indicate that contextual differences were observed in all scaffolding levels with significant F values in each level. Significant interaction between context and scaffolding level was found in all scaffolding levels. The mean percentage of scaffolding behaviors at Level 1 during puzzle games (50.25%) was the highest. This was followed by story retelling and pretend play averages of 21.85% and 8.71%, respectively. This difference indicates that contexts in which mothers and children engaged influenced the mothers' use of scaffolding

Table 17.4
Repeated Measures Analysis of Variance for Within-Context Differences in Levels of Scaffolding

Context	1	2	3	4	F	p
Pretend Play	8.71	26.84	40.94	23.51	13.84	.000*
Puzzle Game	50.25	42.64	4.63	2.48	44.44	.000*
Story Retelling	21.85	13.55	41.27	23.33	7.67	.000*

*p $\leq$ .001.

strategies. A significant difference was also found at Level 2 scaffolding behaviors. Compared to the high standard deviations of pretend play and story retelling at Levels 1 and 2, the standard deviations of puzzle games at Levels 1 and 2 were relatively low. Consequently, these data indicate that scaffolding strategies at Level 1 and Level 2 are mostly used by mothers with low deviations while interacting with their children during puzzle games.

Different from the usage of scaffolding strategies at Levels 1 and 2, maternal scaffolding behaviors at Levels 3 and 4 were mostly used during pretend play and story retelling. More specifically, the mean percentages of Level 3 during pretend play and story retelling were very similar—40.94% and 41.27%, respectively—and much higher than during puzzle games (4.63%). A significant difference was also found at Level 4, with the same pattern as Level 3. The mean percentages of Level 4 during pretend play and story retelling were much alike: an average of 23.51% for pretend play and 23.33% for story retelling. During puzzle games, mothers used 2.48% of Level 4 scaffolding strategies with a very high standard deviation of 5.11. This finding illustrates that mothers used Level 4 scaffolding behaviors more frequently during pretend play and story retelling than during puzzle games.

In order to determine the scaffolding patterns within each context, an analysis of variance with repeated measures was used to test for significant differences among scaffolding levels in each context (Table 17.4).

Consistent with the contextual differences in each scaffolding level (see Table 17.3), mothers did vary their scaffolding behaviors while interacting with their children across three contexts (see Table 17.4). A significant difference was found in proportions of scaffolding levels within each context. In other words, mothers across contexts made use of some levels of scaffolding strategies significantly more than others. During pretend play, there was a significant main effect for scaffolding levels, F (2, 27) = 13.84, p < .001. An average of 40.94% of scaffolding happened at Level 3. A large amount of scaffolding behavior also occurred at Level 2 and Level 4. Maternal scaffolding behaviors during pretend play usually occurred in high levels, showing that mothers guided children's

play both directly and indirectly by explicitly organizing play and joining children's play to enact pretend roles rather than following the children's play
theme.

During the puzzle games, a significant main effect for scaffolding levels was
also found, $F (2, 27) = 44.44$, $p < .001$. Considering Levels 1 and 2 as low
levels of scaffolding strategies, mothers used an average of 92.89% of scaffolding strategies at relatively lower levels of 1 and 2. This finding indicates that
mothers helped their children solve the puzzle problem using general and implicit forms of scaffolding strategies most of the time rather than providing them
with specific directions to put puzzles together. Contrary to the situation of
pretend play, low levels of scaffolding behaviors were predominantly administered by mothers during the puzzle games. These findings suggest that mothers
encouraged the children to perform independently through general positive comments or praise and provided verbal hints for search or operation most of the
time. In other words, mothers refrained from identifying materials or demonstrating an operation in the process of scaffolding interactions.

During story retelling, there was also a significant main effect for scaffolding
levels, $F (2, 27) = 7.67$, $p < .001$. An average of 41.27% of scaffolding behaviors occurred at Level 3, followed by 23.33% at Level 4, 21.85% at Level
1, and 13.55% at Level 2. The interactional style of mothers in using scaffolding
strategies during story retelling was well balanced over all the scaffolding levels,
compared to their distributions during puzzle games and pretend play. Findings
from the context of story retelling suggest that mothers varied their scaffolding
behaviors to help structure children's story retelling by asking different kinds
of questions. Even though mothers' usage of scaffolding strategies was spread
out across all the scaffolding levels, an average of 64.60% of the total scaffolding strategies occurred at Levels 3 and 4, which are considered high levels of
scaffolding. In this sense, the distribution of scaffolding levels used by mothers
during story retelling is more like the one during pretend play, in that an average
of 64.45% of scaffolding interaction occurred at Levels 3 and 4.

As indicated by significant main effects in all three contexts, the findings
indicate that maternal scaffolding behaviors were influenced in significant ways
by the nature of context.

Contingent Shifting of Maternal Scaffolding Strategies

Contingent shifting is a principle of providing less support after the child
succeeds and more support after failure on a task (Wood, 1980; Wood et al.,
1976; Wood, Wood, & Middleton, 1978). Based on this definition, appropriate
or contingent shifts are those that followed the principle of providing more or
less support depending on children's responses. Continuously revised scaffolding techniques followed by the contingent shifting rule predict increased learning
and positive outcomes in children (Wood et al., 1976). In this sense, the effectiveness of maternal scaffolding strategies could be assessed by adapting

Table 17.5
Mean Percentages of Mothers' Contingent Shifting Rule Use and Result of Repeated Measures Analysis of Variance across Contexts

Context Play	Pretend Game	Puzzle	Story Retelling	F	p
Mean	35.80	78.50	41.60	57.979	.000*
(SD)	(4.67)	(12.86)	(9.69)		

*p ≤ .001.

the principle of contingent shifting. The extent to which the mothers provided effective scaffolding was examined by the mothers' use of contingent shifting.

The mothers' effectiveness of scaffolding was highest during puzzle games. During the collaborative sessions of pretend play and story retelling, mothers' usage of the scaffolding strategies was not sensitively tuned and, therefore, was ineffective (see Table 17.5). The results of repeated measures analysis of variance in testing mean percentages of mothers' contingent shifting rule use across contexts revealed that mothers' contingent shifting rule use was different across contexts in addition to maternal use of scaffolding levels. These differences indicate that the contexts in which mothers and children were engaged influenced the mothers' use of contingent shifting rules as well as their scaffolding patterns.

Instead of carefully choosing their scaffolding behaviors according to children's responses, mothers guided children's activities directly and explicitly upon mothers' intention in the contexts of pretend play and story retelling. Using high levels of scaffolding and low amounts of the contingent shifting rule in the contexts of pretend play and story retelling demonstrates that the mothers guided their children with directive and demanding utterances in the contexts without considering the child's current level of mastery on the play situation and story contents. Also, these findings from the context of pretend play and story retelling illustrate that mothers sometimes varied among scaffolding levels, indicating that the mothers did not carefully observe children's performance and did not scaffold children's activities systematically.

During the puzzle games, however, mothers used low levels of scaffolding strategies through indirect and general verbal instruction instead of picking up the right pieces or putting the pieces in the right places by using directive scaffolding strategies. While using low levels of scaffolding strategies most of the time, mothers' shifts between scaffolding strategies were very contingent. These findings indicate that mothers chose their scaffolding behaviors based upon the child's current ability by using low levels of scaffolding strategies, rather than demonstrating operations by identifying materials or placement. Consequently, contextual factors influenced effectiveness of maternal scaffolding.

Table 17.6
Mean Percentages, Standard Deviations, and Analysis of Variance with Repeated Measures for Mother-Control, Mother–Child Joint Control, and Child Control Within Contexts

Context	M-Control	M-C Joint Control	C-Control	F	p
Pretend Play	30.68 (9.49)	62.09 (9.80)	7.24 (6.08)	101.79	.000*
Puzzle Game	18.89 (11.14)	61.56 (12.55)	19.55 (10.74)	45.16	.000*
Story Retelling	33.18 (9.55)	60.17 (10.83)	6.64 (6.26)	86.74	.000*

*p ≤ .001.

Regulation of Mother–Child Interaction

Regulation of mother–child dyadic interactions was explored by the extent to which mother–child dyad interactions were controlled across contexts. Transition of task regulation from the mother to the child is a characteristic of scaffolding. Each episode was coded as one of mother-control (M-control), child-control (C-control), or mother–child joint control (M-C joint control) based on the extent to which mother or child took responsibility in each episode. The proportions of each control category in the three contexts were derived from the ratio of the episodes of each control category divided by the total number of episodes.

In Table 17.6, analysis of variance with repeated measures revealed that mother–child joint control was used significantly more to regulate mother–child interactions in all three contexts. In all three contexts, over 60% of mother–child joint control was used in the transition of task regulation. This finding revealed that mother–child joint control was prevalent over all the other control categories. Following a significant finding on control categories in all contexts, post hoc analyses with Bonferonni adjustments in control categories were conducted to examine which control category was used more often or less often in each context (Table 17.6).

Table 17.7 showed that during pretend play, mother–child joint control was used significantly more than mother-control and child-control; mother-control was significantly used more than child-control. During the puzzle games, mother–child joint control was also used significantly more than mother-control and child-control. However, a significant difference was not found between mother-control and child-control. During story retelling, mother-control was used more than child-control with the fact that mother–child joint control significantly outnumbered the other two control categories. Overall, more mother-

Table 17.7
Post Hoc Analysis in Control Categories for Pretend Play, Puzzle Games, and Story Retelling

	Pretend Play	Puzzle Game	Story Retelling
Control	2 > 1 (p < –.001)	2 > 3 (p < –.001)	2 > 1 (p ≤ .001)
Categories	2 > 3 (p < –.001)	2 > 1 (p < –.001)	2 > 3 (p ≤ .001)
	1 > 3 (p ≤ .001)		1 > 3 (p ≤ .001)

1: Mother-control; 2: Mother–Child joint control; 3: Child-control.

control was used during pretend play and story retelling than during puzzle games.

These findings matched the previous findings in that contextual difference influenced regulation of mother–child interactions as well as maternal scaffolding patterns and maternal usage of the contingent shifting rule.

DISCUSSION

Vygotsky's sociocultural view on development indicated that the social world is the source of all the child's knowledge and that the child's intellectual development is rooted in social interactions (Wertsch & Hickmann, 1987; Wertsch & Rogoff, 1984). The findings are congruous with previous American studies (Fiese, 1990; Rogoff & Gardner, 1984; Wertsch, Minick, & Ams, 1984) in that mothers' input and guidance serve as a scaffold for children's performance during moment-to-moment interactions. This study, focusing on mother–child interaction, supported the positive effects of adult–child collaboration in social contexts. However, this study showed that mother–child interactional styles were highly differentiated depending on social contexts.

Consistent with Vygotsky's zone of proximal development (ZPD), recent research confirms that mothers' direct involvement with their young children facilitates pretending (Dunn & Dale, 1984; Garvey, 1990; Haight & Miller, 1992; Slade, 1987) and helps improve children's problem-solving abilities (McNamee, 1987; Moll & Greenberg, 1990; Rogoff, 1990; Wertsch, McNamee, McLane, & Budwig, 1980). Mothers have long been intrigued by observing playful transformations that provide a glimpse into their child's inner life and with the opportunity to interact with their children within that world (Haight, 1998). In the current study, mothers tended to provide their children with direct and indirect scaffolding at complex levels on a moment-to-moment basis in all contexts. They required children to participate in current situations to play and solve problems. However, general patterns of maternal scaffolding in all three contexts revealed that the highest level of scaffolding strategies was used relatively little.

This observation suggested that Korean mothers refrained from using highly explicit and directive scaffolding while interacting with their children in all contexts.

Contextual differences in maternal strategies for scaffolding children's performance were found in this study. The significant differences found in these interactional scaffolding processes across three contexts are consistent with the description of contextual influences by Newman, Griffin, and Cole (1989). In this study, they claimed that different contexts place different constraints on the participants that potentially influence the nature of resulting interactional patterns in a school setting between teachers and children. Findings in this study confirmed that scaffolding is indeed a context-bound phenomenon. The Vygotskian approach suggests that mother–child interactions are nested within and influenced by contexts. Contextual findings found in this study support Moss (1992) and Stone's (1993) argument that different relationship contexts would fundamentally affect collaborative endeavors with respect to participants' interactional patterns for engaging in joint activities. Most research on maternal scaffolding is limited to a given context. Consequently, contextual differences in patterns of maternal scaffolding behaviors are not apparent from the literature. Further studies of mother–child collaborative activities across contexts are needed.

This study also suggests that cultural differences apparent in maternal play behavior may be related to culture-specific child-raising practices rather than cultural deficiencies. In a Mexican environment, Farver (1993) found that play develops in the context of sibling interaction from a subsequent comparison of mother– and sibling–child play. Interview data in the current study support similarities of mother–child interactional patterns in the context of play between Mexican and Korean cultures. During interviews, seven mothers who have more than two children in their families mentioned that target children play with their older siblings most of the time, rather than with their mothers. They even worried about how to play with their children when the researcher asked them to participate in this study. This suggests that scaffolding or supporting play may be essential to the development of children's play, but who does the scaffolding and how it is done may be culture-specific. Traditionally, Korean parents' values, expectations, and educational goals for children are academically oriented (Kim & Choi, 1994), and Korean parents believe that playing with children is culturally inappropriate adult behavior (Farver et al., 1995). However, parental involvement is necessary to ensure the success of children and is viewed as an essential component for academic, economic, and social success (Kim & Choi, 1994). Even though the value of play in children's learning and development is increasingly recognized by Korean parents, Korean mothers are still focusing on children's academic achievement. Recently, there is growing concern among Korean parents about effective input and stimulation for learning.

Contextual differences in maternal use of the contingent shifting rule were found in terms of effective scaffolding. This difference may be explained by the different characteristics and orientations among the three contexts. This contextual difference explains the Vygotskian paradigm by demonstrating that how the ways mothers scaffold their children are nested within and are influenced by contexts. In contrast to puzzle games and story retelling, pretend play is relatively unstructured. Play activities rarely focus on achieving one particular goal and, instead, allow an unlimited number of alternatives. On the other hand, problem-solving contexts such as puzzle games and story retelling focus on close-ended goals and right answers. Hence, Beizer and Howes (1992) speculated that the nature of scaffolding strategy use with children during pretend play and the ways in which such interactions help children's play may differ from the ways in which mothers assist children to solve problems.

File (1995) argued that locating scaffolding as a single point on a continuum makes less sense than using it to describe an entire continuum. However, this study was based on moment-to-moment interactions between mother and child, so it was difficult to capture an ongoing picture to connect moment actions with previous story lines in all the contexts. For example, it was obvious that Korean mothers were more likely to incorporate child input for guiding play with high levels of scaffolding. Dyadic interactions during pretend play involved more direct and explicit scaffolding about pretend roles and scripts. However, it appeared that mothers were more willing to contribute to pretend play through active behaviors, such as elaborating play frames and assisting play roles. This current study shows that mothers made suggestions or prompted the child's pretending activities relating to the ongoing play process. Consequently, further studies analyzing scaffolding interactions within a script or a frame are needed.

It was expected that mother-control would be prominent in the contexts of problem solving since Korean mothers tend to focus on the academic area. Analyzing three control categories (mother-control, child-control, and mother–child joint control) within contexts demonstrated that mother–child joint control was the dominant type of regulation in mother–child collaborative interactions in all three contexts. Rogoff (1990) and Rogoff, Mistry, Goncu, and Mosier (1993) in their studies of guided participation, concluded that there are universal processes across contexts in the nature of shared activity. In order to communicate and proceed toward common goals, it is necessary to develop some degree of shared understanding and to adjust each partner's involvement accordingly. The finding that mother–child joint control is the dominant type of regulation also supports Rogoff's idea that scaffolding is a universal phenomenon.

Korean mothers played a passive role in the puzzle games by giving more opportunities for the children to perform independently, instead of directly intervening in children's problem solving with puzzle pieces. Korean mothers scaffold their children's play activities directly and actively, and they help children's problem-solving activity implicitly and passively. They even used a play situation as a teaching task by introducing play materials and explaining how to use them correctly. Consequently, there was less child-control than mother-control in pretend play, and mothers controlled the play activity more than the children. This was consistent with the argument that in a situation when the adult focused on teaching roles, the child was unlikely to take a larger role in collaborative interactions (Rogoff, 1990; Rogoff et al., 1993). In terms of adults' role in mother–child play behaviors, however, Chin and Reifel's (2001) study showed age differences in frequency as well as features of scaffolding strategies. They found that mothers of 2-year-olds used maternal directive for pretend actions such as role assignment and object request more frequently than did mothers of 3- and 4-year-olds.

The pattern of findings identified contextual differences supporting a sociocultural view of collaborative interactions. Issues of scaffolding behaviors in mother–child interactions can be discerned from the contextual analyses of how the characteristics of contexts influence maternal scaffolding strategies. Consequently, information about maternal scaffolding behaviors taken separately in each context cannot explain an integrated view of unique cultural meanings. It should be noted that the way that each measure is quantified does not guarantee that scaffolding is really comparable in each of the measures. This study demonstrates that the issues of scaffolding behaviors among different activities need to be considered in sociocultural context within a given cultural setting. This suggests further studies about contextual differences in scaffolding in different cultural settings.

REFERENCES

Beilin, H. (1994). Jean Piaget's enduring contribution to developmental psychology. In R. D. Parke, P. A. Omstein, J. J. Reiser, & C. Zahn-Wasler (Eds.), *A century of developmental psychology* (pp. 333–356). Washington, DC: American Psychological Association.

Beizer, L., & Howes, C. (1992). Mothers and toddlers: Partners in early symbolic play. In C. Howes, O. Unger, & C. C. Matheson (Eds.), *The collaborative construction of pretend* (pp. 25–44). Albany, NY: SUNY Press.

Belsky, J., & Most, R. (1984). From exploration to play: A cross-sectional study of infant free play behavior. *Developmental Psychology, 20*, 630–639.

Bodrova, E., & Leong, D. J. (1996). *Tools of the mind: The Vygotskian approach to early childhood education.* Englewood Cliffs, NJ: Prentice-Hall.

Bodrova, E., & Leong, D. J. (1998). Adult influences on play. In D. P. Fromberg & D. Bergen (Eds.), *Play from birth to twelve and beyond: Contexts, perspectives, and meanings* (pp. 277–282). New York: Garland Publishing.

Bruner, J. S. (1983). *Child's talk: Learning to use language.* New York: Norton.

Chin, J. H., & Reifel, S. (2001). Maternal scaffolding of Taiwanese play: Qualitative patterns. In S. Reifel (Ed.), *Play and culture studies* (vol. 3, pp. 263–289). Stanford, CT: Ablex.

Christie, J. F. (1985). Training of symbolic play. *Early Child Development and Care, 19*, 42–46.

Cole, M. (1985). The zone of proximal development: Where culture and cognition create each other. In J. V. Wertsch (Ed.), *Culture, communication, and cognition: Vygotskian perspectives* (pp. 146–161). Cambridge: Cambridge University Press.

Dunn, J., & Dale, N. (1984). I a daddy: 2-year-olds' collaboration in joint pretend with sibling and with mother. In I. Bretherton (Ed.), *Symbolic play: The development of social understanding*. London: Academic Press.

Elbers, E., Maiser, R., Hoekstra, T., & Hoogsteder, M. (1992). Internalization and adult–child interactions. *Learning and Instruction, 2*, 101–118.

Erikson, F., & Schultz, J. (1981). When is a context? Some issues and methods in the analysis of social competence. In J. Green & C. Wallat (Eds.), *Ethnography and language in educational settings* (pp. 147–160). Norwood, NJ: Ablex.

Farver, J. (1993). Cultural differences in scaffolding play: A comparison of American and Mexican mother–child and sibling–child pairs. In K. MacDonald (Ed.), *Parent-child play—descriptions and implications* (pp. 349–366). Albany, NY: SUNY Press.

Farver, J. M., & Howes, C. (1993). Cultural differences in American and Mexican mother–child pretend play. *Merrill-Palmer Quarterly, 39*(3), 344–358.

Farver, J. M., Kim, Y. K., & Lee, Y. (1995). Cultural differences in Korean- and Anglo American preschoolers' social interaction and play behaviors. *Child Development, 66*, 1088–1099.

Farver, J., & Wimbarti, S. (1995). Indonesian toddlers' social play with their mothers and older siblings. *Child Development, 66*, 1493–1513.

Fiese, B. H. (1990). Playful relationships: A contextual analysis of mother–toddler interaction and symbolic play. *Child Development, 61*, 1648–1656.

File, N. (1995). Applications of Vygotskian theory to early childhood education: Moving toward a new teaching-learning paradigm. In S. Reifel (Ed.), *Advances in early education and care—Social contexts of early childhood* (vol. 7, pp. 295–317). Greenwich, CT: JAI Press.

Garvey, C. (1990). *Play*. Cambridge, MA: Harvard University Press.

Haight, W. (1998). Adult direct and indirect influences on play. In D. P. Fromberg & D. Bergen (Eds.), *Play from birth to twelve and beyond: Contexts, perspectives, and meanings* (pp. 259–265). New York: Garland Publishing.

Haight, W., & Miller, P. J. (1992). The development of everyday pretend play: A longitudinal study of mothers' participation. *Merrill-Palmer Quarterly, 38*(3), 331–349.

Haight, W., & Miller, P. J. (1993). *Pretending at home: Early development in a sociocultural context*. Albany, NY: SUNY Press.

Kermani, H., & Brenner, M. E. (1996). *Maternal scaffolding in the child's zone of proximal development: Cultural perspectives*. Paper presented at the annual meeting of the American Educational Research Association, New York, April (ED396821).

Kim, U., & Choi, S. (1994). Individualism, collectivism, and child development: A Korean perspective. In P. M. Greenfield & R. R. Cocking (Eds.), *Cross-cultural roots of minority child development*. Hillsdale, NJ: Erlbaum.

Lewis, C., & Gregory, S. (1987). Parents' talk to their infants: The importance of context. *First Language, 7*, 201–216.

McLane, J. B. (1987). Interaction, context, and the zone of proximal development. In M. Hickmann (Ed.), *Social and functional approaches to language and thought* (pp. 267–285). London: Academic Press.

McNamee, G. D. (1980). *The social origins of narrative skills*. Unpublished doctoral dissertation, Northwestern University.

McNamee, G. D. (1987). The social origins of narrative skills. In M. C. Hickmann (Ed.),

Social and functional approaches to language and thought (pp. 287–304). San Diego: Academic Press.

Mervis, C. B., & Mervis, C. A. (1988). Role of adult input in young children's category evolution: An observational study. *Journal of Child Language, 15,* 257–272.

Miles, M. B., & Huberman, A. M. (1994). *Qualitative data analysis.* Thousand Oaks, CA: Sage Publications.

Miller, P., & Garvey, C. (1984). Mother–baby role play: its origins in social support. In I. Bretherton (Ed.), *Symbolic play: The development of social understanding.* London: Academic Press.

Moll, L. C., & Greenberg, J. B. (1990). Creating zones of possibilities: Combining social contexts for instruction. In L. C. Moll (Ed.), *Vygotsky and education: Instructional implications and applications of sociohistorical psychology* (pp. 319–348). New York: Cambridge University Press.

Moss, E. (1992). The socioaffective context of joint cognitive activity. In L. T. Winegar & J. Valsiner (Eds.), *Contexts for learning: Sociocultural dynamics in children's development* (pp. 19–42). New York: Oxford University Press.

Newman, D., Griffin, P., & Cole, M. (1989). *The construction zone. Working for cognitive change in school.* Cambridge: Cambridge University Press.

O'Connell, B., & Bretherton, I. (1984). Toddler's play, alone, and with mothers: The role of maternal guidance. In I. Bretherton (Ed.), *Symbolic play: The development of social understanding.* London: Academic Press.

Perez-Granados, D. R., & Callanan, M. A. (1997). Conversations with mothers and siblings: Young children's semantic and conceptual development. *Developmental Psychology, 55*(1), 120–134.

Pettit, G. S., Raab, M. M., & Harrist, A. W. (1988). *Social events coding: Observer training and coding manual.* Bloomington: Indiana University Press.

Pianta, R. C. (1997). Adult–child relationship processes and early schooling. *Early Education and Development, 5*(1), 11–26.

Portes, P. R. (1991). Assessing children's cognitive environment through parent–child interactions. *Journal of Research and Development in Education, 24*(3), 30–37.

Pratt, M. W., Green, D., MacVicar, J., & Bountrogianni, M. (1992). The mathematical parent: Parental scaffolding, parental style, and learning outcomes in long-division mathematics homework. *Journal of Applied Developmental Psychology, 13,* 17–34.

Pratt, M. W., Kerig, P., Cowan, P. A., & Cowan, C. P. (1988). Mothers and fathers teaching 3-year-olds: Authoritative parenting and adult scaffolding of young children's learning. *Developmental Psychology, 24*(6), 832–839.

Reifel, S., & Yeatman, J. (1993). From category to context: Reconsidering classroom play. *Early Childhood Research Quarterly, 8,* 347–367.

Renshaw, P. D. (1992). Reflecting on the experimental context: Parents' interpretations of the education motive during teaching episodes. In L. T. Winegar & J. Valsiner (Eds.), *Children's development within social context* (pp. 53–74). Hillsdale, NJ: Erlbaum.

Resnick, L. B. (1994). Situated rationalism: Biological and social preparation for learning. In L. Hirschfield & S. Gelman (Eds.), *Mapping the mind: Domain specificity in cognition and culture* (pp. 474–493). Cambridge: Cambridge University Press.

Rogoff, B. (1990). *Apprenticeship in thinking.* New York: Oxford University Press.

Rogoff, B., & Gardner, W. (1984). Adult guidance of cognitive development. In B. Rogoff & J. Lave (Eds.), *Everyday cognition: Its development in social context* (pp. 95–116). Cambridge, MA: Harvard University Press.

Rogoff, B., Mistry, J., Goncu, A., & Mosier, C. (1993). Guided participation in cultural activity by toddlers and caregivers. *Monographs of the Society for Research in Child Development, 58* (8, Serial No. 236).

Roopnarine, J. L., & Johnson, J. E. (1994). The need to look at play in diverse cultural settings. In J. L. Roopnarine, J. E. John, & F. H. Hooper (Eds.), *Biology of play* (pp. 1–8). London: Spastics International Medical Publications/Heinemann Medical Books.

Roskos, K., & Neuman, S. (1993). Descriptive observations of adults' facilitation of literacy in young children's play. *Early Childhood Research Quarterly, 8*, 77–97.

Slade, A. (1987). A longitudinal study of maternal involvement and symbolic play during the toddler period. *Child Development, 58*, 367–375.

Stone, C. A. (1993). What is missing in the metaphor of scaffolding? In M. Minick & C. Stone (Eds.), *Contexts for learning* (pp. 169–183). New York: Oxford University Press.

Tudge, J. R, Lee, S., & Putnam, S. (1998). Young children's play in socio-cultural context: South Korea and the United States. In S. Reifel (Series Ed.), *Play and Culture Studies* (vol. 1, pp. 77–90). Stamford, CT: Ablex.

Tudge, J. R., Putnam, S. A., & Sidden, J. (1993). Preschoolers' activities in socio-cultural context. *Quarterly Newsletter of the Laboratory of Comparative Human Cognition, 15*, 71–84.

Turkheimer, M., Bakeman, R., & Adamson, L. B. (1989). Do mothers support and peers inhibit skilled object play in infancy? *Infant Behavior and Development, 12*, 37–44.

Uzgiris, I. C., & Raeff, C. (1995). Play in parent–child interaction. In M. H. Bomstein (Ed.), *Handbook of parenting, Vol. 4. Applied and practical parenting* (pp. 353–376). Mahwah, NJ: Erlbaum.

Vygotsky, L. S. (1978). *Mind in society: The development of higher psychological processes.* Cambridge, MA: Harvard University Press.

Wemer, T., & Kaplan, B. (1963). *Symbolic formation.* New York: Wiley.

Wertsch, J., & Rogoff, B. (1984). Editors's notes. In B. Rogoff & J. Wertsch (Eds.), *Children's learning in the "zone of proximal development"* (pp. 1–6). San Francisco: Jossey-Bass.

Wertsch, J. V. (1985). *Vygotsky and the social formation of mind.* Cambridge, MA: Harvard University Press.

Wertsch, J. V., & Hickmann, M. (1987). Problem solving in social interaction: A microgenetic analysis. In M. C. Hickmann (Ed.), *Social and functional approaches to language and thought* (pp. 251–266). San Diego: Academic Press.

Wertsch, J. V., McNamee, G. D., McLane, J. B., & Budwig, N. A. (1980). The adult–child dyad as a problem-solving system. *Child Development, 51*, 1215–1221.

Wertsch, J. V., Minick, N., & Ams, F. J. (1984). The creation of context in joint problem-solving. In B. Rogoff & J. Lave (Eds.), *Everyday cognition: Its development in social context* (pp. 150–171). Cambridge, MA: Harvard University Press.

Wood, D. (1980). Teaching the young child: Some relationships between social interaction, language, and thought. In D. R. Olson (Ed.), *The social foundations of language and thought* (pp. 280–296). New York: Norton.

Wood, D., Bruner, J., & Ross, G. (1976). The role of tutoring problem solving. *Journal of Child Psychology and Child Psychiatry, 17*, 181–191.

Wood, D., Wood, H., & Middleton, D. (1978). An experimental evaluation of four face-to-face teaching strategies. *International Journal of Behavioral Development, 2*, 131–147.

Wood, D. J., & Middleton, D. (1975). A study of assisted problem-solving. *British Journal of Psychology, 66*, 181–191.

Index

About the Contributors

BETTY A. BEACH is a Professor of Early Childhood Education at the University of Maine at Farmington.

PATRICK BIESTY is a Professor in the Department of Sociology and Anthropology at the County College of Morris, Randolph, New Jersey.

NATHALIE CARRICK is a graduate student at the University of California, Irvine.

LI-CHUN CHANG is an Assistant Professor in the Department of Early Childhood Education at the National Taiwan Teachers College, Taipei, Taiwan.

PEI-YU CHANG is an Assistant Professor at the Center of Teacher Education of the National Taipei College of Nursing, Taipei, Taiwan.

MARGARET CLYDE was formerly Associate Professor in Early Childhood Education at Melbourne University, and now works statewide as an early childhood consultant.

MICHELLE DUCKETT-HEDGEBETH is an Instructor at the Atlanta Technical College, Atlanta, Georgia.

PHIL FITZSIMMONS is a Lecturer in the Centre for Language Education at the University of Wollongong (Faculty of Education), Australia.

JOE L. FROST is Parker Centennial Professor Emeritus in Education at the University of Texas at Austin.

KARA M. GREGORY is an Early Childhood Consultant in the state of Michigan.

DANA L. GROSS is an Associate Professor in the Department of Psychology at St. Olaf College, Northfield, Minnesota.

THOMAS S. HENRICKS is Danieley Professor in the Department of Sociology and Anthropology at Elon University, Elon, North Carolina.

OLGA S. JARRETT is Associate Professor in the Department of Early Childhood Education at Georgia State University, Atlanta, Georgia.

SEUNGHWA JWA is an Instructor in the Department of Early Childhood Education at Kyungsung University, Korea.

AN SOOK KIM is a Ph.D. student in the Department of Family and Child Ecology at Michigan State University.

E. BEVERLEY LAMBERT is a Senior Lecturer in Early Childhood Education at Charles Sturt University, Wagga, New South Wales, Australia.

DONALD E. LYTLE is a Professor in the Department of Physical Education and Exercise Science at California State University, Chico. He also has taught social psychology courses for the Departments of Psychology and Sociology. His research interests surround the world of play, game, and sport as well as embodied knowledge in movement studies. He has been a past president for The Association for the Study of Play (TASP) and writes a column, "Dr. Play," for the TASP Newsletter. He is the Philosophy Chair of the National Association of Sport and Physical Education Council with the American Alliance for Health, Physical Education, Recreation, and Dance.

GRACE MASSELOS is a Lecturer in the Faculty of Education, Early Childhood Studies at the University of Wollongong, Australia.

BARBRA McKENZIE is a Lecturer in Language and Literacy in Early Childhood and Primary Education at the University of Wollongong, Australia.

ROSARIO ORTEGA is a Professor in the Department of Developmental and Educational Psychology at the University of Seville, Spain.

STUART REIFEL is a Professor in the Department of Curriculum and Instruction at the University of Texas at Austin.

JEANETTE RHEDDING-JONES is a Professor of Pedagogy in Early Childhood Education at Oslo University College, Norway.

R. KEITH SAWYER is an Assistant Professor in the Department of Education at Washington University.

JANET K. SAWYERS is a Professor of Child Development and Assistant Department Head of the Department of Human Development at Virginia Tech, Blacksburg, Virginia.

BRIAN SUTTON-SMITH was a Professor Emeritus in Human Development and in Folklore (1987–1994) at the University of Pennsylvania, Philadelphia.

ALICE WHIREN is a Professor in the Department of Family and Child Ecology at Michigan State University.